Quod scriptura, non iubet vetat

The Latin translates, "What is not commanded in scripture, is forbidden:'

On the Cover: Baptists rejoice to hold in common with other evangelicals the main principles of the orthodox Christian faith. However, there are points of difference and these differences are significant. In fact, because these differences arise out of God's revealed will, they are of vital importance. Hence, the barriers of separation between Baptists and others can hardly be considered a trifling matter. To suppose that Baptists are kept apart solely by their views on Baptism or the Lord's Supper is a regrettable misunderstanding. Baptists hold views which distinguish them from Catholics, Congregationalists, Episcopalians, Lutherans, Methodists, Pentecostals, and Presbyterians, and the differences are so great as not only to justify, but to demand, the separate denominational existence of Baptists. Some people think Baptists ought not teach and emphasize their differences but as E.J. Forrester stated in 1893, "Any denomination that has views which justify its separate existence, is bound to promulgate those views. If those views are of sufficient importance to justify a separate existence, they are important enough to create a duty for their promulgation ... the very same reasons which justify the separate existence of any denomination make it the duty of that denomination to teach the distinctive doctrines upon which its separate existence rests." If Baptists have a right to a separate denominational life, it is their duty to propagate their distinctive principles, without which their separate life cannot be justified or maintained.

Many among today's professing Baptists have an agenda to revise the Baptist distinctives and redefine what it means to be a Baptist. Others don't understand why it even matters. The books being reproduced in the *Baptist Distinctives Series* are republished in order that Baptists from the past may state, explain and defend the primary Baptist distinctives as they understood them. It is hoped that this Series will provide a more thorough historical perspective on what it means to be distinctively Baptist.

The Lord Jesus Christ asked, *"And why call ye me, Lord, Lord, and do not the things which I say?"* (Luke 6:46). The immediate context surrounding this question explains what it means to be a true disciple of Christ. Addressing the same issue, Christ's question is meant to show that a confession of discipleship to the Lord Jesus Christ is inconsistent and untrue if it is not accompanied with a corresponding submission to His authoritative commands. Christ's question teaches us that a true recognition of His authority as Lord inevitably includes a submission to the authority of His Word. Hence, with this question Christ has made it forever impossible to separate His authority as King from the authority of His Word. These two principles—the authority of Christ as King and the authority of His Word—are the two most fundamental Baptist distinctives. The first gives rise to the second and out of these two all the other Baptist distinctives emanate. As F.M. Iams wrote in 1894, "Loyalty to Christ as King, manifesting itself in a constant and unswerving obedience to His will as revealed in His written Word, is the real source of all the Baptist distinctives:' In the search for the *primary* Baptist distinctive many have settled on the Lordship of Christ as the most basic distinctive. Strangely, in doing this, some have attempted to separate Christ's Lordship from the authority of Scripture, as if you could embrace Christ's authority without submitting to what He commanded. However, while Christ's Lordship and Kingly authority can be isolated and considered essentially for discussion's sake, we see from Christ's own words in Luke 6:46 that His Lordship is really inseparable from His Word and, with regard to real Christian discipleship, there can be no practical submission to the one without a practical submission to the other.

In the symbol above the Kingly Crown and the Open Bible represent the inseparable truths of Christ's Kingly and Biblical authority. The Crown and Bible graphics are supplemented by three Bible verses (Ecclesiastes 8:4, Matthew 28:18-20, and Luke 6:46) that reiterate and reinforce the inextricable connection between the authority of Christ as King and the authority of His Word. The truths symbolized by these components are further emphasized by the Latin quotation - *quod scriptura, non iubet vetat*— i.e., "What is not commanded in scripture, is forbidden:' This Latin quote has been considered historically as a summary statement of the regulative principle of Scripture. Together these various symbolic components converge to exhibit the two most foundational Baptist Distinctives out of which all the other Baptist Distinctives arise. Consequently, we have chosen this composite symbol as a logo to represent the primary truths set forth in the *Baptist Distinctives Series*.

CHRISTIAN DISCIPLESHIP
AND BAPTISM

CHRISTIAN DISCIPLESHIP AND BAPTISM:

BEING

𝕰𝖎𝖌𝖍𝖙 𝕷𝖊𝖈𝖙𝖚𝖗𝖊𝖘

IN REPLY TO THE THEORY ADVANCED BY DR. HALLEY
IN THE CONGREGATIONAL LECTURE OF 1843.

DELIVERED BY THE

REV. CHARLES STOVEL,

IN THE LIBRARY OF THE BAPTIST MISSION HOUSE, MOORGATE-STREET,
LONDON, IN OCTOBER, 1845.

With a Biographical Sketch of the Author by John Franklin Jones

LONDON:
PUBLISHED BY HOULSTON AND STONEMAN,
65 PATERNOSTER ROW.
1846.

he Baptist Standard Bearer, Inc.

NUMBER ONE IRON OAKS DRIVE • PARIS, ARKANSAS 72855

Thou hast given a *standard* to them that fear thee;
that it may be displayed because of the truth.
— *Psalm 60:4*

Reprinted 2006

by

THE BAPTIST STANDARD BEARER, INC.
No. 1 Iron Oaks Drive
Paris, Arkansas 72855
(479) 963-3831

THE WALDENSIAN EMBLEM
lux lucet in tenebris
"The Light Shineth in the Darkness"

ISBN# 1579786448

ADVERTISEMENT.

When the following course of Lectures was projected, the Baptist Library, in Moorgate-street, appeared to offer the most suitable accommodation; the use of it was, therefore, solicited, and finally obtained; but, in granting that favour, the committee of the Baptist Missionary Society have only acted as trustees to the premises, and neither that society nor any person whatever, except the author, is answerable for any sentence the work contains. This service of the truth was undertaken from a deep impression of personal duty, and it has been performed, deferring only to the Lord.

As the undertaking advanced, it was found that incidental arrangements, necessary to secure the comfort of the audience and the safety of the Mission House and property, would require a constant supervision, and this was confided to the following gentlemen, who kindly consented to act as a Committee for that purpose:—

Rev. William H. Black
    John J. Brown
    F. A. Cox, D.D., LL.D.
    Benjamin Davies, Ph.D.
    James Hoby, D.D.
    Timothy Moore
    William Norton
    Thomas Price, D.D.
    Joseph Rothery
    J. Russell (Greenwich)

Rev. F. Trestrail
Mr. George Bailey
    William Beddome
    William Bowser
    John Danford
    John M. Hare
    George Kitson
    J. Penney
    Thomas Pewtress

Mr. James Whitehorne, Treasurer.
Mr. David M'Laren, Secretary.

To the kindness and wisdom of these gentlemen the author is greatly indebted. A perfect accommodation was secured for the audience, and a tender regard was paid to his own comfort. These helps were not only gratifying, and, therefore, deserving of thanks; but became indispensable, for without them the labour, added to other engagements, and the oppressive feeling of responsibility, could not have been sustained.

David M'Laren, Esq., of Highbury Terrace, who acted as secretary to this committee, has, by his punctuality in business arrangements, his wise, Christian, and dignified suggestions, in everything relating to the delivery of these Lectures, laid all parties under peculiar obligation. His service, both to the audience and to the author, was invaluable.

The work was undertaken by the author entirely on his own responsibility, and at his own cost; and thus the tickets were issued gratuitously; but the committee and friends, who sympathised in the movement, generously defrayed the whole expense incurred at Moorgate-street, with all that attended the previous advertisements.

The Rev. Dr. Cox, and the Rev. Dr. Hoby, to whose affection the author has, in former times, been more indebted than can be here expressed, with Dr. Thomas Price, Dr. Davis, J. Whitehorne, Esq., J. Penney, Esq., W. Beddome, Esq., and the Rev. J. Russell, of Greenwich, afforded important assistance in occupying the chair; and, by their judicious influence, added to the comfort of each attendance, and the accompanying devotional exercises.

To the committee of the Baptist Missionary Society, who granted the use of the room, and to all those parties by whom he was so essentially served while occupying it, the Author hereby presents his sincere thanks, confessing, at the same time, and most devoutly, that words can never express what is due, or what he feels, for acts of love granted, as these were, at a time when conscience was imposing a most difficult and responsible task. He only, in whose cause the work was undertaken, can, by placing them to his own account, sufficiently honour such Christian offices.

At the unanimous request of the audience, which was full, and whose kind and patient attention could scarcely be greater, with prayer for a Divine blessing on the work, the Lectures are now presented to the public.

C. STOVEL.

5, Stebon Terrace,
Philpot-street East, London.
　March 26th, 1846.

CONTENTS.

	PAGE
Preface	xvii

LECTURE I.

INTRODUCTORY.

Introduction	1
The Word "Disciple"	2
Dr. Halley's Interpretation of the Word Disciple	6
The Influence of Parties	7
The Resuscitation of Sacramental Doctrine	9
Dr. Halley's Authority	10
Dr. Halley's Aim and Work	11
The Origin and Position of Modern Baptists	17
Becon's Statement	20
Denne's Statement	23
The Case and Position of Independent Churches	27
The Word *Musterion*, or Mystery	30
The Personal and Practical Nature of Christian Baptism	35
The Perplexing Question and Solutions Proposed	37
The State of the Argument	41

LECTURE II.

JEWISH BAPTISM.

	PAGE
Introductory Restatement	43
Dr. Halley's Hypothesis	44
Dr. Halley's Rule of Interpretation	48
Dr. Halley's Argument	51
The Jewish Baptism	59
The Evidence in Favour of Jewish Baptism	61
The Authorised Expectation of Proselytes	66
The Proof that this Expectation was Just	82
The Summary and Conclusion	85

LECTURE III.

JOHN'S BAPTISM.

Recapitulation	88
Dr. Halley's Admissions Relating to John the Immerser	91
Dr. Halley's Assumptions	93
The Doctrine Affirmed	97
The Declaration of our Lord	98
Intimations Given at John's Birth	100
The Predicted Character of John	102
Prophetical Declarations of his Work	104
The Recorded Character of John	110
The Record of John's Ministry	112
The Practical Result of John's Ministry	120
The Concurring Action of our Lord	123

LECTURE IV.

THE MINISTRY AND EXAMPLE OF OUR LORD.

Introductory Admissions of Dr. Halley	128
The Baptismal Scene	131
The Immediate Effect of his Baptism	133

CONTENTS. xi

	PAGE
The Peculiar Work of the Redeemer	136
The Annunciation and Birth of our Lord	138
The Ancient Prophecies	141
Apostolical Statements	146
The Personal Ministration of our Lord	149
His Messiahship	150
His Rejection of Earthly Influence	151
His Preparatory Object	151
His Treatment of Inquirers	152
His Treatment of Rejected Persons	154
His Treatment of the Openly Profane	156
His Treatment of the Undecided	156
His Treatment of the Baptized Disciples	159
The Instruction of his Disciples	160
The Expressions of his Peculiar Regard	161
The Example of our Lord Himself	164

LECTURE V.

THE ACTION OF THE FORTY-SEVEN DAYS.

An Introductory Case	168
The Argument Stated	173
The Recognition of his Disciples	173
The Personal Intercourse of our Lord with his Disciples	175
The Practical Intention of our Lord	182
The Authoritative Treatmen' of his Disciples	187
The Lord's Commission	190
The Conduct of his Disciples	196
The Pentecost	198

LECTURE VI.

THE APOSTOLICAL EXAMPLES.

Introductory Recapitulation	206
The Limited Theory of Infant Baptism	209

	PAGE
Dr. Halley's Theory without Discriminating Limitation	213
Constructions of the Commission	221
Dr. Halley on the Commission	234
Dr. Halley on the Apostolical Examples	239
The Argument Founded on Epistolary Passages	241
Dr. Halley on the Epistolary Passages	250
Epistolary Affirmations of Baptized Disciples	253
An Illustration	255
The Body of Christ, its Nature—what?	259
The Incorporation	260
Practical Illustrations	260
The Principle of its Discipline	273
Demonstrative Cases contained in the Epistles	274
Classified Examples contained in the Acts	280
Case of the Apostle Paul	289

LECTURE VII.

THE EARLY CHRISTIAN AUTHORS.

Introductory Recapitulation	293
The Object of the Present Inquiry	295
The Witness of Enemies	297
The Discipline Relating to Confessors	299
The Ancient Baptismal Controversy	300
The Catechumenical Discipline	301
The Discipline Relating to Sin after Baptism	302
The Ancient Heresies	303
The Testimony and Use of Ancient Christian Authors	305
The Testimonies from Rome	308
Evidence from Clement of Rome	317
The Testimonies from Greece	336
The Testimony of Theophylact	338
The Testimonies from Asia Minor	345
The Testimonies from Syria	352
The Testimonies from Palestine	354
The Testimony of Justin Martyr	359

CONTENTS. xiii

	PAGE
The Testimonies from Africa	364
The Conclusion from the Whole	371

LECTURE VIII.

THE GENERAL APOSTASY.

The Decisive Declaration	375
Dr. Halley's Transition Age, and the Apostolical Predictions	378
Dr. Halley's Mistakes	380
The Principles Combined in the Apostasy	384
The Love of Power	385
The Assumption of Sacramental Efficacy	385
The State Alliance	386
The Beginnings of their Action	388
The Principal Cause of the Apostasy	390
The Origin of the Assumption of Sacramental Efficacy	393
The Antichristian Error	396
The First Impression	398
The Successful Modification	400
The Rise of Infant Baptism	402
The Canons on Baptism	403
The Multiplication of Sacraments	404
The Monopoly of Sacramental Power	406
The Internal Effort to Reform	409
The Protestant Reformation	412
The Protestant Dissenters	414
The Last Resource	416
The Protecting Modifications of Dr. Halley	418
An Appeal to Christian Candour	421
Practical Inductions	431
Practical Dangers	433
Nature of Christian Faith	434
Modern Technicalities	437
Individual Churches	442
On the Discipline of Disciples	453
The Christian Enterprise	456

CONTENTS.

	PAGE
The Vicarious Service	460
The Labour and Prospect of Home	464
The Missionary Field	468
The Conflict	471
The Individual Requirement	473
A Motive to Fidelity	477

APPENDIX.

		PAGE
I.	On the Act of Christian Baptism	479
II.	English Renderings of "Μυστηριον"	507
III.	On the Ellipsis in the Commission	508

AUTHORS QUOTED IN THIS WORK.

Halley, Rev. Dr., Lectures on the Sacraments, vol. i., Edition I.
Stovel, Rev. Chas., Woolwich Lectures, Edition II.
        Hereditary Claims to the Covenant of Grace Considered and Rejected, Edition I.
        Letter on Baptismal Regeneration, Addressed through Dr. Fletcher to the Independents in 1842, Edition I.
        On Christian Duties, Edition I.
        Hints on the Regulation of Christian Churches, Edition I.
Lardner's, Dr., Works, vols. x., London, 1829.
Becon, Thos., S.T.P., The Catechism, Republished by the Parker Society.
Denne, Henry, A Treatise of Baptism, London, 1673, Rev. Chas. Darkin's copy.
Cicero, Elzevir Edition, 4 vols. in 2, 4to.
Septuagint, Ed. Bos., 4to, 1709.
Campbell, Dr., Jethro, Edition I., London.
Godwin, Rev. J. H., On Christian Baptism, 12mo, Edition I., London, 1845.
Gale, Rev. John, D.D., Reflections on Mr. Wall's History of Infant Baptism, London, 1820.
Meuschen (wrongly spelt *Moeschin*), p. 214, Ed. H. T. F. Braunii, Lipsiæ, 4to, 1736.
Clement of Rome, Ed. Paris, Epistolæ Romanorum Pontificum, &c., 1721.
Ignatius, Ed. by Archbishop Usher, Oxford, 1644.
Polycarp, Ibid.
Justin Martyr, Opera Omnia, folio, Paris, 1686.
Tertullian, Opera, folio, Lutetiæ, 1634.
Moshemii, De Rebus Christianorum Ante Constantinum Magnum Commentarii, 4to, 1753.
Hanmer's Chronographie, in Translation of Eusebius, &c., folio, London, 1619.
Theophylact on the Epistles of Paul, folio, London, 1636.
Clement of Alexandria, Opera, folio, Paris, 1641.
Hug's Introduction, &c., by the Rev. D. G. Wait, LL.D., London, 1827.
Eusebius, Ecclesiastical History, by Hanmer, folio, London, 1619.
Cypriani, Opera, Paris, 1564.
Cramp's Text-book of Popery.
Paul of Venice, His. Coun. Trent, folio, London, 1620.
The English Hexapla, Bagster, London, 1841.
Pindar, Ed. Heyne, 8vo, vol. ii., London, 1821.
Demosthenes, In Oratores Attici, Ed. Dove, vol. xvi.

PREFACE.

UNION is strength, and therefore it will be sought by all who are duly sensible of their own weakness. All objects involving practical difficulty require its advantage; and, the more important the object, the more imperative will be the demand. Hence is seen the value of that bond which toucheth, encompasseth, and joineth into one fraternity, the persons who are hoping for salvation in Christ, and to whom are entrusted the means of promoting salvation in others. No object can be more important than that which is committed to their care; and, in none, can the weakness of human nature be more deeply felt; and, therefore, to none can the attainment of perfect union be more indispensable, and on none can the obligation of promoting it devolve with greater solemnity.

The One Spirit by which Christians are led, and the

one hope of their calling, by which all are sustained and comforted, supply a preparation for that unity which is required. An attraction of moral affinity is thus produced, which naturally awakens the expectation of unity; for, as like loves like through all creation, it is to be expected in the body of Christ.

Had any suspicion rested on the lawfulness of yielding to this tendency, the strong combining influence of Christian principles in mankind would have called for extreme watchfulness and self-denial; but the Lord has spared his people from any such restraint: he has written his command to love one another with as much clearness as can be given to any form of words whatever. To indulge the love of union is, therefore, in the body of Christ, converted into positive duty.

To make this duty the more binding, the Lord, to whom every Christian is indebted for all that he possesses or hopes to possess, has actually combined his own honour with its observance. The wealth, the honour, the learning, the power, and all the things which men are prone to love, seek, and delight in upon earth, are totally disregarded by him; he pronounces his benedictions on the poverty of his people's spirit, and their persecution for righteousness' sake; and, in these their peculiar disadvantages on earth, he says, "This is my commandment, that ye love one another; then shall all men know that ye are my disciples, if ye love one another."

When the position, duties, and enemies of Christians are properly considered, these facts cease to be surprising. They stand where the things of time take hold upon eternity, for the earthly house of their tabernacle hath its aspect altogether in that direction. Each one knows that it looks out upon the sea, and that, when it falls, it will fall into the ocean. Yet the uncertain moment, during which he stands upon the falling precipice of time, is occupied, under the eye of the Redeemer himself, in duties which involve the salvation of other souls; and not one duty can be performed, but in the face of this world's stedfast opposition, led on by the great deceiver. If other men need watchfulness, these need more; they require to be all eyes and all attention, that no opportunity be lost, that no energy be wasted, but that all the resources entrusted to them be perfectly used, at the point and moment of action. It is not only requisite that each should be faithful and diligent, it is necessary that all should be one.

Divine aid is covenanted by the Redeemer, who saith, " I am with you always, even to the end of the world; " yet is that aid so imparted, to each of his servants, that no one is permitted to feel sufficient in himself alone. The Lord deals with his people as with a flock, a family, a body composed of many parts, which cannot be perfect if one be wanting. The meanest is thus essential to the rest; and he who is most exalted in station and endowment, is as nothing without the brethren he is called to serve. Separated from the body of Christ, a believer is an incomplete and an unmeaning existence, resembling an amputated limb.

By a vital union to Christ, and the indwelling of the Spirit, an actual union between all true believers is rendered inevitable; but this is not all that the commandment and the case require. Men are voluntary and moral agents after, as well as before, conversion to God. In the exercise of all their faculties they are to serve the Lord who redeemed them, and brought them to himself. Hence the union of such must be a willing and visible action, recognising the Lord's injunction, and raising, to highest estimation and honour, that work of grace by which each has been created anew in Christ Jesus.

How this union of Christians should be recognised and declared, by each individual, and by the body of Christ, has long been a subject of dispute, even amongst true believers. This is the more to be regretted, because thereby a broken front has been presented to the adversary, and the external fissures of division have been widened and deepened, until the separating of believers from believers has become as much a matter of course now, as in former times and by the law of Christ, was the separation of believers from the world.

Few have paid much attention to Christian affairs, without perceiving this evil ; and none who love the Saviour can see without deploring it. Hence the numerous expedients proposed for its redress. Time, money, and great good feeling, have been expended profusely, but without effect. The church or body of Christ is still divided, though division is deprecated and deplored. The external appearance and the internal working of Christian fellowship declare with too much distinctness for misapprehension, that hitherto a remedy for this evil has not been prescribed.

One cause for this failure may be found in the wrong assumption on which the various expedients have been adopted. It seems to be forgotten that, for such calamities, it is not the province of man to prescribe at all. Human weakness and frailty are congenial with the introduction of moral evils, such as this is, but absolutely fatal to the working out of a cure. Men may divide, but union can only be effected *in* the Lord. All deliverance from moral calamity and wrong must be obtained, if at all, under his direction, and by his aid.

Another cause of failure is to be discovered in the fallacy of the proposed rule of action, by which a greater degree of unity is sought. Charles V. of Germany used his utmost power to produce a quiet resignation of points of difference, and subjection to defined principles and doctrines. He is only an example by which the absurdity of this compulsory effort may be elucidated; but the most remarkable fact is, that union should be sought by proposing the voluntary quiescence on such points now, which, when blood had flowed in rivers, could not be imposed by any power that then or formerly obtained an existence upon earth. It is said, Let the points on which we differ be passed by, and investigation cease; or, in other words, let us cease to learn, that we may be united. To show the fallacy of such a proposal, it is sufficient to say, that by ceasing to learn, we cease to be disciples, and that the pursuit and diffusion of truth can never be relinquished, except by those who do not love it.

A third cause of failure may be seen in the desire to combine incongruous elements. He was a wise Master-builder who said, " What fellowship hath light with darkness ?" The fall of a building and the ruin that attends it, will justly be imputed to the man who, with fraud or carelessness, builded into its walls and arches, blocks of ice for stone. God has decreed that his people shall be separate from the world, and he has endowed them with principles to which the men of this world are positively and absolutely opposed. If, by a forced contact, these unfriendly principles be, for a time, suppressed, the explosion, when it transpires, will be augmented by all the violence that is now employed in restraining them. Nature will, eventually, have her own way. It is a prerogative granted by her Creator.

Hence, it would appear, that union between Christians and the men of this world, is not to be sought as if there were no difference between them. On the contrary, Christians are to come out from among them and be separate. But the union of Christians with each other is to be sought with all perseverance, and since it can only be obtained in Christ, it must be sought by a scrupulous and absolute conformity to his instructions. This must be obtained, not in one particular only, but in all. Moral society, like a vast and complex machinery, is broken and ruined by departing from truth in any one of its centres. When the working is found to be wrong, therefore, he is the kindest and wisest man, who brings the greatest skill, and devotes the most attention, to those parts of the machinery in which the wrong may be, by possibility, detected; for, by securing conformity to Divine law, we secure unity, smoothness, and efficiency of action.

If the investigation, conducted in this work, has not altogether failed, it will serve to illustrate, at least, that simple and most practicable law by which the Lord provided for the union and holy fellowship of his people. The baptismal rite, requiring a credible declaration of repentance and faith, marked and set apart individual believers for the embraces and fellowship of each other. Protected by the discipline which cast out, until subsequent repentance was evinced, every offender against the law of Christ, the baptismal profession and recognition defined a sphere within which the Christian disciple is bound to indulge the affectionate confidence which his regeneration produces, and the cultivation of which his Lord commands. This natural basis and protected sphere for exercising brotherly love and Christian fellowship, is the great desideratum of our time; and nothing can be more pleasing than to observe how directly the efforts to promote Christian union are bringing us back to the law of our Lord, and the practice of ancient times. If Christians are to be one, each one ought to have, and must have, some way of determining who the Christians are. He cannot examine every one; and to give every professor the endearing confidence of Christian love, is to expose with weakness the best feelings of his heart to constant violation and abuse. This the Lord hath nowhere commanded; and nothing can show its impropriety more than that sentimental feeling which, professing to love all mankind as Christians, reveals a mind utterly unacquainted with the nature of that holy principle, from which it has purloined the name. He who opposeth, in nature, the attractions of affinity, as far as in him lies, urgeth a dissolution of all her beautiful organisations, and of all the jewels that enrich her mountains; and he who burlesques the union of Christians with Christians, and yet pleads for Christian unity, pleads, under that phrase, for a restoration of that moral chaos in which God has ever been dishonoured, and from which Christians have been redeemed. The rites and discipline of the Christian church were designed to bring accredited Christians as purely and as closely as possible within the sphere of each other's influence. Thus, like the particles which form a diamond, they are prepared to obey that attraction of moral affinity which produces an aggregated union not to be dissolved.

Dr. Halley cannot receive too high an encomium for the spirit with which he has entered a perplexing and unpopular discussion with this aim. He has ventured in a track not much trodden, and led his inquiry to points from which, if all parties are not instructed by their own observations as well as his, it will be their own fault. If he has failed in his main object, this has often occurred to the best of men, even where the purest motives have led to the undertaking; and should it appear that, in the warmth of his feeling, some departures from cool propriety have occurred, these accidents are too few and insignificant to diminish, in any great degree, the praise which is due to his eminent superiority over writers who have formerly appeared on his side.

Observing the work he performed, and the importance of the investigation, because of its influence over the health and communion of Christian churches, it was felt to be a duty to lay before the brethren of all classes, the thoughts which are contained in the following lectures. To give them the most general character, and facilitate the attendance of all parties, the use of the library was requested and obtained, and admission was granted, by tickets gratuitously distributed, on application. The kindness shown to this individual effort in defence of truth, far exceeds all desert or expectation; and the result is, by request of those who heard the exercises, herein presented to the reader. If an earnest desire to find, exhibit, and defend the truth has led to any undue severity, or the least discourtesy of expression, it is altogether without design, and will, when discovered, be deeply deplored. It was felt that Dr. Halley's theory of indiscriminate baptism and discipleship was not sustained by truth and led to pernicious consequences, by filling the church with elements of disunion, defeating the principal aim for which the Lord had appointed it, and, in the highest degree, endangering the whole interests of personal religion. Whether these views be well supported, the reader will decide. The work, with all its demerits, is presented to him in the hope that its perusal will be attended with a Divine blessing.

LECTURE I.

INTRODUCTORY.

WHATEVER Jehovah is pleased, in his providence, to permit, his people must endure, and improve for his glory. To man, his arrangements may, for a time, be obscure; but they possess a consistency with his Divine perfections which, when rightly perceived, will provoke admiration and praise. Perhaps, too, these darker features of his providential system are essential to our perceiving the beauty we now observe in those which yield us the greatest pleasure: we could not know the patience and kindness of God in teaching, unless we knew how slow mankind has been to learn. If this could be borne in mind, it would relieve and enrich the labours connected with this tedious controversy. To its continuance in the nineteenth century we could scarcely be reconciled, by any thought, other than, that it is for God, and by his permission; but if, in conducting it, we may hope to perceive greater endearments in the operations of his love, this will sufficiently reward whatever trial and exertion it may demand.

ON THE WORD "DISCIPLE."

The very first thought, then, baptizes our whole subject in that element of divine perfection; for the word "disciple" has been chosen by our Lord, to designate those who, under his guidance, were seeking to know the fulness and beauty of Divine love, as exercised towards men; and in whom, by his consent, the hope of its blessings was entertained. Round those individuals, and in their treatment, we find, in the gospel histories, a government which combines, both for protection and improvement, exertions of power which produce dread, and operations of love which command admiration. Human society never presented its capabilities of enjoyment and holiness so perfectly as in that community which was formed between Christ and his disciples; no men have ever possessed greater hopes than those which they were invited to cherish; and none were ever called to a more responsible service than that which they performed. They were the constituents of the reign or dominion of God, in Christ, upon the earth: from them the Lord selected the twelve, and the seventy, who formed his special messengers to mankind; these, collected in assemblies, formed his churches; out of these, and by these, his ministers were chosen: they formed, in fact, a community in themselves, distinguished from all other men, in that they revered and obeyed his authority, and enjoyed his favour. A right interpretation and use of this word, therefore, while it is essential to a correct view of practical Christianity, will lead us into the centre of its speaking mysteries.

The word μαθητης, used by our Lord and the Evangelists, in this case, has, for its synonyms, ακροατης, a hearer, ὁμιλητης, a companion, φοιτητης, an attendant, and γνωριμος, one that has been recognised. All these terms have a relation to διδασκαλος, a teacher; and while each brings into prominence one particular feature in that relationship, its use implies the features brought into prominence by the rest: thus, if the disciple be called ακροατης, a hearer, it is implied that he is also γνωριμος, a recognised hearer; and μαθητης includes all that the relationship includes. In some instances, the disciples of a school used a peculiar name; in other, a peculiar dress. In the school of Pythagoras, at Crotona, the recognition of a disciple was called a beginning of a new life; and his expulsion from the school, for violating its laws, was solemnised as his funeral; after which he was written dead. Each school might have its own peculiar aim and laws; but, in all, the disciple of any teacher was regarded as one who recognised the truth and importance of his doctrine; and who, in order to acquire a proficiency in its knowledge and use, submitted to his instructions and discipline.

Most of the ancient schools which attained to recorded celebrity, rose out of some form, in which the miseries and criminalities of human society enforced attention and claimed a remedy. The good that was promised in each school, whether Jewish or Gentile, was to be obtained by a patient adherence to the discipline of its teacher. The relationship was essentially personal—the benefit sought was personal, that benefit was sought of a person, the teacher; and by a person, the disciple: it brought these persons, therefore, into contact and union for the matter in hand. The forming of such a relationship supposed a confidence in the teacher; and the attainment of its proposed advantages involved a constant exercise of that confidence.

In the discourses of our Lord we find no new definition of the term. The object of his school was, to teach the way of salvation; and his discipline was formed to secure, for his disciples, the full and personal enjoyment of its blessings. His great engagement is, Believe in me, and you shall be saved, sin and mortality notwithstanding; but the requirement of his school is so enforced, that "if any one love father or mother, brother or sister, wife or child, or even his own life, more than me," his Lord and Teacher, "he cannot be my disciple." By this declaration of the Lord himself, the business and law of his community were defined; and those who were recognised in their devotion to him under this rule, became, at an early age, designated Christians.

The recognition of disciples is, in Scripture, and by all who now adhere to that rite, ascribed to Christian Baptism, which Dr. Halley calls "*the badge of discipleship.*" On this recognition, its conditions, and its results, the constitution and government of this whole community depends; for the disciples so recognised are its members. To them are entrusted its oracles and laws; and by them, in the bodily absence of their Lord, these oracles are to be interpreted, and these laws are to be administered. This community, therefore, will be, in effect, what these disciples are: if *they* be sincere, the *community* will be pure; if they be superficial and insincere, the reverse will follow. Hence proceeds the importance of our whole inquiry; for, the influence of circumstances, and especially of religious disputations, has changed the meaning of the word "disciple;" and the action induced by this change in its import, has changed the character of the Christian community, involved the nature of that community, and the constitution of its assemblies or churches, in almost infinite dispute; it has changed the whole aspect of the Saviour's kingdom, modified its procedure in the work of mercy, betrayed its dearest interests, and dishonoured its Author in the eyes of all mankind. The forbearance with which the Lord has endured this injury exceeds our comprehension: and nothing can be more important than the correction of the evil; for words exert an influence over thought and feeling; and action, whether right or wrong, is destined to produce its natural results.

DR. HALLEY'S INTERPRETATION.

Those who profess to be disciples of Christ are bound, by that profession, so to observe his instructions, that the things affirmed, by inspiration, of disciples and churches in the time of our Lord and his apostles, may, in similar cases, be affirmed of disciples and churches now. If they were "*sons of God by faith in Christ Jesus,*" these *ought* to be; if the former were encouraged, and even commanded, to cherish a peaceful expectation of blessings which correspond with that high relationship; the latter, when recognised, should be in a condition to do the same: otherwise, the very reading of Scripture becomes delusive. A deep sense of this requirement has led every party in the Christian world to form some theory of discipleship, and its recognition, by which its own practice might seem to be reconciled with Scriptural affirmations. Some have ascribed to the recognising rite, a power of producing, in its recipient, such a change in personal character and moral qualities as would justify their receiving as such, after baptism, the person who was not a disciple before. Others have assumed an hereditary claim to discipleship, as though individuals descending from religious parents inherited the qualification to Christian discipleship by natural birth. Dr. Halley is not satisfied with either of these theories; and, therefore, in distinctly repudiating them, he affirms that Christian discipleship required no personal qualification at all; but that, by the Saviour's own authority, the recognising baptism was administered without any discrimination whatever. By this means, the modern practice is *not* reconciled to the ancient and inspired affirmations; but these very inspired affirmations themselves, are, by this attempt, placed in clear and open hostility with the practice of their authors, of the Lord himself, and his last commission; for the supposition that the recognising baptism was administered indiscriminately, could never show how every baptized person may be designated "*a child of God by faith in Christ Jesus;*" it would rather show, that the apostle, being indiscreet, had written a sentence which could not, with propriety, be used at all.

THE INFLUENCE OF PARTIES.

Dr. Halley affirms, that his views on this subject have been long entertained by him. This may be the case; but they bear a singular relation to the state of parties at the present time. Where none but accredited believers are recognised in baptism as disciples of our Lord, no difficulty has yet been found in using, under similar circumstances, the language of the apostles: but modern times have imposed, on Christian teachers, the task of reconciling their conduct to the use of that language, when others than accredited believers have been recognised as disciples: both adults, who have neither professed nor indicated, and infants, who are incapable of, repentance and faith. Moreover, this difficulty has been augmented by a diversity of view and profession, in those who advocate the disputed practice. Some profess to do more, and to do it better, than others can dare to promise; and the great Protestant principle obliges an appeal to sacred Scripture. Each would preserve the infant baptism which has, since the reign of Popery, been embalmed in the affections of mankind; but each would give it a different character. One party must have it esteemed the cause of spiritual benefits in the subject: one section claiming to one extent, and another to another, but both pleading for some spiritual gift in baptism; the other party disclaiming the baptismal benefit, but pleading an hereditary condition of discipleship and right to the covenant of grace. Each, with equal justice, pleads against the other a departure from inspired truth, and an incompatibility, in the theory proposed, with the doctrine of justification by faith. During the last ten years, this conflict, between the Tractmen of Oxford and the Evangelical Pædobaptists, has increased in its extent and acrimonious hostility. Nothing could show more perfectly than this conflict, the immutable perfection of truth; for, as each has been compelled to search for support in the divine oracles, each has been found to be wrong. The ceremony to be defended has been placed in danger, by the conflict of its own advocates. The Tractmen profess to administer the rite more beneficially than the unanointed Evangelicals; and the Evangelicals have pleaded that they can administer it as *well*, and more unexceptionably, than their ordained brethren. During the conflict, Baptists, reasoning from their mutual arguments and concessions, have shown that neither party can administer it with scriptural propriety at all. Hence the most urgent requirement of these times has been, a defence of infant baptism, which might, at least, seem to accord with our present knowledge of revealed truth: such a production had, indeed, been called for,* and was indispensable; and Dr. Halley has come forward to meet the demand.

THE RESUSCITATION.

It is not to be understood that the Oxford Tractmen are originals. This they do not profess. They have only given visibility to the doctrine and laws of the English Hierarchy, which differ, on this point, in nothing essential from those of the Lutheran Church and that of Rome. Indeed, wherever the spiritual gift in baptism is taught, and its expectation is entertained, without faith in the subject, whatever name the advocate bears, and whatever his other peculiarities, he falls, with the Tractmen, into the same class of persons advocating baptismal benefits. This elementary error lay, for ages, almost unobserved, in canons, articles, and old controversial writings; few perceiving its malignity, and almost no one dreading its power. When forced upon public attention, by these popular writings, every Dissenter, at least, was ready to smile, and say, The Bible is abroad; we cannot fear anything of this sort *now*. But its way was prepared before it, and its victory has been singular. It has actually appealed to Scripture against the hereditary scheme; and it has not appealed in vain. Its advocates have demanded, in its favour, the high import of Scripture

---

* Stovel's Letter on Baptismal Regeneration, addressed, through Dr. Fletcher, to the Independents, in 1842.

language: and they have urged obedience on the principle of faith only. Angry, as if outraged, the whole body of Evangelical Pædobaptists have protested and declaimed, but failed to meet the just demand of their opponents. Having no canons or councils to confine and regulate them, they have individually quoted Scripture by piecemeal; and, by the variation of their views and declarations, have almost justified the worst allegations of the Papists. The variations of defence and explanation respecting the rite were so great and so frequent, that a friend could find nothing to stand by, and an objector to the theory had nothing tangible and recognised to refute. The same things were so often affirmed and denied, that no common starting point could be found in the discussion; and the inquirer found no pathway in the jungle. The Tractmen were condemned, sometimes with incivility; but the Scriptures were not explained, and their consistent application to modern use, in reference to recognised disciples of Jesus, was not shown. These inconsistencies and sometimes improprieties in its advocates, do not prove that infant baptism is invalid; but they do show, must fully, that its defence and explanation imperatively claimed some such centralising and vigorous effort as that in which Dr. Halley has served the public.

DR. HALLEY'S AUTHORITY.

It will scarcely be supposed that Dr. Halley is, in the highest sense, an *authority ;* because the brethren on his side professedly defer to none but God: yet his

Lectures were delivered under such peculiar auspices, that they cannot be treated as an ordinary production. He was called to that work by the Congregational body. The subject was chosen for him by his brethren. The Lectures, prepared with great deliberation, were heard in the denominational house, in Blomfield-street, with great applause, and even cheering. They were revised with great care, published with a commendatory advertisement from the body, and reviewed, with almost unqualified praise, in the Congregational organs. It is to be hoped, therefore, that he will not be hereafter repudiated by those whom he has come forward to defend: they, at least, will sustain him as far as their consciences will allow: by them surely he will be read with care, and his proposals will be weighed with deep attention: this is due from them: and, after what has transpired, unless his brethren do, openly and avowedly, reject him, we are justified in using these Lectures as an authority from which the general views of Congregational Pædobaptists may be understood; and, for the arguments of which, that body will be answerable.

DR. HALLEY'S AIM.

The work, which has been long before the public, is entitled "*The Sacraments*," and in the first two exercises much attention is paid to the nature and perpetual obligation of the two rites so designated in Protestant churches. To a certain extent his reasoning relates to both Baptism and the Lord's Supper; but, the latter being reserved, and the nature of the case requiring it, his principal attention is fixed upon the former. The propriety of this is obvious; for, the whole question of sacramental efficacy, and also of the constitution of Christian churches, is involved here. In whatever way we answer the question, What is Christian baptism, and who are to be baptized? the effect will follow, by inevitable consequence, through all the constitution and operations of the church of Christ. The interior cannot be arranged until this question of initiation, at its entrance, has been determined.

DR. HALLEY'S OWN WORDS.

"Whether I have been successful or not in pursuing the inquiry with an impartial and unbiassed mind, I do believe that, if other and abler divines on both sides will divest themselves of prejudice, they may bring this dispute to a satisfactory determination. Instead of saying, so quietly and comfortably as some good people do, Let us agree to differ; it would be more in accordance with our respect for the will and authority of Christ, to say, Let us agree to find out the truth, adhering closely to Scripture, seeking all aid in its correct interpretation, assuming nothing without proof, and carefully endeavouring to detect the cause of the error, on whichever side it be, the πρῶτον ψεῦδος which, lurking in the breast of one party or the other, in this, as in almost every controversy, vitiates all the subsequent reasoning, and, ever present in the dispute, colours, with a false light, the arguments adduced on each side of the question; concealing the weakness of some, and imputing a fictitious value to others. Let us reach, if it be possible, the *arx causæ* of this unhappy dispute, and there it surely cannot be difficult for an unprejudiced mind to ascertain the truth. That central position of controversy, respecting infant baptism, on which the whole depends, appears to be, so far as I can judge, whether faith be or be not the proper qualification for baptism. Vituperation and abuse in this controversy have, probably, done more than anything else to obscure the truth. Let every controversialist consider how far he is guilty of obstructing, by the acrimony of his words, the force of his own arguments.

"There is also another controversy on baptism, at the present time, of great importance, as upon its decision, more than upon anything else, depends the settlement of the momentous and agitating question of the day—the doctrine of sacramental efficacy. Upon baptism, we have more full and precise information than we have upon any other ritual observance; and, if baptism be not regeneration; if it do not produce or imply any moral or spiritual change, the whole fabric of sacramental efficacy falls to the ground, and with it, the authority of the priesthood and the mediation of the church; so that, having nothing left for our dependence, we must look immediately and exclusively to the grace of God, through Jesus Christ our Lord. This one point being decided, the whole dispute between Protestant and Catholic, in every form and aspect, Anglo-Catholic or Roman Catholic, vanishes as a mist from the region of theology. Of the importance of this controversy, it is not easy to offer an exaggerated statement."—*Dr. Halley's Lectures,* pp. 112—114.

The concluding words of this passage are most true, "*Of the importance of this controversy it is not easy to offer an exaggerated statement*"—and the spirit of the whole, which for the most part pervades his work, is worthy of the author and his undertaking. He has grasped its central thought, and is right in saying that it is time to meet the whole question with unhesitating boldness. When the Tractmen have occupied nearly all our parishes, and pioneered the way for Popery in all the land; presenting the gospel in a false light, and strengthening heathenism by producing greater absurdities in the name of Christ; it is no time for evangelical Christians to shrink away from light for fear of its effects on some peculiar and favourite practice of their own. The practice which will not harmonise with inspired truth is not worthy of their esteem. Now, if at any time, abandoning all prejudice, the followers of Jesus should come, with all simplicity, to the one inspired and authoritative rule of action in the church of Christ. By its teaching they should search out and correct the original and germ of every error. The stain of a corruption, generated and matured in the dark ages, has been borne upon Protestant churches long enough. It is time to seek the Lord with all the heart. In doing this every disciple is bound to shrink from no scrutiny, and to forsake no truth which comes under the authority of Him to whom alone salvation is entrusted. He is all in all; his authority is supreme; and nothing should be so dear to his disciples as his glory.

Imperfection is an element in human nature, and to be traced in all its actions; he, therefore, who, in the midst of infirmity, aims well, deserves the more respect. This Dr. Halley justly claims. He not only states the rule, as you have heard; he pursues its application, and to an extent which is scarcely equalled in modern times. Having weighed the popular theories of infant baptism, and the common arguments used in its defence, he has found their weakness and, in effect, abandoned them; and, if he has not reached, he has brought this controversy nearer to the origin of modern errors, than any other author writing on his side.

To inquire what baptism is, whether it be the act of pouring or sprinkling water upon a man, or the act of immersing the man himself therein, will not come within our design;* and, therefore, the part of Dr. Halley's work which relates to Dr. Carson, and what has been so improperly designated the *Mode* of Baptism, might have been passed over, had not the spirit of this argument formed an exception to the foregoing commendation. If the Lecturer became, in this case, a little too eloquent for close reasoning, and too sarcastical for the work of convincing, it must be allowed, as an apology, that his antagonist was one of no common order. The materials of that author's work are so vast, and, on every new investigation, appear so demonstrative, that an opponent, not quite convinced, may be excused for being a little irritated; and after the acknowledgment published on the information of Dr. Carson's death, instead of severely rebuking, we should sympathise with Dr. Halley, and rather be admonished by so affecting an incident to treat our opponents, when engaged in controversy, as we shall wish that we had treated them when earthly relationships have been broken by mortality. This is the more

* See a "Short and Easy Method with the Word Baptize," in Appendix I.

to be desired, because reputation for rectitude and good temper is as important to a man while living, as it can be after his decease. On this ground, some of the insinuations contained in page vii. of his Introduction, might have been spared by Dr. Halley with advantage. He says, " If I can succeed in convincing our Baptist brethren, not that we are right, but that we have a case which honest men may honestly maintain without being chargeable with criminally resisting the truth, &c., my chief object, &c., will be attained." Familiar as this jerking method may be to others, it is so far from Dr. Halley's ordinary style, that his usual precision is lost while employing it; for his Baptist brethren have based their whole argument, for free communion, on the supposition, that the practice he has received into the place of that which Christ ordained, may be, conscientiously, so mistaken, and so " *maintained*." The maintaining of these mistakes will not prove men to be honest; but when "honest men" do maintain them, they will do it *honestly*, or cease to be " *honest men*." Dr. Halley's *Baptist* brethren, moreover, are not more likely than other brethren to blame men for " *honestly* maintaining" what they think to be true; but they have long felt, and still feel, that the Divine authority of a rite, enforced on their observance in the name of God, is a far more important consideration to them than the method and spirit employed by other persons in its advocacy.

THE ORIGIN AND POSITION OF MODERN BAPTISTS.

Before the position and feelings of the Baptist brethren can be rightly appreciated, a few things must be considered relating to the origin of their churches. When Tertullian, about A.D. 200,* wrote against the baptism of young people, and persons not duly prepared for that rite and its engagements, he rebuked the practice as a novelty unauthorised by Scripture or the practice of the early churches; but when the Protestant reformers bore their protest against it, the practice was very general, and, supported by the highest ecclesiastical authority, formed a part of those religious errors which are now called Papal. The doctrine of sacramental benefits, without personal faith in those supposed to receive them, had grown to maturity; and, on its delusive influence, the most extensive and powerful religious usurpation had been erected. All through Europe the Reformation consisted in appealing to Scripture against the domination and edicts of this spiritual tyranny. The war began with indulgences, and the outworks of Papal superstition; but the conflict soon involved its central idea, the supposed power of sacraments to convey the grace of God to their recipients, and the absolute necessity of grace, supposed to be so conveyed, to the salvation of men. By this means, the doctrine of the fall, and of original sin, and the absolute depravity of human nature, became illustrated and exemplified, by being turned into essential

---

* Lardner, vol. ii., p. 271.

elements of a traffic the most fascinating and gainful to its conductors. When once the Reformers had broken down its bulwark of anathemas, and assailed this vital part, the Papal power writhed with convulsion, as a monster struggling for existence. By appealing to Scripture, Luther sustained his doctrine of justification by faith only, and thereby repelled, exploded, and overwhelmed with obloquy, the Romish doctrine of justification by grace received through sacraments. In the hands of Wickliffe, Huss, Tindal, Knox, and the Protestant martyrs, the Reformation was the same; it removed the hope of man from grace expected through sacraments, to grace received through faith in Jesus Christ alone. Nothing could sustain this conflict but a wide circulation of Holy Scripture, and a general and direct appeal to its authority. By this means, it was not only proved that justification by faith only came from God, and was his own act, but that, in his Word, only two such rites as those now called sacraments are ever enforced; and that the use of these is justified by God *in believers only:* the Baptism, to recognise their relationship in the family of God; and the Supper, for their edification in its fellowship. It was by advancing this step, and giving a visible existence to this doctrine, that the reforming Scripture students obtained from their contemporaries the appellation " Baptists;" and, on the same ground, they are now designated " Baptist Brethren."

Should Providence, at any future time, lay open for our use the official records of ecclesiastical persecution, much greater information may be expected on the subject now before us. As the case now stands, it is with great difficulty determined, from their confessions, whether many Protestant martyrs were Baptists or no. It is often quite impossible. The conflict with the common enemy was so absorbing, and the common interests of the Protestants were so great, that, until the act of National Reformation had transpired, the appellation " Baptist" was not forced into common use; and the previous existence of those who held this sentiment, is proved only by rare documents and incidents recorded indirectly, in England, indeed, till the time of Wickliffe; but, on the continent, to an earlier period—perhaps, to the age of Paul. But when the act of National Reformation took place, a vital question to be considered was, how the uninformed and unconverted masses of the people might be most peacefully transferred from a Papal to a Protestant government, and most effectually united under its rule? In determining this question, to every worldly politician it would appear, that the less change they introduced in the external ceremonies and popular rites of religion, the more their difficulties would diminish; because the change would thus become less obvious and painful to the subject. Hence, it is said that Luther, and the other Reformers, retained as much of the Papal ceremonies and sacramental doctrine as they could, with any appearance of consistency, defend. But the Bible was abroad, and others could not, they wanted the motive to cease from inquiry, when the legislative

Reformers affirmed that they had learned enough. The Word of God became so sweet, that they would learn it all. There they found a religion that was personal, with everlasting hopes, that expanded to infinity, and whose action was as free as the praise of angels. The legislative Reformers had no design to leave religion to herself, her friends, and God; they deemed her a home-born slave, and shuddered at the thought of her emancipation from their use and rule. Their subjects, therefore, went before them. They still kept reading, and claimed of the ruler what they found written in, the Word of God. It was then that in Germany the terms Baptist and Anabaptist became uttered with scorn; then, also, in the court of Edward VI., the men so designated were called "bloody murderers of infants;" and thus these students of the Holy Word, and their descendants, were loaded with the obloquy and griefs of a second Reformation.

A PASSAGE FROM BECON.

"The best and the chiefest baptism is given to the infants; and shall we deny them the inferior and baser baptism? God hath baptized them with the Holy Ghost; and shall we disdain to baptize them with water? . . . . 'They that are led with the Spirit of God,' saith St. Paul, 'are the sons of God.' The infants of the Christians are led with the Spirit of God, as we heard of the Prophet Jeremy, and of St. John Baptist; and St. Paul likewise calleth the children of the Christians holy and pure; therefore are they the sons of God. Now, if the infants of the Christians be pure, and holy, and the sons of God, shall any man be so rigorous to take that from them which God hath appointed and ordained for his sons?

"God hath instituted baptism as a most certain pledge of his love, mercy, and favour toward his people, and hath commanded it to be received of all that appertain unto him; and shall we, contrary to the commandment and will of God, deny it to the infants whom Christ commanded to be brought unto him? whom Christ most lovingly embraced in his arms? whom Christ most graciously blessed? whom Christ pronounced to belong unto the kingdom of God? whose angels Christ affirmeth to see the face of our heavenly Father? Who seeth not here, therefore, the madness of those apish Anabaptists which, contrary to the commandment and expressed will of God, forbid baptism to be given unto the infants? Our Saviour Christ saith, 'Except a man be born of water and of the Spirit, he cannot enter into the kingdom of God.' What other thing, then, do the Anabaptists, by forbidding the water of baptism to be given unto infants, than utterly seclude and put away the young children, so much as in them is, from the inheritance of God's kingdom, and so to become for ever heirs of everlasting damnation? O most damnable sect! O bloody murderers, both of souls and bodies! As they are of the devil their father, so do these wicked Anabaptists satisfy the desires of the devil their father, 'which was a murderer from the beginning, and abode not in the truth, because there is no truth in him.'"—*The Catechism of Thomas Becon, S.T.P., Chaplain to Archbishop Cranmer, &c., Republished by the Parker Society*, pp. 208, 209.

The language here quoted from Becon is strong, but not abusive; it was intended, after the manner of that age, to define the reputed character of the persons to whom it was applied.* By Cranmer,

---

* In making this apology for Becon, it is proper to except

Becon, and the divines who formed the English Liturgy, and conducted the Reformation under Edward, the doctrine of sacramental efficacy was holden and taught; and Baptists were condemned as murderers of infants, because they withheld from them a supposed benefit, without which it was deemed that their salvation was uncertain, if not impossible. Persons of this persuasion had united in separate church fellowship, and suffered martyrdom for their views, in Britain, as early as the reign of Henry VIII. From Becon's work it is quite clear, that the discussion of their sentiments on baptism had been conducted so as to include all the points now deemed vital in that controversy. Through the long and troubled interval from Edward VI. to the commonwealth, with all its convulsions, the Baptists inherited their uniform portion of obloquy, persecution, and martyrdom. The oldest church now known was formed in Wapping, in A.D. 1633; but no minister of that persuasion was found in the Assembly at Westminster, and that body of divines showed them no favour. Dr. Featley, who sat in the Assembly, and Edwards, have shown their existence and importance by the acrimony with which they treated their teachers and sentiments. Owen, Baxter, and others, followed on the same side, and in the same spirit; but for the language of these,

---

those who have republished this language without any note to guard its application. It will be undignified and inexcusable if moderns recall the ancient dead, that, through their writings, affirmations may be circulated which no living author has the courage either to make or to defend in his own person.

Lightfoot, and other authorities, the apology offered for Becon must be received. They had all to do with a national religion, and they taught, in modified forms, the doctrine of baptismal benefits without faith. The Baptists had to do with personal religion, and they knew of no right use to be made of baptism which did not suppose the previous existence of faith in its recipients; they have, therefore, been regarded and treated as persons withholding from unoffending infants an important spiritual benefit; and their constancy has been sustained by their reverence for Divine authority, and their deep conviction that these supposed baptismal benefits, however taught, are specious delusions, diverting mankind from the only way of personal salvation.

THE STATEMENTS OF EARLY BAPTISTS.

If the words of Becon imply a serious matter in dispute, the views entertained by those whom he condemned were not less serious and momentous. If true, they demanded the utmost decision in defending them; if false, their exposure and refutation demanded a similar zeal from the opponent. A single illustration will suffice to justify this remark. In the work of Henry Denne, entitled "A Treatise on Baptism," published in London, 1673, we find the following passages:—

"If the very act of sprinkling or pouring a little water on the child's head or face (with the charms attending it) must give *grace, regenerate,* take away *sin,* save the *soul,* add to the *church,* and give right to all the *ordinances ;* as Mr.

Pope hath been pleased, sitting in the temple of God, as God, to *ordain* and *decree,* and that with anathemas, too, against every one that shall not so receive it; how naturally must it follow,—first, that Christ's *conversion,* and the powerful preaching of the gospel, his means to effect it, must be *slighted* and *despised;* ignorance and profanity, the true interest of this state, necessarily brought in; Christ's *baptism,* with all the *spiritual ends* and *uses,* outed and contemned; the *Jewish* antichristian *rites* of a *national church* and *high priesthood,* with all the appurtenances, *introduced ;*—secondly, that, as the nations should accept this new project of being made *Christians* and *church members* by the Pope's *christening,* they necessarily oblige themselves, by receiving his law, to *embrace* also his government, and to be ruled in chief by himself (as the greatest part, called Christendom, have done accordingly), who can deny it? To the erecting a *throne* for the *beast,* and to give that vile person (whom blasphemously they call his *Holiness*) cause to say (looking over his goodly fabric, with his father of old, Dan. iv. 30), '*Is not this great* Babylon *that I have built by the might of my power and for the honour of my majesty ?*' And so hath it become the corner and foundation of the *anti-christian* church and state."—Preface, p. 2.

"For, as they who take (as far as they can judge) *living stones* (called the *spiritual seed,* saints by calling, or believers) to build Christ a *house* or *church,* orderly joining them together by *dipping,* do yield obedience to Christ's *command, conform* to the *primitive* pattern of the *New Testament churches,* ascribe *honour* and glory to the Lord Christ, the Institutor; so they who take the *carnal seed,* viz., *ignorant* and *unconverted* ones, to make up the *national* or any *particular church,* joining them together by *sprinkling,* do thereby yield obedience to the *Pope's canons,* conform to the *Jewish* and *antichristian pattern,* and reflect honour and dignity to their sovereign lord the *Pope,* the *contriver* and *imposer* thereof."—*Ibid.,* p. 3.

" But that which is most to be lamented is, that the *Protestant reformers,* who detected and cast away so many antichristian abominations, should yet hold fast such a principal *foundation*-stone of their *building;* though, it is granted, with the rejecting of many of its *superstitions,* and also upon other pretended *grounds:* for, when the rottenness of the *Popish* grounds aforesaid did appear for *infants' sprinkling,* it had certainly fallen to the ground, but for some new contrivances to support it, though therein they have not been so happy to agree amongst themselves in their conclusions."— *Ibid.,* p. 3.

" For some are for *baptizing all children* whose *parents* are never so wicked; others only the children of *professors;* whilst others are for the baptizing the children of such professors only whose parents are *inchurched,* viz., belonging to some particular *congregation.* Some are for *baptizing children* upon their own *particular faith* (which with much confidence it is affirmed they have). Others deny that with great vehemency, affirming they ought only *to be baptized* upon an *imputative faith,* viz., upon the faith of others, though herein, as you'll find, they vastly *differ;* some saying, it must be by the *imputative faith* of the church; others, of the *gossip;* others, of the *parent* or *proparent* in covenant upon the account of *federal right.*"—*Ibid.,* pp. 3, 4.

" So that some are for baptizing upon an *ecclesiastical* faith, some an *imputative,* some a *seminal,* some an *habitual,* some a *dogmatical,* and some a *justifying* faith."—*Ibid.*

" And it is no wonder that such *contradictions* should proceed from such contrary *principles;* for if from *one baptism* (Eph. iv.) Christ would oblige and engage us to *unity,* let it not be thought strange that, from a *baptism* so *different* from Christ's, such *differences* and *divisions* should flow."—*Ibid.*

These passages are followed in the preface with references to the writings of Baxter and others, and the concessions which they have been led to make in their efforts to unite the conflicting parties of Pædobaptists; and, in reference to these concessions to Popery, he says:—

"But alas! whereunto will not men run, left to themselves, who leave the *word* for their *rule,* to embrace the *traditions* and *inventions* of men? Oh! were not these *twenty quæries* so much against the self-evidencing authority of the *Scriptures* in favour of *tradition,* a heinous provocation, to say no more of them?"—*Ibid.,* p. 14.

These twenty questions relate to forms of worship, and are found in Baxter. It is known with what violence he resisted the Baptists of his time, and how numerous were his labours to secure, by mutual concessions, the union of those parties into which his Pædobaptistical brethren had been divided. His aim was good, and his zeal unspeakable. His Directory alone is a herculean labour; but the light in which these conformities were viewed by the Baptist brethren is thus expressed by Denne:—

"And not only so favourable to their ministry, but to many of their ministrations also, of *bowing, kneeling, musick, homilies, apocrypha, vows, holiness of days, times, places,* yea, even *images* and *crucifixes,* also; and, as though by a *monkish zeal* and *confidence,* and some sweet pretensions to brotherly *love,* peace, and *moderation,* with the legerdemain of fallacy and quiddity, and (as Rutherford calls it) *unwashen distinction,* we are at last to be *trepanned* into *Popery,* and persuaded to lick up all the *vomit* again."—*Ibid.,* p. 15.

It is plain, from these quotations, that to Denne and his brethren the proposal of baptizing infants appeared to involve the bitter and fatal consequence of returning by degrees to all the rejected pollutions of Popery; and, in the seriousness which this view of the case induced, they girded on their armour, and contended as for existence.

THE CASE OF THE INDEPENDENTS.

When, by appealing to Holy Scripture, Congregational churches were formed of persons dissenting from both Papal and Protestant hierarchies, the impression under which individuals acted was, that the bodies from which they withdrew were radically wrong; and, that the new associations must be formed in strict conformity with divine law. Some flew to the opposite extreme of sacramental rule, and rejected the rites of Christianity altogether. These will find much to consider in Dr. Halley's remarks on the perpetuity of Christian Sacraments. The Baptists, as we have seen, confined the use of those rites to believers only; but the Independents appear, from the first, to have pleaded for retaining the infant baptism of the forsaken hierarchies in favour of their own children. This seemed to offer a tangible link, by which the family might be united with the church, and parental sympathy become enlisted in its favour. Difficulties were suggested from the beginning, but defences were proposed, from a supposed analogy in the Hebrew dispensations, which seemed to justify the application of Jewish law, and to support an inference in favour of the practice drawn from that perfect silence which is observable, on this subject, in the New Testament; while other advocates boldly pleaded that the children of believers were distinguished, in moral constitution, from those born of unbelievers; and that, for this reason, as being born in the church, their inheritance in the covenant of grace should be recognised in baptism. By many writers on this side, and of this denomination, it has also been pleaded, that, if the regeneration of the child was not certain in the baptism, yet it was possible, and so likely to transpire, "at the very time when baptismal water was falling on its face,"—that the withholding of the rite could, on no consideration, be justified. All these arguments continue to be used for defence, as they were constructed for defence. The rite was found in the hierarchies they left; and its advocates plead for retaining it; but, since the Independent churches have been multiplied, and their activities have brought them out before a reading public, all these defensive expedients have been used with greater caution than in former times. Advocates of the English hierarchy, assuming their apostolic descent, have unclothed the argument for baptismal benefits without faith, and pressed it to a result at which these brethren shudder. Baptists, on the other hand, have shown, that to fulfil the meaning of Scripture produced in this argument by the Tractmen, these baptismal benefits, if admitted at all, must be admitted *invariably*, and to that terrible extent, in which the scriptural doctrine of justification by faith is utterly supplanted; they have also proved, that the analogy of the Hebrew covenants is against the practice of baptizing infants in the Christian church, and that the supposition of a moral difference, by birth, in children of believers, flatly contradicts the words of Scripture, and the doctrine of universal depravity in man, in which the necessity for justification by faith originates. The Baptists have gone further: they have asked their Independent brethren to produce a defence of their practice free from these practical and serious difficulties, and on which may be based a combined action against the common enemy. This was not only so requested, it was demanded by the necessity of the times. Dr. Halley has attempted to meet that demand. Against the Society of Friends, and other anti-ritualists, he has shown that a law binding on all churches in the Apostles' time, must, unless repealed, be binding on all Christians now; and, therefore, that the rites then ordained are of divine authority in the present times. Against the Papal, Lutheran, and English hierarchies, with all other advocates of sacramental efficacy, he has shown, that no such idea is expressed in Holy Scripture, and, therefore, that the doctrine, with the system of ecclesiastical rule which it sustains, must be treated as an unwarrantable human fabrication. Against his own brethren he has shown that the arguments drawn from Hebrew covenants and hereditary claims are, in their chief aim, absolutely untenable; and that, if the practice of infant baptism be retained, some other ground for its enforcement must be provided; and, lastly, against the Baptist brethren he has endeavoured to show, that where adults are concerned, Christian baptism should be administered, indiscriminately, to all applicants, as a symbol of evangelical truth; and that the baptism of infants is to be enforced on the just interpretation and authority of our Lord's commission. He has thus given a definiteness and positive form to the whole subject; and he has further facilitated the investigation by admitting, that the whole question is whether repentance and faith be or be not the authorised prerequisite to Christian baptism. This, therefore, will lead us to deal principally with positive evidence; for if it can be shown that this prerequisite is ordained and enforced by the law of Christ, Dr. Halley is answered, and the authority of believers' baptism is sustained.

THE WORDS "MYSTERY" AND "SACRAMENT."

A further illustration of Dr. Halley's argument will be readily introduced by his remark on the word μυστηριον, or mystery. He is led to this by the word *sacramentum*, or sacrament, the word by which μυστηριον is translated, and by which the rite under consideration is expressed. Words of this kind must, in some cases, be used to prevent an unmanageable circumlocution; but, in this instance, the one chosen is unfortunate. It creates a difficulty by the bad associations into which it has for ages been forced. If Dr. Halley had left this word to his opponents, and confined his attention to the great inquiry, Whether repentance and faith be indispensable prerequisites of baptism? much more positive information might have been obtained, and much *mystery* avoided. From the materials which Dr. Halley has collected, it appears that *sacramentum* was, by the old Latin writers, used for the Greek word μυστηριον; and that both were used to signify an oath of consecration, a thing consecrated, and an indication of some reality which could not be understood without the clue of interpretation supplied by its author. It was not necessary that the things indicated should be divine, for Cicero uses the word in his Letters* with reference to his own communications; and by Herodian it is used in reference to war.† It is also employed in the Apocrypha to signify things confined within the limits of confidential friendship,‡ and for those entrusted to the confidants of kings.‖ Few words appear to have had a more wide and various application; but Dr. Halley traces it to the heathen temples, and thus their rites appear, from his statements, to be the origin of that distinct treatment to which believers and unbelievers were subjected in the ancient Christian churches. In thus depreciating this discipline, the Doctor becomes eloquent, calls the language of the Fathers "*tumid*," and treats it as absurd. But his inductions are made from materials collected at too recent a period; for it will be found

* Ad Atticum, Lib. iv., Ep. 3, and Lib. vi., Ep. 4, "μυστικωτερον ad te scribam."

† Και νυν φυλασσοντες τον στρατιωτικον ορκον, ος εστι της Ρομαιων αρχης σεμνον μυστηριον.—Herod., Lib. viii. Dr. Halley, p. 12.

‡ Ο αποκαλυπτων μυστηρια απωλεσε πιστιν.—Soph. Seirax., xxvii. 16.

‖ Μυστηριον βασιλεως καλον κρυψαι.—Tobit xii. 7.

32   THE WORDS "MYSTERY" AND "SACRAMENT."

that the phraseology and the practice he condemns, existed at a time anterior to the third and fourth centuries, and had the sanction of inspired men. His censure extends also, if admitted, not to the examination of candidates for Christian baptism only, but to all separate incorporation of believers, as such, in any Christian fellowship whatever; for however they may be accredited and recognised, they must be initiated in some way; and, when initiated, they must, in that fellowship of believers, be treated as such. His proposed theory harmonises with this censure; and it becomes the more serious, because it breaks down the enclosure of Christian society, and reduces it to a level with the unconverted masses of mankind.*

Dr. Halley says, " It would be vain to consult the New Testament for any exposition of a sacrament." This is strange. The word " sacrament," or *musterion*, occurs in those writings about twenty-seven times; and, in the Septuagint version, not less than twenty-five. Out of these fifty-two cases, it might, at least, be possible to verify its meaning; especially, as many of these cases contain the relative and cognate words. Moreover, baptism, the rite now under consideration—and now called a " sacrament," or *musterion* —is the one on which we have, in the New Testament, the most specific information.† If there be no case in which Christian baptism is there called a mystery, in direct terms, yet the kingdom of heaven, which Christ established, *had* sacraments or mysteries,

---

* Dr. Halley's Lectures, pp. 9—14.   † Dr. Halley, p. 113.

and it was given to the apostles to know them :*
they also were constituted stewards of those mysteries.† These, therefore, were actions or events in the kingdom of heaven, invested by God himself with a meaning which the apostles were enabled to comprehend, and authorised to explain. Some of these were more simple, others more profound; some were actions of men, others actions of the Deity; some stood by the wayside to enlighten by their import the path of daily obedience, while others rose like promontories looking out upon the sea, where signals were exhibited; and, in them, those who could properly interpret the symbols, might be forewarned of future danger, or contemplate with joy the purposes of mercy. Such sacraments or mysteries supposed the previous existence of faith in God, and some knowledge at least of his will, without which they never could be used; and they propounded a future advantage attendant on their right employment. But Dr. Halley himself affirms, that baptism is " *a symbol of evangelical truth*," appointed by the Lord himself, and, therefore, receiving from him its symbolical meaning : it is, therefore, a mystery of the kingdom of heaven, and the apostles are the stewards of that mystery. To them, therefore, in their holy writings, we must look for the only exposition of this mystery, or sacrament, which can be received as an authority.‡

* Matt. xiii.　　　　　　† 1 Cor. iv. 1.

‡ The English reader will be assisted in forming his own judgment on the case by turning to the schedule of renderings given to the word "musterion," or sacrament, in the six principal versions of our own country.—Appendix II.

When considering the nature of modern rites, called sacraments, if some feature in their constitution be found of which no trace is discoverable in the Word of God, that feature itself, whatever it may be, is positive proof that the church of Christ has departed from the law of her Redeemer. This additional idea, so demonstrative of wrong, will be hereafter defined; but, before advancing to that point, Dr. Halley says, "I am somewhat perplexed in attempting to form such a definition of a sacrament, as will include *Baptism* and the *Lord's Supper*, and exclude every other ordinance of the Christian religion," p. 1. This is likely from the nature of the case. A great number of things have, in Scripture, been called mysteries or sacraments, because, when rightly understood, they indicate the covenanted action and movements of the kingdom of heaven. But the Lord enjoined an initiating rite of baptism, and made it a symbol of evangelical truth. On this account, the ancients who followed him called that rite a mystery. Now, Dr. Halley is perplexed in seeking such a definition of a sacrament or mystery, as will include this one rite with the Supper, and exclude other ordinances, be they mysteries or not. He is wrong in his intention, and subordinates the principal to its adjunct. Instead of defining a sacrament so as to exclude all other sacraments but this, he should define baptism so as to prove its right to be designated a sacrament at all. The ancients who called baptism a mystery or sacrament, supposed that there was something in its nature to justify the application of that word; but never supposed it to be the only sacrament. The Lord's Supper was included with it under the same term. Tertullian speaks of more than a hundred sacraments or mysteries. Origen has multitudes. It was the error of the time, to suppose them where they did not exist. Justin has many, which he names; they are found in the earliest Christian writers; and little less than fourteen are named in Holy Scripture. All these are not to be cast away because this newly-ordained rite asks to be included under their name. Instead of this, the inquiry should be, What is the evangelical truth symbolised in this act? How, and by whose authority? To whom does that truth relate? To the subject, the spectator, the church, the minister, or to God? Is it a truth to be used in time, or in eternity? and by whom? and who placed the mystic symbol in the kingdom of heaven? The controversy respecting infant baptism would have been decided by stedfastly prosecuting this inquiry; the one with which Dr. Halley is perplexed, can only augment perplexity, deciding nothing.

THE PERSONAL NATURE OF CHRISTIAN BAPTISM.

These inquiries become the more important from the personal nature of Christian baptism, and the practical influence it exerts upon mankind. Some of the divine arrangements are more, others less general, but this is the most particular of them all. The proclamation of mercy is made to all mankind, and the promise of its blessings is given to those who believe: before any practical result has been gained, therefore, there must be some personal action in the sinner, an embracing of the proclamation, a believing submission to the truth. Even the Lord's Supper has something general in its character; for the Lord saith, "Eat ye all of it:" and, therefore, if an unbelieving hypocrite has found his way in amongst the disciples, while he remains undetected, he seems to pass under the general warrant given to believers; but, in baptism, the very person himself is taken, and made the subject of an action, with its results, whatever they may be. The language of the minister is, "*I baptize* THEE *into the name of the Father, and of the Son, and of the Holy Spirit.*" The action does away with all hypothesis, and leaves no room for speculation; whatever the baptism communicates, be it grace, recognition, or instruction, or whatever other supposed or supposable thing, it is brought home to the individual baptized. "*I baptize* THEE." To this personal character of the rite we have the most general and convincing testimony. The Scriptures so regard it in all the places; the early Christians so regarded it; Rome, Heidelberg, England, Scotland, and the Assembly, agree in all their documents. Drs. Campbell* and Miller are in harmony: all show, that wha the baptism is, it must be to him who receives it. The persons who receive it, therefore, must, sooner or later, be influenced by it. Spread over all this world, the recipients of one common sign, we are separated

---

* See " Jethro."

from other classes of men, as if to form a community in ourselves. Why was this done? and what does it mean? Have we, under the law of Christ, the privilege and hope of Christians? or have we not? Such inquiries do, and must arise; and the answers given to them must, whether right or wrong, powerfully influence the conduct and character of individuals.

The wide circulation of Holy Scripture modifies and increases the importance of this fact. No teacher can now regulate the operation of his own theory. Before he has uttered it an hour, some individual student of Scripture brings it into contact with inspired truth. The affirmations of inspired men are thus brought into close and frequent comparison with those which uninspired teachers make on the same subject. It is thus with the personal ground and effect of this sacrament. Paul, a steward of the mysteries or sacraments of God, has written his statements on the subject, and modern teachers make theirs. How these can be reconciled, or the declarations of Paul are to be verified, in any ordinary Pædobaptistical assembly, is a question full of perplexity; which must, unless further discoveries in Divine truth be made, increase, until infant and indiscriminate baptism be extinguished.

THE DIFFICULTY AND PROPOSED SOLUTIONS.

To meet this practical difficulty, of reconciling the expressions used in Holy Scripture, with reference to baptized persons, and the community in which they were united, with the present state of so-called Christian churches, the advocates of a spiritual gift in baptism plead, that however the regeneration might have been caused or facilitated, variably or invariably, the grace so received may be sinned away by subsequent transgression. Those who build their theory on hereditary grace, plead the same thing. Both parties argue, further, that the grace received fails of its result for want of proper education: it is *in* the children, they say, but care is not taken to bring it out. Appeals to experience show, that this supposed exception forms, in fact, the rule. No clear case can be produced, in which the fruit of baptismal and hereditary grace can be exhibited. With all the care and the best education that can be used, it is impossible to bring it out. Out of nothing, nothing comes. Dr. Halley has, moreover, clearly and truly shown, that the supposition on which each theory rests, is absolutely opposed to the whole doctrine and spirit of the Inspired Writings. It is inevitable, therefore, that the societies thus formed, on principles contrary to those observed in the apostles' time, should be dissimilar in their character and in their action to those which then existed. The same things could never be affirmed and denied of disciples received on suppositions so essentially false, and disciples who were received on a personal and accredited profession of faith.

As far as the reconciliation of modern practice to the apostolical affirmations is concerned, Dr. Halley's theory makes no other provision than that which is supplied by the defence of infant baptism, founded on the supposed analogy of Hebrew covenants, which he rejects. In both these theories, it is assumed, that the words of Paul are used in a sense so mild and flexible as to bear an application to persons admitted into the church, as Jews were admitted to their community, or even to persons admitted without any discrimination whatever. On this principle, it must be denied that the expressions "faith," "believed," "dead unto sin," "sons of God," "planted together with Christ," "buried with Christ," "risen with Christ," &c., &c., have any meaning by which one man may be discriminated from another, or which supposes that such discrimination has been made. By this means, the gospel system of fellowship is made more indiscriminate than the Jewish system, and less influential on moral character. For Dr. Halley affirms, that baptism is the badge of discipleship; and that, in it a disciple was recognised; and he admits, that the words, "As many of you as were baptized into Christ, have put on Christ," and other similar expressions, were addressed, and had special reference, to these disciples, and their baptismal recognition. But, it is argued, that these and similar words are used in so loose a sense, that they imply no discrimination of character. The faith on which they were accepted is supposed to be no faith at all, as we deem it; and hence it is concluded, that any congregation of baptized individuals may, with as much propriety, be called "sons of God by faith in Christ Jesus, and heirs according to the promise," *now*, as in the apostles' time. This assumption reduces the language of Paul to modern inconsistency; but it does not make the expressions true and proper. Dr. Halley, moreover, declares that this personal recognition of individual discipleship was positively ordained of God, and that it symbolises God's truth; but he pleads, that the symbol speaks to others, rather than to the subject of baptism himself. The baptism is, therefore, made vicarious, and the infant begins to do good before he has learned to speak. That which is symbolised in the subject himself is, the *necessity* of faith and repentance, not their actual existence. The baptism, *he says*, teaches what the recipient *must* be, not what he is. It requires great acuteness to perceive how this assumption could explain how Paul might say, with truth, " Ye, as many as have been baptized into Christ, have put on Christ; ye *are* sons of God, by faith in Christ Jesus." Dr. Halley supposes that the baptism symbolises *ye must be ;* but Paul affirms, " Ye *are* sons of God by faith in Christ Jesus," and supports his affirmation by most powerful argument. The absolute inadequacy of the assumption is obvious, and its discordance with Divine truth will be exhibited in another place.

A hesitating vacillation in the use of terms seems to indicate that Dr. Halley's reasoning is, in his own estimation, not without its difficulties. At page 7, he calls baptism " *the initiatory rite of the Christian church ;*" and at page 120, he says that the Jews, from whom he supposes that rite to have been derived, regarded it as "*a badge or profession of discipleship.*" This difference of expression might have appeared accidental and unimportant; but at p. vii. of his Introduction, he assumes *that baptism is not a church ordinance at all.* This reveals a vital defect in his whole theory. It assumes that, in the apostolical times, the church members were persons altogether distinct from the ordinary disciples; and, to make his reasoning conclusive, he should have shown that *the initiation to a Christian church* was, in the apostolical age and by the law of Christ, an act distinct from the *initiation of a disciple.* It will be seen that this was impossible; and Dr. Halley has not attempted it. By giving up the unsound and inferential theories of his brethren he has done great good; and by clearing out the subject of debate—in admitting that the true question is, Whether the law of Christ requires faith and repentance as prerequisites to baptism?—he has greatly facilitated future investigation; but, at the very point where the argument presses, he fails in flagrant defect. To make way for his infant baptism, he separates the ancient initiation of disciples from all regard to the character of those who received it, and thus invalidates the regard to character which, in their constitution and discipline, those churches which they composed were commanded to preserve. Making his baptism indiscriminate, he makes the assemblies of disciples indiscriminate also. By deriving the authority of this theory from the commission of our Lord, he brings that commission itself into direct hostility with the whole body of revealed truth, and renders it the duty of a Christian teacher and pastor, now, to shun the precept of the great apostle. Instead of taking heed how and what he builds into the walls of Zion, because his work is to be tried with fire, Dr. Halley, appealing to Jewish rites and the great commission, boldly affirms that it is the duty of a Christian teacher, in the name of the Father and of the Son and of the Holy Ghost, to take as he finds them, indiscriminately, the human materials of earthly society, and, whether they be gold, silver, or precious stones, wood, hay, straw, or stubble, to build them up into the temple walls, the prospect of its fiery purgation notwithstanding. To support this terrible conclusion he appeals to ancient Jewish baptisms, and makes them interpreters of the Christian law. The nature and value of his evidence from that source will, therefore, occupy attention in the next exercise.

Nothing now remains, brethren, but thanks for your kind attention, and an earnest request that your sympathy and prayers will sustain this endeavour to extend the truth.

LECTURE II.

ON JEWISH BAPTISM.

THE question which relates to the *act* of Christian baptism has already been dismissed. Whether it be a sprinkling or pouring of water upon a person, or whether it be an immersing of the person in that element, appears to be sufficiently shown in Dr. Carson's work, entitled "Baptism in its Mode and Subjects;" and an English method with the word baptize is given in the Appendix I. It appears, from the evidence thus supplied, that the *act* of immersion is clearly imperative, but that the mode of the immersion is not defined. It may, without any infringement on Divine law, be performed backwards or forward, to a greater or less depth, for a longer or shorter time, provided only that life and health be not hazarded. Those opponents who have encumbered the inquiry with frivolities respecting the mode of baptism have only to consider that the immersion enjoined, like every other act of worship, must be performed with decency and in order. This appears to be the only written law which affects the mode of the immersion; and, if anything further seems required to sustain the authority of its decent and orderly administration, abundant materials are ready on demand. Avoiding embarrassment from this question, therefore, the inquiry before us is, On whom does the duty of submitting to this immersion devolve? and, what characters are the members of Christ bound in that ceremony to receive? Or, conforming to the recent phraseology, If Christian immersion be " the badge of discipleship," who are the men that should wear it?

Some of those serious matters which stand associated with this inquiry will be best introduced by a brief repetition of Dr. Halley's own words:—

" There is also another controversy on baptism, at the present time of great importance, as upon its decision, more than upon anything else, depends the settlement of the momentous and agitating question of the day—the doctrine of sacramental efficacy. Upon baptism we have more full and precise information than we have upon any other ritual observance; and if baptism be not regeneration, if it do not produce or imply any moral or spiritual change, the whole fabric of sacramental efficacy falls to the ground, and with it the authority of the priesthood and the mediation of the church; so that, having nothing left for our dependence, we must look immediately and exclusively to the grace of God through Jesus Christ our Lord. This one point being decided, the whole dispute between Protestant and Catholic, in every form and aspect, Anglo-catholic and Roman Catholic, vanishes as a mist from the region of theology."—*Lecture* iii., pp. 113, 114.

It may well be added, " Of the importance of this controversy it is not easy to offer an exaggerated statement," p. 114. By thus consenting to remove this inquiry from the region of mere circumstantial frivolities, and yielding to it a claim on prayerful and devout consideration, the opponent has performed an essential service to the truth. The hypothesis he has here stated, if fully sustained by his reasoning, will also accomplish all that he promises, and something more: for if it can be proved, as we think it may, that baptism does "*not produce any moral or spiritual change, the whole fabric of sacramental efficacy falls to the ground,*" and all the other consequences named are equally certain; but if it can also be shown that baptism does not "*imply*" any moral or spiritual change, then not only "*sacramental efficacy,*" but *believers' baptism also,* falls to the ground: baptism is then dissociated from considerations of personal character entirely: the badge of discipleship is worn without any qualification; and men, as followers of Jesus, are separated from the world, while yet retaining a fellowship in its treasonous corruptions.

That the word "*imply*" was not accidentally introduced, but designed to express an essential part of the hypothesis, is obvious from the facts of the case. For, First, to this point the greatest force of Dr. Halley's reasoning is directed; and, by maintaining this, he labours to sustain his whole theory. Secondly, in 1842, a year and a half before his lectures were delivered, the close connexion between this baptismal controversy and the vital interests of personal religion, together with the appalling advances of Oxford Tractarianism, had induced the presenting, through Dr. Jos. Fletcher, of Stepney, to the Evangelical Pædobaptists, two questions:—First, " Ought not something more decisive to be done in exposing the nature and checking the progress of this pernicious heresy?" and, secondly, " Ought not you and your brethren, in some more obvious and conclusive way, to clear yourselves, and the ceremony you perform on infants, from your implication in the evils which flow from its extension?" The doctrine here called " a pernicious heresy," is that of the Tractmen, the true exponents of baptismal benefits taught and defended by Scriptural phraseology; and the implication of Evangelical Pædobaptists in its evils, is that which appears, if not in the existence, yet certainly in their mode of defending infant baptism. The requirement was, a defence of infant baptism, which should fulfil the words of Scripture justly used by Tractmen, and yet remain unpolluted with their doctrine. Dr. Halley does not name this communication, but his hypothesis is, if sustained, the only one yet discovered that has any plausible claim to be respected as an answer. The separating baptism from all consideration of personal character whatever, when shown to accord with Scripture, will prepare the way for a defence of infant baptism, free from alliance with Tractarian heresy. But no other argument for this practice at present exists, of which so much can affirmed.

His righteous censure of Joseph John Gurney, the Society of Friends, and all who deny the present authority of Christian rites, leads Dr. Halley to narrow the ground of this inquiry, by confining the authority of infant baptism and the Lord's Supper, to the right interpretation of Divine law. He rejects, with a very proper, though with strong feeling, the use which has been made of Paul's conduct at Corinth, and that of Christ in his ministry. He shows, with great force, that, if Jesus himself did not baptize, and Paul baptized but few;* yet, during the ministration of both, the disciples who acted under them, baptized by their authority: and thus the act was morally theirs, as much as it would have been if performed with their own hands.† "So far *(he says)* as the Apostles' authority extended, not a single convert was unbaptized,"—p. 82. "The Apostles have left these carnal ceremonies (baptism and the Supper) unimpaired to their successors, who, in the next, and in every subsequent age, have scrupulously retained them, as the emblems and memorials of the truth of Christ,"—p. 71. All these expressions include a claim to that Divine authority in the rite for which he pleads. He carries this principle still further, in affirming that "Jesus submitted to [John's baptism] that he might fulfil all righteousness. But righteousness *(he says)* must have reference to some law: of what law" [then could this be a righteousness]? He answers, "The Divine commission which John had received,"—p. 75. Dr. Halley's plea, therefore, is, that, in the case before us, Divine law is the only

* 1 Cor. i. † John iv. 1, 2.

rule of present action; that the Apostles, and even the Lord himself, submitted to its authority; and that this law, when rightly understood, positively requires a separation of Christian baptism from all restrictive considerations of personal character whatever, its free administration to infants, and an opening of the fellowship of disciples, and of the churches they form, and (by consequence) of the ministry they sustain, to the unconverted masses of mankind.

Such, then, is the hypothesis which we have to investigate. We shall now consider the rule of interpretation which Dr. Halley employs; and then, the argument by which that interpretation is conducted to this result.

DR. HALLEY'S RULE OF INTERPRETATION.

In the clearest manner, Dr. Halley admits that the words of Paul, in Rom. vi. 11, Col. ii. 12, Gal. iii. 26, and Titus iii. 1—7, in which, the baptized and baptism are variously spoken of in the relation they bear to personal religion and the body of Christ, all relate to that baptism in water, which we have now under consideration. This is most important; because many have denied this fact, pleading, but most inaccurately, that these passages can only relate to the baptism of the Holy Spirit.* Dr. Halley disavows this subterfuge: and he admits that this baptism in water, whose recipients are here said to have been planted with Christ, buried with Christ, risen with Christ,

* Godwin on Christian Baptism, pp. 142—183.

DR. HALLEY'S RULE OF INTERPRETATION. 49

born again, and to be sons of God by faith in Christ Jesus, derives its whole authority, whether administered to infants or adults, from the commission of our Lord, " Go ye out, disciple all the nations, baptizing them into the name of the Father, and of the Son, and of the Holy Spirit."* This, therefore—the rite now under consideration—which Paul so elucidates, was instituted by the Lord himself, and still retains its moral obligation; because, He had been invested with all authority (power) in heaven and upon earth. But Dr. Halley thinks that the true meaning of this commission cannot be ascertained from its own words, nor from its own words taken in connexion with those of Paul, nor from both united with the practice of the apostolical times. Though this rite is the one on which, he says, the most explicit information is given; yet, it would seem, from some parts of his work, impossible to learn what the Saviour meant therein, or to whom it should be administered, from all that the Lord and his disciples have either said or done: and hence the rule of Dr. Halley is, to interpret the commission by the practice and the notions which prevailed in the Jewish nation, at the time, and before Christ came into the world. This is the precipice, to which Dr. Halley, with great composure, leads the student of Divine law. Let him once plunge from this, and he will soon reach the ruinous conclusion. Only let antecedent Jewish notions and practices be made the interpreters of Christian law, and it will not

* Matthew xxviii. 19.

be easy to form an exaggerated statement of the evils which must ensue.

Before we consider the argument founded on these premises, it is obvious to remark, that it assumes two facts, the most discreditable to any one entrusted with supreme authority: first, that the authoritative communications of our Lord are not intelligible in themselves; and, secondly, that their interpretation has been placed, as far as possible, beyond the reach of those who were required to obey them. All government requires an explicitness, and an independent perspicuity, in its laws; for, without this, the subject can never be without excuse in disobedience. A commandment should be, in itself, as clear as that, " Thou shalt not steal." But, Dr. Halley supposes that the command, " Go forth, disciple, and baptize," cannot be understood by the simple meaning of its own words; but that the words derive their sense from the preconceived notions of the Jewish people. By this one imperfection alone, the wisest and best designs of any ruler must be reduced to utter inefficiency. It would seem impossible to serve one whose own words will not explain what he means. It is still more fearful to consider, also, how generally, and with how much severity, the Lord himself condemns these preconceived notions of the Jews: for, by rendering them the expositors of his law, he would have subjected his whole dominion to the influence of things which he himself most solemnly repudiated. Besides, on what authority does Dr. Halley ascertain the *nature* of these preconceived notions? not from the

New Testament, or the Old, or from any inspired writing whatever—but from the Talmud, and the Mischna, and rabbinical writings, the oldest of which was brought into existence more than a hundred years after the Saviour's death, others more than a thousand; writings which Dr. Halley himself does not read, but isolated parts of which are found in Dr. Lightfoot. He does not seem to know that Dr. Gill, and others, have disputed the truth of all his assumptions, and made the Jewish notions of baptism subsequent to, and imitative of, the Lord's commandment. Our present object does not require that the merits of these respected and learned, though contradictory claims to general confidence, be considered: the fact, that it is disputed by such high authority, invalidates the assumption, and renders it useless as a means of interpretation. If we can never understand the commission of our Lord, until we have read and understood the rabbinical writers, it is not presumptuous to affirm, that most of us will never understand it at all: and where the commission of our Lord cannot be understood, an intelligent obedience to his requirement becomes impossible.

DR. HALLEY'S ARGUMENT.

Premises which frustrate the aim of an argument, increasing obscurity where explanation was sought, invite its rejection altogether. The facts which have been named, therefore, lead us, by a first glance, to expect that the theory they are designed to support will never bear inspection. To this result, however, we must not advance without a careful examination of the author's reasoning. Let all possible candour, therefore, be exercised in this duty; for, Dr. Halley speaks not so much for himself, as for God. The thing sought is, the meaning of our Lord's commandment; and the practice pleaded for, is enforced in the name of God. Dr. Halley himself states that "The symbols of our faith, if not of Divine authority, are profane inventions of men," p. 69. With such an alternative before us, the utmost care should be taken not to lose, much less to reject, one particle of evidence.

The whole chain of Dr. Halley's reasoning may be stated in six particulars:—

1. "Baptism," he says, "is a symbolical representation of evangelical truth," p. 7; and "a badge or profession of discipleship."—*Dr. Halley*, p. 120.

2. "Such a baptism existed amongst the Jews, and it was used by them to initiate the disciples they obtained from heathenism, before Christ or John the Baptist came."—Lect. II., *passim*.

3. "This baptism John administered indiscriminately to all applicants, as a symbol of the repentance which he taught, and a badge of discipleship under his dispensation; and thus, by virtue of his commission from God, that baptism first received its divine authority," p. 160, 163.

4. "The baptism of Jesus was the same as John's; and became a perpetual ordinance by virtue of the commission given to the apostles," p. 121.

5. "The baptism of John was administered without any discrimination, and the commission of our Lord imposed no discriminating condition; and, therefore, Christian baptism is to be administered now with equal freedom to all applicants," p. 602—604.

6. "The Jews, in their proselyte baptism, baptized the children with their parents; but the baptism of Christ and of John was the same, confirmed by Divine authority, without any formal exception of infants; and, therefore, by virtue of our Lord's commission, infants are to be baptized now as they are supposed to have been in the Jewish nation, before the ministrations of John."—*Ibid.*

On these several points Dr. Halley has built his whole theory of infant and indiscriminate initiation to Christian discipleship. A direct and simple appeal to the independent meaning of inspired documents, does not appear in his work. His whole reasoning implies, that this notion of Jewish baptismal initiation, not expressed by the Divine teacher, but understood by the learners of that time, gave its own character and colouring to every utterance and every divine injunction. It passed from the Jewish community into that of John and of Christ, and through all the authorised ministrations of that time, without one mistake calling for observation of any kind from any one, down to the very last of the apostles. It should seem, from the author, that this key to the meaning of New Testament injunctions is so important, that the evangelical history could never be understood till it was found; if this were true, it would make the New Testament a vast enigma, but not prove the result which Dr. Halley intends.

The first point to be sustained by thus referring to Jewish baptism is, that John's baptism "*was indiscriminately administered to all recipients,*" p. 163; and that the commission of our Lord, interpreted by this supposed practice of John, and preconceived notion of the Jews, requires his baptism to be administered in the same way. But the conclusion does not follow from the supposition. In Maimonides, as quoted by Dr. Halley himself at p. 126, it is said, " Whenever a heathen will come and be joined to the covenant of Israel, and place himself under the wings of the Divine majesty, and take the yoke of the law upon him, voluntary circumcision, baptism, and oblation are required; but if the proselyte be a woman, baptism and oblation." The expressions " will be joined to the covenant," " place himself under the wing of the Divine majesty," and " take the yoke of the law upon him," are all discriminating; and the language of Maimonides plainly shows, that such persons only would be admitted to the rite of initiation. No such indiscriminate character, therefore, can be inferred from the Jewish to the Christian baptism. Dr. Halley must find the support of this feature in his theory therefore; not in the antecedent baptism of the Jews, but in those inspired documents which relate to the ministry and precepts of John and of Christ themselves. It is astonishing how little attention he pays to these. His most forcible reasonings only go to render plausible the affirmation, that there is no proof of any discrimination being used or enjoined, because both John and Christ administered baptism in conformity with the Jewish notion; but the Jewish baptism was discriminating, and, therefore, Dr. Halley infers that Christian baptism should be indiscriminate. When such an argument becomes our only defence against the Tractmen and Popery, it is easy to predict their speedy and universal victory; and hence, it is to this point chiefly that attention will be led in the subsequent lectures of this course.

The second object Dr. Halley seeks to gain, is a defence for indiscriminate *infant* baptism. By making the Jewish baptism the precedent and interpreter of Christian baptism, he thinks to bring all infants within our Lord's commandment. If this could be done by any other line of argument, it cannot be by the one here chosen; for if all the facts, supposed analogies, and arguments stood just as he has put them, they would only infer the baptism of children whose parents are baptized, which hypothesis would obviously involve a discrimination of *infants;* while Dr. Halley repudiates a discrimination even in *adults*.

But, further, the premises are not sufficient to sustain an argument for infant baptism at all; for, though it should be admitted that the Jews did baptize their proselytes, and the children of their proselytes, since the baptism was their initiation, it could not be inferred that infants should be initiated into the society of Christian disciples, unless it could also be proved that the association of Christian disciples was designed for the same end, and formed on the same principle, as the association of the Jewish people. If this could be done, if Christianity could be reduced to the character of Judaism, then it might be inferred, if no other reason existed against the inference, that as the children of one who became a Jew were baptized, so the children of one who became a Christian might be baptized. But this identity in the nature and aim of the two systems cannot be shown; and, therefore, this inferential authority for infant baptism falls to the ground. Dr. Halley himself pleads that there was and is a different object and principle of association in the Christian church, and even in John's dispensation; but if he could invert this plea, and make the Christian community in nature identical with the Jewish, because the baptism of the latter was discriminate, in the parents, of character, and in the children, of relationship, the baptism of the former must be discriminate also, which is the very thing Dr. Halley denies.

It was necessary, and even courtesy required, so much attention to the premises and argument taken and considered in their best estate. It is, also, curious to find, that when Dr. Halley's premises are admitted, the two essential parts of his theory destroy each other. To sustain the supposed indiscriminate character of baptism, it is necessary to relinquish the assumed authority for infant baptism; and, in admitting the assumed authority of infant baptism, its supposed indiscriminate character must be resigned. For let it be granted in the argument, that Christian baptism is derived by analogy from the Jewish proselyte initiation, then, because the Jewish was a national and hereditary dispensation, and the Christian dispensation was personal and spiritual, therefore the children which would have been initiated in the Jewish, must be excluded from the Christian, until their personal qualification is attained. On the other hand, let it be assumed that, by the commission of our Lord, the Jewish baptism was so enforced as to include the children with the parents, it follows that only the children of parents who were initiated could be received, and this makes the baptism discriminate. The assumption of Dr. Halley, therefore, annihilates both parts of his own theory. This of itself is enough to indicate that some inaccuracy must have escaped the Doctor's attention, when he was collecting the materials of his argument. Indeed, the hesitancy of his own expressions give positive proof that his own mind was not perfectly at rest with reference to the premises themselves. He says, " Previously to the time of our Lord . . . the Jews were accustomed to baptize the infants of proselytes together with their parents, and so to incorporate them in the kingdom of Israel; and without baptism no Gentile adult or infant could be received into the congregation of Israel, or admitted within the gates of the Temple; . . . or, *if these opinions prove incorrect*, the general expectation of a universal baptism prevailed about the time of the appearance of John the Baptist; and, however it arose, received the sanction of the Divine authority in the institution of John's baptism," p. 160. Here the expression, "*if these opinions prove incorrect,*" plainly indicates a doubt in the author's own mind respecting the Jewish baptism to which he appeals for an interpretation of his Lord's commandment. This is not well. Before an author publishes on such a subject as this, he ought to be himself satisfied with the premises on which his theory is to be based. But he goes further than this, and says, " To those who do not think that the Jews baptized the children of proselytes in the age of our Lord, I leave the probabilities I have noticed divested of that aid; but, as its substitute, the expectation I noticed in the last lecture, of a general baptism of all Israel previously to the coming of Christ," p. 204. Here are four variations of the premises: first, the doubt appears to extend over the whole subject of Jewish baptisms, and the " *expectation of a universal baptism*" is substituted in its place ; then the doubt is fixed on the assumption that the Jews baptized the children of proselytes with their parents; and, instead of this, the expectation of a general baptism of *all Israel* is substituted. From materials of thought so shifting and undefined, how could Dr. Halley, or any other man, obtain a clear and safe conclusion? Does he mean to say, that the "*baptism of all Israel*" is the same thing as " *a universal baptism ;*" and that this expectation, as he says, " *however it arose,*" is to infer the same thing, and have the same power of interpretation, as the supposed Jewish ordinance? This, at first sight, would seem to be inconceivable, and yet he says, "Those who do not believe the one, may take the other." This is not only cutting the knot, when unable to untie it, but it is grasping an axe when the knife fails. It is almost saying, I will have the result by one supposition, if not by another. We dare not follow such a course of complicated and bold conjecture without considering more particularly what it is that Dr. Halley does assume? What is the evidence on which it rests? the authorised expectation with which it was associated? and the legitimate conclusion to which the assumption leads?

THE JEWISH BAPTISM.

The use of existing and long-standing practices to explain the meaning of writers in any age, inspired or not inspired, is by no means to be rejected; but then the illucidating practice itself must be authenticated and definite: an obscure conjecture can, at least, afford nothing further than obscure and hypothetical illustration. It must be admitted, also, that Dr. Halley does himself and his cause injustice by these vacillating expressions; for if they be attributed to modesty of feeling, it is obvious that the modesty of feeling which hesitates in laying down the premises of an argument, ought also to be seen in drawing the inference. But this is not found; though timid and variable in respect to his premises, Dr. Halley is confident and determined in asserting the conclusion. This vacillation respecting his premises, moreover, is quite unnecessary. His whole argument, as well as his authorities for Jewish baptism, plainly distinguish it from circumcision, because it formed, with circumcision and oblation, a separate and distinct part of one initiation. The initiation, if his own authorities be admitted, included the circumcision, the baptism, and the oblation, in men; and baptism, with oblation, in women. Circumcision, therefore, with all the use that has been made of it, is thrown out of the discussion. But a still more important advance is made by Dr. Halley. He distinguishes clearly his supposed antecedent and illucidating baptism from all the ordained purifications of the Jewish temple, and from the baptisms of the Pharisees;* or, in his own words, from "*the legal purifications with water, and the usual frequent ablutions of the Pharisees,*" p. 119 —121. By this distinction he relieves his subject from the cumbrous and delusive argument which has recently been built upon the daringly gratuitous assumption that $\beta\alpha\pi\tau\iota\zeta\omega$, like $\kappa\alpha\theta\alpha\rho\iota\zeta\omega$, is a generic term, signifying, to purify. Dr. Halley shows distinctly and formally (p. 119, 120), that "*neither the daily ablutions, nor the legal purifications, could have been intended when the messengers inquired of John why he baptized?*"† The illucidating ceremony assumed, therefore, is by Dr. Halley himself separated from all Jewish rites traceable by any means to Divine authority. In all the law of Moses, or the Prophets, there is no commandment on which its authoritative administration can be based; but before

* Mark vii. † John i.

the coming of John, at least, it formed, if it then existed, a part of those rabbinical observances of which the Lord himself said, "*In vain do ye teach for doctrine the commandment of men.*"

THE EVIDENCE IN FAVOUR OF JEWISH BAPTISM.

The assumption of Dr. Halley, therefore, is, that "*the baptism of John, and of our Lord, was understood by the Jews to be Proselyte Baptism*" (p. 121). But still the question returns: Did any such baptism of proselytes exist at all before the coming of our Lord? This has, at least, been denied; and Dr. Halley has done but little to confirm the supposition against objectors. The evidence with which he labours to confirm the authenticity of Jewish proselyte baptism, is derived partly from rabbinical writers, of various ages, as far back as to the second century in the Christian era; which writers describe the practice as being one of great antiquity before their time. Maimonides is produced as a principal witness; and his work would give to the supposition a considerable probability, but it is too recent to supply any evidence sufficiently authoritative to decide the question.

"The most ancient part of the Talmud, namely, that which is called the Mischna, was not compiled till about 150 years after the destruction of Jerusalem. Buxtorf says, the Jerusalem Talmud was compiled by Rab. Jochanan, 230 years after Christ: but the Gemara, which is the far greatest part of the Babylonic Talmud, was not made till 500 years after Christ, nor till 311 years after the Mischna: according to

Abraham Ben David, and Ganz, Maimonides lived not till above 1100 years after Christ."* Of those Jewish authorities which are the most ancient, some have actually pleaded that as no immersion of proselytes was enforced by Moses, Jesus Christ had assumed to himself an undue authority in appointing it. This is very much what a Sadducee might have pleaded in our Lord's time against the traditions and rites not written in the Pentateuch. But Maimonides and others, declare the existence of such a practice without any hesitation. By possibility, the circumstance just mentioned might tend to reconcile these conflicting rabbies. It might be, that the practice of baptizing Jewish proselytes having existed before the coming of John, led to the affirmation of those who declare it and explain its nature; and, that its never having been appointed by Moses in his law, led others to reject it, and condemn the Saviour for enforcing such a ceremony. But, whatever becomes of this conjecture, the uncertainty, the conflicting character, and the mixture of all evidence derived from rabbinical sources, with their obvious falsehoods and gross absurdities, positively annihilate all its worth. The clearest assertion made by these authors, ought to be re-examined with care, and taken with suspicion, although it had formerly been holden for truth. The principal service performed by these writings will be found in the evidence which they afford, to justify the severity with which our Lord, in his discourses,

---

* Gale's Reflections on Wall, p. 263.

rebuked the men of this class, as fools and blind, who could put the most absurd construction on the words of God, and make void his law by their tradition. They thus form an admonitory example, showing to what absurdity and sin it is possible for men to advance in using what they revere as a written inspiration from God. Hence, therefore, if the practice supposed by Dr. Halley be admitted, the evidence it supplies is, as we have seen, fatal to his own theory; and, if the rabbinical authority for that practice be examined, it is found to be not worth a straw. Dr. Halley's argument, therefore, is, thus far, an inference, unjustly drawn, from premises both advanced and contradicted by writers, who prove nothing so perfectly as that they themselves are unworthy of confidence.

It is clear, therefore, that, if any authoritative information on this subject be obtained, we must look for it in the New Testament. From it we learn, that there were baptisms of cups, and beds, and of persons before they ate, and when they came from a journey or from the markets. These were traditionary rites; and it is not impossible that some such traditional practice existed in the form of initiating proselytes, at least amongst the Pharisees, and those who favoured their views. From several passages in the Gospel of John, and others of a similar nature, Dr. Halley has laboured to show that some such rite, used in the act of initiation, must have been known to the Pharisees, and have given a character to the message they sent to John the Baptist, inquiring of his ministry and his reason for baptizing. Certainly, there are allusions which seem to look that way; and, for the sake of meeting his argument, we may admit that these passages do refer to a baptism which was used in the act of initiating converts. In that case, the question is, What was its nature, as indicated by this New Testament evidence? If this supposed practice is to become so important to us, all the evidence ought to be obtained that is within our reach. To some passages in the Gospels, Dr. Halley has done ample justice; but, for some reason, there be other passages which he has altogether passed by.

Apart from his inspiration, the writer of the Epistle to the Hebrews was, in all things Jewish, a high authority. When writing that epistle, he also had to deal with Jewish institutions, and to use them as illustrations of Christian truth. He there mentions[*] a "*doctrine of baptisms*" as it existed in the Christian church, requiring "*repentance from dead works and reliance upon God*," followed by "*the laying on of hands*," and united with a hope of the "*resurrection*" and *the future judgment.*" This doctrine of baptisms, with its requirement and privilege in the Christian church, is designated a foundation, in which repentance is laid as the first stone, then reliance upon God, after that baptism and laying on of hands, and these are succeeded by a resurrection of the dead and the final judgment; and baptism, when so designated, as a first principle, requiring no discussion, the author agrees in his argument to pass by for the present. By

---

[*] Hebrews vi. 1—3.

using the expression, διδαχης βαπτισμων, a doctrine of baptisms (plural), instead of the doctrine of our baptism (singular), he seems to indicate that other baptisms existed than that which they received or he administered, but that the doctrine of Christian baptism was so clear that those who had rejected or dishonoured it might be left now as hopeless cases. This passage goes no further than to imply the existence of *other baptisms;* it does not determine whether they were Jewish or heathen; but another expression appears to lead us nearer to the point. Describing the temple, or first tabernacle service of the Jews, he says, " This tabernacle was a figure for the time then being, during which (time) were offered both gifts and sacrifices that were unable to make the worshipper perfect in respect to the conscience, they consisting only in meats and drinks and divers immersions (baptisms), terms of justification for the flesh [appointed] until the time of reformation [should come]."* Here, then, the existence of different baptisms, or immersions, in the Jewish service before the coming of Christ, is distinctly affirmed. But to make a worshipper perfect, τελειῶσαι, is to complete his initiation; and terms of justification of the flesh, δικαιωματα, are things without which a personal participation in the visible service of that tabernacle could not be justified. In these terms of justification the baptisms are included, whether one or more; and, therefore, supposing they refer to the same subject, the words here written agree

* Heb. ix. 9, 10.

with those of Maimonides, who affirmed that whenever a heathen will come and be joined to the covenant of Israel, &c., voluntary circumcision, baptism, and oblation, are required. That is to say, in the words of the epistle, he is not perfectly initiated, or prepared as a worshipper, nor can his presence in the service be justified, until those rites have been performed. Nay, on the supposition that proselyte baptism did exist in that age, the very words of Dr. Halley are thus sustained, without any if or reservation whatsoever (p. 160): "Without baptism, no Gentile adult or infant could be received into the congregation of Israel, or admitted within the gates of the temple of the Lord."

THE AUTHORISED EXPECTATION OF JEWISH PROSELYTES.

Nothing can be more important than to retain in every argument an exact statement of the evidence on which it is based; for uncertain premises can only, at the best, lead to probable conclusions. If it could be positively proved that no initiatory immersion, Jewish or heathen, existed before the dispensation of John and of our Lord, then, of course, all the arguments which advocates of infant baptism have built upon that supposition would fall to the ground. But this positive proof has not yet been produced, and the probabilities shown by Dr. Halley, and in the Epistle to the Hebrews, are too great to be altogether disregarded. There can be no doubt of the initiatory immersions and sprinklings in which water was used by the heathen priesthood, and Justin Martyr affirms that they were borrowed from the Jews. This is not improbable. The sprinkling of the water of purification, prepared from the ashes of an heifer, is clearly an ordinance of the Mosaical law; and, baptizing the whole person before meat, and after a journey, or any contact with other nations, or even the common people, was clearly a practice in the time of our Lord. That the Jews should baptize themselves after a contact with the heathen, and not baptize a heathen when he was initiated, would seem strange. The baptism of a proselyte is, moreover, retained until this day, and practised just in that way which would seem to be implied by the words of Holy Scripture. Still our brother would have served the truth more by advancing to consider the nature of the initiation, rather than its accidental and disputed form.

Instead of hesitating to affirm the necessity of the initiation imposed on Jewish proselytes, Dr. Halley would then have been more accurate in stating, that the idea of forming communities of individuals separated from the mass of society on different grounds, and for different purposes, had, long before the advent of our Lord, pervaded almost the whole of civilised society. Many such communities existed in Egypt. Others are found amongst the Greeks. The school of Pythagoras is an example: and another is found in that association to which men were initiated by the Eleusinian mysteries, of which the oath of mutual fidelity was so sacred, that its violation was avenged by death. Cicero belonged to this association; and states, that therein he learned, not only how to live with joy, but also how to die with a better hope. If this was the expectation of one in a heathen society, therefore, the question is, What would a heathen expect,—what might Cicero himself expect,—after the act of initiation with the Jewish people? Might he justly expect any moral advantage or not? and, if any, was that the same advantage which is propounded in the gospel of Christ? Or, lastly, did not the gospel justly raise the expectation of men in Christ to a felicity and holiness infinitely superior to anything proposed by Jewish, or Gentile, or by any other association of men whatever upon earth?

What modes of initiation were used is not the question. In these they differed from each other; but a various and extensive use of water is traced in almost all. Some baptized, and others first baptized the candidate, and then sprinkled water on him as he fell into the procession. But these diversities are nothing to our point. The initiations were called new births, especially amongst the Jews, because therein persons began life anew, by a new rule, and with new expectations. What, then, might have been the expectation which Cicero would have justly cherished had he been initiated into the nation of Israel? Maimonides saith, " He will enter the covenant of Israel, come under the wing of the Divine majesty, and take upon him the yoke of the law; and in order to this he must willingly be circumcised, baptized, and offer an oblation. Here is an expectation and a condition; and before Cicero could submit to this condition, he must be convinced, that, by submitting to this condition, joining the covenant of Israel, coming under the wing of the Divine majesty, and taking on himself the yoke of the law, in fact, by tearing himself away from his own nation and friendships, and by becoming one with a people whom his countrymen derided for pouring out their prayers into the empty heavens, he would declare himself to be convinced, that, under the wing of this divine, though unseen and insulted Jehovah, he had obtained a better rule for life, and a better hope in death, than that which he obtained in the Eleusinian mysteries.

But this expectation of good, through acting on the covenant, and under the direction of another, is faith. When the person so trusted and followed is Jehovah himself, the faith is faith in God. This, under Moses, is the faith required, before his initiation, of every proselyte to the Jewish religion *now*. This requirement is clearly implied in the words of Maimonides, and on this faith Abraham himself was justified. This, therefore, was the nature of the initiation; it was a recognition on one part, and, on the other part, a declaration of faith in God under Moses. If the initiation contained several parts, all the parts must participate in the nature of the whole. If circumcision was a part of the initiation, then that was a circumcision of believers in God under Moses. If oblation was a part, that was an oblation of believers in God under Moses; and if baptism was a part, that was a baptism of believers in God under Moses. If the children were admitted with the parent (which is by no means certain), it was because of the parent's faith in God under Moses. The language of the proselyte was like that of Ruth, "Your God shall be my God, and your people shall be my people." From the moment of his initiation, all heathen relationships were dissolved; and, as one beginning to live a new life, his age might be reckoned from the time in which he was incorporated with the tribes of Israel. The question, therefore, whether proselytes were or were not baptized is of no moment; the initiation was discriminating, and if baptism was a part of it, the baptism must have been discriminating too.

How far, and to what age, the child of a proselyte could be received with him, is, though the Jewish was a national and hereditary system, very uncertain. But the proselyte initiation itself was unquestionably *discriminating*, it supposed a character which might be accredited, and it imposed a rule of life which was and must be a test of that character. The proselyte took upon himself the yoke of the law; and, being initiated, he became a debtor to do the whole law. Paul not only states this in his argument with the Galatians, he expands the thought in his Epistle to the Corinthians. When the nation was baptized, initiated into Moses, being immersed in cloud and sea, they entered under an authority the exercise of which was destined to secure the glory of the God to whom they were subject.* They were not permitted to return. Their criminalities were punished with

---

* 1 Cor. x. 1—14.

severity, and their covenant was sacred, until its end was accomplished in the coming of the Christ. But one law was for the proselyte and the home-born Jew. This subjection to the law and discipline of God in Israel was one thing that every proselyte was bound to expect, and his willingness to embrace it must have been an indispensable term of his initiation.

It is the nature of Jewish initiation, therefore, of which there can be no doubt, that affects the subject now under debate, and not the use of baptism as a part of the initiation, which has been and is disputed. If it be true that the proselyte was immersed, since the person must have been converted to the Jewish faith before he was initiated with the Jewish people, the immersion included in the form of his initiation, must have been administered on the declaration of that faith. If, in conformity with the national and hereditary nature of that community, his children were initiated with him, then this also must have taken place because of the faith which the parent had disclosed. If other ceremonial observances were used, of which we have no record, which is by no means impossible, the essential nature of the initiation in which they were comprised would have been extended to them also. To determine these is not essential to the matter in hand. It is of no importance whatever. The question is not *how* the Jews and Gentiles initiated persons in their respective associations? but *what persons*, and with *what intent* they initiated them? It is a fact that schools and separate associations were formed amongst the heathen, and it is a fact that the Jews were a people incorporated and made separate from the heathen; and it is an additional fact, that John and Jesus formed an association of persons separate from both heathen and Jews: What, then, was the ground of this separate communion of individuals in each case? The heathen expected an advantage in the Pythagorean school, and in the Eleusinian association; but a member of either of these societies might have become converted to the faith of Moses. What advance did he make by that step? Did God hold out any good for such? Did he justify any expectation in the fellowship and covenant of Israel? It is impossible, with the Old Testament, the law, and the prophets in our hands, to hesitate on this point. He did justify an expectation. The mere forms of initiation were as nothing compared with the good to be obtained by the proselyte in his fellowship with Israel and the service of Jehovah. It is this which gives its character to the proselyte initiation; and the confidence in God which produced separation from heathen idols for his sake, and obedience with his people on the hope of his blessing, was the faith which that proselyte initiation required.

That the expectations of the Jews, even under their own discipline, were not always approved or justified by God, is clear from the Inspired Writings. At one time they were too earthly in their views and wishes, and, at other times, they were too willing to rely on forms. God designed, in their dispensation, to secure a line of progenitors by whom the advent of Messiah might be traced to the seed of Abraham; and through the symbols and forms of worship established with that people, individuals were led to feel the need of salvation, and to cherish the hope of its attainment, through the Messiah, when he came. The fault of that people consisted not in supposing that the members initiated into their society were not separated from Gentiles, with whom they would not eat; but in making their national distinction and their forms of worship too exclusively the ground of their dependence for personal safety before God. Here they were met by their own prophets, by John, and by Paul. They were admonished not to lean on their personal relationship to Abraham, whether adopted, or by natural descent. The author of the Epistle to the Hebrews is very bold. He admits that their initiation made them perfect as to the fleshly relationship;* but clearly affirms, that not all their rites and ceremonies together could make them perfect as to the conscience. The great privilege of their nation he shows to be, the bringing forth of one who, with authority higher than Moses, and sacredness greater than that of Aaron, and in all the power of an endless life, should bring forth, hold, and administer, this perfection as to the conscience, both for Israel and the world.

"What advantage, then, had the Jew over the Gentile? Much every way: chiefly, because unto them were committed the oracles of God." This

---

* Heb. ix. 1—11.

national and hereditary association (separated from all other peoples and societies whatever), was thus exalted and enriched. Their law was a rule for the detection of sin; and the ordinances of their worship symbolised its remedy; while the prophecies foretold the coming of one in whose person and work every blessing expressed by these symbols should be procured and brought into actual use. The national and hereditary association secured the line of Messiah's descent; and the national ordinances of religion secured advantages leading to personal piety, and to faith in the coming Lord. But neither of these could be appreciated by any heathen without a rejection of idol gods in favour of the one Jehovah, and of heathen theories in favour of the Divine oracles. Whatever mistakes of interpretation might exist in Israel, Moses and the prophets must there be supreme; and, by their authority, no Jewish proselyte could bring one of his rejected penates into the congregation of Israel on pain of death. If the ordinances he found in the temple did not make him perfect as to the conscience, by perfecting his fleshly relationship to the Lord's nation, they gave the proselyte a high advantage. Cicero himself would have been thereby exalted. When once imbued with the Jewish faith, he would have learned, before the altar, its sacrifice, mercy seat, and the Shechina, more of the nature of God, than his work now exhibits; aided by the teaching of Divine law, his Offices, if not more valuable in matter, would have become more solemn by the fear of God; the history of God's people would have supplied warmer and more vitalising elements, with which to imbue his theory of friendship; his thoughts on old age would have become more grave and majestical by pondering eternity in the light of Divine revelation; the example of Moses and the predictions of Messiah would have raised and purified his principles of policy; and, powerful as his oratory proved, its moral influence would have been augmented when filled with the words of Jehovah, instead of appeals to Apollo carved in stone. These are not merely possible results, which such an initiation to Moses might have produced, they are results which that initiation and its privileges were intended to produce in every such case. It was intended to produce similar and corresponding results by every initiation with its privilege; and the initiation was administered in conformity with that design. The Jewish dispensation, therefore, though subordinate, was not mean; in moral greatness it had no antecedent or contemporaneous equal upon earth. In it the ancient patriarchal sacrifice, preserved from defiling idolatries, brought down, from paradise itself, the voice of mercy, and symbolised its chief work, annually, in bleeding expiations. The minor rites brought out the central thought of the symbolic system, applying it to the daily, weekly, and monthly necessities of the whole people, its families, and individuals. It marked the whole human existence with blood; and every mark had reference to the coming Saviour. All its symbols seemed to speak its own imperfection, because they could not make the comers thereunto perfect; yet was it filled with glory by its author, and it formed a splendid introduction to that greater system whose glory was destined to excel and to last for ever.

At that point where the Jewish dispensation fails, and on which all the symbols of its worship throw their light, the Gospel unfolds its glorious superiority. The conscience, its burdens of guilt, and the judgment to which it appeals, are the great emergencies which it contemplates. The former system made the initiated perfect as to the fleshly, subordinate, and temporal relationship; but, Christ being come, a high priest of the good things to come, the purchaser and the minister of the better hope, the better covenant, the heavenly tabernacle, by his initiation with its requirements of repentance and faith, and its everlasting privilege, makes men perfect as to the conscience, makes them perfect for ever; and does it through the sacrifice of himself. The meaning of the passage, through its whole reasoning, is that Jesus initiates those who are sanctified, on a ground which reaches the vital solicitude of conscience, and renders their relation to himself perfect for ever. This is the very thing which the Jews and their proselytes were led to expect, the substance of which their own dispensation held the shadows; the desire of all nations; the sovereign and only remedy for this world's guilt and ruin; and hence, by all kinds of argument, the believing Jews are urged not to forego their privilege in this fellowship, but to hold fast their confidence to the end, that is to say, till death and the final judgment.

Whatever the fact respecting proselyte baptism may be, whether it did or did not prevail before the time of our Lord, it is quite certain that it never formed the *sole* initiating rite: for all the authorities join circumcision and oblation with it in men, and oblation is joined with it in the case of women. The circumcision, moreover, is clearly a divine appointment, while the baptism of the proselyte, if it was practised, cannot be traced to any ordination of God granted to the Jews. It is only in the Christian system that baptism is found exalted to the character of an adequate initiation, without any other physical rite or ceremony whatever. Here, therefore, it stands alone, separated from all other ritual observances, but joined with the peculiarities of the Christian dispensation. But in that very passage of the Hebrews, from which the most specific information is obtained respecting the Jewish initiation, and the whole Jewish preparatory system—with its gifts and sacrifices, its diverse baptisms, its terms of justification for the flesh, and the object which the whole was to accomplish—the Jewish system is placed in bold and decided contrast with the Christian. The object of the sentence being to describe the requirements necessary to fellowship in the temple worship, if any baptism of proselytes was used, it must be included in these " diverse baptisms," and its object could go no further than the part it might perform in making perfect *as to the flesh*. But, on this very point, the contrast between these two dispensations is declared and proven. With reference to this very point, the first is made subordinate, and the second the principal; the first is for the time being, the second is final and everlasting; the one makes men perfect as to the flesh only, the other makes them perfect as to the conscience and for ever. But it is inaccurately assumed by Dr. Halley, first, that baptism in both cases formed the sole initiation, and then it is inferred that those who were baptized into each dispensation, constituted its initiated members. Dr. Halley concludes, therefore, that baptism is, in each case, the same thing; and has, in these two dissimilar dispensations, the same condition. This would make the societies both different and identical at the same time, which is absurd. But, contrary to his own authorities, Dr. Halley affirms, that the Jewish, and therefore the Christian, baptism were administered without any discriminating condition whatever; will he, then, affirm, that, in any sense, the adult or infant when baptized, without *any* discriminating regard to his own character, is perfect as the conscience, and perfect for ever? Unless the Doctor himself avow it, we could not dare to affirm this dreadful, though legitimate, conclusion.

But it may be answered, This is arguing from views of the Jewish dispensation which were entertained by Paul and the other apostles, when they had been converted, and long after the Christian community was formed. This could not show *what* the notions of the Pharisees and other Jews were *before* these events transpired. Admitted; but this authority of Paul, and the Epistle to the Hebrews, shows what these antecedent notions ought to have been; it shows that view of the Jewish dispensation, to which, the Christian dispensation was conformed by God himself. But abundance of proof exists to show that this idea of subordination and insufficiency in the one, and of supreme sufficiency in the other, was a prevailing notion with the Jewish people, and ought to have been long before the time of our Lord. Abraham led them to expect in his seed, and in the kingdom which he should form, a blessing for themselves and for all mankind. Jacob, in the inspirations of mortality, in no obscure terms, intimates that Judah's sceptre should be broken before him. Moses plainly declares that his own dispensation and law and people must all submit under this authority. David exalts the kingly character of his Son, affirming that he should dash in pieces, as a potter's vessel, all resisting powers. Isaiah affirmed that he should strike the earth with the rod of his mouth, and effect his purposes with doctrine. Daniel affirms that the force of his dominion should break up and destroy the four great empires upon earth. Some prophecies relate to his personal character, some to his teaching, the treatment of his disciples, and the treatment of his enemies; while others relate to the time of his appearing, and the place of his birth. In these two last points, which are attended with more difficulty than all the others, the Pharisees were informed, and their explanation was accurate. When they sent to John, inquiring of his ministry, it is clear that they expected Messiah to form a community distinct from themselves and from all men, which might be called his own, and into which persons should be baptized. Moreover, in the scenes which attended the birth of our Lord and of John, incidents transpired, and words were used, which show that the kingdom and glory of Messiah was not altogether misunderstood. In the ecstasy of Zacharias on recovering his speech at the birth of John, he said,* " God hath been mindful of his holy covenant, the oath which he sware to Abraham, our father: and thou, child, shalt be called a prophet of the Most High, to prepare his way, that he may give a knowledge of salvation to his people in the forgiveness of their sins, through the tender mercies of God, in which a day-spring, which is to shine out upon those who are sitting in darkness and a shadow of death, hath visited us." These words, which accord with all that is recorded of the Advent, realise, not only the spirit of the ancient prophecy, but also the whole reasoning of St. Paul and the Epistle to the Hebrews, as before cited. They show that the people of the Most High, which is Jesus, whose way was prepared by John, should be a people in whom the Lord would reveal the peculiarity of his mission, by giving to them a knowledge of salvation in the forgiveness of their sins. His people, therefore, were to be made perfect as to the conscience; for, its solicitous references to the final judgment were the subjects of his ministration. When his kingdom was evolved, and its initiation made known, the time and occasion for those rites which

* Luke i. 67—79.

made perfect as to the flesh only, had passed away. The people united in the Christ, were, by his death, to be made perfect for ever. The individual who failed in obtaining this, gained nothing; his existence amongst the Lord's disciples was a violation of his law. But the law of Christ concedes no hope of salvation in the forgiveness of sins, without repentance and faith; and, therefore, none could be initiated into his fellowship without repentance and faith.

But it is pleaded, that these views of Zacharias were confined to the pious few, while the Pharisees were exceedingly corrupt. There is some plausibility in this; yet, it must not be forgotten, that these Pharisees were better at interpretation than in practice. They knew more of the truth than they observed: but they were corrupt, very corrupt, and, for their corruption, they were grievously rebuked both by the Lord and the Baptist. But why, then, should Dr. Halley call them in as expositors of the Lord's commandment? If they corrupted their own worship, perverted their ancient oracles, and made void the law of God by their traditions, what evil may we not expect when the writings of the New Testament are explained by their preconceived notions? If no authorised conceptions of the Messiah's kingdom had, at the time appealed to, existed amongst the Jewish people, this appeal to the Pharisees would have claimed some excuse; but, to turn from ancient Scripture, the Apostle Paul, the Epistle to the Hebrews, and the inspired Zacharias, to those whom the gentle Redeemer designates a generation of vipers, can hardly be allowed without censure. That Tractmen and Papists should seek, for their theories, support in such traditional authority, is quite consistent; but, that Dr. Halley, the magnanimous advocate of Evangelical principles, should build his theory upon such materials, is unaccountable. Judging from his work, it should seem that no personal inclination, but the emergency of his undertaking alone, has forced him into this alliance. If this be the case, it is hoped that this fact, of itself, will induce the advocates of infant baptism calmly and conscientiously to review the authority of a rite, whose defence has imposed upon its noblest advocate so terrible an expedient.

That the idea evolved in the language of ancient Scripture, of Zacharias, the Epistle to the Hebrews, and of St. Paul, and not any other idea supposed to exist amongst the Jewish schools, was acted upon in founding the Christian dispensation, is seen on various grounds.

1. The treatment of Jewish teachers and schools by our Lord and his forerunner, seems to indicate and justify this conclusion. After all that Dr. Halley has said, it is inconceivable that John, while saying, "Ye generation of vipers, how shall ye escape the damnation of hell?" could, without any explanation, make the unauthorised practice of these very individuals a precedent in founding his own discipline.

2. The reason assigned for rejecting Israel as a people of God, leads to the same result. After the Pentecost, the temple was no more God's temple; the ceremonies no longer constituted his worship, and the

incorporated nation was no longer his people. But why?—the Apostle says, because of unbelief.* On what principle of incorporation, therefore, could another people of God be formed, save that of faith, by withholding which the Jews had been rejected? Hence the Apostle himself argues, that each individual who believes is, through his faith, justified by God himself in appropriating all that relates to this incorporated body and its prospects; but that without faith, no one can be justified in appropriating anything that mercy has revealed, or that Christ has purchased.

3. The fact that the baptism of disciples began amongst the Jews, is proof of the position: for, the act itself, as if vocal, said, the coming reign of God will not authorise your national rites and incorporation, but deal with individuals only, and only on its own principle of justifying all through faith, and none without it, or on any other terms.†

4. The avowed principle of Christian incorporation affords a decisive proof. For, in the words of Paul, Christians, though many, are one in Christ Jesus: that is to say, being in Christ Jesus, they become one, and only thus. The being in Christ, therefore, is the principle of their incorporation with each other; but he that is in Christ Jesus is a new creature, because the being in Christ involves a transfer of all interests to his care, and a subjection of all thought to his teaching: this is a double operation of faith, which

---

* Rom. ix.—xii. † Gal., *passim*.

distinguishes its possessor from Jew and Gentile, from all unrenewed men whatsoever.

5. The language used in describing this new character is quite decisive. The Gentile man was deemed the lowest and most forsaken; the Jewish man had his peculiarity and privilege; but, the New man*— the Christian man was distinguished from both, in that, being no more dead in sins, but quickened by the Spirit and saved by grace through faith, he was initiated, incorporated, builded up together with the saints, an habitation of God in the Spirit.

6. The use which is here assigned to this incorporated body gives further proof: for, rejecting the Jewish nation for unbelief, and saying, Ye are not my people, he places his Shechina here, and dwells in them, as a father in a family, a ruler in the midst of subjects, as God amidst his believing worshippers. Here, in all simplicity, but with all grandeur, he, whom none can please without faith, designs to realise in men, the vast but authorised conception of all inspired and uninspired antiquity. Plaintive as the tones may be in which he proclaims his love, they are full of import and sustained by power. Touching indeed, pathetic, and often majestical, are the paintings of his throne in the poetry of prophecy; but his actual glory exceeds them all. When he came, he came unto his own, and his own received him not; he found no faith upon the earth till he produced it, and then he treated it with all endearment, binding its posses-

* Eph. ii., iii.

sors to himself and to each other by his holy sacramental initiation. These are his people: in these he lives apart, separated from all other corporations of men whatever, but contemplating in his sanctuary the deliverance of all. Round his throne are seen, in grateful worship, the sick whom he has healed, the slaves whom he has liberated, the dead whom he has raised, the sinners he has forgiven; and all the believing recipients of his favour are employed under his command. By these he has once transformed all civilised existence, and designs to transform it again. By individuals who believe, he is acting on individuals who do not yet believe; and, by gathering up individuals who are thus brought to believe, and consecrating them, he is, through all its generations, leading, despite all its gloom and criminality, the fainting population of this dying world back to their long-lost paradise.

THE SUMMARY AND CONCLUSION.

In conclusion, therefore, the premises of Dr. Halley are not laid down with accuracy. The initiating immersion in water, which he ascribes to the Jews, as if peculiar to that people, however probable, is disputed in their case; but it certainly was used before the time of our Lord by heathen communities. Separated communities of men were thus incorporated, having different objects and laws of association, and extending over nearly the whole civilised world; and therefore, in using an immersion in water, by which to initiate his own disciples, the Lord could no more be said to imitate the Jews, than any other association by whom a baptism in water was so employed. The nature of each community was determined by its origin, its aim, the term of its initiation, and the discipline of its members when received; and not by the initiating immersion which was common to all who used it. The Jewish community was distinguished from all heathen communities by its Divine origin, its reference to the coming of Messiah, the faith in Jehovah required of each proselyte, and his discipline by the law of Moses. By these peculiarities the Jews and their proselytes were distinguished from all heathen society. In his initiation, however it was performed, the proselyte, being expatriated, was recognised as one dead to all heathen relationships whatever, and received as one without father or mother, by this new birth, to a new life, a Jewish life, in which he became incorporated and registered in the tribes of Israel. The initiation of his children with the proselyte appears to be more disputed than his baptism; and the supposed initiating immersion, if it was administered, not being a legal purification, had no Divine authority, but formed a part of those rabbinical appendages to the Jewish ceremonies which our Lord so often and so severely reprehended. Our Lord, in founding the gospel dispensation, did not act upon the traditions which had made void the law, nor upon rabbinical notions, which he condemned; but, upon that antecedent expectation of Messiah's kingdom, which Moses and the prophets had awakened, which God had preserved and justified, which Zacharias expressed at the birth of John, and which Paul explained in his

Epistles. This expectation was, that while their own relationship' and discipline under Moses raised them above the heathen world, and made them perfect as to the flesh, the kingdom of Messiah should raise them above both Jews and Gentiles, making its members and subjects perfect as to the conscience, and perfect for ever. The appointment of an immersion, as an initiatory rite, was an act of Sovereign and Divine authority, first expressed in the ministry of John, and then by our Lord himself in his commission; and the terms of admission to that rite must be sought in his own words, the recorded practice of himself and his ministers, the antecedent expectation which he justified, the law of incorporation observed, the discipline to be maintained, and the end to be accomplished in his kingdom. Finally, all these sources of evidence concur in proving, that "repentance toward God, and faith in our Lord Jesus Christ," form an indispensable condition of all or any recognising action in the congregation or kingdom of Christ: that where these are possessed and evinced, all personal and relative honours and benefits in the body of Christ may, in conformity with his law, be sought under the justifying protection of God himself: and that, where this repentance and faith are wanting, the man, being included in unbelief, is marked and rejected as an enemy, and, therefore, not distinguished as a disciple.

In the next Lecture, this conclusion will be confirmed by the character and ministry of John the Baptist.

LECTURE III.

ON JOHN'S BAPTISM.

We have already seen, that the use of water, which our Lord appointed in the initiation of his disciples, was no more the preceding rite of the Jewish initiation, than that of any other of those communities which used it with the same design. If any regard was paid to antecedent practice, it will be found in that excessive condescension with which our Redeemer embraced the plainest language of earth, and the most common figures of speech, to make his communication most intelligible and impressive on his hearers. On this principle a reason might be assigned for this divine appointment. His community of disciples was destined to dissolve all others; and, by drawing away and appropriating their materials, to terminate their existence. Apollo and Jupiter, with their separated communities, were doomed, and Athens, Ephesus, Corinth, and Rome, were to be bereaved of all the supposed sanctity they derived from the holy places of their worship and priesthood. In every separate community it would be understood at once, that this Christian initiatory immersion separated its recipient from their assemblies, their fellowships, and all their interests. It was a rite which spake to all parties; and, with most expressive simplicity, it conveyed, to all other priesthoods, the one simple idea on which their death-struggle was to be maintained.

The result of this great practical conflict, in which more blood was shed than in any civil war, is seen in our own and the other museums of Europe. There these ancient deities, or dæmons, are stowed away, hacked and worn, but preserved, in their maimed condition, by public charity, as if to save them from the contempt which surrounds their fanes, and from the rudeness that would burn them into lime. But in their hospitalries these invalided deities are destined yet to perform a great and good service. They are now become witnesses, testifying the hold which they once had upon their votaries, and their former command over all the results of human labour. Every line which Phidias has left carved in the broken fragments of his works is an expressive record of the fact, that these communities, existing at the time and before the Saviour came, were not loose assemblies, but, like the temples they used, were fabricated with skill, compacted with strength, and, like the idols they worshipped, polished with the extreme of elegance. They were practical embodiments of the moral principle which then existed. That moral principle, such as it was, became, by this means, obvious in its age, and to the men of its time. Its advocates, and the individuals submitting to its influence, were, in every case, marked by the initiation; and a social influence was thus formed and concentrated for its support. The support thus obtained for heathen principles was not affected by the Jewish community and its initiatory declarations. By these, the heathen were declared to be wrong in principle and in practice; but by these the heathen systems could not be overturned. In its constitution, the Jewish dispensation thus appeared to be introductory, subordinate, and insufficient of itself to effectuate the Divine intention. By that very hereditary principle of incorporation, which made the children of the flesh heirs with their parents in a system designed to make perfect only as to the flesh, and through which the birth of Messiah was secured to the natural posterity of David and of Abraham, the original element of human depravity was retained in the society set apart, and a society so formed could not, in the nature of things, become effective in overturning societies whose worst errors were all produced by that very original element of human depravity which was so retained. Before these societies could be encountered with effect, and their members could be induced to forsake the worldly splendours and interests therein engaged, another association must be formed, from which should be expelled, by the law of its incorporation and discipline, that original treason of the heart out of which had sprung the formality of Jewish, and the atrocities of heathen, societies. The

Jewish community could not do this, because it had, by the covenant with Abraham, to secure a separate line of natural posterity in which Messiah should be born. For the attainment of personal salvation, in the precepts of their law, which detected sin, and in the symbols of their worship, which explained the operations of mercy, the Jews possessed many and great advantages; but, for the formation of a society, the creation of a *new* man, neither Jewish nor heathen, but "*one new man*,"* made, by a merciful operation, from the human materials contained in both; in whom, and by whose operation, God would overturn all combinations of formality and wickedness whatsoever, and reassert his claim to worship and obedience upon earth, their expectations were fixed on that Messiah himself, and the kingdom to be formed under his administration. That this was the authorised expectation realised and acted upon in founding the Christian community, is now to be proved from the character and ministry of John the Baptist.

ADMISSIONS OF DR. HALLEY.

Here, as in former cases, especial attention must be paid to Dr. Halley's admissions. These, in his own words, are as follows:—"John, the baptizer, the son of Zacharias, was, by his birth, of the sacerdotal office. It is not, however, probable, that he discharged any of the peculiar functions of the priest-

---

* Eph. ii. 15, 16.

hood, for he received his special commission, as a prophet, to announce the coming of Christ, and to baptize into his name, as he was entering on the thirtieth year of his age, the year in which he would, in due course, have been installed and registered as a priest before the Sanhedrim at Jerusalem. It is said, 'He abode in the desert,' the hill country where he was born, ' until his showing forth unto Israel,' which expression may denote, until he appeared to execute his important office as the precursor of the Messiah," p. 161. "He was commissioned" "to teach a new doctrine," "to declare that the kingdom of heaven was at hand." "The older prophets had described the reign of Messiah, John announced his advent." "The near approach of that reign was the new doctrine which attracted the attention of great multitudes, who received baptism from him, and were thenceforth called his disciples." "So closely were the baptism and the new doctrine connected, that the one term seems to be employed for the other," p. 162. It may be observed here, that in these cases it would have been more accurate to have said, that John was commissioned to declare a new event, or a new fact relating to a long-expected event; yet, here is a great difficulty, since neither was the event itself of Messiah's coming, nor the fact that he was coming soon, at all new in Judea. The infants at Bethlehem had been slaughtered thirty years before, in consequence of that impression. The following words of Dr. Halley make this more clear:—" It is true that the baptism of John is called the baptism of repentance; but then the repentance was, in every instance, founded upon the new doctrine, the uniform exhortation, the incessant cry of the baptizer being, 'Repent, for the kingdom of heaven is at hand,'" p. 162. From this "uniform cry of the baptizer," it is obvious, that " the kingdom of heaven is at hand" expresses an assumed fact on which the exhortation, "repent," is enforced, and the new doctrine must have been the necessity of repentance to meet that event with *propriety*, if not with *safety*. But Dr. Halley adds: " It is, indeed, said, that they (the disciples of John) were baptized, confessing their sins; but whether they uttered an audible confession as they stood in crowds listening to his preaching, or their baptism was itself an act of confession, an acknowledgment that they needed repentance, we are not able to ascertain," p. 163. Perhaps *not;* but from these passages, it is clearly ascertained that Dr. Halley does admit a connexion of some kind between their baptism, confession of their sins, and repentance; and, also, that these three duties were so connected with the speedy appearance of our Lord, as to produce, in the ministrations of John, a character by which it was distinguished from all that had preceded him, and by which it "attracted the attention of great multitudes."

THE ASSUMPTIONS OF DR. HALLEY.

But Dr. Halley cannot " suppose that there was a distinct and personal confession, anything like auricular confession, of their several offences made to John, their baptizer;" but affirms that " the baptism of

John was indiscriminately administered to all applicants," p. 163. He rests this affirmation, first, "on the numbers baptized;" secondly, on the supposition that, "of the great multitudes who went out to his baptism, we have not the slightest hint of any person whatever having been rejected;" and, thirdly, "the excitement produced by the preaching of John speedily subsided." All these unguarded assumptions are made to confirm his affirmation that, "To be baptized was (no more than) to be initiated as a learner of the new doctrine—the speedy coming of Christ," p. 162. But this was no new thing in Israel. The coming, the speedy coming of their Christ, was the leading idea in all the calculations of the Jewish people. It had exposed them to diverse and dreadful impositions. Almost any daring adventurer could, by assuming that character, obtain adherents. Nor was it merely a preparation for his coming, that could have fixed and filled the attention of so many minds; from the time of Moses, down to the day of John's "showing forth unto Israel," and especially by all the latter prophets, the necessity of this preparation had been urged in language which could scarcely be strengthened. If anything new, therefore, appeared in the ministry of John to strike the public mind, it must be sought, not in the doctrine that he taught, which was old as Isaiah, nor in the fact which he used, which was known to many,—but, in the discipline which he instituted, preparing by official acts a people for his Lord.

After Dr. Halley had so fully and so positively declared, that baptism was not a purification at all, it is hard to say in what sense the word purify can be used in the following sentence : " As Moses purified the nation preparatory to the descent of Jehovah on Sinai, so it seems to have been the commission of John to purify the whole nation preparatory to the coming of Messiah," p. 164. If the technical and misleading word "*purify*" were left out of this sentence, it would express a great truth. Moses did prepare the Jewish people for the descent of Jehovah on Sinai, by special purifications, which made them perfect as to the flesh; if, by analogy with this event, John was commissioned to prepare the nation for the coming of Messiah, his preparation must accord with the spiritual nature of that kingdom which Messiah came to establish. For Paul has actually brought the two dispensations into contrast on this very reference. The Sinai covenant and incorporation, he calls a son of the bond-woman which is cast out, and which he himself identifies with the Jewish community then existing at Jerusalem ; but himself and his brethren, forming the subjects of Messiah's kingdom, he calls the children of the free woman, the inheritors of the promise, the family of God.* But how did they become so? His own answer is, " We are all sons of God, by faith in Christ Jesus; for, as many as have been baptized into Christ, have put on Christ."† If John, therefore, prepared the nation for that Messiah's coming, it must have been by urging that repentance towards God and faith

* Gal. iv. 26, 27. † Gal. iii. 26—29.

in our Lord Jesus Christ, then called "*the coming one*," on which this Messiah's kingdom must be built. If John *did* prepare a people for him, that people must have had the distinguishing character of his subjects. And of this we have even stronger proof: for, of those who were then in Christian fellowship, and some in the apostolical office, and were so described by the Apostle; that is to say, of these sons of God by faith in Christ Jesus, there were many who had been, before the death of Christ, baptized *by John's baptism, and had put on Christ* in none other. If all, therefore, had so put on Christ in baptism, saving faith must have been an element in that repentance which they professed to John.

The national aspect of John's commission seems not altogether without foundation. He appears to have been sent to none other than the Jewish people, and all who belonged to that nation came within its scope. By him a last effort was made to induce in that erring people such an improvement of religious privilege, as would secure the personal enjoyment of his favour when Christ appeared. With all the flaming energies of his soul, he rushed between them and their approaching catastrophe. In position and deportment he resembled Moses when, beholding the idolatry of his people, he smashed the tables of the law, and, planting the tabernacle without the camp, cried, Who is on the Lord's side? In executing his great commission he forsook a priesthood defiled with all corruption. Therewith his part in ordinary Jewish purifications was relinquished. The professed reformers of his time, both Sadducees and Pharisees, were all abandoned, and all his energies were given to this one work, in which he formed no people or community for himself; he was merely the forerunner of him that was to come, who was just at hand. He made ready a people prepared by repentance, and pledged to his reception. If this work was prosecuted on a vital and essential principle, it gave the Jewish nation one more opportunity of securing, by repentance, the final advantage of their own covenants, in receiving and exalting their own Messiah; and, to fill up the measure of their crime, it required nothing further than the appearance and rejection of that Messiah himself. But it is hard to conceive of anything more delusive and fatal than a mere superficial administration of things already known, at such a time, with expressions such as John used, and the character in which he appeared. His strong language, coarse fare, eremitic garb, and stern separation from the society of his own priesthood and people, combined with a superficial doctrine and an indiscriminatory baptism, would have presented the most ludicrous and despicable of all exhibitions that ever appeared in the history of mankind. Instead of being the greatest of all that before him were born of woman, he would have been the least, one might almost say, the worst, that had ever appeared.

THE DOCTRINE AFFIRMED.

Suppositions relating to the mode of former action, are often made the means of leading inquirers away from those questions which involve and determine the truth. It is not for us to explain in what way John received the confession of sin and the declaration of his repentance from each candidate for his baptism; all we mean to affirm is, that the confession and repentance required, were of that kind which stands, in the dispensation of mercy, connected with the forgiveness of sin; and, that the pledge of submission to the coming Lord, was one on which an action might be taken in Christian discipline. The baptized person was committed to all the intents and purposes of the kingdom of heaven; and, when recognised by baptism, the disciple was excused from none of its duties, and he was excluded from none of its privileges, until he had proved himself to be insincere. The act which recognised his discipleship, separated him for the Lord from all other associations of men, as far as their proceedings were incompatible with his laws and purposes. This dealing with individuals, and setting them apart for Christ, because of their personal repentance and faith, commenced with John—it formed the peculiarity of his ministration; and, by that way which he thus prepared, the Lord himself advanced, consolidating first and then enlarging, his kingdom upon the earth.

THE DECLARATION OF OUR LORD.

The first proof of this doctrine is supplied by our Lord himself. In Matthew xi. 7—24, and Luke vii. 18—35, the subject of John's ministry is brought before us in his own words. The miracles Christ had performed, and the effects of his ministry, had been reported to John in prison; and his disciples were sent to ask of Jesus whether he was the one who was coming, or, whether they should look for another? John, it appears, in those trying moments which preceded his martyrdom, notwithstanding the intimations he had received from God, wished to obtain a clear declaration on this point from the Lord himself. The reply is full of dignity, as if to assert his own superiority: "Tell John the things that ye see and hear; and blessed is he who is not offended in me." Such treatment of their teacher must have powerfully impressed the messengers; but, when they were gone, the Lord's declaration of John is made. This includes four points important to our design. *First*, That the aim of John, and that of our Lord's ministrations, at that time, was the same: to produce repentance in Israel. *Secondly*, That each had laboured in a different way: the servant and forerunner, with ascetical severity; the Lord himself, with forbearance and infinite tenderness. *Thirdly*, It is also affirmed that each was treated with similar but individualised rebellion and injustice: the severe forerunner was rejected as one demonised to extravagant severity; the Lord, as one given to licentiousness. And, *Fourthly*, The repentance which each urged, and which was refused to each, is shown to be that by which the judgment of the last day shall be determined. If, therefore, true repentance is in any case required, it was required in the ministry of John; and, as to the spirit in which it was urged, the Lord saith, What went ye out to see?—a man clothed in soft raiment? Why, he was a man despising all indulgence. But, what went ye out to see?—a reed shaken with the wind? He was more like an ancient oak rooted on some tempest-beaten promontory. A certain inflexibility of character and action is indicated by these two expressive lines; but the Saviour adds, "Of all that have been born of woman, a greater prophet has not arisen than John the Baptist." But, in what can we realise the superiority here implied? It is in this, that he collected all the material for constituting that kingdom of which all the others spake. He was, therefore, equal to, and even greater in office than they, and was therefore called Elijah that was to come. But, it is still added, " He who is least in the kingdom of heaven is greater than he:" but how? It is answered, in the same official dignity, Because he who officiates in a temple, is greater than he who collects the material for building it. But, the materials which lawfully compose a Christian church are, persons who are sons of God by faith in Christ Jesus; this, therefore, or an equivalent to this, must have been the object John sought, and the condition of his baptism.

INTIMATIONS GIVEN AT JOHN'S BIRTH.

But, *Secondly*, This conclusion is sustained by inspired intimations given at the birth of John. When that event transpired, it is said that Zacharias was filled with the Holy Spirit, and prophesied.* In this prophecy, the coming, the character, and work of

---

* Luke i. 67—80.

Messiah, are all pronounced, not as new discoveries, but as things covenanted and expected since the holy covenant, the oath which he swore unto Abraham, was given. Designations of the Messiah are so used as to indicate a clear view of his character and work. The Lord, the Highest, the Day-spring, are expressions which can scarcely be mistaken; which, when used by Zacharias, seemed to create no difficulty with the people who heard him. "The horn of Salvation" not only applies to the Saviour, but points out also the special nature of his work, which is *to save*, and his qualifications to perform it; a horn being an emblem of effective authority. But, this salvation is also said to be effected in his people by a remission of their sins, through the tender mercies of God. In this specific work, it is expressly said, that John would find his holy avocation: " For thou shalt go before the face of the Lord, to prepare his way," " to give knowledge of salvation to his people by the remission of sins." With these intimations before us, it is impossible to conclude otherwise than that the repentance and confession of sin, which John associated with his baptism, were the repentance and confession which God has connected with his own act of forgiveness. This is made more clear by the intimations of the Angel.* He affirms that John should "*make ready*," that is, discover and consecrate, " a people *prepared* for the Lord." If he, knowingly, made ready any others, it was beside his commission. This prepara-

---

* Luke i. 11—17.

tion of the people is also said to consist in their being turned from disobedience to the wisdom of the just, and the result of his labour is thus defined: "And many of the children of Israel shall be turned to the Lord their God." The perfect historical precision of all these Divine intimations, not only shows their Divine origin, but renders it almost impossible to construe them in a second sense. When John died, many of the children of Israel had been turned to the Lord their God; they had been thus prepared for the coming Redeemer; and, having been made ready in their baptism, they received the Redeemer when he appeared, and he received them without any further initiation.

JOHN'S PREDICTED CHARACTER.

Thirdly. In the Lord's declaration we find these words: "And if ye will receive it, this same (John) is Elijah who was to come. He that hath ears to hear, let him hear."* The adjunct to his affirmation was never used by our Lord, but when he had uttered something of great practical importance. A similar expression is used in the angel's address to Zacharias: "And he (John) shall go before him (the coming Messiah), in the spirit and power of Elijah, to turn the hearts of the fathers to the children, and the disobedient to the wisdom of the just; to make ready a people prepared for the Lord."† But both these high authorities refer to a preceding and well-

* Matthew xi. 15. † Luke i. 17.

known prophecy of Messiah's coming. "Behold, I will send you Elijah the prophet, before the coming of the great and dreadful day of the Lord, and he shall turn the heart of the fathers to the children, and the heart of the children to their fathers, lest I come and smite the earth with a curse."* The object of John's ministry, as here defined, was to prevent, by confession and repentance, that fearful judgment with which Messiah would vindicate his honour and rights upon rebellious Israel; and this becomes more clear from the blessing with which it stands contrasted in the same prophecy: "But unto you that fear my name, shall the Sun of Righteousness arise with healing in his wings."† Here all is personal, practical, and vital. The blessing and the curse of the Almighty are suspended on the character which John was to form and recognise in his ministry. He formed and recognised this character by his preaching and his baptism of repentance. His personal character and action were to realise the firm, uncompromising action of Elijah, in the reign of Ahab. A decisive pungency of rebuke, resisting the whole tide of present and popular feeling, and risking all consequences in his mighty work, were requisite in John, to realise a resemblance with his great precursor. As Elijah resisted Baalim, and the errors of his day, so John must resist the formality and corruptions of his time; as Elijah sought the true God, the true worship, and the witness of fire, so John must seek the

* Malachi iv. 5, 6.   † Malachi iv. 2.

true Messiah, the true worship, and his actual appearing. Each ministration was made dependent on an actual event: that of Elijah, on the answer he received from God on Carmel; that of John, on the appearance of his Lord. As Elijah prepared for future events, and then departed, so John, by the will of God, finished his work by preparing for another, and retired with joy when he heard the bridegroom's voice.

PROPHETICAL DECLARATIONS OF HIS WORK.

Such is the authorised antecedent expectation respecting John himself. Whatever light Dr. Halley might think to obtain from rabbinical practices, he, as a Christian teacher, was bound not to pass over, as he has done, those precedent instructions which are given by inspiration of God; and besides these which have been named, two other prophecies exist, from which a *fourth* supply of evidence is placed at our command.

Isaiah predicted the kingdom and coming of Christ in the reign of Hezekiah, king of Judah.* That period was distinguished by singular trials, and by great efforts made by the king, and many of his people, to reform the nation, and restore to its purity the worship of God. The Egyptian and Babylonian policies—each power seeking to obtain supremacy in Judea, and thereby a command of its ports on the Mediterranean sea—had thrown a network of allure-

---

* Isaiah xl. to lxvi.

ment round the Jewish king, while the invasion of Sennacherib had filled the people with dismay. Appeals were often made to their Jehovah, and not in vain. Isaiah, filled with inspiration, moved like a seraph through these active scenes. He declared the word of God, not merely as it supplied direction in the present crisis, his visions reached to the end of time. To encourage the faithful of that age, he declared the glory of Messiah's future reign. He made each of those adherents to truth who surrounded him feel, that their struggle of fidelity was not to be supported in vain. The great principle of faith, and its justified privileges, by which both Jew and Gentile should become one in Christ, is avowed, with its mediating atonement, almost as clearly as in St. Paul; and its final victory is proclaimed with wonderful power and beauty. The birth, life, rejection, death, but final triumph of Messiah, in the spiritual constitution and glory of his kingdom, are set forth with such precision, that his prophecy appears like a history of the events. Nothing can be more clear than that the Holy Spirit in Isaiah was dealing with the vital and imperishable realities of the gospel dispensation. But in the very introduction of this prophecy, John appears, "the voice of one crying in the wilderness."* It seems, the very wilderness in which his ministry began, was that by which the invaders of Israel were presently returning from their conflict with Tirhakah, the Ethiopian, and in which the

---

* Isaiah xl. 3—8.

Assyrians perished by the angel. Isaiah, taking advantage of this, leads the thought down the whole course of time to John's appearing, and there presents him calling upon Zion to rise in her zeal and greatness, because of the blessings her Messiah gave; and proclaim the faithfulness of God in his covenants, affliction, and death, notwithstanding. The attitude he assumes, his words, and the whole business of the prophecy prove, that the herald is dealing with eternity; and, therefore, the baptism he administered, and the repentance it required, must have laid hold on eternity too.

It must not be forgotten, that this application of the prophecy is not only assumed by John;* but another, whose application is authorised by the Lord himself,† gives it a peculiar clearness and strength. Malachi delivered his prophecy in Jerusalem, when Nehemiah was building the wall, and seeking the restoration of his people. The Temple had been restored; and one good effect resulting from the captivity was, the entire separation between idol gods, and the Jews who returned; but the priesthood, the nobles, and the whole congregation, were exceedingly corrupt. Nehemiah complains of this with great pathos; and Malachi mentions eleven gross criminalities in which they indulged against God and his worship. They depreciated the love of God; they withheld his parental honour, and his service as a Lord; they were mercenary in what they

* John i. 23.   † Matthew xi. 10.

did, and his service was a weariness; they departed from the law of their God, and admitted alliance with idolaters; they were guilty of social violence, and said, Where is the God of Judgment? They saw the chastisement of their fathers, and yet adhered to their crimes; they evaded the overtures of mercy sent for their good, robbed God of service and of sacrifice, and became wearisome in their blasphemy, saying, It is a vain thing to serve the Lord. To men affected with these and similar vices Malachi uttered his prophecy: "Behold, I will send my messenger, and he shall prepare the way before me; and the Lord whom ye seek shall suddenly come to his Temple; even the Messenger of the covenant, whom ye delight in: behold, he shall come, saith the Lord of Hosts. But who may abide the day of his coming? and who shall stand when he appeareth? for he is like a refiner's fire, and like fuller's soap; and he shall sit as a refiner and purifier of silver; and he shall purify the sons of Levi, and purge them as gold and silver, that they may offer unto the Lord an offering in righteousness. Then shall the offering of Judah and Jerusalem be pleasant unto the Lord as in the days of old, and in former years."* Now, on this whole prophecy, it is obvious to remark that the persons predicted are, the Lord himself, and John his messenger; moreover, the thing lost by their sins, and to be regained by this twofold ministry, was the favour of God, and his acceptance of their service;

* Malachi iii. 1—5.

and, lastly, that repentance of these sins, by which the favour of God could be obtained, must be produced by faith in him and his Messiah, and be as spiritual and practical as the evils to be eradicated are pernicious. Such, then, was the repentance which our Lord required; and, therefore, such a repentance was required by John, for their work and their requirement were the same.

Taken conjointly, these two prophecies are of the utmost importance to our design. They exhibit one work, in which the Lord and his forerunner were both engaged: the one describing its merciful intentions with greater clearness; the other unfolding more distinctly the searching nature of its process. In each case mercy is the great moving power, and the aim is a practical bestowment of its blessings on mankind. Both prophecies are first addressed to the Jewish people, and, through them, extend to Gentile nations. Isaiah presents the Messiah as a shepherd, gathering the lambs in his arms; a comforter, speaking peace to the broken-hearted; a deliverer, dying for the guilty; a guide, leading those who are in darkness, and—omitting other aspects of his work—a victor triumphing in his work of delivering love. Malachi, assuming all the kinder aspects of his reign, unfolds its moral severity. In his language, the Saviour is a great Refiner, and his ministrations act on men as fire upon silver in the retort; and those who war with his operations of love, are made as chaff and stubble when cast into the flame. To meet all these inspired descriptions of his covenanted work, some one moral feature must be found in which they all harmonise; for this alone can be a preparation for his work; and the people thereby distinguished, must be his prepared people. This feature or state of mind, therefore, is given in the faith of the New Testament. To the believer, and to him alone, he grants the covenant of salvation. In fulfilling that covenant of salvation, he realises every endearing and every searching character presented in prophetical allusions. Give him but your confidence, and he engages that you shall never perish; withhold this, and, in the words of himself and his forerunner, he declares that you shall never see life. This faith is, so to speak, the parent of all other moral states of mind which he approves; realising the faithfulness and competency of the Saviour, it produces confidence; by the good which he has promised, it awakens hope; by the perfections he reveals, it produces love; and, realising the purity of his law and the greatness of our sin, it produces repentance. The last-named is generally the first production of faith, which makes itself perceptible to man; but where this first-fruit is, a preparation is made for all that is to follow. He who believes so much of Divine Truth as to repent, to say, It is enough, I will sin no more; to fall at the feet of mercy, and submit under its discipline, is prepared for the ministration and the use of his Redeemer; and, to make such prepared persons ready, John had only to separate them by their baptism, and leave them to unite with his Redeemer when he came.

THE RECORDED CHARACTER OF JOHN.

But, *Fifthly*, the recorded character of John confirms the truth of this induction. He was just the man these prophecies describe, and eminently qualified for this moral undertaking. He was filled with the Spirit from his birth. In what way its operations were evolved in all the progress of his rising youth, we can only conjecture, for we are not informed. If the veil could be removed from that advancing maturity,—its intercourse with the unrevealed Lord, as festivals and family intercourse brought them into contact,—the deviation from ordinary treatment, which filled him with the Spirit from his mother's womb, would, undoubtedly, present a splendid moral preparation for his future greatness. He drank neither wine nor strong drink, but all the energy of nature was devoted to holy communing with divine realities. At the time when his office in the priesthood might by law have been assumed, he came forth abruptly, like Elijah; in his garb, and habit, and spirit, fixing attention by official acts of preaching and baptizing. He occupied the very scenes in which Elijah had acquired his awful celebrity. Bethabara was at the ford where Elijah had divided the Jordan, and near which he rose to immortality in his chariot of fire; and here, in the Jordan, John baptized. He was called to resist no formal idolatry, for none then existed in Israel; but a formality in the true worship of Jehovah, and a fearful corruption of his law, revealed a general departure from God, which made the nation unfit for Messiah's coming. Resisting this departure from God, John urged an individual repentance, and laboured that the people of his time might be turned to the Lord. It was not so much his doctrine, as his method, discipline, and character, that were new; and his discipline, more than all. Even this was not without its precedent in the history of Israel, for Nehemiah resisted the corruptions of his time, by compacting individuals in a holy covenant, to renounce them and serve the Lord; and Moses called the faithful to himself without the camp: but each of these retained the hereditary covenant, while John renounced that ground of association, basing his whole proceeding on the personal repentance, preparing for that great and final work, in which the nation should be judged, cast off, and recognised as God's people no more. To this new work of urging repentance, and recognising believing penitents, by baptizing them preparatory to the Saviour's appearing, John was appointed; and, in it, all the features of his character obtain a beautiful and harmonious appropriateness. He was just the man to be respected in such a work, and his movements became felt from the throne, through the priesthood, and to the meanest of its subjects. He was resisted, and by many rejected, but he could not be despised. Herod both heard him and feared him, though Herod was not baptized. His ministrations roused the Sanedrim itself, and brought forth messengers to know if he were not the Christ. In less than two years, the labours of John thrilled the very heart of Judea, and so provoked a royal lust that he became a martyr. If the persons

John baptized were spiritual, and his object comprised the interests of eternity, all this appears consistent; and he lies there, a great man sacrificed in a great and worthy cause. But, such an expenditure of moral feeling, and moral greatness, on a mere formality, an indiscriminating and ineffectual baptism, until it has been clearly affirmed of God, must be treated as an absurdity.

THE RECORD OF JOHN'S MINISTRY.

Sixthly, The spirituality of John's commission is shown by the record of his ministry. The brevity of this record leaves no want of information, though it may impose the exercise of patient attention. The message sent by the Priests and Levites, who inquired why he baptized if he were not the Christ,* enables us clearly to determine, First, that the coming of Messiah, his coming about that time, and the probability, at least, of his baptizing a separated people, were no new things to Jews then in high authority; and, Secondly, it shows that John was acting on the people apart from them and their authority, and in the Temple, where sin was confessed, its atonements were offered, and its repentance was enforced. But why, then, should John separate himself from high and recognised authority, teaching repentance, which they also taught, and urging confession, which they also urged? Plainly and unquestionably because their doctrine of repentance and confession was

---

* John i. 19—28.

corrupt, and its fruits were unfitted to attend the Saviour at his coming; but John was commissioned to teach a repentance which was not corrupt, and to recognise a fruit meet for repentance, to make ready a people prepared for the Lord; and, therefore, his baptism and ministry were essentially discriminating, both in principle and in administration.

Moreover, it is said that the Pharisees rejected the counsel of God against themselves, not being baptized of John. But their strict adherence to the counsel of God was the very boast of their own society. That counsel of God, therefore, which they rejected to their own hurt, was the discriminating doctrine which John urged, and the baptism he administered on its observance.

But, it is pleaded that the Pharisees did come to act upon his baptism and doctrine. The words referred to are,* " Seeing many of the Pharisees and Sadducees coming (to act) upon his baptism." And the words do indicate that many belonging to these sects, moved by the impulse of John's ministry, did come to act upon his proposal, and to use a system now rapidly advancing in popular esteem. It is not, however, affirmed that they *were* baptized; and the disjunctive particle which begins the clause, would lead to an opposite conclusion. " Then went out unto him Jerusalem and all Judea, and all the region about the Jordan, and were baptized by him in the Jordan, confessing their sins. *But*, seeing many of

* Matthew iii. 7.

the Pharisees, &c., coming, he said to *them*." "*But he said to them*," in such a connexion, would lead us to conclude that while the former were baptized, confessing their sins, the Pharisees and Sadducees did not confess their sins, and were not baptized. The disjunctive there implies the negative, and this is strengthened by the words that follow: "But, seeing many of the Pharisees and Sadducees crowding upon his baptism, he said to them, Generation of vipers, who hath warned you to flee from the coming wrath? Produce, therefore, a fruit worthy of the repentance, and do not seem to say in yourselves, We have Abraham for our father; for, I say to you, that God is able to raise up from these stones children to Abraham." There is nothing in this to affirm that they were baptized; the whole language is expressive of rejection. He also tells them that the means of their punishment are already in operation. "And even now also the axe lies at the root of the trees: every tree, therefore, that bringeth not forth a good fruit is"—not made ready by baptism for the Lord, but—"cut down and cast into fire." The tree is the man; and, if the tree is known by its fruit, the man is known by the action and result of his professed principles. If this be taken as a cogent exhortation to fidelity, then they must have professed the repentance which was thus to be evinced; but, if they were rejected, which is most certain, then their rejection is based on the inadequacy of their profession. In either case, the discriminating character of John's ministry is proved, and its discrimination is associated with his baptism.

It ought to be observed, too, that those Pharisees and Sadducees who rejected the counsel of God against themselves, were not averse to prominence, for they sought it, or to baptism, for they used it on many occasions; yet, they not only resisted the counsel of God by John, but by the Redeemer also; they did it with such determination, that, eventually, they became his murderers. It should seem, therefore, that in the demands of each there was something incompatible with their habits and interests. Nor is this concealed. They were self-righteous; but John baptized the people who confessed their sins. They were deeply engaged in religious policies; but John required an absolute submission to the Lord. The more this gospel system came to be explained, therefore, the more would these Pharisees and Sadducees be disposed to reject it: and this, of itself, is sufficient to prove that, with hearts unchanged, Jesus and John must have rejected them.

Dr. Halley's reasoning implies that because the Evangelist affirms that "all the region went out," we are to conclude that all the people went out, and were all baptized, Pharisees and Sadducees not excepted. This is not true. All did not go out; many could not, and many would not. Herod was not baptized, Herodias was not baptized; some said, He hath a devil; and others resisted the counsel of God which he declared. Multitudes did go out; but, multitudes were not moved by his lamentations and reproof. Of those who did go out, many were baptized confessing their sins; but, if any confessed their sins with indifference, or resolving to retain them, would these have been baptized? The narrative says, NO. John baptized them into repentance, without which none can be accepted of God in the Redeemer. This is discrimination; but, John adds, "I indeed baptize you in water, but he who cometh after me is more mighty than I, and he shall make this ministry more discriminating than I can. Judea and Jerusalem are his barn-floor, the penitent and believing are his wheat, the impenitent are to him as chaff and straw. The process has begun, he is beating it from the husks, he will winnow out the refuse, and gather up the grain with care; his fan is in his hand, he will throughly purge his floor. I am doing what I can; he will do the work more effectually: he will gather the wheat into his barn (the church), but burn up the chaff in unquenchable fire."

Whether they be considered in relation to the Jewish people, who were first addressed, or mankind at large, who are equally concerned, such words and illustrations can never be intended to describe the Christian ministry and baptism as indiscriminate. They describe a process designed to make the wheat as clean, the society of saints as select and as pure, as possible. If further proof of this were needed, it is found in the last testimony which John gave to his advancing Lord. This treatment of individuals had, from the beginning, reference to a society or

---

* John iii. 27.

kingdom which Jesus should constitute with these disciples. To describe this, he saith, "He that hath the bride is the bridegroom."* This endearing illustration was not only used by John before, but was written by the Evangelist sixty-five years after, the death of our Lord, when that illustration had been long used to represent the society in which Christ was beloved and enjoyed; and, as if to leave no room for hesitation, it is added, "He that believeth in the Son hath life; but he that believeth not the Son, shall not see life, for the wrath of God abideth on him." The repentance, therefore, which John required, must have been based on evangelical faith, and his baptism was believers' baptism.

The proof of this fact is strikingly exhibited in Mark xi. 28—33. Jesus had just returned to Jerusalem, and was walking in this Temple. The high priests, scribes, and elders surrounded him there, and said to him, "By what authority doest thou these things? and who gave thee this authority in order that thou mightest do them? But Jesus answering said to them, And I will ask you one question, and do ye answer me, and I will tell you by what authority I do these things: The baptism of John, was it from heaven, or from men? answer me." By the words " the baptism of John," is clearly intended the whole doctrine and discipline which John enforced; and his answer depended on their reply, for if they admitted that the doctrine and discipline of John were from God, because John testified of him, they must also have admitted that Jesus was from God, and did what he did by divine authority. This did not appear to strike them. "They reasoned amongst themselves, saying, If we allow it to be from heaven, he will say, Why then did ye not believe in him?" The word "believe" is here used in the plain and practical sense of Scripture. In the Sacred Writings, as well as in those of Greece, to believe in any one means, to take his word, and act on his instructions. A strong conviction may exist that what the speaker says is true, at least, as to the principal matter stated, and yet the hearer may not be prepared to follow his instructions in the practical observance of that truth. It is clear that this was, in a great measure, the state of their minds. They were not prepared to meet and expose by refuting the opinion of the people who held John to be a prophet. They were the learned, and the highest in authority, but the stubborn evidence was beyond their control. They dared not to face the people, and say he was an impostor. If there had been proof that John did not act and teach by Divine authority, they must have seen and used it. But they did not. They replied, "We cannot tell." This was false; they could tell. The evidence before them, that John acted on Divine authority, was such that they could not refute. But that irrefutable claim to Divine authority they would not obey. By this they rejected the counsel of God *against* themselves; and, on this rejection of Divine counsel, the Lord rejects them. He would not even answer their question. "Neither tell I you (he says) by what authority I do these things. That authority by which I do these things is the same which you knowingly reject in John.. But this is called "not believing in him:" the opposite of that faith which John required. John, therefore, did require faith, and the faith which he required was no superficial act of the intellect merely, but one which ruled the heart and formed the character. How could it be otherwise? John came from God, and acted under Divine inspiration; the faith which he required, therefore, must have been the faith which God approves.

The right understanding of this word is of great importance, and the two works of Aristotle on this subject are, hence, of unspeakable value. His "Treatise on Rhetoric" is expressly designed to show in what way a speaker may produce faith in his hearers; and that designed for Alexander explains how he might produce faith in his soldiers, and the people he had subdued. The faith of the citizen was gained when he was prepared to go with the orator, in voting for his law, and carrying it into effect. The faith of the soldier was gained when his confidence in the general prepared him to rush on the pikes and masses of the adversary. The faith which John required was gained when, in repentance for sin and hope of its forgiveness, the hearer consented to enter on a new life in John's baptism. All inquiry and conviction that fell short of this, fell short of the faith which John demanded. His doctrine and discipline were, therefore, called the baptism of repentance. But repentance, without faith, is absurdly impossible; for how can one repent of sin who does not believe that he has committed it? and how can the nature of sin be felt, unless we have faith in God? Lastly, who would forsake his sin at the suggestion of another, and on the hope of its forgiveness, unless he believed that the ground of forgiveness propounded was sufficient, and that the promise of forgiveness was secure? These suppositions are all against nature, as they are against the intentions of Divine mercy. The requirement of repentance in baptism, therefore, involves the requirement of faith; and the acknowledgment of these priests and lawyers, that they did not believe in him, is an acknowledgment that, against their own convictions, they did not submit to Divine authority in him; but impenitently held on in the course of their rebellion. When this was made clear to themselves and to all, Jesus rejected them; he not only would not baptize, he would not answer their inquiries. With treasonous impenitence he would have no fellowship; his disciples, therefore, were baptized on a repentance by which it was rejected. But the baptisms of Jesus and of John were, at that time, the same; and, therefore, the disciples of John not only admitted the truth of his words, and the divinity of his mission, but submitted to his demands, in penitent and obedient expectation of the kingdom.

THE PRACTICAL RESULT OF JOHN'S MINISTRY.

Such a man, proclaiming and administering a baptism of a repentance for a remission of sins, must have produced effects in which the nature of his work and doctrine might be exemplified. Hence, we find them pointed out in the history, first, as they appeared in the inquiring multitudes, and then in the people made ready for his Lord. The general excitement and spirit of inquiry was not a trivial result. It proves that the cold habits of indifference and resistance had been disturbed. All religious teachers find this a first, and often a heart-breaking, difficulty to be overcome. Men will not easily be forced from an ordinary and fixed line of conduct, which has reference to religion and God. When once the existing order of thought and action has been disturbed, difficulties present themselves in every station of society, which seem to form apologies for neglecting the new doctrine and discipline. Had John demanded no discriminating features of conduct in those he set apart, no one would have felt a difficulty, perhaps few would have been disturbed; but the words of Luke* show each class in society questioning how its own disadvantage might be overcome by individuals acting upon his instructions. Soldiers on the march, passing the ford at Gilgal, came within the influence of his ministrations, and said, What can we do? Toll-collectors were convinced, and came to be baptized, but pressed the inquiry, What can we do? The crowds of oppressed people said, What, then, can we do? Each seemed convinced that John was right, yet each wanted direction, for in each case the discriminated character was loaded with difficulty.

* Luke iii. 10, 14.

The answer of John was, in effect, the same to all. He seemed to say, Let each one evince his repentance by rectitude in his station, and wait there until the Messiah comes. Let the multitudes give up their selfishness, the publicans their fraud, and the soldier his violence; and let each expect direction and deliverance. The words which follow, "I, indeed, baptize you in water,"* do not apply to these inquirers, but to the conjectures entertained respecting his person, and form a part of that sentence in which he declares that he is not the Christ. The inquirers might have been baptized or not, as each conformed, or failed to conform, with his requirements. To this particular the deponent answereth not; but the same chapter presents, in Herod, a case in which the instruction was individualised with awful daring; but the person instructed was not baptized: he rose up and murdered the teacher.†

Dr. Halley's treatment of these histories is unworthy of himself. He first rushes to the conclusion, that John baptized everybody in Judæa; and then, from the general conduct of the Jewish people, two years afterwards, he infers that John's baptism must have been indiscriminate. The learned opponent ought to have been more careful in stating the facts; he would then have escaped this unsound conclusion. The angel who announced his conception, said, that through the ministry of John "*a prepared people should be made ready for the Lord.*" The period of

* Luke iii. 16. † Luke iii. 19.

his ministry was very short—perhaps, not more than two years—and the nation in which he laboured was one vast conglomerate of religious error and vices; yet this result was gained. He was rejected by many, by some called a devil, and was murdered at last; but yet, he left behind him a people made ready for the Lord. Dr. Halley finds nothing to serve his purpose but the Pharisees, the publicans, and their criminality; he might have found those who heard John say, "Behold the Lamb of God, who taketh away the sins of the world," and followed Jesus thenceforth: Andrew, Simon his brother, Philip, Nathaniel, and John the Evangelist, are all mentioned in the history; and the Doctor might have explained the principle on which these and others gathered round the Lord at his appearing. These were prepared men, and ready for his use. Subsequent events show that these were not few, and that the advantage of their existence was not small; for by these the way of the Redeemer was prepared in all the cities of Israel. If this result had not been secured, the Divine authority of John's commission might have been suspected; but when this had been predicted at his birth, and recorded as the chief result of his existence, no diversity of opinion ought to have existed respecting the nature of his ministry and baptism: they were, by necessity, discriminating.

THE CONCURRING ACTION OF OUR LORD.

But, lastly, all testimony is exceeded by that of the Redeemer himself, whose words and actions are decisive. His concurring movement, therefore, resting on John's discriminating baptism, may be seen, first, in his treatment of the disobedient Jewish people; and, secondly, in his treatment of those disciples who came to him from John. In both he realised all the prophetical exhibitions of his character and ministry. While John remained at large, Jesus laboured with him, preaching the same repentance, administering the same baptism, and preparing, in the same manner, for the kingdom of heaven, which was just at hand; but, when John fell in martyrdom, Jesus moved forward to the front, ordained the twelve, and then the seventy, extending his operations of mercy on the Jewish people. He assailed their impenitence and unbelief by movements that were wonderful, in cities and in their fields, in families and in their temple. No moral tactics could be more profound or more decisive than those which he employed. He came to that nation as his own; and, though his own received him not, he forced on their regard his merciful proposal of repentance, till they, in solemn judgment, had renounced all mercy, and, round his Golgotha, invoked his utmost wrath. This was the limit of his mercy. They were his no more. To individuals he preserved a door of hope; but the nation, the priesthood, the religious establishment, he would own no more. He rent their veil, exposed their holy things, degraded the community, became a consuming fire; he burnt their throne, their mercy seat, their temple; and the fierce burning of his wrath was unquenchable. Nothing has been more discriminating since the beginning of time; and nothing will be more discriminating till the judgment-day. The same on the other side. The men baptized by John, who gathered round the person of the Lord, obtained in him all that Isaiah had predicted. He led them like a shepherd, gathered them in his arms, laid them in his bosom; he instructed them; he preserved them; and often, when they saw his acts of love and power, were forced to say, What manner of man is this? Nothing within the range of human thought, excepting heaven, has ever presented so secure and so sublime a scene of friendly intercourse as that between himself and his disciples. There, goodness and authority secured happiness and subjection, as Deity alone is able to combine them. The society was on earth, and composed of men, and, therefore, was not perfect; but it was separate and distinguished by his favour; he abode in it; he blessed it with his presence, cheered it with his smile, conducted it by his wisdom, and, with all-sufficient grace, brought its members (Judas only excepted) through all extremities and convulsions, until, himself at God's right-hand, he sent them forth, with pentecostal fire, from conquering to conquer.

CONCLUSION.

On this brief statement of the case, therefore, it is observed, that to call the ministry and baptism of John "indiscriminate," is most unwarrantable. To say "that John's baptism was administered indiscriminately to all," is not only to affirm what cannot be proved; it is to make an affirmation which the ancient and latest prophecies, the record of John's ministry, the words and actions of our Lord himself, all positively declare to be absolutely untrue; and if the affirmation had been true, all the evidence derived from these sources would have demonstrated that the administering of John's baptism, without discrimination—the thing assumed and affirmed—would have been contrary to the purpose and will of God who sent him. This corner-stone of Dr. Halley's whole argument, therefore, when exposed to the light, and subjected to fair investigation, crumbles into dust, leaving the whole fabric of his reasoning to perish for the want of its support. The Jewish initiation, before John's time, was shown to have been discriminate, separating the proselyte from the heathen by his faith, his privilege, and his obligations: now, the initiation of John is seen to be discriminate, separating penitent believers, both from Jews and Gentiles, by their faith, repentance, privilege, and obligations, under the Messiah in his kingdom. Two discriminating systems, therefore, can scarcely sustain, they positively demolish, the indiscriminating theory now proposed. But Dr. Halley is concerned about the infants, and says, "Why should John, for the first time, distinguish parents from children in the religious rites of the Jews?" It is answered, The baptism of repentance which John administered, was not a religious rite of the Jews, it was a rite the authority of which began with his own commission; and children could not be admitted to that rite, because their unmatured minds were incapable of that repentance by which John discriminated, and was bound to discriminate, the people whom he thus made ready for the Lord. Lastly, it will be seen hereafter, that the moral and spiritual advantage of the rising generation will, in all ages, be promoted by the observance, more effectually than by the violation, of Divine law.

LECTURE IV.

ON THE EXAMPLE AND MINISTRY OF OUR LORD.

"The dispensation of John," it is said, "was a law of God, without submission to which, Jesus, being a Hebrew of that age, would not have fulfilled all righteousness," p. 75. "John was commissioned to declare, that the kingdom of heaven was at hand," p. 162. From these two statements of Dr. Halley, it appears, that the kingdom of heaven, which Jesus himself announced, and the preparatory movements of which he conducted through his ministry, was also the object of John's dispensation. It follows, therefore, that John and Jesus were devoted to the same work. But John was to make ready a people prepared for the Lord: this was his portion of that work: this he did; a people prepared for the Lord was made ready, and set apart in baptism, for the Lord: and, when the Lord appeared, he took this people made ready for him, united them with himself, employed them under his direction and care in preparing others—making them ready, in the same immersion, for that full administration of his government which he himself was about to exhibit and sustain.

Besides that ministry of preparation which our Lord conducted, and which comprised his own work of atonement for sin, Jesus had to occupy the supreme seat of legislative and mediatorial power in that kingdom itself. This power could not be perfectly revealed until he had been offered up and accepted as the great sin-offering for mankind. From him, therefore, this kingdom of heaven derived all its holy peculiarities; and its subjects were to be united under his care, the good Shepherd, who laid down his life for these, his sheep. His ostensible and personal devotement to that kingdom, in which he had to perform so high and important functions, our Lord himself calls " entering by the door into the sheep-fold."* The immersion of John was so important, that Dr. Halley himself says, without submission to this, " Jesus, being a Hebrew of that age, would not have fulfilled all righteousness," p. 75. If, therefore, it can be ascertained on what grounds this initiation became necessary to the Saviour, so that, at the time of his baptism, and not before, it should be said, " Thou art my son, this day have I brought thee forth;" this will enable us to use the whole force of

* John x. 1—18.

his example in elucidating the initiation in which both he and John baptized.

By Dr. Halley's own concession, therefore, the baptism of John had a twofold aspect: first, as it looked back upon the past, and was called a baptism of repentance; and, secondly, as it looked forward to the coming reign of heaven, and became a badge of discipleship in that community. The question, therefore, is, In which character did this baptism become a necessary part of righteousness to the Redeemer, so that even he could not be justified in taking his place in the kingdom of heaven without its observance? In the first case, from his known character and divine perfections, as well as from the words of John, it is certain that the baptism was *not* necessary; and, as a *symbol*, could have *no* meaning. He had no sin, and could require no repentance. On the contrary, John, knowing the purity and devotion of his early life and manhood, said, " I have need to be baptized of thee."* But, if he required no repentance, and could not profess any, his being baptized could not be a symbol of its necessity, but rather of something else, in which the repentance of those who needed it was supposed to have transpired. Here, therefore, the question returns; for if the baptism of Jesus was not received as a profession and symbol of repentance, how could it be received as a badge of discipleship, since, in that kingdom of heaven, he was to become, not a subordinate and a learner, but the

* Matthew iii. 13, 17.

sole teacher and Lord? It is answered, Every initiated penitent, who wore this "badge of discipleship," declared in the immersion itself, not only that his past rebellion was wrong, and its results to be feared; but, also, that he approved the coming reign of God, had hope in its operation, and willingly submitted himself under its authority. This each disciple did in his place, whether sincere or insincere, high or low, safe or exposed, prominent or secluded: his "badge of discipleship," or incorporation in this kingdom, was a symbol of those moral elements on which the kingdom itself was based. This is not only appropriate to the Redeemer and Lord, since in any kingdom nothing could be more unseemly than neglect of its own laws in the person of its supreme ruler; but, it was more needful in him, than in them; for they, in their devotement, became the recipients of good; but he, in his devotement, became the victim of wrath, and the price of their redemption; whatever might demand of them, therefore, the expression of *their* approval, hope, and submission in the reign of God, the declaration of *his* became needful to show the justice of God in his vicarious punishment, and to encourage the faith of a ruined world, whose hope must be built on his voluntary atonement.

THE BAPTISMAL SCENE.

With this clue to its import, the Jordan, in which our Lord was immersed by John, presents a scene of vast moral splendour. A compact of self-devotion is ratified there, which involved every hope of the Redeemer, and every hope of man, with all the glory to be acquired by God himself in dispensing mercy. If vain and flippant imaginations could be laid aside, the devout observer might perceive, in that form which comes up straightway out of the water, something more than human seriousness and majesty. The countenance is reverently turning heavenward, as if this soul conversed with the Eternal Father; the cheerful thought within is sombered with a deeply-sorrowful reflection; his features reveal a soul contemplating some vast and terrible design; and every step he seems to say, " Lo, I come to do thy will, O God." John has already perceived the dove descending over him, and in that sign beholds his own commission more than half fulfilled. The Great One is prepared, by inspiration from on high, to meet both earth and hell in man's redemption. The supernatural voice, "This is my beloved Son, in whom I am well pleased," not only seems to imply the existence of other sons so born, but leads us to the prophecy in which his own pre-eminence is described.* Led by Paul to the second Psalm, we there find the resisting powers described, Jehovah holding them in derision, and uttering the decree, " Thou art my son, this day have I brought thee forth: ask of me, and I will give thee heathen for thine inheritance, the utmost part of earth for thy possession. Thou shalt break the resisting powers as with a rod of iron, thou shalt dash them in pieces like a potter's vessel: be

---

* Hebrews i. 5—14.

wise now, therefore, ye princes; be instructed, ye judges of earth: kiss the Son, lest he be angry; ye will perish from the way when his wrath is kindled but a little."

THE IMMEDIATE EFFECT OF HIS BAPTISM.

The prophecy and the facts combine to show that this was no thoughtless and indiscriminating transaction; but an event in which something was doing and done. His personal work, preparatory to his administration in the reign of heaven, begins forthwith; and four things, at least, are accomplished:—

1. The Lord, by this act, declares his approval of John, and the baptism he administered. Though Jesus had a different part to perform, and chose to employ a different method, yet he found in the forerunner nothing to condemn. His rebuke of sin had not been too severe, and the repentance for sin which he urged was not too deep and distinguishing. This act of the Redeemer is, in effect, saying to John, "Well done, good and faithful servant," thy ministrations shall be supported, extended, and perpetuated by him who ordained them.

2. The Saviour himself became identified by this event. He who sent John to baptize, had said, "Upon whom thou shalt see the Spirit descending and remaining upon him, the same is he who immerseth in the Holy Spirit."* From this moment, therefore, John assumes the individual expression.

* John i. 33.

Pointing to the Lord himself, he said, "Behold the Lamb of God, who taketh away the sins of the world!"* "This is he of whom I spake."† His disciples are at once directed to him in whom their promise of subjection must be kept; and the enunciation, The Messiah is come, "We have found him of whom Moses and the prophets spake,"‡ spread like intimations by a beacon fire, announcing the very person to whom they were consecrated.

3. The personal subordination of our Lord in the kingdom of heaven, is here both declared by himself, and accepted of God the Father. He had no sins to call for repentance, but he had an unspeakable interest in this dispensation; its issue must exalt him in the midst of his redeemed people, or sink him for ever in the ruin they deserved. This alternative hung upon the service he had to perform; and, therefore, he thus took upon himself the form of a servant in the kingdom of heaven.§

4. The whole light of his example is thus thrown upon the Christian life. When thus set apart as a servant, his action shows in what way the service of obedience should be rendered. His work, in its substance, may be different from theirs, and each of his followers may have a specific duty; but, that which is to form the distinguishing and common feature of the whole incorporated body, is the perfect and uniform fidelity which marked his whole official

---

* John i. 29. † John i. 30. ‡ John i. 35—41.
§ Phil. ii. 5—11.

career. Being once devoted to the kingdom of heaven, he lived henceforth for nothing else. He took upon him the form of a servant; and he served with such perfection, that all Christian duty whatever seems to be included in his one expression, "Follow me." Heb. xii. 1—4. Rom. xii. 1—9. Phil. ii. 5—11.

Dr. Halley says, "He being a Hebrew of that time," John's immersion formed a part of all righteousness in which the submission of our Lord was necessary. The expression, "*he being a Hebrew of that time,*" might have been struck out by the learned Doctor; for, if Jesus had been a Gentile of any age whatever, it would have been equally necessary. For the ministry of John must have been approved, because Christ had to carry it forward; the person of our Lord must have been identified, because he was to become the object of universal reliance; the personal subordination of our Lord must have been confessed, because, without this, the proceedings of that kingdom could not be justified; and, if Jesus had never been initiated into the kingdom of heaven, he could never have become the example of its subjects. This acknowledgment of facts, of person, and of moral principle, constitutes a necessary basis of all action in the social compact he came to form. But, these acknowledgments of baptism are alike incompatible with the undeveloped faculties of infancy, and the unrenewed condition of impenitence. In the first case, their profession would be absurd; in the other, hypocrisy. But, hypocrisy and absurdity are both condemned by the words and example of our Lord: and, therefore, the baptism he so approved, must have been discriminating, and confined to those in whom this acknowledgment of moral principles could be obtained. If, as Dr. Halley says, the discriminating baptism was indispensable to the Jew of that time, since the Jew had already been set apart from the Gentile, it was indispensable in all; and the kingdom of heaven was composed of individuals who were recognised in baptism, as separate and distinguished from all mankind by their voluntary and intelligent submission to Divine authority in the hands of Christ.

THE PECULIAR WORK OF THE REDEEMER.

The peculiar work undertaken by our Lord in the reign of God, and the ends thereby to be accomplished, derive a melancholy interest from their relation to our guilt; and they thus give to his example an augmented power. The work which was assigned to John, in leading Israel to repentance, formed but one small part of the Redeemer's undertaking. He came to do the will of God in making an atonement. Before he could say, "It is finished," the final propitiatory must be raised, where God could meet the chief of sinners in his kindest acts of mercy; and then its benefits must be proclaimed through all the earth until the judgment. By his subjection to the Father, the law, which we had broken, must be honoured; and the curse, which we had merited, must be endured. No sin could be forgiven, and, therefore, no sinner could be saved, till this had been performed; and, the ratification of all the past with all the future acts of mercy contemplated in the purposes of Divine compassion, were suspended upon that event. If he failed, all failed: if he succeeded, the chief of sinners might rejoice in hope. His immersion in water, therefore, pledged and symbolised his immersion in woe. His personal act in Jordan was the ordained, the righteous beginning, of that series of public and personal acts relating to the reign of God, by which he advanced through all the intervening conflict, to Gethsemane, the Judgment Hall, the Golgotha, and the Sepulchre; and which he is still performing within the veil, at God's right hand. On those who feared his name, this Sun of righteousness rose at the Jordan, as in the morning of his first day, with mild but penetrating radiance; his unobstructed course flamed in the splendour of his earthly life, until his setting was observed on Calvary, with earthquake and crimson glory, penetrating heaven's darkest thunder-clouds. The day in which we live is produced by his distant and refracted beam, the orb itself remaining unperceived. His third day, when it dawns, shall have no cloud or termination, but be bright for ever. Through all his course, he has *an* action which we must not imitate, because it belongs to him only; but, his constant faithfulness, his patient, uniform, untiring perseverance, his personal and unreserved devotedness to the cause in which he was initiated and consecrated in his baptism, supply an example to which it is ordained that every disciple shall conform. This is the very law of the kingdom he has constituted. His course of action in the sphere of human duties, and to which he was committed in the ordinance of initiation, forms one single case through which the laws of God are brought out from the region of abstraction into that of human sympathies and practice. In those events which led him from the Jordan to his cross, a spirit is unclothed, often grieved with man, not often glad; but yet, a spirit in which all possible perfections harmonise, and dwell, and operate—a spirit so mild, that we can meet it; so condescending, that we can enjoy its fellowship; so powerful, that we can use and trust it; and so exalted, that in him we are united to Divine perfection. " Be ye holy, for I am holy," thus becomes, when uttered by him to his people, a word awakening hope and joy: the most defiled, accepted in his mercy, must desire it, and the most feeble may aspire to its enjoyment. The ignorant he will instruct, the feeble he will strengthen, the exposed he will protect, the tempted he will succour. Let the case be committed to his hands, and this baptized Deliverer has, by his conduct, shown a willingness and power to deliver to the uttermost; but, unbelievers he will *not* save. They cannot copy his example, and cannot, without absurdity, be designated his disciples.

THE ANNUNCIATION AND BIRTH OF OUR LORD.

But these conclusions, it may be argued, are drawn from *our* notions of Divine truth: what where those entertained by the Jewish people who first saw these events, and to whom the first lessons of our Gospel were delivered? In answer to this, it must be remembered that the whole authority of rabbinical traditions has been disposed of. The authorities are too late, and they have been too severely censured by our Lord, to serve the purpose for which they have been produced; so that, though the whole of their evidence, such as it is, falls on our side, we cannot use it. The expectation in Israel, as authorised by God himself, is, with more certainty, expressed by inspired messengers at the annunciation and birth of our Lord. In the prophetical address of Gabriel to Mary, the words "He shall be great, and shall be called the Son of the Highest, and the Lord God shall give unto him the throne of his father David, and he shall reign over the house of Jacob for ever, and of his kingdom there shall be no end,"* can have no meaning that accords with rule in natural society, because this he never possessed: but, that dominion over believing and converted men, in which David calls him Lord, fully meets the sense of the predictions. In the song of Mary, the mercy received by her is plainly recognised as shown to them that fear God, in obvious distinction from the proud, who are scattered in the imaginations of their own hearts. This mercy, also, is identified with that which God spake to Abraham and his seed for ever;† which, by the authority of Paul, can mean none other than the seed who are

---

* Luke i. 32—34. † Luke i. 46—56.

subjects of Abraham's faith.* The words delivered to Joseph, the husband of Mary, "Thou shalt call his name Jesus, for he shall save his people from their sins,"† having no merely national application, can only refer to his compact and work of salvation in believers. The words addressed to the shepherds near to Bethlehem, " Unto you is born this day, in the city of David, a Saviour, which is Christ the Lord,"‡ can only be true in the evangelical sense; for Jesus resigned the nation to its punishment. And the chorus of angels who sang, " Glory to God in the highest; on earth, peace, good-will to men !"§ must have been contemplating the mercy God was now to exercise in Christ, to penitent believers. " Thy salvation," which Simeon adored, " prepared before the face of all people, to lighten the Gentiles, and the glory of thy people Israel,"‖ can only be found in Christ, as he becomes the covenanted and ordained object of personal confidence in repenting sinners. That other and earthly expectations were entertained, is certain, from the murder of the infants, and the errors rebuked by our Lord in his ministry. But from these the Redeemer hid himself, and loaded them with the heaviest reprehension. The only expectation he justified and fulfilled, was that of a kingdom founded on the faith of a repenting people, and supported by the power which he exerted in their midst, and on their behalf. To this the first

---

* Rom. iv. 11—13.   † Matt. i. 21.   ‡ Luke ii. 10, 11.
§ Luke ii. 10—15.   ‖ Luke ii. 29—33.

learners of Gospel truth were directed, by the interventions of Deity, and by the messages from God which have been named. It is this, the expectation on which Christ himself acted, which Christians are bound to use in elucidating his words; and, by the light of this central thought, in all preceding dispensations, we are forced to conclude that, not his initiation only, but all the discipline, polity, and proclamations, both of mercy and of judgment, must be based on the discrimination of individuals, by the absence or the exercise of personal repentance and faith.

THE ANCIENT PROPHECIES.

After what has been advanced,* the Divine intimations, given at the birth of John, may now be passed by; but these, harmonising as they do with those given at the Lord's annunciation and birth, and taken with them, occupy a most important place in the Divine dispensations. They form a connecting link between the ancient prophecies and the statements of St. Paul. That great authorised expectation which was made so clear and prominent in all those intimations which attended the Redeemer's advent, became expanded in the prophecies from which the words are quoted, and confirmed in the apostolical interpretations. Of those two inspired witnesses, thus brought to testify the nature of our Lord's dominion, the first to be considered is, that of prophecy. Here,

* Lectures II. and III.

however, the field is too wide for full investigation; and the thought must rest on those prophecies which have been, in these Divine intimations, or the early teachings of our Lord, brought home in application to himself and his dominion. Of these, the most general is, that of Simeon,* which seems to express a conception, authorised by the whole scheme of prophecy, but rests on the gathering of the Gentiles, so fully and so variously predicted by Isaiah. The words of Mary and Zacharias lead to the covenant made with Abraham, and the final predictions of Isaiah; while the angel, in speaking to Zacharias, fixes the thought on Malachi's prediction of the great Refiner, and on the spirit of his Messenger. Here, then, are various predictions of one person, and of one kingdom in which he should rule. Moreover, the person to whom they all refer is identified; the only question is, How may these be made to harmonise in his kingdom and work? Suppose, then, for a while, that his work and kingdom are to us unknown, what would—what ought—these prophecies to lead us to expect? Would they lead us to expect the formation of a society built on some supposed communication by merely ritual acts? The prophets had no such conception. Do they indicate that the society or kingdom should be formed on hereditary relationship? This was the old thing cast off and done with when Christ was born. Do they lead us to expect an indiscriminate association?

* Luke ii. 30.

Why, the very gist of the whole prophetic voice is, that man shall be distinguished from man by blessings and curses whose effects are everlasting. In some prophecies the *good* is made more prominent; in others, the *evil*: the one class of prophecies being formed to encourage, and the other to admonish. The covenant made with Abraham has no definite sense until the expression, " In thy seed shall all nations of earth be blessed," comes to be united with the promise of deliverance from sin, which God declared in Paradise; and then its fulfilment is obtained in sinners who are justified by faith in Jesus Christ our Lord. He is also plainly identified as the Messiah of Isaiah, the King who should rule in righteousness, the victim of our transgressions, and yet the conqueror of all sin. As his appearing, treatment, and victory form the great theme of Isaiah's chief discourse, it is natural to expect that some intimations would be given of his people, their treatment, their character, their privilege, or their calamity. Such, then, is the case. The fortieth chapter opens with a discriminating expression: " Comfort ye, comfort ye my people."* And through the whole of the subsequent discourses, to the sixty-sixth chapter, the same discrimination is observed, through all the variety of aspects in which this people and their Lord are presented to our view. Isaiah clearly distinguishes this people from the ordinary mass of Jewish society;† and also includes, with

---

* Isaiah xl. i. † Isaiah lxvi. 1—14.

them, children from the Gentiles.* They are described as being more dear to him, their Saviour and Lord, than an infant to its own mother; and his word of covenant with them is declared to be more permanent than the ordinances of nature.† Their gathering, and the coming of their Lord to his kingdom in their midst, form the glad tidings which Jerusalem had to proclaim; and the chief glory and joy of Abraham, and his seed, are shown to consist in their participation in the gathering and incorporation of this peculiar people, and in their permission to unite with them on the appointed terms. Could the entire phraseology of Isaiah be brought before us, with all its bold and delicate imagery, nothing could be more perfect than the portraiture which is drawn of these the children and the subjects of the Prince of Peace; but, passing by these beautiful details, they are discriminated as fearing the Lord, contrite in heart, and trembling at his word;‡ and, in comparison with them, the formal worshipper is presented as one who offered swine's blood, or cut off a dog's neck. This is not a mere hasty allusion; through twenty-six chapters the operations of this kingdom, and the action or suffering of its subjects, are so presented as to bring out these moral features in all the variety of their modifications, so that, even now, it is difficult for any sincerely penitent believer to be placed in any condition in which the action and treatment of his penitence

---

* Isaiah liv. 1—17. † Isaiah xl. 1—11. ‡ Isaiah lxvi. 1—17.

and fear of God will not be found with wonderful preciseness described in the prophecies of Isaiah. It is this which makes the book a favourite with repenting sinners throughout all time. Suppose, then, that it were announced to us, as in the days of John, the Messiah is come to incorporate and glorify his people, initiating each one by immersion in water, in the absence of all other information, what character would these prophecies of Isaiah lead us to expect in those whom he initiated? Could we, from the information here supplied, expect that he would initiate as his own the formal and impenitent, whom, by his wrath, he himself declares, that he will make an abhorring to all flesh? Should we not be compelled to expect that his initiation would rather embrace the broken in heart, who are called his own, to whom he is devoted, and of whom it is said, " As one whom his mother comforteth, so will I comfort you"? It is unquestionable. This, then, was the antecedent and elucidating idea which Jews and Gentiles were bound to use. This, too, the baptismal incorporation of believing penitents as his own, realises, in the details of its working, all the scheme of prophecy, presenting an association or community of men, of which every declaration relating to the kingdom of Messiah may be re-affirmed. But this conclusion is made yet more decisive by the words of Malachi. While he therein appears as a Refiner of silver, heating his furnace to refine the mass, could he be expected to baptize into his retort the perishable refuse of this filthy world? This were contrary to every design declared in the discourse, or suggested by the illustration. The Refiner doth not put the mountain into his retort, but the ore he findeth *in* the mountain; and over *this* he sits till it is purified: so the Lord doth not place the world in his church, but the penitents he obtaineth in the world, and over these he sits until, by their purification, his likeness is reflected, and they are thus prepared for his final and everlasting glory.

APOSTOLICAL STATEMENTS.

Our Lord himself leads us into the very heart of this predicted system, as set forth at his advent, and expanded in the ancient prophecies. In the synagogue at Nazareth,* after reading from the sixty-first chapter of Isaiah, " The Spirit of the Lord is upon me, because he hath anointed me to preach glad tidings to the poor," &c., he closed the book, and said, " This day is this Scripture being fulfilled in your ears." His discourse on the grace here predicted, by which the hearers were so impressed, has not been recorded; but, the passage read, forming only a part of those discourses in which Isaiah unfolds the spiritual nature of Messiah's kingdom—if this part was then being fulfilled by him, he must have been commencing a dispensation in which the whole would be eventually realised. But, the Messiah of Isaiah was the seed of Abraham; and, in the kingdom of that Messiah, the blessing to all nations upon earth, covenanted by that seed, was also fore-

* Luke iv. 18.

APOSTOLICAL STATEMENTS. 147

told; and both predictions are united in Christ, and in the kingdom he has founded. How all these prophecies harmonise, and obtain fulfilment in the Christian church, the apostle Paul explains. He affirms that the seed of Abraham is Christ;* the sons of faithful Abraham are believers in Christ.† These, though sinners, being in Christ, have no condemnation;‡ but are justified by faith, and, on their parts, by faith alone.§ Their faith comes by hearing, *not* by baptism; and hearing by the word of God,‖ *not* by human traditions and reasoning. The whole system, therefore, is so built on the personal exercise of Abraham's faith, that Abraham's own offspring were rejected, cast off, not justified in using the rites, and bearing the name, and cherishing the hopes that we have in Christ; but, actually and openly renounced. The words, "Ye are not my people," are, by Paul, taken from the ancient prophecy, and confirmed by the very words of Isaiah.¶ The reason, too, of their rejection is clearly given: they were rejected because of unbelief. Their Jewish descent was neither a ground for their exclusion or admission: they were rejected because of unbelief. The *national incorporation* was rejected because of unbelief, and *individuals* were rejected because of unbelief; and all who were received, were received because of their faith, and stood by their faith, and were justified by their faith. The

---

* Gal. iii. 16. † Gal. iii. 29. ‡ Rom. viii. 1.
§ Rom. v. 1—6.   ‖ Rom. x. 1—18.
¶ Rom. x. 21; xi. 20, 21; ix. 25—33.

whole polity of this kingdom, therefore, rests on this personal qualification. The believer is justified by God himself in doing all that Christ commands his people to do, in using all that he has purchased for his people, and in seeking to enjoy all that he has promised; but, the unbeliever is condemned already, and, therefore, justified in nothing. But, he who is justified in nothing, cannot be justified in wearing the badge of discipleship; if justified in nothing, he cannot be justified in being initiated; else, by the reasoning of Paul, the unbeliever would be initiated and rejected at the same moment, in the same community, and by the same God, which is impossible. Hence, by the figure of engrafting, this Apostle associates with the rejection of unbelievers, the initiation of a penitent believer; and makes both acts rest on this discriminating regard to their personal character. He makes the future effects dependent on this discrimination: for, the initiated only stand by faith; and the rejected become eligible when they repent and believe. He does more than this: he brings his argument home to the very rite of initiation; for, as many as have been baptized into Christ, have put on Christ,* which is an act of faith; they were planted together with Christ,† given up with him to the same inheritance, to live or perish in the same soil and by the same elements. They were even planted together in the likeness of his death, which, whatever it mean, must imply faith. It im-

* Gal. iii. 26—29.   † Rom. vi. 1—14.

plied hope also, for they were planted together in the likeness of his death, that, like as Christ was raised from the dead by the glory of the Father, so we, also, might rise to newness of life. It is this new attested life of God, which believers enjoy in Christ, and which is recognised by their baptismal initiation, which forms, in the estimation of Paul, the visible fulfilment of Abraham's covenant and Isaiah's prophecy. It is in this community that Jesus reigns. Its merciful, enlargement is the aim of all ordained aggressive action; and, in its perfection and final glory, all the hopes that inspiration has ever yet awakened in the breast of man, shall be more than realised.

THE PERSONAL MINISTRATIONS OF OUR LORD.

As sin cannot be forgiven without repentance, so the ministration of Christ cannot be used without faith; and, every one, justified in entering his community, therefore, needs a qualification in which both these moral elements are combined. Repentance without faith, and faith without repentance, are equally imperfect; but, the man in whom both unite, is separated alike from Jewish formality and heathen corruptions. In Christ Jesus he is a new creature, not Jew or Gentile, but, in the words of Paul, one "new man."* The kingdom of heaven, or body of Christ, or family of God on earth, is the incorporated body of such new men, or persons so renewed. This

---

* Eph. i. 13; ii. 1—8; ii. 11—18; ii. 19—22; iv. 1—6.

discriminating incorporation of individuals, based on this individual character, was, to Jew and Gentile, a new thing. It provided a sphere for spiritual worship, and a basis for fraternal confidence and moral discipline, in which the Divine perfections might appear with greater glory than hitherto had shone upon this earth. The propriety of expecting it, we have shown; the fact of its having been expected by the Jews, is also clear. The woman of Samaria said, "When the Messiah hath come, he will teach us all things." * And Matthew, speaking of our Lord's ministry, said, "The people that sat in darkness saw a great light."† His words are quoted from that part of Isaiah in which the Lord is designated, "Wonderful Counsellor, the Mighty God, the Everlasting Father, and Prince of Peace, on whom the government should rest, and of whose dominion there should be no end."‡ These notions, existing in the public mind, must have met the Lord in his teaching; and his treatment of them ought to decide our question for ever.

HIS MESSIAHSHIP.

First, then, his office as the Messiah, though not so openly avowed before as after his resurrection, yet, during his ministry, was not concealed. To the woman of Samaria he said, in plain terms, "I that speak unto thee am he."§

---

* John iv. 25.   † Matthew iv. 16.   ‡ Isaiah ix. 1—7.
§ John iv. 26.

THE REJECTION OF EARTHLY INFLUENCE.

Secondly. On more occasions than one, his mighty works produced the intention of making him a king, or of investing him with earthly authority. His influence with the people might have been turned to great political account, either with the priests or the Romans; between whom, with little care, he might, in a short period, have holden the balance of power. The only thing to be remarked here is, that, in every form, with friends and foes, every such opportunity was stedfastly rejected. His whole conduct is explained by his own expression, "My kingdom is not of this world;" and, therefore, it could not have been constituted on this world's principles of association. It could not, therefore, be hereditary; and, if not of this world, it must have been discriminating, and discriminating, too, on such points as involve eternity.

THE PREPARATORY OBJECT.

Thirdly, Great as our Lord appeared in his ministry here, he did not enter on the full administration of his kingdom while on earth. He showed the disciples, going to Emmaus, and from the ancient prophecies, that the Son of man must first have suffered, and then enter into his *glory.* Moreover, the seventy and the twelve, in all their preaching, still used the expression of John: " Repent, for the kingdom of heaven is at hand." His object, therefore, was, to collect and prepare individuals for that full administration of his kingdom when it came. In this work, too, he made and baptized many disciples; at one time, more than John. And since the duty of collecting and initiating disciples for the kingdom of heaven, is that which occupies our attention now, it is incumbent on us, at least, to examine how he addressed inquirers? how he treated the disobedient? and how he distinguished his disciples when initiated?

THE TREATMENT OF INQUIRERS.

All that can be collected, having reference to his treatment of inquirers, ought to be considered in the light of his own example; because he was actually going before them in the very character which each applicant for initiation was wishing to assume. By this one fact alone, the whole work of initiation must have been invested with solemnity, and have been made to call for the deepest reflection. His stedfast mind rested so seriously on his ulterior object, that every individual proposing to be joined with him, was, by the very habit and condition of the teacher, admonished to consider with himself, whether any object demanded, and whether he had sufficient principle to sustain, an alliance with one whose peculiarity had separated him from all other associations of men; and yet who had not, in the association he himself was forming, "where to lay his head." The Lord did not conceal this admonitory and discriminating aspect of his own administration. It was deepened by his own words,

"No one who placeth his hand upon a plough, and looketh back into the things that are behind, is fit to enter into the kingdom of God."* A ploughman, to turn up his furrow cleanly and straight, must have but one object before him, fixing his whole attention; and this simplicity of aim, ever enforced by our Lord, is, by the figure, demanded for that kingdom which the Lord was revealing to men; and the incompatibility of its claims with that anxiety for the affairs of his own house which the candidate had expressed, is most forcibly exhibited. To one who wished first to bury his father, the Lord said, "Let the dead bury their dead; but, go thou and proclaim the kingdom of God."† All were admonished to count the cost, because an unprincipled attempt could only result in ridiculous exposure, and increase of blame; ‡ and when great numbers pressed round him, he said, "If any one come unto me, and hate not his father and his mother, his wife and children, his brothers and sisters, and even his own life, he cannot be my disciple."§ Some of these cases are so mentioned as to indicate that the persons became his disciples, notwithstanding his admonition, and the hazard which attended their devotion to his cause; in others, the result is not indicated; but the using of such admonitions, to such persons, and at such a time, plainly indicates a careful and discriminating initiation. It shows that the only characters he designed to be

* Luke ix. 61.   † Luke ix. 59.   ‡ Luke xiv. 29.
§ Luke xiv. 26.

united in his fellowship were those who perceived and recognised in his service a duty and a hope which justified them in subordinating all worldly interests to this one pursuit. With this " good seed," "the children of the kingdom,"* he planted this sacred inclosure of his mediatorial reign; and if others, as tares, not having the character of his children, be introduced, his practice and his doctrine forcibly declare, that this is the work of an enemy, and done in opposition to his law.

THE TREATMENT OF REJECTED PERSONS.

Besides a clear declaration of this fact, our Lord's parable of the tares† contains a declaration of its cause and treatment. He who sowed good seed, initiated, and caused believers to be initiated and set apart for himself in the world, is the Lord himself; he who sowed tares, insinuated, and caused unbelievers to be insinuated, amongst the children of the kingdom, is the devil: he did this while men slept. Not while the Lord slept; but while the men, who were his servants, slept. The infirmity or indifference of Christians and Christian ministers, therefore, in regard to their own community, has been, as here predicted, used by the adversary of God and man to corrupt the society of believers; and the remedy for this evil is prepared by further discrimination at the final judgment, when the tares shall be consumed, and the corn preserved.

* Matthew xiii. 38. † Matthew xiii. 24.

The prediction of our Lord, in this case, presents a striking instance of that perfect precision by which, in the absence of systematical formality, all his instructions were administered. Believers may, they are bound to, separate themselves from unbelievers for his sake, even while they are continued in this world; but they must not root unbelievers out of the world. Decision is their duty; but judgment is the work of God alone. They may, also, exercise love in the admission of persons to their fellowship; but those who have been admitted in conformity with divine law, can never be expelled, except in the cases and in the way which that law defines. Hence is manifested the great importance of faithful treatment at the outset. The persons who form a church are supposed to know, and ought to know, more of the Redeemer's will, than those who are appearing at its entrance in the character of converts from the world. All experience shows, that mistakes committed on either side, at that time, lead to moral results which human power is unable to prevent. Tares in a wheat-field will choke and smother the corn. It is the province of the labourer, therefore, to keep them out, if possible; and whatever the reasons he might have for permitting the defective ministration of his servants here predicted, the Lord has clearly exempted himself from its approval; and this will become still more manifest from his own treatment, both of those whom he rejected, and of those whom he received.

THE OPENLY PROFANE.

The common and authorised terms of admission being so definite and radical, it is not necessary to divide the persons received into classes—all are comprehended, with sufficient clearness for practical purposes, under the one term "believer;" but those whom the Lord rejects, are so distinguished from each other, that they receive, so to speak, a different kind of rejection. In the open and hardy treason of the Jewish rulers, the Pharisees, and the Sadducees, a perfection of crime demanded and received from the Redeemer, even here, a forcible and unsparing reprehension. During the first two years of his ministry, he shows them all possible kindness, and meets their objections, that they may have no excuse; but when he had left them without any cloak for their sin, his compassion is inflamed, and he rises to an indignant majesty of rebuke. Some of his sentences, united and harmonising with his flowing tears and convulsive grief, must, in the circumstance, have been sublime: and, at last, when merciful forbearance had performed her utmost, crying, "O Jerusalem, Jerusalem," he retired to the circle of his chosen ones, to meet this rejected people for purposes of mercy to them no more on earth for ever.

THE UNDECIDED.

Those who stood around the Lord on that day when, from Olivet, he declared against Jerusalem and the corporation seated there, that now repentance could not be received at their hands, would not have said that in the Saviour's ministrations of mercy there was no discrimination. He himself discriminated in his very words: he said, "Thy door of hope is shut, and thy house is left unto thee desolate, because thou wouldest not be gathered by my teaching, and knewest not the time of thy visitation." But, this discrimination becomes the more remarkable in those cases which were marked with lovely features, and which yet fell short of his requirement. "What good thing shall I do," said a young man whom Jesus loved, "in order that I may obtain the eternal life?" * In thus taking the end as implying the means, he confessed his knowledge of the object to be gained, by the reign of God, in all its faithful subjects. It is the eternal life which Jesus promised. The Lord's reply, "If thou wilt be perfect,"† supposes the truth of his professed obedience in the law, and wish to be initiated with his disciples. His own requirement is given in the words, "One thing thou lackest yet: sell all that thou hast, and give it to the poor, and thou shalt have treasure in heaven; and come, *follow me.*"‡ His peculiar demand, in this case, was just one exercise of that authority to which all his disciples declared their subjection. Hence the difficulty which the love of riches creates for those who are entering the kingdom of heaven. Others, though convinced that the claim of this Redeemer was just, yet failed to avow it, because they loved the praise of men more than the praise of

* Luke xviii. 18.   † Matt. xix. 21.   ‡ Luke xviii. 22.

God. Nicodemus exhibits a timidity, which it is hard to account for on any other principle. He confessed that Jesus was a teacher come from God, but he came by night to see him, as if to avoid being detected in the act. Jesus replies to him, " Except a man be born again of water to a new life on earth, and of the Spirit by which that life may be sustained, he cannot enter the kingdom of God."* My fellowship cannot be conducted in secrecy, and no one loveth darkness rather than light whose deeds are not evil. The whole argument of this discourse goes to show the sovereignty and justice of this arrangement. To those who received him he gave a power,† a right, to become sons of God; but, the reality of their faith was not to be credited, if, from the fear of man, or love of wealth, that privilege was resigned. Hence the cogent reasoning in John xii. 37—50. Here the refusal of his claims is ascribed to that corruption of heart which Isaiah had predicted:‡ yet, it is added, " Many of the rulers believed on him, but would not confess, because of the Pharisees. But Jesus cried out, and said, He who believeth on me, believeth not on me, but on him that sent me. I, a light, have come into the world, that every one who believeth on me might not remain in the darkness." This remaining in the darkness, was the conduct which those affrighted believers chose to pursue; and that coming into the light, which Jesus urged, was their yielding the confession which they now refused,

---

* John iii. 1—21. † John i. 12. ‡ Isaiah vi. 9, 10.

and publicly resigning their interests and persons to his merciful governance and care. If they believed, this was essential to the consistent operation of their faith; and, in thus violating the convictions of their own minds, they dishonoured him and God who sent him. The personal confession, therefore, founded upon personal faith, is urged by the Father's authority, the Pharisees and their excommunication notwithstanding. To make this confession was to begin, and to sustain it was to continue, a new life by faith in Christ Jesus; and the beginning of that new life by baptism was, by Dr. Halley's own confession, the new birth out of water urged on Nicodemus.

THE BAPTIZED DISCIPLES.

With all that these undecided cases have for approval, therefore, they stand, in the Saviour's ministration, without the Christian community, and are not recognised amongst his followers. Nicodemus is nowhere called a disciple; but one who came to Jesus by night. Joseph of Arimathea was a disciple; but secretly, for fear of the Jews; and, like many Arimatheans in our own time, submitted to the truth, concealing the act of obedience as much as possible. In all, therefore, we obtain the illustration and evidence of one rule, carried, in its application, through the whole work which Christ performed. Those whom he rejected as profane, were, as long as forbearance continued, urged to repent and believe; and those who repented and believed were, with as much decision, urged to confess and be baptized. Where the condition was wanting, it became the subject of discourse; and where the condition existed, the open consecration was enforced; but where they were both conjoined, he rested in his confidence, and proved the discrimination of his ministry, in acts of love.

THE INSTRUCTION OF DISCIPLES.

Partly from the distance of the time, and the difference of circumstances in which we read them, the evangelical records appear to us greatly confused and indistinct; but when they have been collated with care, a unity of design presents itself, in which all incidents harmonise with the universal purpose of Divine mercy. As the disciples he collected were chosen to constitute the kingdom in which, by his administration, he was hereafter to reveal the glory of Divine grace, as might have been expected, a large portion of his labour was given to their instruction and training. Wherever the mind rests on these lessons of his own family, of disciples, servants, followers, friends, and brethren, as he variously calls them, the lessons imply the existence of faith; the fact of their repentance is taken for granted; and the whole force of his teaching is directed to the evolving and perfecting of that character which had been recognised in their initiation. On the indiscriminating supposition, this could not have occurred. Had the disciples been baptized as persons in whom repentance was needful, this would have been no distinction, because repentance is needful to all the human race; and then, also, the baptized disciples must have been urged, by various arguments, to repent; but now their faith is encouraged, their hope is raised, their peculiar responsibility is elucidated, their danger is predicted, and the provision made for their protection and final victory is explained. When he retired from all the world besides, he committed himself to them, as to individuals who were authorised to expect his confidence, until, by some overt act, it had been forfeited. Hence, the very treatment of Judas himself, who was not expelled on any suspicion, however strong, is positive proof of that discriminating law on which the fellowship of these disciples was based. It was only when positive offence had ripened to incorrigible impenitence that they were permitted to treat a brother as if he were a heathen man or a publican; and this law of discriminating privilege was not only imposed upon them in their activities, it was actually observed by the Lord himself, in his teaching, in all his intercourse, and in suffering himself to fall by the treachery of Judas.

HIS EXPRESSIONS OF PECULIAR REGARD.

In his addresses to unrenewed men, his infinite and varied kindness is always the result of compassion; he came that they might not perish, and he pitied them as ready to perish. But, in the midst of his disciples, no idea of perishing is entertained. His admonition is, "Abide in me, and let my words abide in you; you shall not then be fruitless. I come that you might have life, and that you might have it more abundantly; because I live, ye shall live also."

Could he have used such expressions in speaking to Caiaphas, to Herod, or to the unbelieving and impenitent masses of mankind? He could not; he did not. In speaking to them, he said, "Ye will not come unto me that ye might have life." He could not say to them, Abide in me; he could not say that they *were* in him; and it is against nature to abide where we are not. Nor is this discriminating method of treatment observable only in a case or two: it extends through his whole ministry. At the beginning, in his first address to Peter and Nathaniel, he entered at once into the very sanctuary of their tenderest affections, and produced the acknowledgment, Thou art the King of Israel, thou art the Son of God. With others who heard John say, " Behold the Lamb of God," and followed him, he acted in the same way; not urging their repentance, but calling forth their promised reverence, and then responding to its exercise in words and acts of love, which find no parallel in merely human intercourse. Many of the incidents by which this affirmation is sustained, are recorded with the utmost brevity, as matters of course; as if, neither enemies nor friends of the Redeemer could suppose that his recognised disciples would not receive from him a marked and discriminating expression of esteem. But, passing by a thousand elements of proof, and, amongst the rest, that family of disciples in which, at Bethany, he raised Lazarus from death, and seemed so perfectly at home; a single case supplies all that our argument requires. In that upper room, where he ate the last passover with his disciples, the essential peculiarity of his intercourse with them is perfectly demonstrated. He therein not only proves that this society was formed and set apart for holy purposes, but calls the man by whose perfidy this sacred inclosure was first violated and profaned, "the son of perdition;" and declares that it were better for him that he never had been born. During this interview, everything done and said implies the existence of faith, and a willing self-consecration of each, by its exercise. Hence proceed their equality as brethren; the common law of brotherly affection by which the whole fraternity is united; their common and intimate relation to the Lord himself; their inheritance in the love of God the Father; their peculiar privilege and certain hope in prayer; the promise of peculiar manifestations of regard, both from God the Father and God the Son; their exposure to the hatred of this world, from which they had withdrawn, and the promise of their certain victory and joy; the promise of the Holy Spirit, their Comforter, not to lead them to repentance, but to prepare them for their great work of leading others to repentance; and the promise that in this their victory shall be even greater than was that of their Lord. The discriminating endearments of this holy interview, comprehend displays of Divine perfection, exercises of Divine prerogative, manifestations of Divine complacency, and exercises of sympathising care, which Jesus never granted to the men of this world, continuing in impenitence and unbelief. He plainly tells these consecrated men, that the world will hate them, and adds, because they have not known the Father nor Me. He does more: for, lifting up his eyes to heaven, he blessed the Father for those whom he had given him out of the world. In this character, he placed within their consecrated circle the rite which symbolised his dying love, and said, "Eat ye all of it." He declares, that, for their sakes, he had consecrated himself; and prays that they also may be consecrated in the truth. He would not have them taken out of the world, but prays that they may be kept from the evil. He not only discriminates, but shows the ground of his discrimination; saying, "Neither pray I for these alone, but for all those who *shall* believe on me through their word." His disciples, therefore, were distinguished by their faith, and the recognition of a disciple is a recognition of his faith. But, the Saviour still adds, "Father, I will that those whom thou hast given me be with me where I am, that they may see my glory:" and, therefore, the faith which is recognised in a disciple, is the faith on which the alternative of judgment is suspended, the whole polity of the Mediatorial kingdom is reposed, and whose discriminating influence is, by our Lord himself, extended through that bright though terrible hereafter, in which our thought is drowned.

THE LORD'S EXAMPLE.

Against this positive proof of vital discrimination in the initiating and treatment of our Lord's disciples, Dr. Halley brings nothing but his unsustained argument, resting on a disputed rabbinical ceremony, which we reject. The effect of his argument, if sustained and carried out, would be to place the facts of our Lord's ministration and life in absolute hostility to his own commandment. If Dr. Halley cannot understand the evangelical record without this rabbinical light, the man must be very learned who can explain it with. One single axiom will afford a far more certain means of elucidation. Let it be assumed that the Redeemer always means what he says; and then, his own words and actions will explain each other. Hence to this very point he says, "My meat and my drink is to do the will of him that sent me, and to finish his work." And, again: "The words which I speak, I speak not of myself, but as the Father hath commanded me, even so I speak." His words and his works, therefore, were the words and the works of God. His meaning is, that what he spake and did, he spake and did by Divine authority, and for the glory of the Father. His own will was not his rule of action, witness his Gethsemane; his own good or honour was not his pursuit; his everlasting power was not even used in his own defence. From the time of his baptism till his death, he lived the life of a consecrated being. He made it his business, his pleasure, his meat and drink, to perfect and fulfil its consecrating vow. This appears in the facts, and is expressed in his words. His example, therefore, must explain his law. The faith which unites a sinner to himself, is, and must be, the term of initiation; for the initiated have, with him, one life, one hope, and one eternal glory.

It is not requisite to dwell on minute particulars in such a case. The most expressive outline and essential principle and end of the Redeemer's life prove, that he cannot be followed without faith. Some features in his example relate, it is true, to duties which must be performed in scenes with which we are familiar, and where our present sympathies may be indulged; but these are the first steps of his holy progress, the end of which is at the right hand of God. His principal wish respecting his disciples is, that "they may be with him where he is;" that "they may see his glory." This, the end of his purpose, must be the great object of pursuit in all those who follow Him. But, if they follow Him to the end, it must be through the several steps by which he attains the end. His life was regulated by no vague and sentimental reference to the Father and his dominion; the Word which expressed his will was exalted to the character of Divine law, and, in every action, whether outward or secret, he bowed before its dictate, saying, "It is written, it is written." Led by the Word and the Eternal Spirit, he advanced to the place of mental conflict, active service, self-denial, and personal exposure; and, through every one, his word is "follow me." In his solitary retreats for midnight prayer, his transforming converse with eternity, and in the holy fellowship of his disciples, he still saith, "Follow me." Some of the scenes through which he leads his people are beautiful and grand in action, enjoyment, and in prospect; but these are often introductory to other scenes and services, which find their features in his mournful hours—his Gethsemane—his judgment-hall —perhaps, his Golgotha. Still, the voice saith, "Follow me," though anguish or mortality resist: and as he rises up from Olivet, in his ascension, the rapt disciple sees his lovely form, and hears the last echo of his voice, still leading onward to his place in glory. This is no exaggeration; but beneath the facts of history and truth. But what has this to do with unbelief and impenitence? It writes their condemnation as in words of fire. It proves that professions of esteem for these eternal realities offered by unbelievers in his ordinances, dishonour the Lord himself, degrade his worship, and prepare the greatest moral calamity that has yet befallen this guilty world.

LECTURE V.

ON THE FORTY-SEVEN DAYS.

A SINGLE collation of evangelical facts will set before us, in the clearest light, the peculiar relationship which our Lord sustained, first, to the unconvinced and unconverted masses of mankind; and, secondly, to his recognised disciples. After an extensive and laborious circuit through the cities and villages of Galilee, it is said,* that "Jesus, seeing the multitude, was moved with compassion, because they were fainting, and scattered abroad as sheep having no shepherd." This was no merely passing impression; for he said to his disciples, "The harvest truly is great, but the labourers are few; pray ye, therefore, the Lord of the harvest, that he may thrust out labourers into his harvest." At that time, it is said,† that "he retired to a mountain to pray, and continued all night in

* Matthew ix. 36—38.   † Luke vi. 12. Matthew x. 1.

prayer to God." It appears that the effect of his words brought many of his disciples with him into this retirement for devotion; so that they remained in the glen, while he went farther up the mountain alone. Hence, when it was day, he came down to the disciples who awaited him; and having called them to him, he chose from their number twelve to be his apostles:* he then delivered an impressive discourse to them, describing the duties of their office.† After the apostles had been thus chosen out of the disciples, and set apart for their work, "He came down with them,"‡ and stood upon a plain place—a little flat or plain in the mountains—and there a great multitude of his disciples having gathered round him, directing his eyes into the midst of these disciples, he began the discourse to them which is recorded in Matthew v., vi., vii. The matters contained in this discourse, though differing from that delivered to the apostles, are, nevertheless, such as indicated in his disciples a peculiar people, for he calls them "lights of the world," "salt of the earth," "subjects of the kingdom of heaven," the very objects of its establishment and ministry.§ In the whole of this discourse the instructions imply and enforce, not only a separation, but a superiority, to which they were committed in preparation for the kingdom of heaven; and, as if this were not sufficient, it is added, that besides these disciples to whom

* Luke vi. 12, 13.   † Matthew x. 5—42.   ‡ Luke vi. 17.
§ Luke vi. 17—49.

he spake, "many came to hear him, and to be healed of their diseases. Here, the Lord supreme, the ministry around and under him, the initiated subjects of his reign, the uninitiated hearers, and the compassionated multitudes, are all brought before us at one view; and each one occupies a position which demonstrates the discriminating spirituality of the reign of God.

A collection of parables, which appear to have been delivered at different times, is preserved in the thirteenth chapter of Matthew, as if to teach the same doctrine. They all relate to the kingdom of heaven, of which on earth Jesus was preparing to leave the administration with his disciples. The parable of the sower, delivered by himself to the multitudes who came to hear him, elicited the inquiry put by the disciples,* "Wherefore dost thou speak to them in parables?" The Saviour's reply is, "Because to *you* it is granted to know the mysteries of the kingdom of heaven," and you do not need such illustrations; but to them it is not given; and if they be not moved from their present position, they will lose what they do possess. In seeing, they do not see; and in hearing they do not perceive what is enforced. The grossness of heart predicted by Isaiah,† hath so possessed them, that they will not turn that I should heal them. Hence, they were urged to take heed how they heard; because no fruit could spring from any heart not softened and purified

---

* Matthew xiii. 10.   † Isaiah vi. 9.   Matthew xiii. 11—18.

by repentance, and consecrated to the culture of his truth. The value of such a fruit is exhibited as a pearl, so precious that it justifies a purchase by the sacrifice of all other things — as a treasure which makes him rich who retains nothing besides. The society or kingdom formed of such devotees, is said to have a vitality like that of mustard-seed; and a transforming power, like that of leaven in the meal. The members of that community are separated from the rest of mankind, as fish in the net, from others in the ocean; and the imperfection which attends the ministrations of men, is provided for by the sorting time, and still more perfect discrimination of the judgment. The kingdom is exhibited as one adapted to the present state of things; and its law of discrimination is suited to the human agency our Lord was intending to employ. It engaged all minds in that one great work, of exercising faith and inducing it in others. The kingdom, as here described, is a moral husbandry, contemplating spiritual fruit through faith in the Saviour's word; and the recognition of that faith is such as leaves the unbeliever and hypocrite without excuse, and the true disciple without any dread, in the final judgment. Hence, the very words of our Lord, "Blessed are your eyes, for they see, and your ears, for they hear."*

The disciples of our Lord, therefore, were separated from the world by the law of his kingdom; and the

---

* Matthew xiii. 16, 17.

application of that law was based on their personal perception of his truth, and submission to his will in hope of salvation in the world to come; and since their baptism was their badge or recognition of discipleship, this must have been administered on the declaration of that character which was therein recognised. The proof of this fact, as stated in the last exercise, was obtained from the incidents of our Lord's example and ministry, as spread over three years of various and devoted exertion. The scope of our present inquiry is comprehended within forty-seven days. Between the crucifixion and the Pentecost there were fifty days. On the third he rose from the dead. From that time, " he appeared to the disciples* through forty days, declaring the things which concerned the kingdom of God." From the day of his ascension to the Pentecost, therefore, were seven days; and between the resurrection and the Pentecost, forty-seven. In this brief period, his resurrection was demonstrated, his atonement was accredited, his executive authority was declared, the preparation for his reign was perfected, his commission was granted to the disciples; and ascending up on high, and seating himself at the right-hand of God, he fulfilled the promise of the Father, imparted the power from on high, baptized his disciples in the Spirit, completed his merciful revelation, and commenced the perfected administration of his mediatorial reign. Within this brief space all methods

---

* Acts i. 3.

of expressing Divine authority are combined, and harmonise in confirming the doctrine we have stated.

The argument by which this affirmation is sustained rests on seven particulars. *First*, the unaltered recognition of his disciples at this time; *secondly*, the exclusive intercourse with which they were favoured; *thirdly*, the practical intention of our Lord as explained in his own words; *fourthly*, the authoritative treatment to which the disciples were subjected; *fifthly*, the import of our Lord's commission; *sixthly*, the conduct maintained by the disciples themselves; and, *seventhly*, the illustration which is granted at the Pentecost. From all these particulars it will be seen, that these disciples are treated as no unbelievers could be treated; that they evolved a character which unbelief could not sustain; that their work could not be performed by unbelievers; that their interests were ruined by the incorporation of unbelievers; that by law, and in fact, they were separated and set apart for the Lord.

THE RECOGNITION OF HIS DISCIPLES.

Dr. Halley says, that Jesus took the baptism of John as he found it, and made it his own by his commission. This is of no importance; but the facts before us show, that Jesus took *the baptized* as he found *them* at his resurrection; and, without any discriminating process whatever, proceeded with them to commence the administration of his mediatorial reign. Whatever discrimination his government involves, therefore, is equally involved in his initiatory baptism. Some have treated these events as though they related to apostles only; and others have supposed " *a church within the church ;*" but with most powerful inducements to discriminate between disciple and disciple, no such discrimination appears. Peter had grievously sinned, and might have been placed aside; others had fled to their homes, or to hiding-places; and of all baptized into his kingdom, not one appeared on his behalf in the court of Israel, or in the judgment-hall. Of the people there was none with him. Dr. Halley would seem to infer from this, that they had no faith, as we understand the term. He is wrong: the Lord intended that his passion should be a scene in which he must stand alone. Of the people none could be with him. This fact would seem to indicate that strength of faith which bows down under a most terrible necessity. That this submission was their duty, then, seems implied in the words of our Lord:* " Of those whom thou hast given me, I have lost none ; except the son of perdition, that the Scripture might be fulfilled." Besides the fulfilment of Scripture prophecies, by permitting the case of Judas, the Lord brought home to his disciples, and to the apostles themselves, the dreadful possibility and consequence of defiling the sanctuary of their association. It was seen by that case, that unbelief, in their society, would

---

* John xvii. 12 ; xiii. 36—38.

not only mar their peace and destroy their confidence, but betray his own dearest interests, and even his very person to death. While they were writhing under the bitter reflections attendant upon these dreadful realities, Jesus rose from the dead. He did not confine his communications to apostles, or to a favourite few; he began with the sisterhood, and sent them especially to Peter, met the disciples five hundred at once, and, without any discrimination, recognised them all. His word is,* " Go, tell my brethren, I go before them into Galilee; and there shall they see me." What is this, but saying that they were his brethren now; and that the principle on which their relation to himself was recognised, made them so?

THE PERSONAL INTERCOURSE OF OUR LORD.

It seems to have been a fixed rule with the Redeemer, that, in the fellowship of his disciples, the equality of brethren should prevail; but, that between them and the world a clear line of demarcation should be drawn and observed. Hence, when he rose from the dead, he gave no expressions of partiality, save those which met the peculiar weakness and solicitudes of his followers. To the women he appeared first, and sent an especial message to Peter, whose spirit was likely to be grievously depressed; but otherwise, all his disciples were treated alike, each being held under subjection in his own appointed office. He acted towards them like a king.

---

* John xx. 18. Matthew xxviii. 10.

In his intercourse, he exhibited a power to which all laws of nature were subordinate; he appeared and disappeared, under circumstances which proved a superiority in his action to the laws which regulate the resistance and movements of material bodies. When the disciples were shut in together in their private room, he became visible at once, as if his being were entirely spiritual; and yet, to convince Thomas, he said, " Reach hither thy hand, and thrust it into my side. By this intervention, he showed his design to break down all unbelief in the fact of his resurrection. In this great event his disciples were all interested, of this they must all testify, and on this each one must build his hope. Suspicion, therefore, was pursued and annihilated, that those who had trusted him until his death, might rise to greater confidence in the power of his endless life. The effect of these interventions on his disciples may serve to show, with what tremendous effect the same kind of power might have been exerted on his adversaries. When the priests and elders were receiving the depositions of the soldiers,* and bribing them to falsify their own report, and, by constructing a still deeper policy, were devising how they might still sustain their war with truth and mercy, in the Son of God—as he appeared to his disciples, saying, " Peace be unto you," he might also have become visible in the midst of these enemies, confounded them with his presence, and crushed them

---

* Matthew xxviii. 11—16.

in the operations of his power. Every reproach, with which they had insulted his person in grief, might now have been returned upon themselves, charged with rebuke like streaming fire. Many objects might thus have been attained, and these not unimportant to his purpose. He might have broken up their plans, forced the acknowledgment of his resurrection from their own tribunal, procured the testimony of Pilate, of Caiaphas, of Herod, and the Pharisees; or, he might have broken all their powers at once, using as he did a faculty and attributes they could not reach. Why, then, did he not do so? The answer is, He had a more godlike purpose; and, with sovereign majesty, adhered to it against all human calculations. He would not crush them with his power, because he had purposes of mercy to individuals even amongst them; and yet, he would not see them, because, as a nation and an authority, they were now rejected, and, as individuals, they retained a state of impenitence and unbelief, to which no mercy can be shown. He would not see them, because they were not his; he would not accept their testimony, nor personally encounter their devices. He was in Jerusalem, as one who despised their power; and he contemplated mercy only in his own way, combining it with purposes of awful vengeance. He must have witnesses and agencies, authorised ambassadors negotiating peace between him and traitors; but he sought them not among the faithless and impenitent, he sought them amongst his recognised followers. His baptized disciples, therefore, formed the only circle of his personal appearance after his resurrection. Here he appeared like one at home; but, he appeared to no one else. The soldiers at his grave did not see him; they only saw the angel. His judges did not see him. We have no more accounts of intercourse conceded, in courtesy, to Pharisees or rulers; a line of demarcation is drawn, over which he never passed, and, by that line, the sphere of his personal intercourse was determined, and confined to his believing people. By them he would speak to unbelieving men; but, by no other means. His oracles and laws were all given by their inspiration of the Spirit; and all negotiations of mercy were conducted through them, as his ambassadors. These were the elements, the constituency, the subjects, and agents, of his reign on earth. In this society, therefore, he appeared, and in this alone. Here he declared his will, arranged his government, devised his missions, and acted as a ruler in the seat of his dominion; and thereby he declared, more forcibly than words can express, that these, his recognised associates in the reign of heaven, had been discriminated by a principle, a faith, without which, no mercy can be received; but, through which, all the operations of his love shall be conducted till the close of time.

Dr. Halley is eloquent in urging the defects of believers in the apostolical times; as though the faith recognised in them, was no faith at all, or, at least, not such faith as we exercise in our time. In using such an argument, especial care should be taken not to depreciate examples which God himself has approved. These men, who are, for controversial purposes, said to have had no faith, are now perfected in glory. They laboured, suffered, and died, for the truth and for its Author; and, if they had not faith when they were received, Dr. Halley should have shown when, and by what means, they came to be believers; and how, if not in their initiatory immersion, they became recognised as believers. But, passing these considerations for the present, and making all possible allowance for undetected insincerity: on what ground can it be said, that the rejected parties were distinguished and cast away, so that the risen Lord, invested now with all power in heaven and in earth, whose whole delight and office now consisted in the administration of mercy, would not even meet these victims of transgression? They had many and grievous criminalities; but these did not close the door of hope, because subjects of the same criminalities were admitted and saved. They had perverted the law, broken its precepts, and dishonoured God; but, these are not named in their condemnation. The Lord himself said, weeping over their city, "Thy door is shut, *because thou knewest not the time of thy visitation.*" The distinguishing feature of their crime was the rejection of him. With the heart they did not believe unto righteousness; and, therefore, could not confess him with the mouth unto salvation.* By this decisive

---

* Romans x. 9, 10.

feature of their sin, they were prepared for the discriminating feature of their punishment. By this rejection of their Messiah, the whole system was consigned to utter ruin. When Jesus thus withdrew from that society, its preservation became impossible. It was broken like a ship at sea, on fire, and dashed upon the hidden rocks: and, every fragment of that Jewish wreck, now seen scorched and floating on the stream of time, testifies, with a fearful distinctness, that their distinguishing criminality of unbelief, however modified, defended, or concealed, renders a legitimate confession of their Lord impossible, and positively frustrates all the ordained purposes of his merciful administration.

Ignorance is not the mother of devotion; but, personal confidence may co-exist with limited knowledge. This was the case with the disciples of our Lord. They had many things to learn; but, till the time of his crucifixion, they had an unlimited faith in his personal love and power. By this, as by other events, that faith was tried; and often, the sudden and unusual character of the events confounded all their calculations. Walking on the sea, and stilling its tempests by a word, were things they had never heard of; and to make his own crucifixion and return from death, a part of his merciful design, was equally beyond their thoughts. Those who had said, "What manner of man is this, for even the winds and the sea obey him?" had now to look on him in a still more unusual attitude, and say, What manner of man is this, for even death and hell obey him?

Hence the first object to be secured in their minds was, a fixed belief that he was risen from the dead. It was his being numbered with the dead, that shocked them; and, because they could not cease to believe that he came out from God, confounded them. It is plain, that the two going to Emmaus knew not what construction to put on the facts before them; they knew not what to think, or how to reconcile the conflicting elements. The great reconciling fact was that of his resurrection from the dead. Let them be once convinced of this; and though he should remain, after his ascension, concealed from all bodily eyes whatever, yet if they had faith in him before, its action would return with vital power, and gain the victory. But, this itself supposed the existence of a faith united to repentance. If they, like the Jews, saw such evidence that Jesus came from God, as made them fear the operation of his truth, and yet were not repentant for the treason of nature, so as to submit under his authority, this would not be to them a source of joy; but, as in the case of the rejected rulers, form an occasion for renewed resistance. The elders knew that he had risen from the dead; else, they could not have bribed the soldiers to say, at the hazard of their lives, that the disciples had stolen him while they were asleep on guard. But, this knowledge of the fact did not make *them* rejoice in the resurrection; because they were not reconciled to the person and dominion of our Lord. *They*, in impenitence, *retained* their treason; the *disciples* did *not*. This essential and moral distinction was recognised by the Redeemer, when he said, "Go, tell my brethren and Peter, that I am risen." By calling them brethren, he plainly declares that they were no longer traitors, but friends. It is proving that in him they were prepared to honour God as God: and, though they might have much to learn, and require great compassion, yet they had in them the germ and element from which might grow all that his fellowship required. They were the persons prepared by repentance, and made ready, by its baptismal recognition, for him; and in their midst, therefore, and with them alone, his glory was revealed and his throne erected. In eleven cases, specifically recorded, he appears with them, and with none besides. He appears to them without any discriminating exception, because they are his; because they are his brethren in the reign of God; because they were prepared for him; because their wishes were reconciled to his purpose, their persons were subjected to his authority, and their hopes were all built upon his life and favour; and, his so appearing to them exclusively, and to all of them without any discrimination, proves that, on the credible profession of this personal and vital repentance, all had been incorporated for his use.

THE PRACTICAL INTENTION OF OUR LORD.

The initiating immersion may be called "the badge of discipleship;" and this may also be "a symbol of repentance;" but, if so, it symbolises a repentance that has been previously ascertained. This is not only clear from the fact that, in all the interviews before named, the necessity of repentance is never urged, but also from the additional fact, that the great business contemplated in all these interviews rendered its accredited existence absolutely necessary. His one expression, "And ye shall be my witnesses in Jerusalem, in Samaria, and to the uttermost parts of the earth,"* contains within itself a positive demonstration of this truth; for the commission of our Lord was not given exclusively to his apostles. All his disciples were to teach and testify, each in his own place, and to the extent of his own endowments. Indeed, every Christian is a witness for Christ. The great question is, What can he testify? and in what particular can the personal testimony of each believer be taken through all time? The fact of the resurrection was testified by the disciples, as long as any one remained who saw the Lord after he had risen from the dead; but that testimony could last no longer; those who followed might prove, but they could not testify, the truth of that event. Moreover, the fact of our Lord's resurrection is not now the thing in which the Lord is most concerned. In describing the work of that Spirit by which his disciples were to be endowed, Jesus himself said,† "He shall convince the world of sin, of righteousness, and of judgment: of sin, because they believe not on me; of righteousness, because I go to the Father; and of judgment, because the prince of this world is judged."

* Acts i. 8. † John xvi. 7—11.

The great cause in which they were to be engaged, therefore, was that in which the character of our Lord had been impeached. He had been accused of falsehood and of blasphemy; and his resurrection was important to men chiefly as showing that he was true in his declarations, and sacred in his person. The disciple who is to become a witness, must have some practical and personal deposition to make on this great question. It is not enough for him to reason and prove: others can do this as well as he: the witness must have something to state, and something to the point. This the apostles had, this the disciples had, and this all disciples have, when legitimately recognised in that character. The apostles said, "The things which we have tasted and handled, of the word of life, these things declare we unto you."* We have tried the matter, and our experience is testimony. Paul said, " It is a faithful saying, that Jesus Christ came into the world to save sinners,"† I can testify, for I have obtained mercy. It was this personal experience of divine mercy, through the Redeemer, which qualified them to be his witnesses, more than the personal knowledge they had of his resurrection. They did the things which Christ commanded; and, therefore, knew of his doctrine that it was from God.‡ By this, the subjection of the disciple, therefore, they were qualified for the work of the disciple. They had the experience, and, therefore, they could testify. But those who have the ex-

---

* 1 John i. 1—4. † 1 Timothy i. 11—17. ‡ John vii. 16, 17.

perience of mercy, must have repentance and faith in Christ Jesus; and in calling his disciples to that work, without distinction, the Lord has shown that in this character alone they had been recognised as his.

The church of Rome is not wrong in affirming an unity in the body of Christ; it is here seen, that persons of one character, combined in one work, and subjected in that work to one common Lord, must be frequently, and in many respects, spoken of as one. The apostle thus affirms of himself and his fellow-disciples, that "we, being many, are one body *in* Christ."* But, then, if one body in Christ, each member must *be* in Christ, in order to be *one* with the rest. "But if *any* man be *in* Christ Jesus, he is a *new* creature; he has not only faith, but faith has produced a difference of action, of aim, of hope, of joy, of all that constitutes the moral man. When this has been effected, he can testify of Christ in his own way, and in his own sphere, and never without effect; and he becomes one in a body of witnesses who testify of the grace of God. But the testimony of an unbeliever is worth nothing; it merely provokes the reply, If you wish me to believe, believe yourself. Hence the error against which we plead. By incorporating unbelievers in its own body, the church of Rome has ceased to be a church of Christ. It is not an assembly of believers at all. The believers in

* Romans xii. 1—9. 1 Corinthians vi. 15; x. 16, 17; xii. 12. Ephesians iv. 4—16.

it are merely adjuncts to a corrupted principal. The same must be affirmed of every body formed by an indiscriminating rule. Men not distinguished by their experience of the Saviour's love, and truth, and power, can never be his witnesses; and any number of such men, baptized or unbaptized, be they incorporated how they may, by bearing the Christian name, and affecting to testify of Christ, instead of promoting his aim, can only facilitate, and have only facilitated, spiritual corruptions and infidelity.

As long as the Redeemer spares this world from judgment, and entertains a purpose that requires the faith of men, besides the Word in which his will is written, examples will be required, in which his will shall be obeyed, and his promises fulfilled. Such were his disciples when he entered up on high and as he left them incorporated in their baptism, and sent them forth to incorporate others. Perfect they might not be; but their exalted and general consistency and devotedness commanded the attention and esteem of all mankind. No gainsayer ever ventured to affirm, in that age, that this body of disciples were not in earnest and sincere. No persecutor of that time ever impeached their integrity. All we know of their imperfections is from the stern and searching discipline observed in their own body. A martyr-spirit imbued this fraternity, and the whole course of action in their time has proved, that the faith of those whom Christ ordained his witnesses and disciples, prepared them to live and to die for his sake.

THE AUTHORITATIVE TREATMENT OF THE DISCIPLES.

Moreover, the authority exercised by our Lord during these forty-seven days is so absolute, and is so perfectly acknowledged by the disciples, that both their separation from the world, and their subjection to the Redeemer, became therein not only declared, but seen. Nothing short of a confiding and absolute subjection to him could have produced the spectacle here found of calm and sovereign dictation on his part, and joyful, unlimited obedience on theirs. He spake and acted as one to whom all power in heaven and on earth was confided; and they acted as persons who deferred to all its operations. Some of his appointments relate to himself, his kingdom, and the conduct of its ministry, in which it might be expected that his word would be reverenced; but some of them relate to the disciples themselves, the extent of information to which they were admitted, and the treatment of their own persons, even so far as to imprisonment and death. The Lord appears seriously acting upon his own affirmation, "He who loveth father or mother, or even his own life, more than me, cannot be my disciple." His position is taken so near to eternity, and all his actions and appointments have so direct a relation thereto, that none who had not formed their whole calculations on the hopes of an unseen world, could find any consistent place in this community. This is not confined to the apostles, but extended through the whole body of his disciples. From the unconverted people of this world he has altogether retired; he will not see them. Mary, when overwhelmed by his appearance, must not touch him, because he had not yet ascended to his Father. The places, times, and methods of his appearing are all dictated by his own supreme will, never by their request. He appears as one who occupies the centre of infinity, and is actually dealing with all its elements, spiritual and temporal, present and future. One thing he concedes, which shows that his servants had faith before the crucifixion: he destroys every scruple or doubt in their minds respecting the fact of his resurrection; but, when this is done, in all other things he commands. The apostles stand round him in exalted privilege, and all enjoy the clearest proofs of his eternal love; but the highest and greatest are so treated as to imply the absolute and avowed subjection of all. The case of Peter,* by the sea of Tiberias, is full of instruction and evidence to this point. Peter had sinned, and he had also repented; but the Lord had further things to teach, and Peter must endure the process. " Lovest thou me ?" is forced on his heart, compelling a threefold answer, by which it is seen that each question had entered a different sinus in his wounded breast. The appellation, " Son of Jonah," contained a severe rebuke. The injunctions, " Feed my lambs ; feed my sheep," carried it still deeper, and defined his duty. The prediction of his martyrdom, declared an authority to be exercised over his natural life; and the

---

* John xxi. 1—24.

expression, "Follow me," combined with the rebuke of his curiosity respecting John, extended the exercise of that authority over all his present action in body and in mind. Here, therefore, is a case which stands out, as if to show what Christian discipleship is in its nature and in its action. Peter makes no complaint; and, in his submission, neither he, nor any, nor all the disciples together, assume, in any case, the attitude of persons consulting with or counselling their Lord. They must not even know the times or seasons, or his ulterior plans: they are acting under orders: the part they have to do is explained, and they do it, leaving the event with him. They were not to legislate or to command, but to hear and to obey. The nature of their discipleship is thus demonstrated. The action of this period not only implies their faith, it also proves that the character in which they treated him was one in which he commanded, by their own acknowledgment, the absolute consecration of themselves.

That this acknowledged subjection was not a mere incident, having reference to individuals, and the particular juncture merely, but formed a constitutional arrangement in his kingdom, extending throughout all time, will now be seen from the very words of our Lord's commission, and those inspired authorities with which it is connected, in the discourses which our Saviour delivered at this period.

THE LORD'S COMMISSION.

The first form in which his commission appears, is rather explanatory than imperative.* The disciples were still confused by passing events. But he said to them, "These are the words I spake unto you while I was yet with you, (saying) that it behoved all things written in the law of Moses, and in the prophets, and in the Psalms, concerning me, to be fulfilled. Then opened he their minds, that they might understand the Scriptures; and he said to them, So it hath been written, and so it behoved the Christ to suffer, and to rise from the dead on the third day; and that upon his authority (name) a repentance and forgiveness of sins should be proclaimed; (the proclamation) beginning (and proceeding) from Jerusalem into all the nations; and ye are witnesses of these things." This, then, was their official character and their work; and in testifying of repentance and forgiveness in his name, or on his sole authority, they were now to realise that one idea of Messiah's kingdom, which filled the whole scheme of ancient prophecy. They were not only to proclaim, but also to testify, which they could not do without experience.

The second form is more imperative; and therein the proclamation of repentance and forgiveness on the authority of Christ, is called the "glad tidings."†
"And he said to them, going out into all the world, Proclaim the joyful tidings to every creature. He that

---

* Luke xxiv. 44—48.   † Mark xvi. 15, 18.

hath believed, and hath been baptized, shall be saved; but he who hath not believed, shall be condemned." The past tenses of the verbs, believe, and believe not, have reference to the proclamation before named; as if written, "He who believeth not, when that proclamation is made, shall be condemned; he who, when that proclamation is made, believeth and is baptized, shall be saved." The future covenanted work of being saved continues from the time in which, by faith, the sinner submits to the Lord, and is separated by baptism from the world. The future covenanted work of condemnation begins when the proclamation is heard in unbelief, and continues till the unbeliever is in hell. Hence the apostle teaches that sinners are justified by faith; because, when men believe, they are justified in every gospel act, and in cherishing every hope which it awakens; but, as the Lord here affirms, he who believeth not, is being condemned from that moment. The judgment is going against him through all his life; he is not accepted or justified in any one thing. Because he hath not believed in the only begotten Son of God, he is condemned already, and his judgment is coming out into greater distinctness and effect until the last day. His condemnation beginning with his unbelief, therefore, renders his baptism, by the law of Christ, impossible; because baptism is a badge of approved and justified discipleship.

The third form is, for the most part, explanatory.*

* John xx. 21.

"He said, therefore, unto them again, As the Father hath sent me, I also send you;" which means, with full authority in the same work. And hence the apostle saith, "We beseech you, in Christ's stead, be ye reconciled to God." They were, therefore, witnessing ambassadors, negotiating the reconciliation of sinners to God; and thereby realising, upon earth, the predicted reign of the Messiah; and their baptism was the initiation of subjects to his kingdom.

The fourth form is chiefly imperative. It commands, but yet it explains, the nature of the Lord's authority, comprising all power in heaven and on earth, and the duration of his design, he being with the disciples even to the end of the world.* It is in conducting the final dispensation of mercy, therefore, that the disciples are engaged; and this final dispensation of mercy must reveal the predicted spiritual kingdom of Messiah. Their part in the administration of this kingdom is altogether subordinate, and defined in this commission. By this they were commanded to go out, as before shown, into all the nations; they must not wait till the people come, but go to them; their work, therefore, both was and is aggressive. They were to make disciples, as explained before, by proclaiming the joyful tidings; negotiating the reconciliation of men to God; and thus inducing the repentance and faith on which their own forgiveness and discipleship had been granted; in short, to induce in other men the same

* Matthew xxviii. 16—20.

confiding subjection to the Christ as that on which they themselves were acting. They were to teach the disciples they made to observe all things whatsoever the Lord had commanded them to observe; and, therefore, the disciples so made were to be both capable of, and eligible to, the duties they had to discharge, the privileges they enjoyed, and the hopes they cherished in the body of Christ. They were further commanded to initiate the disciples, for βαπτιζειν εις, in such a connexion, means, to initiate, not into Moses, to act under his authority, but into the name of the Father, of the Son, and of the Holy Spirit, to act under their authority, conjoined in the kingdom of heaven. Each disciple, therefore, was to be initiated with those disciples, with whom the apostles were justified by God the Father, through faith, directed and redeemed by Jesus their Mediator, and led by the Spirit, presently to be poured out on their assembly. Lastly, the object of these aggressive labours was, the whole human race, all the nations; and they are bound to pursue this work of discipling through all the nations, under the law of self-consecration, acknowledged in their own discipleship. In this work, all their personal interests must be subordinated; and all their energies must be employed, as long as there is one man on earth without faith in Christ, or who has not been initiated as a disciple and believer. If death arrested them, they were not guilty, though all men were not convinced; if some had not the faculties needful to understand the truth and acknowledge its claims, the disciples were not bound by their commission to create them; and if some, though able to understand the truth, resisted its claims, and refused its blessings, the disciples, being faithful, were yet clear from their blood. The commission imposes no impossibilities, for it was given in love; and no absurdities, for it was dictated by infinite wisdom: it merely engages believing and devoted men in producing, and in recognising when produced, faith and devotedness in others. It organises, in the work of Divine mercy, its own recipients, who are still continued upon earth for that end.

The whole conduct of the Saviour clearly proves that his intention was to leave the population of earth with only one means of salvation, and this one only ministration of man by which that means of salvation should be enforced. This fact itself leads us to conclude that he certainly must have made that ministry as perfect as human nature would admit. Such a merciful care appears in his own words and actions; for, when his disciples had been discriminated by their faith, trained by his teaching, and encouraged as directed by his example, he still commands them not to act, even in his name, before they had been immersed in the Spirit. He thus acted, in all respects, as one who was preparing in the best way an only means of deliverance for this lost world. For this object he had sacrificed himself; but his own blood could not save unless it were appropriated, and it could not be appropriated without faith. On this one vital point, therefore, he concentrated all his movement. He collected examples of its exercise and power, gave them a commission to act in his name, and entrusted to them a message and a testimony more than sufficient to justify unshaken confidence of salvation in the chief of sinners. Hence the discrimination of John's baptism, in making his prepared people ready; hence the discrimination of his own ministry of that same baptism; and hence his peculiar care in training his disciples for their work. He would have the men employed in this one hope of mankind to be such, that he himself might work with them in signs and wonders. Hence the order of his injunctions, and the spirit of his whole commission. The work of the disciples is made aggressive; they proclaim the joyful tidings of salvation by repentance and faith in him; they are prepared, from their own experience, to testify its accessibility and value; they are forbidden to cherish any hope of success until the objects of their compassion are led to believe; they are assured that every recognised believer shall certainly be saved, and that their just administration of his mercy shall be sanctioned in heaven; they are authorised to make disciples, to initiate them, acting under the authority of the Father, of the Son, and of the Holy Ghost, and to enforce on the initiated an observance of all the things which Jesus had commanded his disciples to perform and keep: he promises to be with them himself, and grant them his Spirit to abide with them for ever; while he, at God's right hand in glory, engages all existence in this service, and harmonises the universal action of his government in the great design. In fact, this whole aggressive action of his kingdom upon earth is a warfare with that criminal unbelief which generates the treason of this earth, and the total character of his arrangements would infer that any moral concession in his servants to that unbelief, which he determines to destroy, is not only contrary to his law, it is a clear violation of his principal commandment, a treasonous departure from his chief design.

THE CONDUCT OF THE DISCIPLES.

That baptism is not the cause of faith in its recipients, is proved by this law, which prepares for the production of faith by a rational and authorised teaching, and makes the existence of faith an indispensable condition of any hope or fellowship in the kingdom of heaven. That baptism is not a symbol showing the necessity of faith and repentance in the baptized, is also proved by the same law, and on the same ground; and still further, because, on that supposition, the baptized only would appear to need repentance, while the law has already, in every word, and in all its spirit, and in every injunction, taken the necessity of repentance and faith in all mankind for granted. The persons, therefore, to be baptized into the name, or initiated under the authority, of the Father, and of the Son, and of the Holy Ghost, must be those who become, through the ministration of Divine mercy, willing to act under that authority, and to commit their everlasting interests to the event. No clearer illustration or proof of this declaration can be given than that which appears in those very disciples to whom this commission was first entrusted. They were to make disciples, and they were disciples. How, then, did they act? and what qualification would their action indicate? It is not assumed that they were perfect; for John, the loveliest of all who were then present, wrote, sixty years after, "We know not what we shall be," because he was expecting still an undefined advancement in moral perfection; but he also wrote, "*Now are we sons of God*," and in that expression conveyed the idea of a most exalted state of privilege. This common inheritance of the disciples, which was also combined with a spirit of subjection to the Lord's will, realises the most perfect idea of moral power. They had many things to learn, but in their Teacher and his work they had perfect confidence. After his ascension they returned to Jerusalem with great joy, their doubts were all destroyed, the resurrection was proved, his ascension they had witnessed, they had felt the force of his authority, and now, for seven days, they were left to themselves. During this period they passed the test of all discipline. With adversaries around them, amidst the false reports and slander of themselves and of their Lord, and having the great command to bear witness for him, they had to remain inactive, waiting for the promise of the Father. The calm, thoughtful, and devotional subjection of that period was, of itself, sufficient to indicate something to the purpose when they did move. This passive obedience to the will of Christ seems more demonstrative of character than more active scenes. Men who can bear this can bear anything; yet this is only the essential feature of discipleship brought out into use. Subjection to this great Teacher implies a subjection of our whole nature to his will. When faith has yielded this, all other things are certain; and without this nothing can be gained. In this the Lord himself became their example, and on this subjection to himself he builds, in his church, the whole fabric of his spiritual power; and this, therefore, must be the qualification of his servants.

THE PENTECOST.

But, were these men converted? If, after all that has resulted from their personal devotion to the Lord, such questions must be made the subject of serious inquiry in this age, the answer is, There can be no real subjection to our Lord without it. While the treason of our fallen state remains, there may be political formality, exercised with specious and gospelised selfishness; but this has no conformity with the Saviour's will. It is the voluntary purpose which constitutes the character as estimated by the Searcher of hearts. By this, the use of all advantages is determined; and to produce this in conformity with his will, and, when produced, to guide and train it to maturity of fruitfulness, becomes the object of all religious discipline as ordained of God. His word is, "Give me thine heart:" and, where this is done, all needful guidance and support are mercifully covenanted by himself. Hence the very words of our Lord show that, in his view and recognition, these disciples were so converted, in the turning of their hearts, their willing and best affections, to himself. He commands them to wait for an endowment necessary in their work; but he does not say, they shall be converted and made penitent; he says, they shall have power. But power would only help them to accomplish what they *desired* to accomplish. If their hearts were not *right* with *God*, the giving them power would neither promote his design nor their good. If they were still traitors, through impenitence and unbelief, the less power they had the better; and to make the Holy Spirit an agent in giving them power would, in that case, be to bring the Holy One himself into alliance with their treason. Nothing can be further from our Lord's design than this. He positively affirms that the old threadbare vestment of formality could not be mended, and that the rebellion of this world could not be united in his service: both must be cast away; and when he pledges power to these disciples, he, in effect, affirms that they had been cast away. His own promise thus becomes a clear and positive exponent of his law; it shows that these disciples, however blasphemed by others, were, in his estimation, persons recognised as being sincerely and unreservedly devoted to himself.

The Spirit which descended at Pentecost was the Lord's own gift; and its bestowment formed a first act in his mediatorial reign. By that event, the glory of his exaltation and power was manifested to his own servants first, and through them to surrounding peoples. By that event, the perfected administration of his reign on earth began. Could we avoid diverting and superficial frivolities, the contemplation of this one event would bring each spirit into contact with an absolute revolution in Divine government, designed for our good, necessary to our salvation, confirming the mercy which God had formerly shown to men, and pregnant with results in which that mercy shall appear more glorious than any other attribute of Deity. The action of that day, though it has no parallel in the history of man, is yet no more than a single surge breaking on our earthly shore, which indicates a movement extending through the ocean of infinity. A reign had actually commenced, under which, till Jesus shall again resign the kingdom to God, even the Father, all intelligent existence, created and uncreated, is used, or overruled, for purposes of mercy; and all official acts in the Divine government are made to further that design. From the fall of man, to this day, all the dispensations of mercy were preparatory; but that which now begins is definitive and final. The patriarchal dispensation showed the fatherly character of God, and Moses explained his justice, while the prophets enforced repentance from the arguments it supplied; all predicted future revelations of mercy in the Christ: John enforced repentance, and baptized the penitents for him, because he was near; the Lord himself, during his ministry, did the same, because he was soon to begin the full administration of his kingdom: but, now he is enthroned, he hath purged our sins, and sat down at the right hand of God; he hath ascended up on high, and led captivity captive, and is actually giving gifts to men; now, therefore, his own royal action must explain his law. .

First, then, His spiritual gifts did not produce, but implied, the conversion and faith of his disciples. The power of speaking in many different languages, was rather likely to feed, than subdue, the natural pride of man. The tongues of fire were but symbols of their gifts; and their immersion in the Spirit subjected them to his guidance in their actions. By this, their faith was directed, *not* produced; it was invigorated, but its existence had been shown before. The whole energy that acted on them and in them, did not produce tears of repentance, but joy and zeal, with decisive action in leading others to repentance. A power was given to the intention they before had of bearing witness to the grace of God in their Redeemer and Lord. The whole aspect of the scene was one adapted and designed to fix attention, to produce faith in others, and to lead them to repentance. The Lord appeared now, working both in and by his servants; and the whole operation demonstrates that they had not only been set apart, but that they had also been prepared in their moral condition for his use.*

Secondly, The effect produced reveals the moral

---

* Acts ii. 1—13.

aim on which the whole arrangement had been concentrated. Custom was broken through, indifference was destroyed, men were roused from the lethargy of sin, and made to feel the action of a power which had no affinity with their principles. The first mistake was followed by inquiring attention. They were convinced, conscience was made sensible and testified against them. They were pricked in the heart. Their position as rejectors and murderers of the Christ was seen and felt; they cried, "Men and brethren, what shall we do?"* This is precisely the step to which the ministrations of Divine truth lead: the message of mercy invites every sinner to prayer, and the declarations of justice urge on him its absolute necessity. The propitiatory is raised for this very use; and Christ is seated on his throne of grace, to the very intent that sinners, oppressed with their guilty necessities, may be so received.

Thirdly, The practical direction obtained by their inquiry is personal and radical; for their repentance must refer to that in which their guilt was seen and their alarm originated; and the exhortation is to every one. The expression, "Be ye saved from this untoward generation," leads them, also, to an individual separation from their fellowship in crime.†

Fourthly, The result obtained is decisive. As many of them as joyfully received this same word, namely, the word which called on them to separate themselves from that untoward generation, were

---

* Acts ii. 37, 38.   † Acts ii. 37—40.

baptized. They were added to the disciples; they continued in the Apostles' doctrine, the fellowship, the breaking of the bread, and the prayers. Their number adds to the glory of the result; it formed a splendid beginning of the Saviour's reign. They were all believing on the Lord; the love of property was subdued, and they had all things common; they were day by day with one accord in the Temple; and breaking bread from house to house, they took their food with joy and singleness of heart, praising God, and having favour with the whole people; and the Lord added to them daily such as were being saved.*

Fifthly, The impression made on the people is positive proof of their consistency; for, those who withdraw from a nation, as from a body of murderers, and yet evince no difference of character, can only provoke contempt; while these disciples had favour with all the people.†

Sixthly, The promise of the Spirit to those who repented, were baptized, and thus separated themselves from the polluted and rebellious world, is proof that the repentance urged before baptism must have been taken to be sincere; since the man whose heart was not right with God, though improperly baptized, is said, by an apostle, to have no part or lot in that matter.‡

Seventhly, The position rendered it absurd, and the difficulties all but impossible, to assume, and certainly to sustain, this separated character, without a faith in

---

* Acts ii. 43—47.   † Acts ii. 47.   ‡ Acts viii. 21.

Christ, by which his daily assistance might be obtained. The apostles, also, knowing from their Lord the conflict to which they were advancing, could not, without great injustice, have received any in whom they did not believe to exist the faith which leads to salvation.

Eighthly, The clear and direct appeal of Peter to Joel and to David, connects this actual beginning of Messiah's reign with the whole scheme of ancient prophecy.* By means of its great central thought, this event transpiring seven days after our Lord's ascension, is so united with his predicted dominion and victory, as to form a key to the fulfilment of all prophecy relating to him, delivered from the fall to his advent. He is here before us, the holy One, the slaughtered One, and yet the living, the exalted One; his disciples are testifying, his truth is prevailing, the administration of his kingdom has commenced. The idea of a spiritual government on earth, whose Ruler is in heaven, whose palace and temple looks out upon eternity, and the subjects of which are governed by its terrible realities, has now produced an actual result; and Peter affirms, that this is the thing foretold. Here, repenting sinners, rejoicing by faith in an exalted and redeeming Lord, separated in baptism from the world, and so united as one body in Christ, are actually engaged in leading others to repentance and faith; and then, by the same rite, incorporating them also in the same separate and devoted body.

---

* Acts ii. 14—36.

For this, the preparation was made by Jesus and by John; and now the reality appears, it forms the centre of Divine action, the seat of Divine glory, a sphere of moral conflict, till the close of time, where all events, prosperous and adverse, unitedly reveal the authorising, the directing, the sustaining, the protecting, and the ever-conquering hand of God Almighty.

LECTURE VI.

ON THE APOSTOLICAL EXAMPLES.

The dispensations of mercy have all one aim; they have, also, but one Author; and they all originate in his sovereign love for men. God first proclaimed his purpose at the fall, and afterwards expounded his proclamation, speaking as a father from the patriarchal altar in the rites of that dispensation. On Abraham, the promise of the great Deliverer was so entailed, that the nations who were before expecting a blessing, should now be blessed only in him. Moses was appointed to institute the laws by which this posterity were preserved from amalgamating with the nations, until this promised Deliverer came. The prophets unfolded the nature of his person and work; predicting, under him, a kingdom differing from all others, and destined to rise above all others, and to stand for ever. The essential difference of this kingdom has been already found, in the character of its subjects, the spirituality of its governance, and the glory of its consummation and joys. It is a kingdom in which Divine authority is reverenced through the Messiah; a family, in which God is honoured and enjoyed as the Father; it is a corporate body, of which Christ is the head; it is called a spouse, devoted to him in love, and to whom he himself is so devoted, in the covenant of mercy, that its words are more firm than the ordinance of nature, and in her treatment and fellowship he reveals the praise of the glory of his grace to all generations.

All the prophetical hints relating to this incorporation lead us to expect, in its members, individuals differing from other men in the moral principles by which they are actuated, and in the character which those principles have formed; hence they are said to fear the name of God, to tremble at his word, to be humble and contrite, to be circumcised in heart; and being recognised as his people, they are also represented as recognising Jehovah to be their God. In conformity with these intimations, John and Jesus both, when making preparation for this reign, urged a repentance for sin, and a personal submission to God in the kingdom, on all the Jewish people; baptizing those who received the Redeemer in this high authority and penitently renounced their past transgressions. This baptism of penitent believers was their initiation; so that none were called disciples without their being baptized, and all the baptized had, without discrimination, the equal privilege of brethren in that society. And, lastly, the disciples so set apart for the kingdom of heaven, were, when the Saviour rose again, taken without distinction, instructed, and sent to instruct and incorporate others; and these, at the Pentecost, began the visible reign of heaven upon earth.

It is clearly ascertained, that the only initiation spoken of in Scripture, is the immersion in water we call baptism; without which, in this kingdom or body of Christ, none are called disciples; and after the reception of which, each has, in the community, an equal privilege with the rest, as each is bound to obey all its laws as far as they apply to his individual conduct. The positive evidence which has been considered is admitted, even by our opponents, to justify every penitent believer in claiming the initiating rite, as also his perfect share in the service and fellowship of this kingdom; and, on the same positive evidence, it is clear that, when the repentance and faith of an individual has been credibly avowed, neither the incorporated disciples, nor their official agents or ministers, have any right to withhold the initiation and fellowship so claimed in the name of Christ. This is admitted by Dr. Halley and by most. The only question is, therefore, whether any, who are not penitent believers, who do not, cannot, or even will not, acknowledge that their former position was wrong and unsafe, that the one prescribed by Jesus is both right and secure, and do not engage that, in this kingdom, their persons shall be devoted to him, can, by the law of the Redeemer, be admitted, by this initiation, to the fellowship of his recognised disciples?

At times, the initiation is treated as a distinct and separate thing, having no relation to the fellowship; but no ground for this is discoverable in Scripture. There the body of Christ is represented as being formed of the initiated disciples, and none besides; and the initiation involved the fellowship of the person received, until, by actual sin, his position was forfeited. Both questions, therefore, go together; and it is pleaded, by Dr. Wardlaw and Dr. Owen, first, that believers are to be initiated; and, secondly, that the children of these same believers should be initiated also: but Dr. Halley, advancing beyond them, pleads that any one who *wishes* it may claim this initiation; and, also, that it may be claimed for every infant whatever, without any discrimination.

THE LIMITED THEORY.

The authors just named are chosen by Dr. Halley to represent the more limited use of baptism, which he repudiates. Dr. Owen " baptized the infant children of believers, because they are in their parents' covenant of grace; he did not baptize the children of unbelievers, because they, like their parents, are not in the covenant of grace."—*Dr. Halley*, p. 546. On this supposition rests the whole argument designated " the hereditary claim to the covenant of grace." Dr. Halley justly remarks on this assumption, that "if it is meant that the children of unbelievers are, with their parents, and for their parents' unbelief, excluded from the covenant of grace, and, dying in infancy, perish inevitably, this, I am sure, is nowhere asserted in Scripture," p. 546. This is just. Anything approaching to such an assumption can never be found in Scripture. Yet every limited use of infant baptism implies such an hereditary distinction between the children of believers and unbelievers; while the advocates of baptismal regeneration imply, and many of them teach, that infants unbaptized are, if not lost, in great danger and disadvantage. The error involved in all the cases here named is twofold. It is supposed, first, that the guilt of Adam's sin, which was forgiven when he repented in Paradise, is still, unjustly, punished in all his offspring. This can never be proved. Death continues to be inflicted, in infants, as in believers who are justified by faith; but it only forms a means of removing them from this earthly sphere of discipline and trial. Through the death and mediation of Christ they obtain, in the presence of the Lord, and in the article of death, all that is needful for their transition to everlasting glory. By this act of sovereign grace they obtain immense advantage, and the recipients of mercy are thus multiplied, in all lands, beyond all human power of calculation. If this fact could be well considered, it would remove much of that unconfiding and sentimental solicitude which first originated, and now sustains, more than any argument, the practice of baptizing them. The second error supposed in these cases relates to the nature and object of the reign of heaven and its initiatory rite. The intelligent character and social aim of the rite, and the fellowship to which each recipient is inducted, are left out of the calculation. Both are designed for the use of men, whose period of probation is to be spent here on earth. Infants are taken away from it when they die; and those who live are not prepared for it until they be grown up, and are capable of knowing the import and obligation of what is done, and of what they do. The intellectual and moral character of fellowship in the body of Christ is quite forgotten in the argument; and one of the greatest evils attending this controversy is, its terrible effect in obscuring and diminishing the influence of this feature in our fellowship, wherever the gospel has become known.

Dr. Wardlaw's theory rests on the hereditary principle, as he supposes it to be taught in the covenant with Abraham. It stands thus: "Before the coming of Christ the covenant of grace had been revealed; and under that covenant there existed a divinely instituted connexion between children and their parents, according to which the sign and seal of the blessings of the covenant were, by Divine appointment, administered to children; and there can be produced no satisfactory evidence of its having been done away."—*Dr. Halley*, p. 535, 536. It is replied by Dr. Halley, with great justice, "No one is bound to produce 'satisfactory evidence of its having been done away' until some one produce satisfactory evidence of its having ever existed," p. 536. It was his connexion with Abraham that was marked by circumcision; not the connexion between the child and his immediate parent as such. A Jewish father might incur the forfeiture of his privilege, or, at least, neglect to recognise it in the rite; but this did not prevent the child, who, through him, was a son of Abraham, from claiming his privilege in that relationship; and it is clear that this was the idea in the minds of the Pharisees, when John and Christ admonished them not to deceive themselves by saying, " We have Abraham to our Father." Besides, it was not Abraham's children merely, but his servants also, his whole household, that were circumcised; and Ishmael as well as Isaac. Moreover, the glad tidings, as proclaimed to Abraham, and on which his covenant was based, had two parts: first, the ancient and general, which was that the nations should be blessed; secondly, the new and particular, that the nations should be blessed *in him*. The second was hereditary by its very nature; and the first is, by its nature, not hereditary. The one privilege was secured by a relation to Abraham, the other is secured only by a relation to Christ. But a personal relation to Christ is only to be attained by faith in him; and, therefore, if the analogy prevail at all, it can only apply to the baptism of such as are justified by faith in Christ Jesus.

The steps of this argument are stated almost entirely in Dr. Halley's own words; and it is hard to conceive how he could have escaped the conclusion. He further adds, " To notice the argument in favour of inducting children in this commission, founded upon the Jewish practice of baptizing the children of proselytes with their parents, may be thought necessary for the completeness of this inquiry," p. 575. "In a few words, it may be thus proposed.—' If,' as Dr. Lightfoot says, ' the Jews were as familiar with the baptism of infants as with their circumcision, the commission to baptize the nations could have been understood in no other sense than as including their children.'" "On this reasoning let me observe, whatever weight it may have, it rests ultimately, not upon Scripture, but upon a custom of the Jews," p. 576. These are Dr. Halley's own words, and they are most important, as showing his own estimate of his whole argument, examined in the second Lecture; and resting upon that presupposed existing idea by which the words of John and of our Lord were to be interpreted. It is a Jewish custom, set, as we have seen, directly against the expectation raised by ancient prophecy and inspired intimations given at the Advent; but now Dr. Halley, shifting the counter, adds, "I decline the aid of the Rabbi, who comes to me with his rolls of venerable parchments, to tell me that his fathers always baptized the children of their proselytes—I am not disposed to endorse the gospels with a superscription of Chaldaic authorities. This commission (of our Lord) is best illustrated by the subsequent conduct of the apostles. Their sense of the words is to be ascertained from their own practice," p. 577.

THE PROPOSED THEORY OF DR. HALLEY.

If the just rule of explaining the commission of our Lord by his own, and the words and practice of the Apostles, had been adopted, without any modifying appeal to proselyte baptism, from the beginning of Dr. Halley's work, much unnecessary trouble might have been spared to himself and to his readers. A single reference to Lightfoot, and the authorities collected by Moeschin, would have been sufficient to have shown the nature and source of the whole reasoning contained in the very large portion of his work devoted to this " Chaldaic endorsement," if not of the Gospel, certainly of his argument for infant baptism: for he does not even profess to find it in the words of Scripture; but, having assumed that he has found it in the practice of the Jews, he pleads now, that it is not excluded from the Lord's commission. It is not expressly stated there, Go and baptize children and grown persons, without any discrimination; but he pleads that the commission, as now to be explained by the practice of the Apostles, does not exclude the infants, but actually includes them, by implication, if not expressly. It commands the apostles (he says) to baptize all the nations, and all the nations must have included infants; it commands them to baptize all the nations, without assigning any restriction; and, therefore, it was, and is, the duty of Christians to baptize all the nations, literally if they can. The words of Dr. Halley, as relating to infants, are,—

" Every Gentile now, as distinctly as was every Jew, is born entitled to the external privileges of the Gospel. Dying in infancy, he is saved by the death of Christ; surviving, he has an inceptive right, conferred by grace, to salvation by faith in Christ, the forfeiture of which he incurs by unbelief, or by what may be considered the guilty act equivalent to unbelief, which, in heathen darkness, leaves him without excuse," p. 544, 545. "We restrict neither the sign nor the grace, but believe that all infants are reckoned, not unto the covenant of their parents, but by the first covenant of death unto the first Adam, and by the second covenant of life unto the second Adam, the Lord of heaven," p. 548. "In that state of covenanted privilege, whatever it be, in which Dr. Wardlaw places the children of believers, do I, without respect of persons, place the children of all men," p. 544. And, further, "I maintain, on the terms of the only command to baptize, that to baptize an infant is just as much the duty of the church, and a duty resting upon just the same authority, as to teach a Hindoo," p. 495. "Let it, therefore, be understood that, in our opinion, the great argument for the baptism of infants is the plain grammar of the only commission which we have received to baptize at all," p. 494. And, lastly, he adds, "This commission is best illustrated by the subsequent conduct of the Apostles. Their sense of the words is to be ascertained from their own practice," p. 577.

On these declarations of Dr. Halley, it is admitted that all Gentiles, as well as Jews, who die in their infancy, are saved by the death of Christ. The whole question relates not to those who are by a sovereign act of God removed from this earthly sphere of action, before they can partake in its duties; but to those who are retained here. The case of infants who die before actual sin, and the case of believers who die after justification, show that the fallen state is so under the influence of sin that Divine mercy itself cannot accomplish its aim without either death, or a transformation of fallen nature, equivalent to death. If all who are saved do not die, all must be changed, even where no wrath is designed. But, how is this personal change to be enforced on those who live? Dr. Halley says, baptism symbolises the necessity of repentance. How?—when the infant does not understand it? And with what effect?—when the unbeliever does not believe in it? And still further: when the Doctor affirms that "baptism is the sign of this covenant relation" (p. 553), unto which Jews and Gentiles are now born, and in which they are "reckoned by the covenant of life unto (Christ) the second Adam, the Lord from heaven," p. 548—if baptism were the sign of "this precious birthright" (p. 543), from which Dr. Halley says, that the unbelief of the parent cannot exclude the child, and from which the child cannot be excluded but by his own unbelief, or some equivalent sin—instead of symbolising the necessity of repentance, it would symbolise a state in which no repentance is needed, and the importance of so continuing in this state, that the bitterness of repentance may be avoided. On this view, the baptism proposed is not a baptism of repentance, but a baptism superseding repentance. It is initiating the child on the supposition that actual sin has not called for its exercise; and, the whole object of a teacher would, on the hypothesis, be to urge the rising infant never to allow of a suspicion respecting his personal interest in Christ, but to take the matter for granted from his natural birth. That is to say, the theory of Dr. Halley, in exact opposition to the words of Paul, declares, in the most extensive sense, that the children of the flesh are inheritors of the promise, " of the covenant of life," in " the second Adam, the Lord from heaven."

The wide extension and pernicious influence of this error, which contains all that is bad in Dr. Wardlaw and Dr. Owen, exhibits, in a painful light, the importance of this controversy.* It is diverting the whole attention from the fact of human depravity; and it is superseding the original necessity for personal regeneration by the word and the Spirit of life. Its very aim is to baptize all; and thus to destroy all distinction between man and man, until some actual and open transgression has called for church discipline, and, thereupon, for repentance. It identifies the church with the world; and makes it incumbent on the church to prove the unbelief of individuals seeking fellowship, instead of making them declare and testify their own faith. In fact, this controversy involves the whole question, whether there shall be a people set apart for Christ, a kingdom of heaven upon earth, or not.

But, Dr. Halley says, every Gentile, as every Jew,

* Stovel's Lectures on Baptismal Regeneration, pp. 181—214.

has "an inceptive right, conferred by grace, to salvation by faith in Christ; the forfeiture of which he incurs by unbelief, or by what may be considered the guilty act equivalent to unbelief, which, in heathen darkness, leaves him without excuse." What Dr. Halley can mean by "the guilty act equivalent to unbelief," is not clear from his work; in Scripture, no such guilty act is named. If it existed, however, one would think that its perpetration in gospel light would render it as fatal as when committed "in heathen darkness." But this unbelief, and its unknown equivalent, involve (Dr. Halley says) "the forfeiture" "of an inceptive right to salvation by faith in Christ." This is new doctrine. The Scriptures say that the blood of Christ cleanseth from all sin; and, that while the opportunity and will to believe in Christ co-exist, salvation is sure, previous unbelief and criminality notwithstanding. Dr. Halley says, The right is *inceptive;* that is, a right to begin salvation by faith in Christ. But why say, A right to *begin* salvation? The favour granted by God to man is not inceptive, but absolute; the proclamation is, He who believeth shall be saved, perfectly,—not begin to be saved, but go on to final glory. It requires immense care to extract an evangelical meaning from sentences of this kind, and especially a meaning on which an appeal for confirmation may be made to the grammar of our Lord's commission; yet, since the appeal is made, it would be well not to submit under discouragement too soon. Let us suppose, therefore, that a privilege, or right, is granted by free grace to salvation, by faith in Christ Jesus; then the "*inceptive*" privilege, or right, so granted, is the privilege, or right, of beginning salvation by faith in Christ Jesus. How, then, may a sinner be said to begin his salvation by faith in Christ Jesus? It is answered, Only in two senses: *first*, internally, when the sinner at first, in the action of his faith, subjects himself to the Redeemer and his work; *secondly*, externally, when the sinner, declaring his faith in Christ, openly separates himself on that ground from this sinful world. God has, in mercy, granted each sinner the privilege of doing these two things: he may secretly commit himself to Christ for perfect salvation, and he may openly declare that fact to the church and to the world; and God engages to honour both these acts by his own providence and judgment. The one is the inceptive, or the commencing point, of personal experience; the other is the inceptive, or commencing point, of personal fellowship: for, believers can only commune with believers, as believers become known. When Dr. Halley's words are translated, therefore, they declare, as the two essential elements of fellowship in the body of Christ, that God has granted to men, to all men who will use it, the privilege of becoming united to Christ by faith, and of being united to his people by a confession of that faith; for, with the heart man believeth unto righteousness, and with the mouth confession is made unto salvation. There, in each case, personal salvation begins.

If Dr. Halley had simply meant this, and stated

his meaning clearly, no room would have been found for controversy with us; because it is this beginning of salvation, first in the heart and then in the life, that the commission requires us to recognise in baptism; but under this hard conglomerate of words, the germ of an evil and bitter thought is manifest. The phrase "inceptive right" is intended to harmonise with a former phrase, " Every Gentile now, as distinctly as was every Jew, is born entitled to the external privileges of the Gospel." If it be asked what those privileges are, the former analysis of Dr. Halley's own words reply, They are first to hear of Christ, then to believe in him, afterwards to confess him, and then to be recognised as his member, child, servant, brother, co-heir in the favour of God. The privileges to which the word *external* may with strictness be applied, are those which are ordained for the production of faith, the recognition of faith, and the regulation of its activities; but neither of these are, as ordained of God, what Dr. Halley means. If he intended to say, that every human being is born entitled to the external privileges which lead to the production of faith, this would have been admitted; but, in order to place his infant baptism here, he must make it a means of producing faith, and become an advocate of sacramental grace; and, then, the affirmation of Scripture, " Faith cometh by *hearing*," would have been denied. Hence, therefore, in direct opposition to the natural and proper sense of his own expressions, he intends to affirm that, not only to those external gospel privileges which are ordained for the production of faith, but to those, also, which are ordained for the recognition of faith and the guidance of its action, all men are entitled, without any faith at all. This is the position he wishes to establish, by appealing to the commission of our Lord and the practice of his Apostles. Dr. Halley knows that the only badge of discipleship a believer is commanded to receive is that of baptism; and with this knowledge, he pleads that this should be administered without discrimination to all applicants. The effect of this would be to render the separate fellowship of believers extinct: but as the authority of the commission is pleaded, it is requisite to consider, first, the evidence thence derived; and, then, to review the practice of the Apostles.

THE COMMISSION.

In his appeal to the commission, Dr. Halley dwells with as much triumphant repetition of the English pronoun *them*, and the phrase " grammatical sense," as can with ease be reconciled to modesty. In the sentence, " Go ye forth, disciple all the nations, baptizing them into the name of the Father, and of the Son, and of the Holy Ghost, teaching them to observe all things whatsoever I have commanded you." * The word *them*, which follows the words baptize and teach, is used to translate the word αυτους, which is a masculine pronoun, and falls under

---

* Matthew xxviii. 19, 20.

the rule that a pronoun agrees with its noun in the antecedent proposition in number and gender, but derives its case from the verb in its own proposition. But the antecedent proposition here is, "Go and disciple all the nations;" the nations being neuter: by this rule, the masculine αυτους, *them*, cannot agree, therefore, with this antecedent noun. If the course of the reasoning seemed to require it, and exceptions to the rule could be found, to justify the referring of αυτους to the neuter antecedent, Dr. Halley should have produced the cases, to justify his departure from the rule; but he has not done so, he appeals to grammar, and in grammar he fails. It is believed that no example, to justify such a departure from this rule, can be found.

The facts of the case are recorded as history by Clement of Rome, who, writing in Greek, and at so early a period, may be admitted so far as evidence. He says:—

"The Apostles proclaimed to us joyful tidings from the Lord Jesus Christ,—Jesus, the Christ from God. The Christ, therefore, was sent forth from God, and the Apostles from the Christ; and, consequently, both became duly authorised by the will of God. Therefore, having received promises, and becoming bold through the resurrection of our Lord Jesus Christ, and confiding in the word of God, with a complete assurance of the Holy Spirit, they went forth joyfully, proclaiming that the kingdom of God was at hand. Having preached, therefore, *through regions and cities, being directed by the Spirit*, they ordained the first-fruits of their ministry to be bishops and deacons of those who might afterwards believe."—*Clemens Romanus, Epist.* i., *Sect.* 42.

If these facts of the case, as recorded by Clement, be brought into comparison with the several injunctions of the Lord, they will remove all obscurity from his intention. Clement tells us what the apostles did, and since they were under the guidance of the Spirit, this explains the meaning of our Lord when telling them what they ought to do. Since they were preserved from error by inspiration, their actions render certain what was the import of the instructions they received. But if Dr. Halley live to publish a second edition of his Lectures it will be requisite for him to guard his reasoning here from an appearance of special pleading, in which it is sometimes allowed that advocates may run for shelter to real or apparent difficulties. In the examination of Divine truth, however, he who has recourse to such a means of defence, should take especial care that no one set fire to the jungle in which he hides, for this will always prove, in the end, a greater calamity than any that can follow from open-hearted and fair investigation. The distance of time and the change of circumstances, since the Saviour used these words, may have created a difficulty in their explanation, especially as we now employ a language so very different from that in which he spoke, or that in which his words have been recorded; but it is not well for us to make the most of it, creating perplexity where it has no existence. We are quite sure that the phrase must have had a popular and obvious meaning, and one which the disciples understood and followed after his ascension;

for, in acting on his words, they had the testimony of his approval in signs and wonders wrought by Divine power and gifts of the Holy Spirit. This fact alone might lead us to the meaning of his words; for of all the possible interpretations that may be given to them, that should have the preference which regulated the disciples in their duty, and thus obtained this express Divine approbation.

Let it be supposed, then, that παντα τα εθνη (all the nations), is, as Dr. Halley affirms, the antecedent to *them ;* the question is, in what sense can εθνος (a nation) be taken, which will appear to have been acted upon by the apostles, and also approved of God?

In its first and primary sense, the word comprehends the organised parts of any people, incorporated under one government, as the Roman people, which means, the senate, the officers, and citizens of Rome, including every member of that republic who has arrived at age. These parts make one whole, the εθνος, or nation, of Rome. The nation of the Jews was often spoken of in the same way as one whole community. The children under age were rather the property than parts of the nation. If the command be, Go and baptize a nation, or the nations, or all the nations, in this sense, it is clear that the apostles never understood it so. The incorporated nation of the Jews was rejected. The attempt to baptize a whole community by one act, was absurd, since the act was clearly impossible, it was never attempted; and, indeed, the idea of national religion, as it is

CONSTRUCTIONS OF THE COMMISSION. 225

discussed in our time, never entered into the minds of the first disciples; they dealt exclusively with individuals, and laboured to produce, not national, but personal religion. Let Dr. Halley himself say how he could literally baptize, by one act, the English nation. If he use the word baptize, as if it meant to initiate, the initiating of the English nation into the church must involve an act of the government, and place the church in alliance with the government, which is utterly opposed to the words of Christ and the doctrine taught by his apostles.

A second and very popular sense in which the word εθνος (nation), and especially the phrase τα εθνη (the nations), was used by the Jews, is to signify *the heathen*. It then comprised all the people, belonging to any government whatever not included in the tribes of Israel. In this sense, the nations—that is, the heathen—with the Jews, make up the whole population of the earth. If the words be taken in this sense, the command would be, "Go, disciple all the heathen, baptizing them in the name of the Father, of the Son, and of the Holy Spirit, teaching them to observe all things whatsoever I have commanded you." It is quite clear, that this is not the sense in which the disciples understood the commandment; for, until the case of Cornelius occurred, they did not feel at liberty to baptize any heathen whatever. They were ready to disciple and baptize any Jew, residing among the heathen, but not the heathen themselves. It is also clear that the Lord did *not* use the words in this sense, as

Q

meaning the heathen, and not the Jews; for then no Jew could have been received into the church with his approval, whereas, so many of his people were, at the first, belonging to the tribes of Israel, that, amongst the heathen, the Christians were called Jews, and regarded as a part of the Jewish nation. The national sense, therefore, and the heathen sense of τα εθνη (the nations), must be alike given up.

A third sense of this phrase depends upon the word *all*—παντα τα εθνη, "*all* the nations"—if thus taken in the literal sense pleaded for by Dr. Halley, would mean, the heathen and the Jews taken together; and the command would then mean, Go, disciple and baptize all the Jewish and Gentile nations, or all the nations, Jewish and Gentile. But this, in the national and literal sense of Dr. Halley, will not hold good. For, first, the Jewish nation, as a community, was rejected: it was said, "Ye are not my people," and that saying is acted upon to this day; secondly, no national initiation of any people has ever taken place by Divine command; and, thirdly, the Apostles did not, at first, conceive that any heathen could be discipled and baptized into Christ. Hence the national and universal sense of the words must be relinquished; and these are the only senses which can be given to the words when, as Dr. Halley proposes, the law of grammar is broken, and *the nations*, a neuter antecedent, is made to join with *them*, a masculine pronoun.

A fourth sense is given to the phrase by assuming

what has been called the pronominal attraction. By this expression is meant the power which Greek pronouns appear to exert in drawing out of a foregoing noun of multitude, or of wider meaning, the part of its constituent elements, which forms the natural antecedent to the pronoun. Thus, in Acts viii. 9, it is said, " Simon astonished the nation, εθνος, of Samaria," to whom, it is added, " *all* gave heed, from the least to the greatest, because he had astonished *them*." Here " *the nation*" goes before the adjective and personal pronouns, *all* and *them ;* but *all* and *them* are plural and masculine, while εθνος (the nation) is singular and neuter. What, then, can the words *all* and *them* refer to in this sentence? The history shows, at verse 12; for, continuing the same arrangement of words, it is added, " But when *they* believed in Philip, proclaiming the joyful tidings which relate to the reign of God, and the name of Jesus the Christ, *they* were baptized, *both men and women*." The "men and women," therefore, who composed the nation of Samaria, were the persons referred to by the *all* and *them* whom Simon astonished, and who adhered to him; and they, the men and women who composed the nation, when they believed in Philip preaching, &c., were baptized. These " men and women," therefore, contained in " the nation," are the natural antecedents of *all, them*, and *they*, the pronouns of the sentence; and these pronouns are said to exert the power of attraction, by which these natural antecedents are drawn out of the foregoing and more comprehensive noun. If this construction be used in reference to the Lord's commandment it will stand thus: "Go forth, disciple the men and women who compose all the nations, baptizing *them* (the men and women you disciple) into the name of the Father, and of the Son, and of the Holy Ghost; teaching *them* (the men and women you disciple and baptize) to observe all things whatsoever I have commanded you." This construction, though not without its difficulties, has a great advantage over that propounded by Dr. Halley.

Lastly, the *common sense* construction of our Saviour's words consists in joining them with other expressions used by him with reference to the same design; as, for instance, that recorded in Mark xvi. 15, "And he said to them (the disciples), going forth into all the world, Proclaim ye the glad tidings to every creature: he who believeth, and is baptized, shall be saved; and he who believeth not, shall be condemned." If no puzzling twistification, arising out of controversy, had warped our judgments, common sense, looking at the whole case, would lead us to conclude, that these words, relating to the same subject, and uttered by the same infallible Lord, must harmonise with those recorded in Matthew. In both cases, therefore, it is said, "*Go forth!*" But where? The words of Mark say, "Into all the world;" and "*all the world*" must include "*all the nations*" in the world. But what are you to go for? It is said, "Make disciples." And how shall this be done? "Proclaim the joyful tidings to every creature." What, then, are these joyful tidings? Unquestion-

CONSTRUCTIONS OF THE COMMISSION. 229

ably, the tidings of salvation through the crucified Jesus. But who, then, shall be saved? He that believeth and is baptized. Who, then, shall be condemned? He that believeth not, *ipso facto*. Though the glad tidings of salvation be proclaimed to him, not having believed, he is condemned notwithstanding. "He shall not see life," "the wrath of God abideth on him." What, then, is a disciple? "If any man love father, or mother, or his own life, more than me, he *cannot* be my disciple; then are ye my friends, when ye do whatsoever I command you. If any man be in Christ Jesus he is a new creature; old things are passed away, behold, all things are become new." What, then, is it to make a disciple? To make him a new creature, a creature prepared to forsake all for Christ, and to do whatsoever Christ commands. How can this be done? Proclaim the joyful tidings to every creature; "faith cometh by hearing, and hearing by the word of God;" "with the heart man believeth unto righteousness, with the mouth confession is made unto salvation." But believing in the heart is not a *national*, it is a *personal* act. The disciples, therefore, must be made man by man; that is to say, each individual must be made a disciple, or made to believe, in his own person; or, wanting this, he is a condemned, a lost man, without refuge or appeal. This, then, is the command of our Lord, "Go, make persons disciples by proclaiming the joyful tidings of salvation, and convincing them of their truth and value." To this work, therefore, the apostles and the recognised disciples were called; but where was it to be performed? Mark says, "Go into all the world and do it;" but "*all the world*" contains "*all the nations*," and going into all the world, they must go through all the nations; before they have gone into all or every part of the world, they must have penetrated all the incorporated bodies of men whatever, and the leaven, by this activity, would leaven the whole mass of human society.

If this common-sense view of the case be taken, the words of our Lord, in Matthew, harmonise with those recorded by Mark and others: and they speak a definite sense, which must have been obvious to those who heard the words pronounced. The preaching designed to convert souls is plainly understood to be the means of making disciples; and the command would be, Disciple wherever you can, beginning at Jerusalem, and extending your labour through every nation into all the world. Disciple the persons: baptizing them, is added, because no disciple was to be recognised in any other way; but the disciple must have an existence before he can be recognised. Before he can be baptized "*into the name of* the Father, and of the Son, and of the Holy Ghost," he must be willing to bear that name and to act under its authority; and he must be like the disciples and friends of Christ, before he can keep all things which Christ had commanded them to keep. He must be a believer, therefore, to be a disciple; he must be a disciple before he can be a baptized disciple; he must be a baptized disciple before he can use the privilege and perform the duties of baptized disciples. The words of our Lord, therefore, on this view, contain a command to make and baptize believers in every nation throughout the world. He thus charges them with the fulfilment of his own purpose, as expressed in Luke xxiv. 46: " Thus it is written, and thus it behoved the Christ to suffer, and to rise from the dead on the third day, and that a proclamation of repentance and forgiveness of sins be made on his authority, beginning from Jerusalem, and" extending "*into all the nations,*" εις παντα τα εθνη, the very phrase, with *into*, which is used in Matthew's gospel.

This construction of the Lord's directions, derived from a plain and simple view of the whole case, has also this advantage: *It agrees with both the first and second interpretation of the Apostles, and shows how their actions could be approved by God himself, both before and after the case of Cornelius.* With respect to their judgment as well as their moral feelings, in the case before us, it is assumed that the Apostles were not blameable, because God was bearing them witness with signs and wonders and gifts of the Holy Spirit; and, therefore, as they were acting upon our Lord's commandment, the Divine approval is obtained to their interpretation of it. But since God did approve, and express his approbation so fully, it should seem that there must have been some sense in which the words could be taken, which would be true and valid in both cases, including, before the case of Cornelius, so much of the whole meaning as it was requisite for them to act upon, until that case expanded their view; this sense, also, in which the words were then taken, remaining true and uncontradicted, after the case of Cornelius had conveyed the additional information, on which they afterwards acted, receiving similar and continued expressions of the Divine approval. On these data there should be no dispute, and from them the conclusion is obvious; for the Gospel is a power of God unto salvation in every one that believeth, but in none other; and its power unto salvation was proved first in the Jews, but afterwards in the Gentiles. This seems to have been the design of our Lord in "beginning from Jerusalem:" he would first verify the power of his mercy in the place of his personal injury and sacrifice, and then extend its operation through the world. That their mission related to individual persons, and was to extend through all the world, appears to have been understood by the Apostles from the first; but the Jews were scattered through all the nations, and by making Jews the disciples of Christ, and baptizing *them* through all the nations, or in all the world, they would be obeying the commandment of our Lord. Hence their attention was, at the beginning, confined to Jews; and, as they were to begin with the Jews, this was approved. It was taking the words of Christ in a legitimate, although in a limited sense; but, when the time came, the case of Cornelius was produced to show the wider application of the law. By this, it was shown that they should make disciples through all the nations of the world, not of the Jews only, but of the Gentiles also. This mystery was "at the beginning *hid* in God," though it was comprehended in the Saviour's words. And since the action of the Apostles was sustained by the approving exercise of Divine power, both before and after the case of Cornelius, it should seem that this common-sense rendering of the words, which applies to both cases, must be the right one. In either case, they were making disciples in a way that might begin at Jerusalem, and extend through every nation into all the world; and this the Lord both commanded and sanctioned.

Lastly, This common sense rendering of the commission has the advantage of obtaining support from Dr. Halley's appeal to grammar. When he appeals to the word *them*, and says, with so much triumph, What is intended by *them?* in referring it to "*all the nations*," in the foregoing clause, because *them* is masculine and *the nations* is neuter, he violates the rule of grammar which determines that a pronoun must agree with its antecedent in gender, number, and person; and the learned Doctor gives no reason for this violation of grammatical law. But it is a law that pronouns may be used *absolutely*, an antecedent being understood, agreeing with the pronoun in gender, number, and person. Such a noun, too, is obviously suggested by the foregoing word. Μαθητης, *a disciple*, is masculine, and derived from the foregoing word, μαθετυειν, to make disciples; this would be a third person, and might be supplied in the plural number, which would make the sentence, if written throughout, stand thus:—" Go, make disciples, baptizing the disciples into the name, &c., and teaching the disciples you baptize to keep whatsoever I have commanded you." This not only shows the sense, but shows, from the otherwise unavoidable tautology, a reason for using the pronoun instead of the noun. Moreover, as we have seen, by making "*all the nations*" the subject of the verb baptize, the command is made to enforce an impossibility; since no man can baptize a nation at once, and national incorporation with his church was never the design of our Lord. But, by making "all the nations" the moral and social sphere in which the work of making disciples should be performed, all the instructions of our Lord are made to harmonise; and the language he uses is sustained by the highest Greek authorities.*

None of the foregoing constructions may be without their difficulties; yet, the idea of our Lord is plain. He sent his disciples to secure the conversion of other men as far as they were able, to recognise their converts in baptism, and to continue this work as long as the door of mercy remained open to one sinner who had not so entered it. This is clear, whatever difficulty may now attend the translation of our Lord's expression. But the proposal of Dr.

* Appendix No. III.

Halley, by violating the rule of grammar to which he appeals, makes the commandment, in its literal sense, an absurdity; while by observing the rules of grammar, as they do apply to the case, the commandment becomes, in its literal sense, at least practicable, and perfectly consistent with all the operations of the Lord's kingdom, and with every other expression of his will. But it is not in grammatical niceties only that the learned Doctor has failed: by using the term commission, not found in Scripture, he has formed his argument as though the words recorded by Matthew were all the instructions given by our Lord to his disciples, during the forty days in which he was seen of them, after his resurrection, many times, and spake to them concerning the visible kingdom just then about to be commenced. The word commission is very well, if carefully used, but it must not be allowed to conceal a multitude of facts essential to the argument. Call them the commission, or what you will, these words must be taken in harmony with, not in opposition to, the other instructions of our Lord, given at that time and on the same subject. It has been shown that these instructions include three acts, which naturally precede baptism: to proclaim the glad tidings, to bear witness to their truth and value, and to make disciples. These instructions all imply that faith comes by hearing, that faith justifies a man in becoming a disciple, and that such disciples must be made by teaching and testifying, before they can be baptized. The next part of these instructions require the

Apostles to baptize, or initiate, the disciples so made; and to teach them to observe all things which Christ had commanded his disciples to observe. The last part is a covenant, first with the disciples themselves, that the Lord would be with them in this work; and secondly, with their converts, that those who believed and were baptized, should be saved. They were thus justified in hoping, under his rule, for all that salvation could include. And thirdly, in respect to those who believe not, he covenants that they, from that very fact, shall be condemned; and, if condemned from that fact, of course not justified in anything, much less in becoming sons of God, in company with his disciples. Here, therefore, are at least ten articles of instruction given by the Lord himself, at the same time, and in relation to the same work; and Dr. Halley, crying out, The commission, the commission, I appeal to the commission! modestly takes three injunctions as the basis of his argument, and treats the rest as if they had never been given. It is painful to remind such a man that the whole body of truth, on any subject, cannot be complete without all its limbs; and that no reasoning based upon only three-tenths of the evidence, can be expected to obtain an universal belief.

But this is not all. Dr. Halley not only puts aside the proclaiming and witnessing, by which sinners are to be convinced and disciples are to be made, and then leaves out of his consideration the covenant made both with the disciples, their converts, and respecting unbelievers; so that nothing more remains than the three terms of Matthew, disciple, baptize, and teach—not using the other seven terms at all to explain them—but, as if this were not enough, he virtually casts the first of these away, and, as with a sword of glass, slashes at his opponents on the assumption that the Lord had only commanded the apostles to baptize and teach. Thus the making of disciples is thrown out; and he then gravely asks, why baptism is put before teaching, and answers that he is not compelled to explain.

It requires great courage to occupy such a position before a reading public; but Dr. Halley is more daring even than this: he evades the fact, that to baptize into (in such a case) means to initiate; and that to be initiated into the name, or under the authority, of the Father, and of the Son, and of the Holy Spirit, must require a willingness to act under the authority of these persons in the blessed Trinity; moreover, he positively conceals the additional fact, that the teaching *after* initiation relates to those things which Christ had ordained for the special, if not exclusive, observance of his initiated followers; and he plays upon the word teach, as if it related to those instructions which, in proclaiming the glad tidings and bearing witness to their truth, lead to the production of faith, or the making of disciples. This is very remarkable; for, after resting all his argument on the commission, and, in order to secure this limited ground, casting away seven other instructions on the same subject; when he has retained only three instructions instead of ten, he still, out of the remaining three, casts one more word aside, and then interprets the other two in a wrong sense; so that, when he seems to triumph over his own brethren, as well as his adversaries, it is found that not one term of the commission to which he appeals, is, by him, either rightly interpreted or properly applied.

It is this fact, more than his professed appeal to grammar, that seems to have filled the imagination of our brother, and given a most painful character to his work; for if, contrary to the rule, that every relative must agree with its antecedent in gender, as well as in number and person, we concede to Dr. Halley his demand, and let all the nations (*neuter*) be in disagreement joined to αυτους, *them*, the (*masculine*) pronoun;—unless we allow him, also, in the way we have described, to change the sense of the other words in the sentence, his cause is not served by the anomaly. For, let the three words stand together, though the seven other intructions of our Lord be all, for the moment, and for the sake of trying the argument, laid aside, these three words, disciple, baptize, and teach, are so placed as to render it impossible to change the import of our Lord's injunction, without, as our beloved brother has done, changing the import of the last two, and casting the first of them away. If the verb disciple be suffered to remain in the text, it must speak its own meaning, and enforce the action it describes, which is, so to influence the parties named that they may become disciples. If it be said, So influence all the nations that they may become disciples, the meaning must be, So influence the individuals who compose these nations that they may become disciples. What it is to become a disciple must be learnt from the Saviour's own words; but Dr. Halley himself says that baptism is "the badge of discipleship," and, therefore, the word baptize must apply to those who become disciples. But we have shown that repentance and faith are essential to discipleship, and, therefore, the command to baptize must apply to those who become penitent and believing; and this process of making persons believe and repent, and of baptizing the penitent and believing, may go on until all the people of all the nations have become baptized believers. This, however, is not what Dr. Halley means, nor can the thing he means, with any shadow of plausibility, be obtained, until he has not only broken the law of grammar, but actually perverted the meaning of every word which this injunction of our Lord contains.

THE APOSTOLICAL EXAMPLES.

Dr. Halley says, "The symbols of our faith," "if not of Divine authority, are profane inventions of men," p. 69. If such be the fact, in his own judgment, how can he be justified in thus treating those Divine instructions by which that authority is expressed? This is also the more inexcusable in him, because, while ostentatiously appealing to the positive authority of Scripture, and dexterously seizing every apparent support for his own theory, he rejects the elements of proof by which the whole subject under consideration is determined. The rejected instructions show, first, how the disciples are to labour in producing faith, and in making other disciples, by all the persuasion they can use, in proclaiming the joyful tidings of mercy, and in adding the testimony of their experience to the declaration. These rejected instructions show, also, the point at which the covenanted mercy justifies the hope of salvation, and the privilege of Christian fellowship—that is to say, when the hearer's faith prepares him to cherish that hope and to accept that fellowship in God's own way; the declared condemnation of unbelief shows the one only state of mind in which no Christian hope or privilege is justified of God; the evaded sense of baptize into or initiate under the authority of the Father, and of the Son, and of the Holy Ghost, shows the authority under which all Christian action must be performed, and all Christian hope must be entertained; and the instruction, " teach them to observe all the things I have commanded you to observe," clearly proves that each initiated disciple is to be placed, under Christ, on an equal footing with all whom he finds incorporated in the body of Christ. These instructions of the Lord are to be harmonised in the practice of the church, not rejected or evaded. In this rejection of elements essential to prove the matter in hand, Dr. Halley is the more inexcusable, because he has adopted the same method in those great practical examples which show the sense in which the instructions of our Lord were taken and acted upon by his inspired apostles. In the Pentecost, the event, the effusion of the Spirit, the character of the hearers, the doctrine of Peter, the conviction produced, the inquiry what shall we do? the exhortation, the promise, the result, are all important elements of proof; but Dr. Halley rejects them all, except the exhortation to repent and be baptized: and because Peter exhorted *every one* to repent and be baptized, Dr. Halley infers, that every one should be baptized *without* repentance. The same course is adopted with the case of the Samaritans, the Ethiopian, of Saul, of Cornelius, of Lydia, the jailor, and the twelve who were re-baptized at Ephesus. In each case, the decisive circumstances being left out, the argument is rested on a fraction of the evidence: if the cases be examined in connexion with his reasoning, they speak for themselves; and if they could have the advantage of speaking through a perfected translation, no answer to his work could be so perfect as those sacred documents to which Dr. Halley is at last obliged to appeal.

THE ARGUMENT FOUNDED ON EPISTOLARY PASSAGES.

These passages will be considered separately hereafter. The argument founded upon them may be briefly stated in four particulars. *First*, it is assumed and admitted by Dr. Halley himself, that these passages do refer to that baptism in water which constitutes the rite by which Christians were initiated as disciples of our Lord. *Secondly*, from the passages themselves, it is clear that the hope of salvation, and the privileges of God's children, were recognised in the persons who had been baptized. Indeed, such persons are never supposed to require conversion to God, or a regeneration of the soul, unless their sin and unbelief after baptism had implicated their sincerity. Hence, *thirdly*, it is inferred that baptism must have either implied the existence of personal regeneration and faith, or it must have produced it; but the Apostle affirms, that faith comes by hearing, and not by baptism; and, therefore, the baptism must have implied its previous existence and development. *Lastly*, the typical descriptions of baptism are such as imply the pre-existence of faith, and cannot be true to nature unless the authors of those passages had assumed that each baptized person had been received on the credible profession of that faith which indicates and proves a regeneration of the soul. The elucidation of this last statement will be obtained by considering each typical affirmation made of baptized persons separately.

First, 1 Peter iii. 20—22, "They are saved by water." To save, is to separate from a cause and state of ruinous evil. The water, in this case, is the instrument; the flood is the type. The old earth is a type of worldly society; the new earth, of the church. The water lifted the ark up off from the old earth, and landed it on the new; so baptism taketh a man up from worldly society, and places him in the church. This is not done by washing away the filth of the flesh; but by the answer of a good conscience towards God. But the act of a good conscience towards God, in separating from the world, for his sake, cannot be performed without faith. The infant has no consciousness, and, therefore, no conscience in the act at all, good or bad. The man who professes to do it, without possessing faith, is a hypocrite, and can have no good conscience towards God.

Secondly, Titus iii. 4—7, "They are saved by a washing of a new birth." The new birth relates to the new earth, or the church, into which the disciple is born; but to be born, implies that the thing brought forth has life, and is not an abortion. To be born, is to be brought forth alive; to be *still-born*, is to be brought forth dead. But a person who has no faith in Christ cannot be called a subject of spiritual life. Moreover, baptism does *not* save by a removing of the filth of the flesh, which might be done without faith, but yet it does save by a washing of a new birth: the washing of the new birth, therefore, must mean the answer of a good conscience towards God, which cannot be secured in putting away sin, for God's sake, without faith, because to have no faith in God is itself, of all others, the damning sin.

Thirdly, Romans vi. 3, "As many as have been baptized into Christ, have been baptized into his death." Now, the life of Christ on earth was an entire and absolute separation from all fellowship with the rebellious world, as his death was a submission to its mortal malignity rather than participate in its treason. To be baptized into his death, therefore, is a very strong expression, by which our Apostle describes the entering into fellowship with that holy and merciful decision of character by which the Saviour came to his crucifixion. Hence, it is repeated, we are crucified to the world, to sin, &c. Not merely borne away from the old earth, or worldly society, but separated by covenant through a mortal hatred of its spiritual treason and defilements. A further type is added in the words, being "planted together in the likeness of his death;" for the slips that are planted together, live or die in the same soil, and on the same elements; and, hence, the Christian enters into fellowship with the mortal decision of our Lord, as one who intends to live or die, to grow or perish, with him, by the same principle, and through the action of the same elements. The other part of the idea is also expanded; for the disciple is not only born into a new world, but enters it with a new intention: "as many as were baptized into Christ, were baptized into his death; that like as Christ was raised from the dead, we also might rise to newness of life." To suppose that this mortal decision could exist, in separating from the old sinful world, and that the energy of a new life should be brought into the new world, the church, without faith, is absurd.

Fourthly, Colossians ii. 12, "We are buried with him in baptism." This refers to the persons who are separated from the old earth, the sinful world, as Christ, when he was buried, exercised his decision in submitting to the action of death, and we, in baptism, enter into fellowship with that decision; and that decisive separation from the world, has reference to the entrance into the church, which is called a rising from the dead. So that it would be more consistent for a living man to appear and act as a dead and rotten body in the tomb, than for Christians to conform to the world from which they are separated. The nature of the case, therefore, implies the necessity of faith; and, besides, it is said, that this very act of rising from the dead is performed by the faith of the operation of God, who raised Christ from the dead; and this rising, by faith in the operation of God, is said to be a rising from sin, and it is connected with the forgiveness of sin.

Fifthly, Galatians iii. 27, " As many as have been baptized into Christ have put on Christ." This putting on Christ is a type expressing the character or livery assumed in the new world, the church, and this is not a mere profession, but an actual privilege; for, he saith, " Ye are all sons of God." But this privilege of being a child of God is placed by Paul, in Romans viii., in constant union with justifying faith, and here he adds, " Ye are all sons of God by faith in Christ Jesus."

Without descending more fully into particulars, therefore, we see here a typical exhibition of baptism which necessarily combines it with the action of faith, and the existence and fruit of spiritual life. The disciple is lifted up from the old earth, and placed in the new; taken out of the world, and put into the church. He is separated from the world by a mortal decision, and he enters the church with vital devotedness. He is separated from the world as one that is buried; and he enters the church as one that has risen from the dead. This rising from the dead is performed by faith in the operation of the Divine power; and it is explained to be a rising from sin for God's sake, by Divine aid, and with Divine forgiveness.

Lastly, This entering the church is bearing the likeness or livery of the Redeemer, and enjoying the privilege of *sons* of God. It is impossible that baptism should be so represented without faith. If any one could suppose it, the words of Paul decide the question; he saith, " Ye who have been baptized into Christ, have put on Christ, and are sons of God," —*all*, for he adds, " Ye are all sons of God." But how ? By baptism without faith ? By no means; for he saith, " Ye are all sons of God, by faith in Christ Jesus."

These sons of God, therefore, had baptism and faith too; and it only remains to show which precedes the other. Does the baptism produce the faith ? or, is faith required in baptism ?

This argument, as stated in the Woolwich Lectures, delivered on Baptismal Regeneration, in the year 1843, consists in the following brief propositions. It would have been kind in Dr. Halley, if, while engaged on the subject, he had considered its force, or shown its fallacy. It has been rendered notorious by the wrath it has provoked amongst his brethren, and these " Lectures on the Sacraments" which Dr. Halley delivered, appear to be presented as a shield to them in this extremity. This, however, they cannot be, unless the argument be answered; because it is clear, from what has gone before, that, in these epistolary passages, faith and baptism go together. Which, then, goes first? Does baptism produce faith? Dr. Halley says, "No;" and he is right, as these passages prove. For,

1. It must be admitted, to the Tractmen, that the question is one which must be decided by Scripture alone; and not by any human reasoning whatever.—*Woolwich Lectures*, p. 94.

2. It must, also, be admitted, that those passages in which the inspired writers themselves have declared the condition of all baptized persons, in their time, are of the greatest possible importance.—*Ibid.*

3. It must be conceded that these passages, 1 Pet. iii. 20—23, Rom. vi. 3—13, Gal. iii. 27, Col. ii. 10—15, and Titus iii. 4—7, are all precisely of this kind. Dr. Halley himself allows, distinctly, that these do refer to baptism; and, therefore, that they do describe the assumed condition of baptized persons in the time of the Apostles, and in their estimation. —*Ibid.*, p. 95.

4. It must be admitted, that these passages describe the supposed and recognised condition of *all* baptized persons in the Apostles' time; "as many of you as were baptized into Christ," means all who were baptized into Christ.—*Ibid.*, p. 96.

5. It must be admitted, that the affirmations made of baptized persons, in these passages, involve the

whole business of salvation. If they were truly sons of God by faith in Christ Jesus, their salvation was secure; if they professed this in hypocrisy, without repentance and forgiveness, and continued so, their salvation was lost.—*Woolwich Lectures*, p. 97.

6. It must, also, be admitted, that all these affirmations were personal, and not vicarious. It was the baptized person himself who put on Christ; he did it for himself, and in his own person; he did not become a child of God by another, or for another, but by his own faith, and for his own good.—*Ibid.*, p. 98.

7. It must, also, be admitted, that it is nowhere implied in Scripture, that any Christian had not been regenerated, or that persons could be admitted as dead members into the body of Christ, and then afterwards be for the first time quickened. The truth of these affirmations is proved by these passages, because the actions said to be performed are such as involve the personal exercise of a spiritual life, which is contrary to the supposition.—*Ibid.*, p. 99.

8. It is also clear, that all these affirmations are made absolutely without any reference to time, or subsequent incidents, that could in any way produce a change in the hearts of baptized persons. They are as true of persons baptized ten minutes, as of persons who were baptized ten years ago, and of all alike.—*Ibid.*, p. 103.

9. It is also clear, that the affirmations here made necessarily imply the existence, development, and use,

of personal, intelligent, and voluntary action. The putting on of Christ, and putting off the world, can mean nothing less.—*Woolwich Lectures*, p. 104.

10. These actions of separating from the world, putting on of Christ, becoming crucified to sin, to the world, rising into newness of life, &c., are such personal actions as involve faith, and whatever God hath required as the condition of salvation; and they lead to whatever he has promised in the element and experience of salvation.

Dr. Halley, therefore, is perfectly right in saying, with all the eloquence and emphasis he employs against the Tractmen, that baptism is not here represented as the means of producing faith, because the things said to be performed in baptism imply the existence, and involve the exercise, of faith. If these passages be true, there could have been no proper *reception* of baptism where faith did not exist; and there could have been no proper *administration* of baptism, where that faith was not credibly professed. To say, therefore, that baptism produced faith, is to say that baptism provided its own pre-requisite; it is as much as to say that it produces itself. Dr. Halley is quite right in saying that baptism is not a regeneration, because all these views of baptism suppose the regeneration to have previously taken place; for how can a child be born who has never been generated? and can a man be born again who has never been *re*generated? Existence must precede action; and, therefore, it is not only true that baptism does not produce regeneration and faith, but it is also true that the indiscriminating theory of Dr. Halley, by which faith and regeneration, the ancient and authorised pre-requisites of baptism, are laid aside, is a clear and absolute violation of the doctrine which these passages contain and teach.

Such is, in brief, the argument founded on these epistolary passages, as it was delivered at Woolwich, in 1843. It is necessary to go no further into that argument now, because the subject is taken up, in this course, just where the inquiry then terminated. All that is required here, therefore, may be comprised in this brief individualisation of that argument.

DR. HALLEY'S TREATMENT OF THE EPISTOLARY PASSAGES.

The necessity for the foregoing recapitulation will be seen in Dr. Halley's treatment of the argument so educed, and of the passages themselves on which that argument is based. His words are, "A baptized infant was as competent to put on Christ, as a circumcised infant was to do the whole law; but this reasoning on passages which manifestly refer only to the parties addressed, *as many of you*, is undeserving the trouble of serious refutation," p. 528. Perhaps it may be undeserving of *refutation* at all; but if he appeal to the practice of the Apostles for an illustration of their Lord's instructions, in the kingdom of heaven, it cannot be undeserving of careful study. Without these passages, moreover, the evidence sought on the subject Dr. Halley has undertaken to explain will be incomplete. These passages, also, deserve to be the more carefully considered by him, because on them, and the connexion which they show between vital religion, personal salvation, and the baptismal initiation into the kingdom of our Lord, the advocates of baptismal regeneration have built their strongest fortress. Baptism is so connected with personal religion, in these passages, that the Tractmen have argued a power in that rite to produce it. If it be right to baptize infants, which Dr. Halley has undertaken to prove, he is bound to show how his baptized infants can be so spoken of as these passages so applied would indicate, without assigning to the rite of baptism the power of communicating grace, which these, his brethren, demand for it. By delaying to consider the argument founded on these passages, Dr. Halley has abandoned the very thing he had undertaken to perform. He and his brethren have no right to condemn the Tractmen until their arguments have been refuted. This unfortunate practical error has already betrayed a large portion of the English public into the hands of Catholics and semi-Catholics. Before Dr. Halley breaks the chain of this delusion, frees his own practice from its alliance, and finds and exposes that elementary and first error of this controversy, which he professes to seek, he must not only give these epistolary passages a careful study, but show how they, with the apostolical practice recorded in the Acts, the instructions given in the Lord's commission, the preparatory labours of Christ and John, and the predictions of ancient prophecy, harmonise in that conglomerate of individuals, which, without any common and distinguishing principle of union, he proposes to form by his indiscriminating baptism. He will have much to consider, and to refute, too, before this has been effected: and if, foreseeing the difficulty, he refuse the undertaking, having gone so far, he is bound to produce some other system, in which all these elements of Divine instruction will harmonise; although it should be found at last, in the long but undeservedly dishonoured practice, of baptizing accredited believers only.

The fact is, Paul's affirmations relate to baptized persons, as such, and therefore show the nature of their action in the rite they had received; moreover, the affirmations are in the past tense, and show the action to have been performed when they were baptized. He says, therefore, to the Galatians, " Ye are all sons of God by faith in Christ Jesus; for, as many of you as were baptized into Christ have put on Christ." If there were amongst them some sons of God by faith in Christ Jesus, not yet recognised in their baptism, this would not affect the argument; for, his affirmation is, that all who were baptized into Christ had put on Christ. This was the thing, then, done; sincerely or insincerely, it was done; and the doing it was the thing referred to in the whole argument of Paul. But Dr. Halley says, that every baptized person is *to* repent and put on Christ; and *to* become a son of God by faith in Christ Jesus. His expression is *future*, the Apostle's is in the *past* tense. The one says it is to *be* done, the other says it *was* done, and in that act; the affirmation of Dr. Halley is inconsistent with himself, because he supposes a ground of baptism which requires no repentance. But, besides its inconsistency with itself, it falls at once before these passages of St. Paul; and, the argument from which he turns, as being " undeserving the trouble of serious refutation," is one against which his system has no defence.

If four passages* only be collated, the affirmations made of baptized persons amount, at least, to nineteen; and not less than seven practical inductions are drawn from the facts so stated. Whatever these might be, they ought to be considered. But the character of the facts and inferences render this even more imperative. Those who are baptized into Christ, are said to be baptized into his death, buried with him, planted with him: their faith is said to have come, they are sons of God by faith in Christ Jesus, they have put on Christ, are one in Christ, a seed of Abraham complete in Christ, circumcised with the circumcision without hands, buried with him, risen with him, quickened with him, forgiven their sins, saved by the washing of a new birth and by a renewing of the Spirit, justified, and heirs according to the hope of eternal life. Whatever the Holy Spirit may mean by these affirmations, and however wrong the Baptist brethren may be

* Romans vi. 3—13. Galatians iii. 25—29. Colossians ii. 10—15. Titus iii. 4—7.

supposed to be in affirming that such affirmations can only be made on the supposition that the persons baptized were accredited as the subjects of saving faith; it would have been kind in Dr. Halley to have shown how these affirmations may be made, without alteration, of infants and unbelievers, whom he has baptized without any discrimination. It is the more important that he should do this, because every baptized person is now likely to read these words; and it is the more important that he should know how they can apply to himself, because the apostle who makes these affirmations, infers from them the obligation to walk with Christ in newness of life, the hope of being planted in the likeness of his resurrection, of being freed from sin, and of being under grace; he infers, also, the duty of retaining, without any change, their position in Christ, their freedom from human judgment and reprehension on rites and forms of worship, and their obligation to maintain a character distinguished from the ordinary habits and customs of this world, and to risk eternity on the position they occupied in Christ. Surely these are matters deserving serious thought and explanation. Besides, the Tractmen are affirming with many voices, and in many ways, that the baptism with which these affirmations are so associated, is the appointed means of producing that change of character and state, with which alone the affirmations and inferences do harmonise. Why should Dr. Halley pass by such an opportunity of blunting, if not breaking, this great weapon of sacramental error. His book proves that such an explanation could not have been withholden from indifference or from unkindness, nor yet because the arguments of the Tractmen are unanswerable; because, as we have seen, a glance at these facts which Paul affirms, will show that many of them are moral, and intellectual, and voluntary acts, and must have been performed by the persons who were themselves baptized; and, therefore, that they imply a previous consideration and belief. This might be so said as to prove that all the Tractmen affirm to be the effect of baptism, was, in the Apostles' time, and by the Apostles themselves, deemed *the indispensable conditions* of baptism. Dr. Halley might thus have broken their system on their own heads; but he has not done it. It is easy to see that if he had, in breaking their system, he would have smashed his own, by proving that all these apostolical authorities oppose and condemn the baptism of infants and unbelievers altogether. But Dr. Halley has declined this task, and says that the argument is not worthy the trouble of serious refutation.

AN ILLUSTRATION.

It is worthy of careful remark, that this line of argument has not altogether escaped Dr. Halley himself. When dealing with the evidence brought by Tractmen from the Fathers, he clearly shows that, in some cases, the vital change of heart required in our salvation is declared to have preceded baptism. This is admitted, most distinctly, in the following words, which relate to Tertullian : " Sometimes conversion is declared to have preceded baptism, and baptism is only the sealing, or assurance, or act of faith; as, when Tertullian says, 'The laver is the sealing of faith, which faith begins from the faith of penitence. We are so washed, not that we may cease from sinning, but because we have ceased, since we are already washed in heart, for this is the first baptism of the hearer.'"—*Dr. Halley*, p. 268. This is very correct, and the argument comes home upon the Tractmen; for, if conversion was a prerequisite or condition of baptism, it could not be regarded as an effect of baptism. It is in vain that the Tractmen distinguish between regeneration, the beginning of the spiritual life, and conversion, the act of a regenerated person; for, if conversion, the act of the regenerated person, be a pre-requisite to baptism, then regeneration must also be a prerequisite, because the act cannot be performed until the person has been regenerated. In fact, if conversion be a pre-requisite of baptism, then, no one, infant or adult, ought to be baptized, whose conversion to God has not been credibly avowed. This argument, and the facts on which it rests, are admitted by him most fully with reference to Tertullian, who afterwards comes to be abused. But, though the facts are equally clear in Justin Martyr, the admission of Dr. Halley is more cautious. His words are, " Although he (Justin Martyr) speaks of obtaining remission of sin by the water, he represents the person as having previously repented, making this remission consequent upon his repentance. Although he calls baptism, regeneration" *(a new birth)*, " yet elsewhere he distinguishes them, for he speaks of the washing, εἰς ἀναγέννησιν, for regeneration" *(new birth)*, " and, therefore, distinct from it. Would it not appear that he calls baptism, regeneration, merely as a symbol of regeneration, the true and inward baptism?"—*Dr. Halley*, p. 252. Here regeneration is confounded with *the new birth*, and an obscurity is produced by introducing the phrase " for regeneration," or for a new birth. The fact is, Dr. Halley elsewhere refers to another part of the same paragraph, where Justin describes the baptism and the privilege of the baptized disciple. This mode of treating Justin's words would lead a reader to conclude that his writings are full of contradictions; and yet, this is not the case. It only requires the admission, which has been so clearly made with reference to Tertullian, that conversion and regeneration are declared to precede baptism, and that baptism is the new birth of the converted person; all will then be perfectly clear. It is very remarkable that the concession should be made so fully in favour of Tertullian, and when the facts are equally clear, with so much caution, in respect to Justin; yet Dr. Halley does, even with respect to Justin, say " he represents the person as having previously repented, making his remission consequent upon his repentance." On this admission, therefore, regeneration and repentance must have preceded baptism; and baptism was the new birth of a regenerated penitent. This is very near to the truth; and if this sense of the words be carefully preserved, many passages of the Fathers will cease to be either heretical or absurd. But how shall we explain the fact, that Dr. Halley could see and use this reasoning fully in Tertullian, admit it with great caution in Justin Martyr, but reject it altogether in the writings of St. Paul? There, nineteen statements are made which can be true of none but regenerated persons; baptism is called their new birth; the regenerated persons are said, in their new birth, to put on Christ, and become sons of God; it is expressly stated, that they were sons of God by their faith in Christ Jesus; while John says, that Christ himself gave the power or privilege of becoming sons of God to all who believed on his name. In fact, the truth is set forth with greater variety of expression and use in Paul than in either of the two Fathers which have been named, and yet Dr. Halley cannot see it. Whatever be the reason of this, it is to be regretted, because, until the truth can be seen in St. Paul, as well as in Tertullian, the question never can be settled. It is easy to cast Tertullian overboard, and to call him a son of Jonah; and then the truth, which can be seen in his pages only, falls under his disrepute; but when the fact, as it stands in the writings of St. Paul, comes to be admitted in all its force, it will be found that he also represents the baptized person as having previously repented and believed, and, therefore, as having been previously regenerated. It will then be found that regeneration and the first act of regenerated persons, are, by Paul, made pre-requisites of baptism;

and, therefore, cannot be regarded as effects of baptism. The Tractmen will then be answered, and then it will be proved, from Paul and Tertullian too, that no person who has not been regenerated, and in whom the first acts of the new life have not been credibly avowed, whether an infant or an adult, can be eligible to Christian baptism.

THE BODY OF CHRIST.

All these expressions of Paul imply a moral and personal compact, founded on the profession and recognition of individual repentance for sin, and a confiding subjection to our Lord Jesus Christ for time and for eternity. The disciples, united by baptism, in this fraternity, are variously called the body of Christ, the family of God, the elect and peculiar people, the one new man in Christ, and the kingdom. The churches were assemblies of these disciples meeting, under the law of Christ, for edification and worship, in different places, choosing their own servants and ministers, as the case might dictate. The baptized disciple was received, when accredited, in any church or assembly of disciples whatever; and, wherever he met with them, he bore the responsibility, and claimed the privilege, of a disciple. The action, interests, and inheritance of this community, had so little to do with time, that the disciples were said to be baptized on the hope of the resurrection of the dead. From its very constitution and aim, therefore, having all its life in Christ, and all its hope in heaven, this body could have no place or affinity for men who did not believe, or infants who could not understand, the things of Christ and of eternity. The Lord offers, for disciples so united with himself, his mediatorial prayer recorded in the seventeenth of John; in which he says, "Neither pray I for these alone, but for all those who shall believe on me through their word."

THE INCORPORATION.

Through the whole of our Lord's ministry on earth, with that of his forerunner, the community of disciples was forming. The last instructions relating to it were given seven days before Pentecost. The incorporation of the community was perfect, therefore, when the Lord ascended up on high; but its aggressive action commenced when the Spirit came, and under his influence. Indeed, this incorporated body of disciples is the seat of the Holy Spirit's ministrations; and every one rightly admitted into its fellowship has a baptism in water for his initiation; a baptism in the Spirit for his guidance and support; and a baptism in fire or trial, to exercise, evolve, and purify his principles.

PRACTICAL ILLUSTRATIONS.

From former statements it has been seen that, previously to the Pentecost, the disciples acted as a body set apart preparatory to a particular design. They waited through the interval between the ascension of the Lord and the gift of the Holy Spirit prayerfully attending to the business of their own community, and electing another apostle instead of

Judas, who had fallen, which was done by vote, first submitting the choice to a casting of lots, and then resolving on the appointment of him on whom the lot fell.* In this posture of mind they waited for the promise of the Father until the day of Pentecost was fully come. The promise of the Spirit was then fulfilled on *them*, and not on others who were not disciples. By this act of Divine mercy and power, the highest possible sanction was given to their views and previous action; and the action to which they were led by the Spirit explains more fully the Divine intention. By this holy unction they are exalted in their separated character, and efficacy is given to their operations, in this incorporated body, as far as they could influence the men of this world, from whom they were separated. The baptized believers are endowed with gifts which prove them to be in favour and union with God in Christ; the unbelieving and unbaptized mass of society is addressed in the character of rebels against God, and murderers of Messiah. On this ground they are called to repentance of their sin, to faith in his promise, and an open devotion of themselves, in baptism, to his fellowship and service. All the arguments of Peter go to this point; and whether the gift of the Spirit which endowed the disciples, or the power which was given to the truth, be considered, the hand of God becomes visible in both, conferring its holy and divine sanction to the principle of their fellowship. The fruits of their

* Acts i. 26.

faith proved its reality, as well in the first disciples as in their converts. They "gladly received the word;" they united with the despised followers of Jesus; "they were stedfast in the Apostles' doctrine, and the fellowship, and the breaking of bread, and the prayers;" "they were together, and had all things common;" "they sold their possessions and goods, and parted them to all as every man had need; continuing daily with one accord in the Temple, and breaking bread from house to house, they ate their meat with gladness and singleness of heart, praising God." This is not said of a few, but of "all that believed," that gladly received the word and were baptized. The force of their conduct was felt by observers, they had favour "with all the people;" and "fear came upon every soul." If these things are not sufficient to elucidate and confirm the truth, we have, besides, a continuous and twofold confirmation of the Divine approval; for the signs and wonders wrought by the Apostles were Divine acts, and it was the Lord, who "added to the church daily such as were being saved," Acts ii. 41—47.

THE FIRST APPREHENSION OF PETER.

The healing of the lame man, Acts iii. 1—9, forms a single case in which the Divine power gave its sanction to all the operations of the church. The attention thereby awakened was a natural and designed effect; and the defence of Peter, when seized by the authorities, is founded on the same constitutional principles with those on which he acted and spoke on the Pentecost. He addressed the rulers in the same way as that in which he had before addressed the people. He pleads the exaltation of the crucified One, declares that he was sent, and so exalted, "to bless them in turning every one of them from his iniquities."* The action which he urges on this ground is the same: "Repent ye, therefore, and be converted, that your sins may be blotted out, when the times of refreshing shall come, from the presence of the Lord."† This was their word or doctrine; this many heard and believed; and the number is stated to have been about five thousand.‡ The nature of their faith is seen in the difference of their action when compared with that of the rulers. The latter threatened, and forbade the teaching; the former submitted, avowed their faith, and joined the disciples. The obedient disciples, not only separated from the rulers and the impenitent, they appealed to God, and pleaded his covenant in the second Psalm. Their appeal was made on the great struggle of their negotiations, and the resistance which opposed them. They said, "Now, Lord, behold their threatenings, and grant unto thy servants, that with all boldness they may speak thy word, by stretching forth thine hand to heal, and that signs and wonders may be done by the name of thy holy child Jesus."§ There is a definiteness in the prayer, which shows that it was offered under a conviction that this society acted

* Acts iii. 26. † Acts iii. 19. ‡ Acts iv. 4.
§ Acts iv. 29, 30.

in recognised union with the exalted Lord; and there is a promptness, as well as a distinctness, in the answer which God gave; the house was shaken, they were filled with the Spirit; the thing they asked was done. With great power gave the Apostles witness of the resurrection of the Lord Jesus, and great grace was upon them all. Indeed, the movement of the time was the action of Jehovah, more than that of the men; and his action affords Divine testimony that the association included the recognition of a faith which he himself approved, Acts iv. 23—37.

THE CASE OF ANANIAS AND SAPPHIRA.

The awful visitation of God in punishing the crime of Ananias and Sapphira is a further illustration of the principle on which the church reposed its union. They both were, without doubt, baptized as disciples. They were united in this common fellowship, and joined in that common struggle to which all the disciples of our Lord were, at that time, appointed. Their sinful peculiarity is found in the deficiency of their faith. They could not trust the Lord with all their interests; and the withholding from him a part involved a peculiarity on which they could not face the general feeling. The order of the society was that of absolute devotedness, and they would feel reproached by any appearance of reservation. This induced the lie for which they died. If such an event had passed unnoticed, it might have been supposed that the association, and its baptism, were indiscriminate; but scarcely a more powerful proof of discrimination can be supposed than that which is here given, where an insincere professor of devotion dies, by the visitation of God, because the profession he makes is deemed a lie against the Holy Spirit dwelling in the society. How this struck the half-convinced observers is clear from the history: "of the rest," like Ananias and Sapphira, "no man durst join himself unto them."* The fear of their avenging God attended the disciples in their action and their fellowship. "The fear of their God came especially on all the church."† The church became solemnised, and "terrible as an army with banners." The Divine realities with which believers had to do invested their profession with an awe which struck the unbelieving with dread; and yet believers were the more added to the Lord, "multitudes both of men and women."‡ How can these things be reconciled? The church was both dreadful and attractive at the same moment. This is true; but not to the same individual characters. To the fearful, the impenitent, and the unbelieving, she was dreadful, because God was in the midst of her; but to the penitent and confiding, she was lovely, because her God was the God of their salvation.

THE SECOND APPREHENSION OF PETER.

The whole action which originated in the punishment of Ananias affords a further illustration of the polity which God had appointed in the body of Christ.

---

* Acts v. 13.   † Acts v. 11.   ‡ Acts v. 14.

The hand of God, so clearly seen in that event, solemnised and invigorated the disciples, awed the insincere, and encouraged the converted; so that believers were the more added to the Lord, "multitudes both of men and women." The consequence was inevitable: Jerusalem was moved, the adjacent cities were moved; the multitudes crowded in to hear; through the streets sick persons were brought out on couches, that the shadow of Peter might fall on them as he passed. The leaven of Divine truth, and the principles of our faith, were in active operation. The authorities could not rest. The Sanhedrim was convened, the Apostles were seized, and the common prison was used for their confinement. The matter was brought to a crisis; authority was opposed to authority; the two communities were brought into open and hostile collision. With this fact, so clearly written, who can doubt that the disciples were separated from the world? and when they are delivered from the prison-house by miracle, who can deny that they were separated by their faith?

This scene shows what the Holy Spirit intended by that beautiful figure, "God hath made bare his holy arm in the eyes of all the nations." A visibility and effect were given to the action of Divine power, which no one could mistake. The occasion and the object for which it was revealed, are rendered indisputable by the words of the Angel: "Go stand and speak in the temple, to the people, all the words of this life."* "This life" can mean nothing but the

---

* Acts v. 20.

life in which the disciples were united, and to which they were devoted in their profession. "The words of this life" are the instructions under which that profession was assumed, and the law by which it was regulated. If "this life" had no peculiarity, why should it require a specific law for its direction? and, if its peculiarity was without faith, how can we account for these interpositions, since, without faith, it is impossible to please God? Their declaration to the people, in defiance of their rulers, is proof that those words of this life were intended to produce faith in individuals; and this production of faith in individuals, was the very thing which these rulers intended to prevent. The facts and doctrines of the Gospel they do not dispute; the visitation of Ananias and Sapphira, which might have been brought against the Apostles, is not named; it bore with too much distinctness the mark of Divine interference, and, therefore, the whole proceeding of the elders is based on an appeal to their own authoritative injunction, "Did not we strictly command you that ye should not teach in this name? and, behold, ye have filled Jerusalem with your doctrine, and intend to bring this man's blood upon us."* But how could the blood of the crucified Jesus be brought upon them, except the teaching which they prohibited had produced a faith which led the possessors of it to act in his behalf? It was this, the devoted zeal of the converts, which was before their

* Acts v. 28.

eyes, and that joined with their consciences in producing this guilty dread. They saw a faith in the Redeemer growing up and avowed by individuals through Jerusalem and the adjacent cities, whose practical energies they were unable to control. To them it was a dreaded and practical reality, and when produced, it defied the resistance of human power; the only method of self-defence that presented itself to them was that of possible prevention; if they could subdue the teachers, and prevent the production of this faith, they seemed to have hope; but, to control the faith when it had been produced, was beyond all their calculation. This explains their threatening and violence; and it is a declaration that in their view, at least, there was a deep practical sincerity in this association of believers. They did not deem it promiscuous; it was, in their view, so decisively discriminating, that they had to struggle against it as for existence. The point of their struggle is also made most clear by Peter's defence.* "The God of our fathers raised up Jesus, whom ye slew and hanged on a tree, him hath God exalted with his right hand to be a Prince and a Saviour, to give repentance unto Israel and forgiveness of sins. We are his witnesses of these things, and so also is the Holy Ghost, which God hath given them that obey him; we ought, therefore, to obey God rather than men." What are witnesses for but to testify? But why is any testimony borne except

* Acts v. 29—33.

to produce faith? and what faith can be more perfect than that which obeys its author and object? But, lastly, what testimony can be more positive than that which God himself has borne to the faith of these disciples, when he gave the Holy Ghost to them that obeyed him? The God who gave, and the Spirit that was given, are equally above the possibility, either of deceiving, or being deceived. Gamaliel trembled at the evidence before him; he rose in the Sanhedrim, because he feared lest its action should be taken against God, for he saw that the people were trusting in him, and the facts seemed to justify their confidence; and hence, the Apostles, when scourged by the affrighted rulers, "departed from the council, rejoicing that they were counted worthy to suffer shame for his name."*

THE CASE OF SIMON IN SAMARIA.

Every word of the history is fraught with elucidating testimony, showing, in every possible way, the regard which was paid, in this community, to faith as the basis of all its action and of all its privilege. Hence the mercy which compassionated the world rose to a sublime friendship in the fellowship of these disciples, giving the poor a claim to fraternal support, which was honoured by the rich, the apostles themselves, and by the whole body of believers, in their appointment of deacons for their especial attendance and service.† This regard to a poor

---

* Acts v. 41.   † Acts vi. 1—7.

believer would have never existed, if disciples had not been recognised as believers. The majestical scene of Stephen's martyrdom recalls all the former proofs of every kind. His vision of the Saviour, standing at the right hand of God, as if risen up to receive the suffering martyr, leads us into the secrets of the heavenly kingdom, and of that gracious oversight to which its suffering children are confided; while the point of Stephen's rebuke to the elders brings the thought again to that Divine peculiarity of the brotherhood, by which the recognition of its faith was sealed: "Ye stiff-necked and uncircumcised in heart and ears, ye do always resist the Holy Ghost; as your fathers did, so do ye."* It is plain that Stephen refers to the resistance of the Spirit in the prophets; and, to complete his thought, the Spirit in the disciples is presented as the object of present resistance and insult. The fathers resisted the Spirit in the prophets; the rulers, to whom Stephen was then speaking, resisted the Spirit in the disciples. What this Spirit in the disciples was, is shown by Paul, who said, "After that ye believed, ye were sealed with that holy Spirit of Promise, which is the earnest of your inheritance of the promised possession."† Thus it appears in the case of the Samaritans. The ravages of Saul and the martyrdom of Stephen, scattered the flock of believers, who, because they were believers, bore their faith with them; and, in every place to which they were

---

* Acts vii. 51.   † Ephesians i. 13, 14.

driven, the ground of their faith, and the consistency of their conduct, must have proved their sole defence in the eye of strangers. At Samaria, not only was their constancy in suffering justified; the words and miracles of Philip fixed the attention of that people, and faith ensued. The believers were baptized, united with the outcast disciples, and there was great joy in that city.* Thus far the effect of their initiation is revealed at home; the next consequence of their initiation was the visitation of Peter and John, and the gift of the Holy Ghost by their means, which was a seal of their personal inheritance,† and a witness for God in his people.‡ It was in this matter of so great practical importance, that the true character of Simon became unclothed. He had heard with the rest, he had seen the evidence of Divine truth, he had believed and acted on that evidence, as far as man could examine, he came to the very point at which the gift of the Spirit bore its testimony: this was a criterion that went deeper than the eye of man. The faith of Simon might have been sincere as far as it went, but it did not put the heart right; and this fact the brethren did not perceive till then; but when it was perceived, Peter said, "I *perceive* that thy heart is not right with God!" But what effect had this discovery? did it pass as a matter of course? It did *not*. The man in whom the discovery is made is called to repentance, if,

---

* Acts viii. 1—8.　　　† Ephesians i. 13, 14.
‡ Acts v. 32.

peradventure, the thought of his heart might be forgiven. The expression, "Thou hast neither part nor lot in this matter, for thy heart is not right in the sight of God," is equivalent to a declaration that, where the heart is not right with God, the acceptance of a disciple can never be justified. That men may be mistaken, is supposed through the whole system; but, the giving of the Holy Spirit " after they had believed,"* "which was granted to those that obeyed him," and "which became God's witness in his people upon earth," was a Divine act, performed under the guardianship of Divine perfections, and marked that point in the life of an individual, from which his final perseverance was sealed. Salvation was promised in the overture of mercy to those who believed; and it was sealed by the Spirit after they had believed. The promise and the seal of God, therefore, had reference to the same faith. But baptism is joined with faith, too; and the baptized believers expected the Spirit without any exception;† and, therefore, the faith which the promise required, the baptism recognised, and the Spirit sealed, were supposed and accredited to be real: and he, whose heart was found to be "*not right with God,*" is, therefore, positively told that, in this state, he had no part or lot in the matter.‡

* Ephesians i. 13, 14.   Acts v. 32.   † Acts viii. 14—17.
‡ Acts viii. 18—25.

THE PRINCIPLE OF DISCIPLINE.

The kingdom of heaven is altogether *merciful*, recognising no merit in its subjects; it is altogether *voluntary*, employing no force in their subjection; it is *moral*, for all its persuasions are addressed to the conscience, as well as the affections and judgment; it is *prospective*, for each subject of this kingdom is expecting to be conformed to the likeness of his Lord, both in happiness and purity; it is *demonstrative*, for by the treatment of this willing people God will show forth his glory on this earth, especially the glory of his mercy; and it is, in its preparation for judgment, *absolutely final;* it leaves each man at liberty to meet the judgment, if he will do so, on the appeal to justice, and the plea of his own innocency, but it proposes and urges the appeal from justice to mercy in the work of Christ. The person who submits to its appeal is placed under the direction of Christ and the Holy Spirit, and so his expectation of eternal life is justified; by his personal and open devotement in baptism he is committed as one subjected to the Saviour, for this end, and with this hope; and as the Israelites, when initiated into Moses, were not permitted to return, but compelled to go forward or die, so the baptized hypocrite is marked for peculiar vengeance; he has no place amongst the common damned, he advances to eternal life, or falls, as if to prove that God in Christ means what he says, and means to be reverenced. There is not one part of this kingdom which is not discriminating; the very word which its subjects have to obey is a discerner of the thoughts and intentions of the heart; and, when its administration ceases to discriminate, the kingdom ceases to be.

DEMONSTRATIVE CASES.

To mention the whole of those practical recognitions by which this personal, spiritual and discriminating government in the body of Christ is proved, would be to transcribe the whole of the New Testament. The Apostle affirms, that when Jesus ascended up on high, and gave it pastors, teachers, and so forth, it had one Lord, one faith, one baptism, one God and Father of all, one body, one Spirit, and one hope of its calling; and each member, with whatever gifts he might receive, is commanded to walk worthy of his calling;* and to seek, in his place, the enlargement and perfection of the whole community. The author of the epistle to the Hebrews declares, that this visible fellowship, as upon a foundation, rests on the first principles of repentance, faith in God, baptism, the laying on of hands, the resurrection of the dead, and the final judgment; and that those who have on these principles been enlightened, are, if they fall away, in worse danger than ordinary sinners, having exhausted those resources of mercy with which man has been entrusted.† To bring them again to repentance is the hopeless thing; because, in their apostacy, they have overcome the means by which they were brought to repentance; and by

---

* Ephesians iv. 1—16. † Hebrews vi. 1—8.

repentance, in which their first step toward fellowship had been taken, their return must be effected, if at all. James teaches, that this society was a result, not of accident, but of deliberate council, in conformity with which, God begat its members, produced the first elements of their character and action, not by baptism, but by the word of his truth;* and the members which then existed were a first-fruit of all his creatures, a sample of what was to follow. Paul affirms, that the grace of God was thus made manifest to all men, subjecting the members of this body to a childlike discipline, in order that, abjuring its ungodliness and worldly lusts, they might live righteously and godly in the present world, expecting the blessed hope and the appearance of the glory of the great God, and their Saviour Jesus Christ, who gave himself for them, in order that he might redeem them from all things unlawful, and purify for himself a peculiar people, zealous of good works.† He declares, that they were separated, saved from their alliance with this evil world, by their washing of the new birth, and a renewing of the Holy Spirit, poured out upon them richly through Jesus Christ their Saviour, in order that, having been justified by his grace, they might become heirs according to the hope of eternal life.‡ He earnestly pleads, that they were not initiated under the authority of Paul, or of Apollos, or of any other man, but baptized into the name of Christ only; and that the faith in that name was so indis-

---

* James i. 18.   † Titus ii. 11—15.   ‡ Titus iii. 4—7.

pensable, that his attention had been given principally to its production, while the rite in which that faith was recognised had been administered by inferiors under his authority.* The persons so initiated, and so believing, are said now to be sons of God, and to be looking for higher enjoyments which are not yet fully revealed.† John informs us who had the power or privilege of claiming this distinguishing inheritance in the body of Christ. "To as many as *received* the Saviour, to them gave he power (authority) to become sons of God, even to as many as *believed* on his name.‡ Being admitted on the ground of their faith, and in the right of their Redeemer, they are treated as sons of God in him until the reality of their faith is brought in doubt by some open violation of his law. Hence the affirmations of Paul, which have been enumerated; for if faith had been professed by them, and publicly recognised by the church, it is just that they should be treated by their brethren as believers, until some good reason could be shown to the contrary. They might also be urged to sustain the character they had so openly, and willingly, and solemnly assumed, and in which others were implicated with themselves. Hence, combined with these affirmations of Paul, we have his cogent moral instructions. Being sons of God, they were not to return to the beggarly elements, they had so justly forsaken;§ having risen with Christ, they were to seek the things which are

---

* 1 Cor. i. 10—17. † 1 John iv. 1. Rom. viii. 1—39.
‡ John i. 12. § Galatians iv. 9—11.

above, where Christ sitteth at the righthand of God.* Having been recipients of the tender mercies of God, they were to present themselves as living sacrifices, holy and acceptable to God;† and, to pass over a multitude of cases, which memory may easily supply, they are urged to feel, that they are not their own;‡ and commanded to act, each one in his place, as a subordinate part of one great whole, in which multitudes were, and were still to be, included by the same faith. Each, therefore, is to fill his place as an organ and a member, performing his appointed function with the vigour and ease of unconscious health; each is to sympathise with the rest, in labour, in sorrow, in joy; they are to aim at the same great object, and to be of one mind; each derives a moral benefit from the association, but buries his selfishness in the general interest of his Lord, and of his people, just as a rain-drop, possessing a constitutional likeness, loses its individuality, and imbibes a saltness, by being baptized or plunged into the ocean.

But what communication hath light with darkness? There can be no union where there is no affinity. The rain-drop unites with the ocean, because it is water; and in ceasing to move as a rain-drop, it commences a fellowship with the tides, the surges, and all the wondrous action of the body in which it is absorbed; stones and heterogeneous substances are cast into the sea, but they are not absorbed, they are deposited in its sediments, or cast out upon its shores.

---

* Col. iii. 1—4.   † Rom. xii. 1—9.   ‡ 1 Cor. vi. 19—20.

So it may be with the body of Christ. Through the imperfection of men, but mostly while they sleep, persons who have no faith are brought into its fellowship; this is not the rule, but the exception, the accident. The ocean is the gathering together of the waters, though other things may be cast into it; the body of Christ is the gathering together of believers, though other men may be intruded. Moreover, the ocean itself is not a more striking or necessary instance of Almighty power, in physical nature, than is this body of Christ in the universe of mind. It has no life in itself; but, being moved by a living and unseen power, that acts upon it and through it, a visibility is given to attributes possessed by him, who hideth himself in excess of glory. When moved by this spiritual agency, millions of voices are heard in every land, like swells or surges upon every coast, sighing forth the sympathies, or pronouncing in thunder the admonitions of the living and invisible One. Disobedience may face its movements like a shore of stone, and stand against its action till the fiery consummation of the last day; yet, it will be known that mercy, by this means, and for ages, had sustained its war in terror and in tenderness with man's rebellion. What God designs beyond the judgment-day, is not now fully known; but such a separated and organised community of believing men, influenced by himself, giving visibility to the action of his moral power, bringing it home to the objects he designs to influence, recovering them in mercy, or rendering them without excuse, and thus forming an organisation through which his merciful intentions may be uttered in the ear of traitorous and fleshly-minded sinners, is just what this world wanted. Such a body would be to him as the voice of many waters, uttering his judgments, or expressing his sympathies. Separated by their recognised moral character, and yet made to permeate and surround the rebellious masses of mankind, these new men would admonish by their example, and influence by persuasion, wherever they were placed; and when the awful reserves of unseen strength are brought into operation, the visible and united organisation would act upon a centre, as when an inundation overflows the land. Sovereign mercy has given a written word, which men despise; they want the living voice and its persuasions. Sovereign mercy has also acted, without these intermediate arrangements, directly on the minds of men themselves; but this, however it may display his power, will not justify his judgment. Some arrangement to glorify the verdict of eternal death, something opposed to rebellion, as obvious, as constant, and as majestical, is required, as this ocean which sighs and groans before a precipice, without subduing it. If the stubborn fortitude of human treason were not unclothed, final damnation would seem too severe. This, therefore, is the thing we wanted: a society to speak for God in every land, divested of terror that men might not be afraid, yet raised in character, that the word might be respected; speaking with men in the fervour of human sympathies, and laying hold on God in the bond of an eternal covenant. This the world required, this the prophets foretold; for this John and the Redeemer made solemn preparation; this the Lord began at Pentecost; and the operation of this body has produced the facts which are found in the Apostles' teaching. The epistles are communications between the parts of a body, so separated from other men, and so united in covenant with God, as to move with terrible effect against the masses of corruption to which it was opposed. It was a body of men reconciled to God; and it became mighty, through God, to the pulling down of strongholds. Its Divine authority stands on no doubtful minutiæ of argument; its barest outline is expressive of infinite wisdom; it lies, like the sea, where no man could place it; and its operations declare the presence, the approval, and the power of God.

CLASSIFIED EXAMPLES.

The examples given in the Acts, as far as they relate to the Jewish people, have the additional advantage of not only evolving the nature of the whole polity, but also of exhibiting the Divine approval. As its action proceeded in opposition to authorities whom God had now rejected, a stedfast perseverance in acting upon individuals is shown by the Apostles, who urge them to be saved, separated, from that untoward generation. In doing this, the rulers are set at defiance and the appeal is made directly to God.* The builders who rejected the

* Acts iv. 1—17.

corner-stone, are now themselves rejected; and the corner-stone is exalted upon the ruins of their power, because, under heaven, no other name is given by which men may be saved. They make their appeal, not to the profane, the vulgar, the untaught, only, but to the learned, the refined, and those who feared God; and these are urged to repent, to separate themselves, and to be baptized. It is not clear that the persons present at the Pentecost were other than the best-informed and most devout, assembled out of all nations, at that solemnity, having the faults of their age, but being the best of their age, and related to the nation now implicated in the murder of Messiah. The source of their peculiar errors was the expectation of Messiah, under wrong impressions of his reign; and the rejection of him, who justly claimed their reverence in that character. Peter and his associates declared that the crucified One was he;* that the Pentecostal power was his gift; that, for his sake and service, Jew must separate from Jew, because he was dealing with nature in ruins, and formed his design for its perfect recovery. It was not a mere sectarian classification, without any radical basement of solemn truth and obligation; but a moral and personal action, began with faith, matured in repentance, and declared and ratified in baptism.† The incidentals are of no moment in this case, compared with the solemn promise, "Ye shall receive the Holy Ghost."‡ This

---

* Acts ii. 14—36.   † Acts ii. 37—47.   ‡ Acts ii. 38.

was a testing point, a provision by which the baptized believer might become a living witness for the approving God. The action shows, in the result, that this was the case; for the society became a dwelling-place of God, through the Spirit. The ordinary bonds of society and motives to action, were all overpowered by that superior and uniting influence which pervaded this body of Christ. The first act of the convert was a dreadful test; he stood out in solemn appeal to God, as one devoted to the Nazarene, whose blood was but now reeking on the stones of Golgotha, and whose murderers were exulting in their power and victory. We have no such test of sincerity now in the profession of repentance and faith. But the stream into which they were plunged, consisted of similar events. The personal separation involved a personal loss of all things on the part of many; in a short time, the absolute bankruptcy of the whole community followed; the endearing ties of domestic life were so broken by the act, that the bitterest afflictions resulted in social life. The word required them to forsake all in following him, and they joyfully received the word; they took joyfully the spoiling of their goods, the insult of their persons, their imprisonment, and chains. In that assembly, waiting daily in the temple, there was a speaking seriousness, which indicated more than superficial excitement; motives and principles were brought into action, which suffering and mortality could not subdue. And, more than all, God was with them; and, when they, in their affliction, appealed to him in prayer for his holy child Jesus, and against the rulers from whom they had withdrawn, God answered them in awful but soothing tokens of his presence; the house was shaken, they were filled with the Holy Ghost, the Apostles bore witness with great power, and great grace was upon them all.* The hand of God was there, to mark their association and its policy, as his own.

From all the record supplies, it does not appear that the apostles ever supposed that a system so deeply discriminating in its application to the Jewish people could be represented as indiscriminating when applied to the Gentile nations. Their ideas all went the contrary way. From the case of the Samaritans,† which will come before us in another place, it is manifest that they conceived the extension of Divine mercy to them an unexpected proof of Divine munificence. Instead of supposing that sinners could be initiated as sons of God, without faith and repentance, they were filled with joy when, by peculiar interpositions of Divine power, it was proved that God had granted to the Gentiles also repentance unto life. The case of Cornelius brought this point so fully before them that no doubt could be entertained. Peter was called to teach this individual, and compelled to concede his baptismal initiation by a threefold expression of Divine authority: first, in his own vision;‡ secondly, in the vision of Cornelius;§ and, thirdly, in the

---

* Acts iv. 23—37.   † Acts viii. 4—21.   ‡ Acts x, 1—16.
§ Acts x. 17—33.

extraordinary gift of the Holy Spirit to him *before* baptism, which was ordinarily given to believers *after* baptism.* It could no longer be doubtful whether the faith of a Gentile would be accepted, when the promise of the Father, the earnest of the inheritance by which they were sealed unto the day of redemption, was granted to Cornelius, and the Gentile believers with him, before his eyes. Peter bowed at once before these insignia of Divine authority and power. Who can withhold the testifying water, he said, when God hath granted the testifying Spirit? The earthly recognition of faith, and its hope in Christ, is justified by their heavenly recognition. These reasons, which justified his act to his own conscience, justified it also to the brethren who were witnesses from Joppa, and to all the apostles who heard the case in Jerusalem.† The great fact burst upon their minds, that this gospel of Christ with which they were intrusted, was a power of God unto salvation to every one that believeth—to the Greek as well as to the Jew; that is, to all mankind. The argument of Paul in the Hebrews places this doctrine against the whole chain of Jewish rites and sacrifices; in the Galatians, against the Judaising doctrine that converts to Christ must become proselytes to Moses; and in the Romans and Ephesians, the same doctrine is maintained against all human scruples or reasonings whatsoever. The idea of initiation without faith is never entertained; the whole

---

* Acts x. 34—48. † Acts xi. 1—18.

argument is directed to the one point, that personal faith is the one, sufficient, but indispensable, term of justification in the body of Christ.

The success of Divine truth in Antioch, and the argument of some that Christian converts should be proselyted under Moses, brought this whole matter before the apostles in a decisive form. The question then was—not whether faith might be admitted in a Gentile, but—whether faith in Christ alone would justify their hope of mercy and fellowship in the body of Christ. It is not argued, in that assembly, that baptism is a substitute for circumcision; for that rite, though not enforced on the Gentile, was retained by the Jew. But it was argued, by Peter, that God had chosen to cause, through him, the heathen to hear the gospel and to believe; and that the same God, who searcheth the heart, had borne testimony to them in granting them the Holy Spirit, as he did to the apostles, making no difference between these heathen and them; and that, through the grace of our Lord Jesus Christ, both could be saved by believing in him (only).* James carried the thought further, by saying that this was foretold by the prophets, who said that all the heathen should seek the Lord. He defines the aim of Divine mercy in this to be, to take out of the heathen a people to act in his name.† Paul narrated what wonders God had done to confirm their work;‡ and all the assembly, having resolved on affirming the sufficiency of faith

---

* Acts xv. 6, 11. † Acts xv. 13, 21. ‡ Acts xv. 12, 13.

alone, and recommended a careful avoidance of things which would grieve the Jews, sent their resolution to their *brethren* in Antioch, Syria, and Cilicia, who were from the heathen.* Here the whole argument turns upon the predicted purpose of God: the authoritative movement of his mercy, the hearing, the faith, the turning to God, the acting in his name, and the hope of salvation in Christ, of those whom the assembly calls brethren "*from the heathen.*" These brethren, taken from the heathen to trust in and act upon the name of God, have one privilege and hope of salvation with those who are brethren taken from the Jews. In fact, the distinction of Gentile and Jew in this assembly is merged in the one discriminating term, *believer.* The whole action declares them to be a body of recognised believers, and nothing else; and, therefore, their initiatory immersion must have been an immersion of believers.

If it could be proved that, in baptizing the jailor, Lydia, and Stephanas, and the believers in their several families, Paul had baptized individuals without faith,—which is not affirmed in any part of Scripture, but which is only inferred, against the recorded facts,—yet, if this could be proved, it would only show that Paul had, in these cases, acted contrary to the resolution of the assembly in which he himself sat; and the whole meaning of which was explained by himself, several years after, in his epistle to the Galatians. Nay, more; it would prove that he

* Acts xv. 22—29.

acted in direct opposition to his own words; for his expression, "as many of you as have been baptized into Christ have put on Christ," might as well have been sent to Philippi as to Galatia. But practical inconsistency is not to be charged on such a man without more proof; and, besides that which has been adduced, more evidence against the supposition is actually supplied in the treatment of the twelve Sabeans whom he re-baptized at Ephesus. Had he been indifferent to the faith of individuals received into fellowship, these would have been instructed and set forward, as Apollos was; who, like them, knew only the doctrine and baptism of John. Apollos had become a disciple before, but these after, the Pentecost; the former, therefore, was right, and they were wrong. It was not only needful, in his esteem, that they should have faith in God—because, without faith, it is impossible to please God, since whatever is not of faith, is sin—but it was indispensable that their faith in God should be exercised through the appointed Medium. It must be a faith in God, through Jesus Christ our Lord, now come, now sacrificed, yet risen, at God's right hand, making intercession, and pouring out his Spirit on his people. Such scrupulous regard to the object of faith, renders offensively absurd the affirmation, that he baptized without any regard to its actual existence.*

But the system of fellowship and initiation which

---

* Acts xix. 1—7.

Paul observed, is made unquestionable by comparing this passage with the first four chapters in his epistle to the Ephesians. By this case it is clear, that the baptism and laying on of hands precede the gift of the Spirit; as also that faith in the ascended Lord, who granted the Spirit, preceded the baptism. Hence, without naming the two intermediate steps, he said, " in whom ye also, after that ye believed, were sealed with that Holy Spirit of promise which is the earnest of the promised inheritance ;"* and then he advances, to show the glory of the administering Lord, the previous state of his converted people, the dignity of their fellowship in the body of Christ, the indwelling of the Spirit, the simplicity of its ordinances, being one Lord, one faith, one baptism, one God and Father of all, who is over all, and in you all. Nothing can be more clear than that he was dealing with a vast reality, whose centre was in Christ, at God's right hand; and whose radiating movements were traceable wherever believers became consecrated in his service. He brought this system into contact with all the local peculiarities of civilised society in Asia and Europe; where the mysteries that set men apart in a select society, with new hopes for life and death, in the temple of Eleusis, had their operation; and in the vicinity of Diana, who was great with the Ephesians; in the literary refinements of Asia and Greece; and before the rugged war-gods of Rome; in all societies, Paul sustained, with this simple rite, the

---

* Ephesians i. 1—12.

open separation of believers from the world, and their holy espousal, as virgins, to Christ. John followed him on the same ground in Asia and Ephesus; and all the contents of his gospel show, that while an apostolical spirit remained upon earth, the same essential term of fellowship and salvation was their chief concern.

One source of error in this great inquiry is found in the contracted view which is taken of recorded facts. The few remains of apostolical action can form but a small part of what was done and said in those soul-stirring times, by men so absorbed and devoted in their work. If what is stated seem so impossible to some, how could we bear to look upon the whole of their action, the convulsions it produced, and the operations of Divine power it so constantly displayed? Before we begin to reason on these events, it is incumbent on us to remember that nothing which the Spirit has recorded can be too hard for God to have performed. Constant appeals to impossibility are absurd, when placed against the constant working of Divine power. He who was with these holy men is able to do more than we can ask or think. It was their confidence in this which gave the firm and cheerful action to the disciples of that time, and guided them through darkness. The Searcher of hearts confirmed to Peter the fact of Cornelius' faith; the Spirit directed Philip to the chariot and the Æthiopian; and Ananias was guided by God himself to the converted Saul. An indwelling and guidance of the Spirit characterised their times, which finds no parallel in ours. They moved as the Spirit led them, and spake as the Spirit gave them utterance; and if these splendid peculiarities could, by returning to their simplicity, be now procured, though they might bring the furnace of their trial with them, the unearthly acquisition would be well regained.

A boastful appeal to those baptisms in which it is said, that God, who searcheth the heart, had given witness for the recipients, in order to establish a rule by which all regard to personal character is to be set aside, would, it might be thought, prove sufficiently confounding of itself, without selecting, as an especial case, the baptism of St. Paul. One might pity the observer whose eye became dazzled beneath the splendour of that example. Of all the cases that could be chosen to justify initiation without faith, this is the worst. The personal interference of the Lord himself places it beyond the range of merely human action. If there were no evidence of his faith but that afforded in the declaration of the Lord himself, this would be enough for Ananias, and show, as far as this example is concerned, that without such authority more caution and inquiry should be exercised. But was there no evidence of Paul's faith when Ananias found him? He was praying, and to the Lord, whom he had persecuted too; he had been three days without food in his supplications; his blinded and emaciated prostration would speak volumes, and more eloquently than words. Why did he not seek assistance of the physicians? Why did he not obtain succour of the Rabbis, to whom he had his letters of commendation? Why did he not complain of his personal injury, and charge the Nazarene with using violence? The simple answer is, he *had* believed. In his own words, "He was not disobedient to the heavenly vision." He saw that Jesus *was* the Christ; and he had no hope now but in his mercy. Paul was not ignorant. His knowledge in the Jews' religion wanted only this one centralising point, and it would soon form a perfect system in conformity with its law. Jesus was the true centre of all the elements which Saul had collected in his youthful study. Hence, when once relieved by an acceptance in Christ, he was prepared for action. His sins he saw in the rejection and persecution of the Lord, at whose feet he was now prostrate, fasting in prayer. The messenger reminds him that these sins must be disavowed, washed away, in the baptism by which, as a believer in Jesus, his alliance with rebellion must be broken for ever. Was it mere excitement? He did it. He did it deliberately; he did it as the Lord approved; for the Lord removed his blindness in the very act. Was this mere excitement? He went into the synagogue and confounded the Jews by proving there that this Jesus is both Lord and Christ. Yet it is said, that this was mere excitement, and not faith. There might have been excitement felt, and justly, for the events were wonderful; but it remained until, in danger of his life, the disciples procured his escape by a window in the city wall. That excitement remained until he had penetrated Arabia, and returned;

it was not quenched by the trials of Jerusalem, of Ephesus, of Philippi, or of Rome; it sustained him on Mars Hill, and in the shipwreck; it continued till his martyrdom: but it was more than excitement; a moral principle was implanted and evolved in his breast which never could expire; and hence, on terminating his triumphant career, he said, "I have finished my course; I have kept *the faith.*" St. Paul was a baptized believer.

LECTURE VII.

ON THE TESTIMONY OF THE ANCIENT CHRISTIAN AUTHORS.

By submitting, in the body of Christ, to any authority but that of its founder, we violate the essential law of its constitution. If, therefore, we now turn to ancient Christian writers, it is not to obtain an authority which demands obedience, but an illustration of that law which has been granted by the Redeemer himself, who is the head and centre of all voluntary action in his own community, and from whose words no one can depart without his reprehension. Without any other authorities than such as are justly called divine, it has, in the foregoing exercises, been shown that the purposes of mercy included and required the formation and employment of a society, distinguished from the world by its faith in the Redeemer, and by its subjection to his control. The relationship therein established is essentially personal: first, between each member and the Lord; and, secondly, through him, and under his authority, the relationship is formed between each member and all others admitted into fellowship. As the case might lead us to expect, so the law is found to explain, that the qualification to fellowship should be personal, voluntary, and moral; comprising a subjection of reason and conscience, in repentance for past transgression, in confidential reliance on the personal authority and ministration of Christ, in devotion to his service, in hope of the eternal life to be perfected at his second coming, and in the use of all such means as he, in his word and by his Spirit, appoints for perfecting individual character, and preparing his people for his fellowship in heaven. The privilege of each member, in this community, is altogether of grace; and his baptismal initiation declares his personal belief of its freedom and sufficiency in Christ, his willing subjection to the law and discipline of Christ, and his personal separation from the world for his sake. As the inheritance expected is to be perfected in heaven, and the Saviour he embraces is God over all, so the devotion of each believer is required without any modifying reservation in favour of temporal circumstances or even of mortality itself. He is baptized on the hope of the resurrection from the dead; and, in the discipline of the body of Christ, he is treated as one whose personal consecration hath reference to eternity in its chief design. The believers so devoted, who form separate assemblies, and convene in different places, are parts of the whole, devoted to its extension, and entrusted with its interests where they meet; the person admitted to one assembly being, by that assembly, accredited to all, or to any one, of the rest. The whole body forms a republic of faith; and, separated from the world, is, in the hands of Christ, and under his Spirit, a witness and instrument of mercy to the end of time.

If this be the ordained constitution and use of the community, into which disciples of Jesus were formed, it is clear that, to initiate persons without discrimination, is to violate its law by corrupting its constituency; and to originate a test of discrimination between disciple and disciple, is to change the whole constitution of this community, and to frustrate the design of its existence. The question is, whether Christ shall have upon this earth a body of baptized believers, set apart for his use, in urging the necessity of faith on other men?—or, whether he shall not? The prophecy foretold it; John and our Lord prepared for it; a general expectation favoured it; at his ascension, the Lord commanded it; and in their ministrations, the Apostles formed it, God working with them with signs, and wonders, and gifts of the Holy Spirit: and the evidence thus supplied is pre-eminently of Divine authority. If no other book existed, therefore, and no other authority could be supplied, this would determine our practice: but, when another witness is brought in to be heard, his depositions may be taken and considered. It is in the character of witnesses, therefore, only, that the ancient Christian authors are entitled to be heard; and their testimony is taken principally as to the matter of interpretation. As they lived near the Apostles' time and spake the language in which the Apostles wrote, it may be ascertained from them, whether they found, resulting from apostolical labour, any such separated society of believers, or no; and whether, in their view, this society was conformed to the law of the Redeemer? If there was such a society; if it was formed by appeals to the Saviour's law; if it was found by those who immediately followed the Apostles; if it was recognised, in that light, by enemies, as well as friends; if these believers in Christ were so separated from the rest of mankind, that they would not submit a dispute respecting property, amongst themselves, to the decision of an unbelieving judge; if this association and separated society of believers was produced by similar means, and recognised by one initiatory immersion, wherever the gospel prevailed; and, lastly, if the severest trials and discipline of the church were all treated with reference to this one rule of absolute devotion in recognised believers, and all these testifying facts be found up to the time when the Apostles died, the conclusion will be, that in pleading for such an exclusive and discriminating fellowship of believers, so accredited and baptized, we are imitating the Apostles, and rightly interpreting the law of Christ.

THE WITNESS OF ENEMIES.

The period over which this inquiry extends, is that of about 240 years from the death of the Apostle John to that of Constantine. He was about the thirty-ninth individual, who, either alone or with others, occupied the throne of the empire from the time of Augustus, in whose reign the Saviour was born.* Of this succession, one Emperor only is said to have been a Christian, before Constantine legalised the arbitrations of the church, and formed its alliance with the civil power. Several Emperors were humane, and sought to spare the individuals brought up for martyrdom; the greater part were fierce and cruel persecutors. Some of their efforts to subdue, if not to extirpate, the believers in Jesus, were very extensive, employing the highest authorities, and reaching the furthest limits of the empire. As the Romans were not averse to the creation of new gods, or to the worship of gods revered by nations they subdued, there must have been some peculiar motive influencing the public mind, to which these general movements against the Christians must be ascribed. The individual and exclusive character of the Christian community supplied that motive. Jesus could not be honoured by a place in the Pantheon, and his followers could be implicated in no other worship than that which was offered to Jehovah through him. Their devotion to Christ involved their actual separation from all other bodies of worshipping people

---

* Hanmer's Chronographia.

whatsoever. In their community there was neither Jew nor Greek; they were all one in Christ Jesus. If they could have conformed to other communities, they might have retained their faith in Christ; and if, at an early period, they could have kept their faith to themselves, they might have been protected. But, the individuality of their profession involved an individual exercise of zeal: by individual exertion, individuals became convinced; the republic of faith forced its operations into every part of society, its action was felt in the rural districts and in the cities, in the family and in the market, in the army and in Cæsar's household; individuals convinced of the truth, and repenting of sin, were retiring from the temples, the traffic, the conflicts, the polluted customs and the alliances of the world, until the temples were forsaken, sacrifices could not be sold, land became reduced in value, incense had no market, the priesthood became impoverished, and artists had no employment, because gods and shrines were not in demand. A terrible reality was working its way through all the conglomerate of human treason and defilement. Men were alarmed; they contended, as for existence; and, if they could be so deranged as to contend thus with men who did not themselves believe their own doctrine, or trust in their own Redeemer, the followers of Jesus could never have endured those storms of persecution through which they had to pass, without full conviction that their hope of eternal life was sure, and that their personal expectation of its blessing was justified of God.

THE DISCIPLINE OF CONFESSION.

The observers of their time were often astonished at the readiness with which Christians of that age endured, and even invited, death; but it does not appear that they were ever supposed to be without faith in Him for whom they suffered. If anything more than the nature of their trial could be needed to defend them from that reproach, the order and law of their own communion would supply the demand. No one was received into fellowship without the confession made in baptism; and, though this might be more or less private, the attempt to conceal it was against the law and contrary to the aim of their fellowship. If, even at the hazard of life, the convert of yesterday refused to confess, there was no protection from the church's discipline; the latest convert and the oldest labourer were subject to the same law of excommunication. It appears, from the words of Paul himself,[*] that this principle was so set before the mind of the convert at his initiation, that each one confessed his belief in the resurrection from the dead, and was baptized on the confession of that hope. There was not only an appropriateness in such a rule —it was necessary to the imitation of their Lord; for he strictly commands that his followers should count the cost of their profession, and nothing could support them in the prospect of a violent death for him except the hope of a glorious immortality by his means. This rule of discipline is itself a proof, therefore,—

[*] 1 Cor. xv. 29.

since it applied to every baptized disciple,—that the baptism could only have been administered where the faith was supposed to be sincere.

THE BAPTISMAL CONTROVERSY.

Several passages in Scripture, which have been already noticed, state that believers are saved, or separated, from this evil world by baptism; and others state that believers are justified by faith only. These are reconciled by the fact that the faith which justifies begins to appropriate its privilege and to embrace its obligations in the appointed use of its initiatory confession. The trial which attended their confession of faith naturally led the ancient believers to magnify this difficulty. No one appears to have pleaded for an initiation without faith; but many pleaded that faith, without confession, might secure salvation. The argument employed to meet and condemn this error was, *not* that baptism communicated faith, but that the faith which shrunk from baptism was deficient in the good works which it was designed, by the Redeemer's law, to produce as its appropriate fruits. The imperfect faith was, therefore, rejected, and its rejection on that ground forms an additional proof that the faith on which the Christian fellowship of that time became based became discriminated as sincere, uncompromising, and connected with final salvation; and the constant requirement of its avowal before men proves, that this society was still governed with a particular regard to that testimony of his believing people which Christ ordained as a principal means of producing conviction in the minds of others.

THE CATECHUMENICAL DISCIPLINE.

A body of initiated believers, devoted to each other and to their Lord by a law which required the spirit, and, in many cases, imposed the act of martyrdom, must, in all cases, have peculiar interests, and, in a time of fierce persecution, be exposed to peculiar danger. It was not the law of the ruler they dreaded so much as the lurking informer, animated by personal vindictiveness. Where converts had been made in a household, or worshippers had been drawn away from some popular temple, the offended relatives, or the impoverished heathen priests, would seek revenge by bringing the successful disciples before the tribunal of the ruler. The disciples, therefore, must have confided in the sincerity of each other. It was a rule to suffer death rather than betray that confidence; because each one, when charged with his faith, must die, rather than deny it or dishonour it. Death stood at its very entrance, as if to be a guardian of the church's purity. If, by his terrors, one of the baptized failed in his confession, the Lord himself was dishonoured, and all the brethren suffered shame. Nothing could be more important, therefore, than that each inquirer should be well instructed, and, by the Lord's own rule, reckon up the cost of his profession before he made it. Hence the persons who became impressed by the truth were placed under instruction as catechumens. The most effective teachers were employed in conducting their studies. They were made familiar with gospel facts, and the hopes and obligations of believers in Christ. Under the care of the church they were prepared for its service and fellowship. Dr. Halley defames this practice. Let it be allowed, for the present, that he is right, and the ancient fathers wrong; still, the practice itself proves that they were not indifferent to the faith of those whom they baptized.

OF SINS AFTER BAPTISM.

An engagement formed in obedience to overtures of mercy which God hath proclaimed, and openly avowed before men in the name of the Father, and of the Son, and of the Holy Ghost, must, by every conscientious man, be deemed sacred; and every violation of such a contract should be regarded with abhorrence. Hence the ancients pronounced those sins which were committed after baptism to be most flagrant, because they were committed against a confessed knowledge of the Master's will, and a covenanted subjection to his governance. Paul uses the same argument in his Epistle to the Hebrews: he makes it stronger by showing the mercy which, in this case, is abused, and the despite which is done to the Spirit of grace. Both agree with the Lord, who affirms that "of him who hath received much, much shall be required;" and "he who knoweth his master's will, and doeth it not, shall be beaten with many stripes." Paul and the ancient churches affirm also, that persons who have broken through this restraint are in a more hopeless condition than those who had never heard the truth. It is not the present intention to defend the Apostle and those who followed him from the modern abuse and ridicule to which their doctrine has been exposed; the doctrine is now adduced to prove, that the baptism on which this reasoning rests must have been both administered and received under a thoughtful and credible declaration of personal faith in Jesus Christ our Lord; and that the discipline of these churches held each baptized person responsible for the covenant therein ratified.

ANCIENT HERESIES.

Every great principle existing and operating in the human mind will have its own legitimate results, and give its tinge to other subjects with which it comes into combination. It has been thus in modern times. Where faith has been regarded as an indispensable qualification to Christian fellowship and a hope of eternal life, the great question has been, How shall faith be produced? Here men split into parties, one using one portion and others using another portion of the Divine word. The same question rose in the ancient time. The necessity for faith was assumed; the object was to show how faith was produced, and how its various operations and results were secured. They saw and recognised the difference between believers and unbelievers, and they wished to comprehend the physiology of the difference. They brought the eastern learning to their aid, and laboured to explain the mystery, by a supposed operation, of spiritual seeds. They did not wish to relax the bond of a baptized believer, but drew it tighter, as they thought, until their effort failed in the exposure of their folly. Whatever excuse might be afforded, in their want of books and general reading, they were wrong; the early churches, and the apostles Paul and John, pointedly condemn the absurdities which were advanced, and the teachers who advanced them. Yet they afford a painful testimony to the truth we seek; for no such efforts could have been originated in order to explain the production and operation of faith, if faith had not formed the basis of Christian fellowship at that time.

These are not so much the testimonies of ancient authors as the testifying features of their times. They lead us to expect what will, what must be, the testimony of the authors themselves, and show that the indiscriminating theory now proposed could not then have had any recognised existence. No mention is made of it; no author affirms it; and these general features of the time show, that it could not have formed the basis of Christian fellowship. No such indiscriminating discipline could have provoked the persecution which raged, or have endured its trial; the idea of binding men to die, for one in whom they have never believed, is absurd and unjust; the refusing to acknowledge a faith that would not be confessed, is proof that they recognised it only where they considered it sincere; their catechumenical discipline exhibits the caution and labour they used in fulfilling the Lord's command; their doctrine of sin after baptism, like that of Paul, proves the personal intelligence and solemn nature of its compact, and even the heresies of the time confirm the conclusion. These facts declare the Christian fellowship of that time to have been a great practical reality, whose chief and essential element was, a faith that laid hold on God; to which God himself responded; and which, in all its features and operations, declares the indiscriminating theory now proposed, not only untenable, but presumptuously absurd.

THE ANCIENT AUTHORS.

Nothing can be more important than to keep carefully in mind, through our whole inquiry, the point on which information is sought. Much stress is laid on the fact, that no children are mentioned whose parents were Christians, and who were not baptized. This is likely, because there is no authentic mention of children or unbelievers having been baptized at all. The practice is not mentioned until Tertullian issues his rebuke of it; and then it has been produced by the notion of baptismal efficacy, and combined with the appointment of sponsors, to see that the grace is not only put in, but brought out also, as Pædo-baptists plead in the present age. Besides, suppose it were possible to find amongst the ancient Christian authors an approving notice of infant baptism, since this has been proved to be opposed to all that Scripture contains in the Old or New Testament respecting the kingdom of our Lord, it would be our duty to obey the Scriptures, and resign the

Fathers. But this is not the case. If any authentic and approving notice could be found, Dr. Halley would have produced it. It is quite legitimate, therefore, to ask if the Christian writers of this age contain any traces of that baptismal recognition of believers which is found inculcated in Scripture. Did they know anything respecting it and its origin? Is there anything in their writings to testify that, in their judgment, the interpretation we have given to the Sacred Writings is correct?

In these early Christian authors, references to the Apostles and their writings exist, which indicate a profound reverence for their authority and instructions; their familiarity with the language the Apostles used, and the circumstances under which they wrote, gave them also great advantage as interpreters of their writings; the rules of interpretation were not unknown, and though the common people suffered the want of books, and learning was not widely diffused, yet the most classical of all the works now known were then in use; and some of these evince a profundity of thought which has never yet been exceeded. St. Paul's writings show an acquaintance with the literature of Greece; and to many of the early Christians this must have been familiar. The authorities of that time, therefore, must not be treated as ignorant men; and before the canon of Scripture was completed, their references to the different books which that canon now comprises, proves that they were not indifferent. Could the minute proceedings of those times be unveiled, many would, unquestionably, be seen traversing sea and land to consult and to copy the autographs of inspiration. Liberties were taken by individuals, which could not be justified; but their condemnation, as heretics, proves that the churches contained in the body of Christ were worthy of esteem in their testimony to the import of Scripture, and the practical institutions of Apostolical times.

Moreover, it is well known that every important assembly of the brethren was influenced by a desire to trace its origin, either to the Apostles themselves, or to some of the disciples who laboured under their immediate direction. This foible has been transmitted, through the worship of relics, down to the present day. Wherever a genuine epistle of Paul, or any inspired autograph existed, this feeling must have been strengthened. In two hundred years of eventful struggle, crowded with martyrdoms and victories of the truth, these inspired remains must have assumed an inconceivable value. Experience proves that their loss or decay has mercifully prevented much idolatry. But this veneration for the document, while it retained its healthful character, served to guard it from corruption, and heighten the value of local testimonies. Where such a document existed, especial care would be observed in following its instructions. Hence, when no obvious objection can be found, the ancient Christian authors who lived near the Apostles' time, and wrote on the spot where their autographs were preserved, became the best witnesses of their import. On this principle, the information to be collected may, for the sake of perspicuity and force, be digested in a geographical arrangement. Rome was one depository of Inspired Writings, and it had early writers who bear testimony to the justness of our interpretation of them; Greece and Asia Minor were also honoured with such documents, and they have witnessing authors; Palestine and Syria the same; and Africa, though it was the depository of no Inspired Autographs, yet there the Septuagint version of the Old Testament, generally used in the Apostles' time, was produced and studied, and there the Gospel obtained some of its most splendid and earliest victories. The Ethiopic church, on the Upper Nile, was, not improbably, founded by the Eunuch whom Philip baptized; while Alexandria was a school, as well as market, for the coasts of the Mediterranean sea. If the evidence to be collected at each place be first digested in the order of time, the whole may be combined to exhibit the testimony of the universal church, as recorded in that age, on the matter in hand.

TESTIMONIES FROM ROME.

The first portion of the New Testament brought into use in Rome, was Paul's epistle, addressed to the Christians in that city, A.D. 58. It was dictated by Paul while he was labouring in Achaia. The persons to whom it was addressed are "beloved of God, and called saints."* They were recipients of "the tender

* Romans i. 7.

mercies of God," and formed with him and other believers " one body in Christ."* This body is called the people of God, " the good olive-tree."† Each engrafted member is said to occupy his position by his faith, by which he is justified in that position; he is therein freed from all condemnation, a child, an heir of God, and a joint-heir with Christ. In him they are expecting the adoption, the redemption of their bodies.‡ Their faith secures their justification by appropriating the atonement and mediation of Christ.§ Their faith comes by hearing; believing in the heart, they become justified; confessing with the mouth, they become saved.‖ They had in faith obeyed the Gospel, and been baptized into Christ; baptized into his death, were buried with him by baptism into death, that, like as Christ was raised from the dead by the glory of the Father, even so they also should walk in newness of life. They were freed from the law; freed from sin, being under grace, which justified the hope of final and perfect victory.¶ These expressions are so constructed as to include the Apostle himself, and all other persons truly initiated into the body of Christ.

The second document brought into use in Rome includes the Gospel of Luke, and the Acts of the Apostles, which Professor Hug has shown to be two parts of one treatise, prepared for the use of Theophilus, and probably when Paul appeared before

---

* Rom. xii. 1—9. † Rom. xi. 24. ‡ Rom. viii. 1—23.
§ Rom. iii. 21—26. ‖ Rom. x. 9, 10. ¶ Rom. vi. 1—14.

Cæsar in Rome, the first time in A.D. 64—5.* If this conclusion be admitted, all the acts of baptism recorded therein must be united with the doctrine stated by Paul in his epistle to this church.

Besides these Inspired Autographs, Paul wrote from Rome several epistles to other churches, in which his views are variously expressed, and from which may be inferred what were the doctrines he taught for two whole years in his own hired house in Rome.†

Whether written from Rome, or some other place, the epistle to the Ephesians places the whole subject of Christian fellowship on precisely the same ground as that on which it stands in the epistle to the Romans. The members were sealed by the Spirit after they believed;‡ were separated from the world, both Jewish and Gentile.§ They had one Lord, one faith, one baptism, and one hope of their calling;|| were the endowed instruments of the Redeemer's merciful dominion, and builded together as an habitation of God, through the Spirit. The body they formed is exalted by the grace and majesty of the Lord;¶ and each of its members is exhorted to act, in the service of truth, and the resistance of sin, as an armed soldier under Divine command.**

In A.D. 62—3, three other epistles were written

---

* The 9th or 10th year of Nero.—*Hug's Introduction*, vol. ii. p. 332.

† Acts xxviii. 30. ‡ Eph. i. 13, 14. § Eph. ii. 3—22.
|| Eph. iv. 1—16. ¶ Eph. i. 11—23.
** Eph. vi. 10—20.

from Rome, which show, not only what Paul taught at the time, but what he taught while there: that to the Philippians is chiefly important to us now, as showing the full beauty and confidence with which the love of Christ circulated in the body of his disciples. It was an union that had life. Paul writes to them in the spirit of a hero, and calling the initiated brethren "*the perfect*," he cheers them on to higher perfection and greater victories.

The epistle sent to Colosse, in the same year, resembles much the one sent to Ephesus. The Lord and his glory are therein presented in the same light. The people under his care are also brought into comparison with the unconverted world. Their society was, in the former letter, as a place of holy festivity, compared with a charnel house; in this it is as a kingdom of light to one of darkness. The subjects of this kingdom are said to have put away the body of their sin, to have been buried with Christ in baptism;* the believing compact of which involved an appropriating use of the Lord's circumcision and atonement; wherein, also, they were risen with Christ, through the faith of the operation of God. It was this faith in the power of God which led them to the baptism, and gave it all its sacredness; and hence, as men forgiven and risen with Christ, they are urged, without further discrimination, to sustain their dignity of moral character, and seek those things which are above, where Christ sitteth at

* Colossians ii. 9—15.

the right hand of God. They are addressed and advised altogether, as men who had passed from a state of death and darkness, to one of life and glory.*

Paul's epistle to Philemon, by Onesimus, written from the same place, and probably in the same year, A.D. 62, breathes the same spirit, and brings the same principles down to individuals. The returning slave is to be received as a brother, because of his conversion and faith in Christ; and Philemon is urged to exhibit his own faith in Jesus by forgiving and emancipating the repentant culprit.

If the language of these documents appear to be wanting in systematic consistency, it can only result from a misconception in the reader. Paul writes and acts like a great man devoted to one great cause, and labouring to induce a similar devotion in those who were recognised partakers of like precious faith in the same Redeemer. He was himself the pioneering evangelist of his time; and knowing that faith comes by hearing, laboured to produce it by the declaration of Divine Truth. One word of sacramental efficacy is not to be found in all that he has written; but every statement in his writings indicates a profound reverence for that confiding compact of separation from the world, and devotion to his Lord, which baptismal initiation under Christ comprises. Stronger expressions cannot be found in any language than he employs to describe the transition through which a baptized believer has passed, from darkness to light;

* Colossians iii. 1—17.

from the power of Satan to God; from death to life; from the kingdom of darkness to that of God's dear Son. Instead of being mere rhetorical figures, to be taken with limitation, the more closely they are examined, the more the reality in his mind appears to extend in greatness and value beyond all power in human words to describe. He speaks to the parts of one great community, and reasons with each part, whether it be an individual or an assembly, on principles and assumptions which prove that no one could find a consistent or lawful place therein who had not given its claims and polity a mature deliberation, and embraced its bond of servitude, confiding in the grace and power of its Redeemer and Lord. There, hypocrisy, indifference, and apostacy, were judged as crimes; and no man, without faith, could have submitted to the discipline Paul enforces in the name of Christ. Whatever Rome became in after times, it then received instructions from a stern believer, who fought the good fight and kept the faith in that very city, until martyrdom advanced him to his great reward. He spake to that church, and from that church, as one who was addressing recognised partakers in the same principles, privileges, and obligations with himself.

One hundred and two years afterwards, A.D. 164, Justin Martyr suffered for the truth. About the time that Antoninus Pius began his administration, A.D. 140—2, Justin left Samaria, his native place and charge, to visit Rome, and had his dwelling on the Viminalian-hill, in that city. Through nearly the whole empire, his Christian brethren were suffering from the vigorous measures used by Adrian to suppress the truth, and destroy the reign of the Redeemer. Justin's object in Rome was to plead for his suffering brethren with the senate and the Emperor. Two apologies, as if one were addressed to each of these authorities, are still found in his works. In presenting these, he must be regarded as speaking the sentiments, and describing the practice, at least, of the assembly of the disciples in Rome; because not only has no counter-statement been produced, but, if not correct, he himself must have known that its inaccuracies would be detected, and pointed out against him, to his ruinous disadvantage, both in the Senate and before the Emperor. Here, therefore, we have the same system of fellowship, formed on the same principles, and for the same end, and with the same discriminating rejection of the world that we find in the writings of Paul. The Apostle spake *to* the disciples, and Justin pleaded *for* the disciples; but, in the estimation of both, discipleship was the same rational, penitent, confiding, and self-devoted subjection to the Lord Jesus Christ. Each exhibits a like subjection in suffering and in death, as forming the required characteristic of recognised believers. But Justin has to do with details, and to give explanation. The method used by the brethren in his time to extend the faith, and recognise believers, is, therefore, pointed out with great minuteness. It was by teaching, that believers were produced. Those who believed the things they taught, and declared that they were prepared to live as Christ ordained, were the persons they then initiated. These were taken to a place in which there was water, and, having been immersed therein, were, with fasting, prayer, and laying on of hands, united with the Christian disciples. These formed, not a crowd of heterogeneous characters, but an union of like with like, through one common bond of union, to the same Lord. Justin declares that their law of self-devotement admitted of no limitation, let the Emperor and Senate do whatever they might deem proper. He describes the exclusive participation of these believers, so baptized, in the Eucharist, or Supper of the Lord. This Supper of the Lord was not only used exclusively by persons baptized into Christ; but it also required them to be living as Christ had appointed. This church, like the sea, cast out upon its shores the corruption that might have been thrown into its waters; and, in fine, the description of the worship and discipline of that time would, with little variation, describe the operations of Baptist churches now. And, where the practice of Justin's time differs from the practice of that in which we live, it becomes more discriminating, more devoted, more careful in the cultivation of Christian character within the body of Christ; and, consequently, a more general union of all its parts, in the great design of its existence, is everywhere seen.

But this evidence was given seventy-six or perhaps seventy-eight years after the Apostle wrote his Epistles from Rome. Be it so: but Justin came from Palestine; and the silence of the whole body of disciples on the point proves that no essential corruption had been then introduced at Rome. Besides, the link of evidence is supplied by the Epistles of Clement, who lived in that city, was an overseer of the disciples, and guided their devotions. The evidence supplied, by that Epistle which is undoubtedly genuine, goes to confirm all the points which are material in the question before us. It is written from the whole congregation of believers in Rome, to the whole congregation of believers in Corinth, recognising and exemplifying the fraternal compact of mutual fidelity in which believers are united by the law of Christ. The passages it quotes from the New Testament combine its whole reasoning with those laws which have been already explained, relating to the admission of members into the Christian community, and their government therein. All the great motives to obedience are urged with fraternal freedom, in order to induce in the brethren at Corinth a termination of strife. Paul's argument, in 1 Cor. i., is quoted and pressed on their attention, in which, by the Spirit, the Apostle had affirmed that, since they were baptized into the name of Christ, no division should be allowed for the sake of him or Apollos. Every argument supposes the confessed and recognised faith, both of those who are speaking, and of those who are addressed. It was written about A.D. 96, which is forty-four years before the apology of Justin, and about thirty-four after the first imprisonment of Paul in Rome; and so unites the declarations of each, as to show that, with all the advantages they possessed for forming a correct idea of what Christ intended his church to be, this whole community deemed it an incorporated body of baptized believers, subject to the law, protected by the care, and nourished by the love of their Redeemer and Lord. And, not to mention other proofs, the constitution of the conclave in which the Pope is chosen, by election of the majority, is a remnant of its ancient constitution, which, though broken by convulsion and change, like the architectural remains of antiquity, displays its origin and former use by carvings which time, though aided by the terrible apostacy, has hitherto been unable to deface.

EVIDENCE FROM CLEMENT OF ROME.

But, the evidence from Clement of Rome should be taken with greater fullness, because it will exemplify the nature of the testimony on which, in similar cases, we must depend. Of course, the existence of statements formed to meet the particular point of this controversy, is scarcely to be expected, because such a controversy had, at that time, no existence whatever. At a period so near to the Apostles' time, no one could have doubted the obligation under which he was bound, if a believer, to avow his faith in baptism; and, then, from a passage to be presently produced, the idea of baptizing infants, whose faculties were undeveloped and whose faith was not evinced, had not yet been entertained.

As soon as it was entertained, in Africa, it was condemned by Tertullian, and disputed by others. As no idea was, in this case, entertained of evading Christian baptism, Clement would not be expected to write for its enforcement; but, some centuries after, when the duty was evaded, the obligation of the rite on believers was enforced by epistles written and circulated in his name. It is remarkably the case in those works which have passed under the name of Dyonitius, the Areopagite, the convert of Paul, in Athens. No genuine works of his exist at the present time. Those which pass under his name can be traced no higher in antiquity than to the fourth or fifth century. All we can infer from these and the forged epistles of Clement, is, that the men who in that age wrote these tracts, it might be as works of fiction, plainly declared that, in their view, this was the doctrine and practice of the time and of the persons, whose language they imitated and whose credit they used. Such productions contain, in fact, no more than the evidence of the age and parties who produced them. The genuine Epistles of Clement are, like those of Paul, constructed altogether on the assumption that the churches of Christ were formed of accredited believers, recognised in baptism, and devoted by their own confession to the service and praise of the Redeemer. The first Epistle begins thus:—

"The church of God resident in Rome, to the church of God resident in Corinth, who are called (persons) consecrated in a will of God, through our Lord Jesus Christ;

grace to you, and peace, from God Almighty, through Jesus Christ, be multiplied, upon you individually, and successively."—*Epist. I., Sect.* i., *p.* 9.

Here the term "consecrated" marks the character of the persons who formed these assemblies, and the word "called" intimates that they were so deemed and designated.

The Epistle had been delayed by afflictions which had befallen the church in Rome, but it had been requested by the "brethren," the "beloved," in Corinth, in consequence of a disturbance produced there by individuals who were seeking official pre-eminence.

"Through occurrences and painful events which have happened to us, brethren, we have been reluctantly compelled tardily to make an observation concerning the matters, beloved, which have been earnestly requested from you; and the alienation and strangeness in the elect of God, the base and unholy rebellion, which a few persons having precipitately and daringly countenanced, they have kindled up into so much frantic rashness, that your venerable and celebrated name, worthy to be loved by all men, is greatly blasphemed. For, what individual, sojourning with you, has not verified your faith, filled with firmness and all virtue? who has not admired your humble and well-regulated godliness in Christ? who hath not proclaimed the bountiful habit of your hospitality, and blessed your perfect and safe knowledge? For ye did all things without respect of persons, and ye walked in the ordinances of God, being subject to your leaders, giving the appropriate honour to those who were elders with you. Ye recommended the younger persons to regard things moderate and reverential; and the women, in a blameless and solemn and pure conscience, ye exhorted to perfect all things, loving, and, in the rule of obedience, observing their own husbands, as they were bound to do : ye taught them, with universal modesty, to conduct with reverence the household affairs."—*Epist. I., Sect.* ii., *p.* 8, 10.

In this short passage, it is not only obvious that the rule of the church was to deem its members the subjects of faith ; but, that this church, notwithstanding the calamities which befel it through individuals, was eminent in the faith which its members had evinced. The words of this Section comprise, in their import, the greater part of Christian duty ; and show a systematic method of urging it, which is worthy of imitation now. The fraternal fidelity of the one church, which had been solicited by the other, is positive proof that each must have been regarded by the other as a company of recognised believers, devoted to their one common Lord. But this is not left to be inferred, it is clearly expressed in the following words:—

"Behold, the Lord shall take to himself a nation (εθνος) from the midst of the nations (εθνων), as a man taketh the first-fruits of his field ; and from that nation or people (εθνους) shall proceed things that are most sacred. Seeing, therefore, we are a part of a consecrated people, let us perform all things that belong to the consecration" (in which we have participated).—*Epist. I., Sect.* xxix.

This passage not only shows that the disciples formed an incorporated association, or nation, but that their nation, or society, was separated from all others upon earth, and for most holy purposes. The first part of the passage, also, is a prediction from

Deut. iv. 34; and the constitution of the Christian church is presented as a fulfilment of that prophecy. Lastly, the church at Corinth and that at Rome, are said to be together a part of that holy nation, (1 Peter ii. 9), and are, therefore, urged to perform all things included in their consecration. Clement has taken the idea and the word from Peter, who calls the same body of disciples a chosen generation, a royal priesthood, a holy nation, a peculiar people, that they might show forth the praises of him who hath called them out of darkness into marvellous light. The principle on which this is based and approved is shown from the following:—

"All, therefore, are honoured and elevated, not through themselves, nor through their own works, nor through the just actions they have performed, but by the will of him (our God). And by his will, therefore, we, having been called to be in Christ Jesus, are not justified through ourselves, nor by our own wisdom, or learning, or godliness, nor by the works we have performed in holiness of heart; but through the faith by which the Almighty God hath justified all his people from eternity, to whom be glory for ever and ever, Amen."—*Epist. I., Sect.* xxxii., *p.* 24.

The honouring and exalting of disciples here spoken of, consists in their incorporation and fellowship in the body of Christ. This they enjoyed through their faith; this was justified by God through their faith, and not through any other action they performed, whether in body or in mind. All the privilege of a Christian disciple was, in the view of Clement, a gift of grace, and received by faith only, and, of course, recognised whenever that faith had been avowed and accredited. If the privilege had been recognised where no faith was professed, or believed to exist, its enjoyment could not have been justified by faith only. But, he saith, "The Almighty God hath justified all his people through their faith," and "through that faith the Christian disciple is justified" in his privilege; but, when justified in holding and enjoying the privilege of a Christian disciple, the believer became an εργατης (a labourer) under the direction and employment of the Christ who redeemed him. The nature of his service will be seen in the following passage:—

"The good labourer takes with confidence the food of his own labour; he who is slothful and negligent cannot look his employer in the face. It behoves, therefore, that we be zealous to engage in a good work, for all things are from him. Moreover, he hath said to us beforehand, 'Behold the Lord, and his reward is before him, he shall give to every man according to his own work.' He urgeth us, therefore, to fix the whole heart upon this, that we may be neither indolent nor negligent respecting any good work. Our glory and our confidence should be in him; we should be subjected to his will; we should consider the whole multitude of his angels, how, waiting round him, they perform his pleasure. For, the Scripture saith, 'Ten thousand times ten thousand wait upon him, and thousands of thousands serve him;' and they cry, Holy, holy, holy Lord of Sabaoth, all creation is filled with his glory. Therefore, we also being gathered together, in one mind, for the same purpose, should cry unto him with one consent, as with one voice, continually, to the end that we may become partakers of his great and precious promises; for, he saith, 'The eye hath not seen, and the ear hath not heard, nor have come upon the heart of man, the things which God hath prepared for those who wait for him.'"—*Epist. I., Sect.* xxxiv., *p.* 25.

It is necessary to our object that Clement's distinction between the gifts of grace which are known, and those which are not known, should be clearly kept in view. Hence he saith:—

"How blessed and wonderful, beloved, are the gifts of God! Life (ripening) in immortality, personal honour (possessed) in justification, truth (sustained) in boldness, faith (exercised) in confidence, continence (realised) in sanctity; and all these fall within our own knowledge. What, then, are those things which are *prepared* for those who wait for him? The holy Founder and Father of the dispensations himself knoweth their nature and their beauty."—*Epist. I., Sect.* xxxv., *p.* 26.

From these passages, it is quite clear that Clement regarded the body of Christ as one community of believers in him. Of this community the churches in Corinth and Rome were fraternal parts, or rather assemblies of persons, each of whom was, by his faith, a member in the body of Christ. But he is more explicit in the following words:—

"Let, therefore, the whole body of us who are in Christ Jesus be preserved; and be ye every one subject to his neighbour, as also it is determined in his gifts. The strong must not treat the feeble with contumely, but the weak should respect the strong. The rich should be bountiful to the poor; but the poor should give thanks to God, because he hath given to him (the rich brother) that by which his own necessity may be supplied. The wise should show his own wisdom, not in words, but in good works. The humble should not bear testimony to himself, but leave the testimony to be borne to his humility by others. He who is holy as to the flesh should not exult, knowing that his continence is given to him by another. Consider, therefore, brethren, by analogy, from what material we have been produced; what kind of persons we come into the world, as from the sepulchre and darkness; he having created and formed us, led us into this, his own world, having made ready his kind provisions before ever we were formed. Having all these things from himself, therefore, we are bound in all things to give thanks to him, to whom be glory for ever and ever, Amen."—*Epist. I., Sect.* xxxviii., *p.* 27.

To analogise, is to examine by comparison, or to consider by analogy. Our entrance into the world is thus made to represent our entrance into the church. In the body of Christ, all his merciful provisions were made and fixed, before we were born into its fellowship; as the blessings of providence were made ready before we were born into the world. Hence the following injunction:—

"Brethren, let every one of you give thanks to God, in his own proper place and order; preserving a good conscience, in solemnity; not breaking through the determined law of the service. Not in every place, brethren, were sacrifices continually offered, either of thanksgiving, or for sins and transgressions, but in Jerusalem only; and even there, not in every place were they offered, but before the temple at the altar, the sacrifice having been inspected through the high priest, and the ordained ministry. Those, therefore, who performed anything, except that which was agreeable with his counsel, received the mortal punishment. Observe, brethren, by how much more full the knowledge is which we have been counted worthy to receive, by so much the more" (in a similar offence), "shall we be exposed to danger."—*Epist. I., Sect.* xli., *p.* 28, 29.

Here we have a further illustration of the authority by which the body of Christ was governed. As men by nature are subject to the law of God in nature and providence, and as Jews were subject to the law of God by Moses, so Christian disciples are, in the body of Christ, subject to the law of God by their Redeemer. The believers, therefore, were both a privileged and a subjected body, each member holding his privilege, and yielding his submission to God, in Christ. Which Clement describes thus:—

"The Apostles brought joyful intelligence from the Lord Jesus Christ, Jesus the Christ from God. The Christ, therefore, was sent out from God; and the Apostles were sent out from the Christ. Both, therefore, were appointed in due order by the will of God. Therefore, having received authoritative instructions, and having been firmly convinced by the resurrection of our Lord Jesus Christ, and having been entrusted with the word of God, with a complete certainty of the Holy Spirit, they went forth bearing the joyful intelligence, that the reign of God was at hand. Having, therefore, preached through regions and cities, being directed by the Spirit, they appointed their first-fruits, for pastors and deacons of those who were about to believe. And this was no new thing; for, truly, many ages before, it had been written concerning pastors and deacons, 'I will appoint their pastors in righteousness, and their deacons in faith.'"—*Epist. I., Sect.* xlii., *p.* 29.

Here we see, not only the Divine fountain of all authority in the body of Christ, but also, as Clement viewed it, the channel through which it flows to us. The Christ, as his title imports, is from God; the Apostles, as their titles import, are from him; and the ministry of pastors and deacons has followed, by the election of churches, through all time. But these are perfectly subordinate to the supreme authority of the Redeemer. See this in Clement's own words:—

"Consider the Epistle of the blessed Paul, the Apostle. What did he first write to you in the beginning of the Gospel? He truly sent to you, by inspiration of the Spirit, concerning himself and Cephas and Apollos, on this account, that then also ye had been made partisans: but that party-feeling entailed on you a smaller sin, for you adhered to persons proved to be apostles, and to men who had been attested with them. But now, consider with yourselves who they are that disturb you, and defile the splendour of your celebrated brotherly affection. It is shameful, beloved, —it is greatly shameful, and disgraceful to the fellowship we have in Christ, to be heard that the most firm and ancient church of the Corinthians has been, by one or two faces, stirred up into rebellion with its elders. And this report hath not only reached us, it hath also advanced into those who are opposed to us; so that blasphemies are brought upon the name of the Lord, through your folly, while danger is created for you yourselves."—*Epist. I., Sect.* xlvii., *p.* 32.

The spirit of this passage is beyond all praise. The generous boldness of its fidelity is sweetly softened by fraternal affection. All classes are recognised in its argument: the elders, the members of the church in Corinth, and the unconverted world opposed to Christ and his kingdom. Clement had just been suffering for the name of Christ, and he burns with tender solicitude for its honour. His fervour makes him eloquent, and his appeal to the Epistles of Paul to the Corinthians is proof that the system and object of Christian fellowship, which roused the energies of these two great men, must have been the same. In appealing to personal magnanimity, Paul said, "Why do ye not rather suffer wrong?" In urging a similar concern for the body of Christ, the words of Clement are:—

"Who amongst you, then, is noble-hearted? who is compassionate? What man is filled with love? Let him say, if through me rebellion, strife, and schism be produced, I will depart wherever you may please, and I will do whatever may be appointed by the whole body to be done; only let the flock of the Lord, with its appointed elders, be in peace. He who doth this, will gain for himself great honour in the Lord; and every place will receive him: 'for the earth is the Lord's, and the fulness thereof.' These things, those who maintain the unblameable citizenship of God, have performed and should perform."—*Epist. I., Sect.* liv., *p.* 35.

What can this be, but the act of a believing man appealing to believing men, and stirring up their moral sensibilities to nourish and protect thereby an interest which all had declared to be more dear to them than life? It is earnestness appealing to earnestness, and, with intense charity, labouring to retain the judgment of integrity where faith had been professed and error indulged. Here is no compromise of principle, but a holy and tender anxiety to recover the brethren from practical mistakes. This solicitude shines in the gentle simplicity of his style, as morning sunbeams glitter in the drops of dew which hang, like tears, upon the face of nature. "Observe," he says, "observe, beloved brethren, what an example hath been given to us; for, if the Lord so humbled himself, what should we do who have come under the yoke of his mercy?"* "See to it, beloved, lest the kindnesses of the Lord, which are so many, be for a judgment against us all, if our conversation be not worthy of him, performing with unanimity the things which are beautiful and pleasing before him."† There is a deep feeling in these passages which suffers immensely from being cut out of their connexion. Clement writes like one who had before him a defined and pledged people. Individuals might be wrong, and prove themselves to be insincere; but the principle of the fellowship, and the constitution of the community, for which he is concerned, are before his mind with a distinctness which cannot be concealed, and he, like a great man, fitted to be a leader of brethren, follows the application of this principle, with unerring exactness, through almost infinite detail:—

"See to it, beloved, lest the benefits of (the Lord) which are many, should be for a judgment to us all, unless, having our conversation worthy of him, we do those things which are beautiful and pleasing before him with unanimity. For he saith in a certain place, 'The Spirit of the Lord is a lamp, scrutinising the secrets of the belly.' Mark how near he is! and that nothing is hid from him, either of our thoughts or of the investigations that we make of them. It is just, therefore, that we do not leave our place by departing from his will. Let us offend the unwise, ignorant, and exulting men, who boast in the arrogance of their word, rather than God. Let us reverence the Lord

---

* Epist. i., Sect. 16. † Epist. i., Sect. 21.

Jesus Christ, whose blood was shed for us. Let us honour our leaders; let us respect our elders; let us administer to the youth the training which is based on the fear of God. Let us lead our wives to that which is good; let them exhibit that habit of purity which is worthy of all love; let them show the sincere desire of their modest kindness; let them make manifest the modesty of their tongues by the character of their speech; let them exercise their love, not with partial attachments, but with equality, in holiness to all who fear God. Let your children partake of the discipline that is in Christ. They should learn what strength there is in humbleness with God; what a holy love is able to do with God; how the fear of him is beautiful and great, and saveth all those who, in a pure heart, are holily exercised therein. For the Searcher of our thoughts and councils is he whose Spirit is in us, and, when he please, he taketh it away."—*Epist. I., Sect.* xxi., *p.* 20.

Τους νεους means, not only the youthful part of the church, but the new converts; and the ποιδειαν is the instruction and training by which the Christian was to be advanced to a greater perfection in knowledge and Christian habits. This was contemplated by Paul in himself, and in those churches the care of which fell upon him daily. This was called the discipline or knowledge of the fear of God, because it consisted in explaining the reasons for cherishing that fear with the actions and habits to which it should lead. This was the business of a disciple, and because he had this to learn he was called a disciple. It is here, probably, more than at any other point, that the arguments against believers' baptism, and the communion of believers, reveal their fallacy. By neglecting the individualised, spiritual education of the early churches, the language which described their polity has become, to modern readers, inexplicable, and even absurd. Christians are now treated as men who have nothing to acquire, rather than as disciples, whose avowed business is to learn the truth of God, and to form the habits necessary to his service and fellowship. Hence those passages in the ancient writings, which describe those acts of church discipline and church worship, have been supposed to refer to persons introduced into the fellowship of churches before they believed in Christ, or were Christians at all. This is absolutely wrong. The act of faith by which a man becomes a Christian is only a first step, introductory to that training by which a Christian is to become a *man* in Christ Jesus. It is this faith which is recognised in Christian baptism, and, by neglecting the subsequent training of the convert, the baptismal recognition of his faith is reduced to absurdity. Hence it is made to appear, that the baptism should be applied to infants and unbelievers without discrimination; not because the ancients baptized without an accredited declaration of faith, but because we have so much neglected the spiritual cultivation of baptized believers. It is this which Clement and the ancients enforced with so much zeal and determination. The trials through which they had to pass, made them feel that untrained troops were not competent to their warfare; and, therefore, that to neglect their discipline was to betray the hosts of Israel into the hands of their enemies. That very care which they cherished to make each baptized believer perfect in Christ, would lead them to baptize none but those whom they deemed believers. All the foregoing passages show, that, in Clement's view, these believers formed a society in themselves, a peculiar people, a consecrated nation, recognised in their baptism, as in the world, but not of the world. Their wives were not always Christians, for many had been married before their conversion from heathenism and unbelief; but they were to have an advantage from being so nearly allied to persons recognised in Christ. The Christian husband had a Christian's duty to perform in that relationship, whether his wife were converted or not; if not, that her conversion might be effected; if she were a convert, for her edification and joy in the Lord. The children of a Christian were not necessarily Christian, they were not so deemed until their conversion; but the Christian father had a Christian's duty to perform towards them. He might make them partakers of the instruction and discipline which he himself received in Christ. His children might thus, by his means, be made to "learn how much humility prevailed with God;" "what a holy love was permitted to do with God;" "how the fear of him is beautiful and great, and saveth those who, in a sincere heart, are therein holily converted." By this means, the household of the Christian would become the nursery of the church. To carry out this design, and aid individuals who might feel incompetent, the churches formed their catechetical classes, and in them employed her best-instructed members. The aim of the church was to neglect no advantage brought by Providence within her reach. The Christian was bound not to neglect his wife, his children, nor his neighbour; but, by every means, to seek the production and development of that faith on the profession of which the church might receive them in her holy baptism. All preaching, all evangelising, all domestic influence, and public teaching, was consecrated to this end; and the light in which that baptism was esteemed by Clement, is obvious from the following words:—

"Brethren, it behoveth us to think, concerning Jesus Christ, as God, and a Judge of the living and the dead. And it behoveth us, not to have low thoughts respecting our salvation, for in that which we lightly esteem we expect to find little advantage. And we sin who are hearing (his word), as if it related to matters of no moment, not knowing from whence we are called, and by whom, and into what place, and what things Jesus hath patiently suffered for our sakes." "For he had mercy; and, having greatly compassionated, he saved us, seeing in us great delusion and ruin, and that we had no hope of salvation except that which comes from him."—*Epist. II., Sect.* i., *p.* 40.

"The Christ desired to save those which were lost, and coming, he saved many, and having called, (he saved) us who were already perishing. Exercising so great mercy toward us, therefore, (he caused) first, indeed, that we, who are living persons, should not sacrifice to dead idols, and not worship them; but that, through him, we should know the Father of truth. What is the knowledge which pertains to him except this, that we should not deny Him through whom He is made known to us? But he saith, also, 'He who confesseth me before men, him will I confess before my Father.' This, therefore, is our reward, if we confess him through whom we are saved."—*Epist. II., Sect.* iii., *p.* 41.

"But if those who were so righteous (Noah, Job, and Daniel,) could not, by their own righteousness, deliver their own children, unless we keep our baptism holy and unblameable, with what confidence can we enter the kingdom of God? or who shall be our advocate, if we are not found maintaining holy and justified works?"—*Epist. II., Sect.* vi., *p.* 43.

"What think ye?—he who corrupted the conflict for incorruption, what should he suffer? For of those who preserve not the seal (baptism), he saith, 'Their worm shall not die, and their fire shall not be quenched,' and they shall be for a spectacle to all flesh."—*Epist. II., Sect.* vii., *p.* 44.

"Hereupon, therefore, he saith this, 'Keep ye your flesh holy, and your seal (baptism) unpolluted, in order that ye may receive the everlasting life.' "—*Epist. II., Sect.* viii., *p.* 44.

In these passages the baptism is called a *confession* and a *seal;* and in both characters it forms the ground of a powerful personal admonition. How, then, could it be called a confession, unless the subject of baptism had faith to confess? Or how could it be called a seal, except as an acknowledgment of privileges which believers only are justified in using? Lastly, if nothing was confessed by the baptized disciple, and if no privilege had been sealed to him in his baptism, how could the following sentence have been written?—

"Therefore, brethren, let us confess the Lord in works (which he commands), in this, that we love his people; in this, that we do not commit adultery; that we do not defame each other; that we do not envy; but that we be temperate, merciful, good: and we ought to sympathise with each other, and not to be avaricious; and in good works we should confess God, not in those of a contrary nature. It behoveth us, also, not to fear men; but rather to fear God. On this account, of those of us who do these things (which he forbids), the Lord saith, 'Though ye were with me, collected in my bosom, and do not the things which I command you, I will cast you forth, and say to you, Depart from me, I know you not whence ye are, ye workers of iniquity."—*Epist. II., Sect.* iv., *p.* 42.

"Wherefore, brethren, leaving the conversation of this world, let us do the will of him who hath called us, and not fear to come out from the men of this world."—*Epist. II., Sect.* v., *p.* 42.

It is not the accidental and superficial features, but the heart and soul of this system of fellowship, which, in the hands of Clement, pours its flame of convincing testimony upon our argument. These believers in Rome, through their pastor, are dealing with their brethren in Corinth as with persons separated from the world, confessed and sealed in baptism, who held their exalted privilege on the ground of their faith, and who are called to maintain a conduct consistent with their faith by appeals to the judgment of him in whom they trusted. Mark the spirit of what follows:—

"Let us serve God, therefore, in a pure heart, and we shall be justified; but, if we do not serve through not believing the promise of God, we shall be most wretched. For the prophetical word saith, 'Wretched are the double-minded who are divided in heart, and are saying, all these things we have heard from our Fathers, but we, expecting day by day, have seen nothing of them. Unwise men! Compare yourselves to a tree—take a vine, for instance—first, indeed, the leaves unfold, then the shoots are started, after these the sour grapes appear, and then the fruit becomes perfected; so, also, my people have disturbances and afflictions, but, afterwards, receive the advantage. So that, brethren, we should not be double-minded, but, cherishing our hope, continue steadfastly, in order that we may obtain the reward. For, he who has promised that he will give to every man according to his work, is faithful. If, therefore, we perform that which is justified before God, we shall come into his kingdom, and receive the promises which ears have not heard, and which eyes have not seen, and which never have come upon the heart of man."—*Epist. II., Sect.* xi., *p.* 45.

This solemn demand of consistency in character and action demonstrates the constitutional element of Christian fellowship. Clement not only assumes that the disciples were believers; he also states that, if their faith fail, their obedience must fail too. In his view, therefore, all practical things in the church of Christ depended upon faith, without which no one could be justified or saved. How, then, did they become believers? It is answered, by preaching, teaching, and the attendant blessing of God. The idea of making men believers by baptism does not so much as enter his thoughts. How, then, could he assume that the church was composed of believers? Unquestionably because the accredited profession of their faith was the term of their baptism. On this principle, his writings are clear as the most lucid stream; and, however blasphemed by ministerial rashness and levity, the fervent, devoted spirit with which the holy father carries out and applies his thoughts is deserving of all admiration. His perspicuity is such as almost defies misconstruction. The obscurities and absurdities attributed to him are the productions of modern imaginations, heated with impatient zeal to find in his pages some reverent authority for infant baptism. This expense of feeling, and its fretful consequences, might be spared; the brethren seek for evidence to sustain their practice where it cannot be found. It is of no use to search the writings of Clement for such evidence: it is not there.

THE TESTIMONIES FROM GREECE.

By concealing dates and shrinking from the labour of calm investigation, polemical advocates have beguiled themselves, and thought they could perceive in this antiquity the shadows of every absurd notion. If the thing affirmed of these times were true, the great first action of Divine mercy would stand disgraced with failure in the face of all mankind. The deeds of mercy would not then sustain our faith in its magnificent promises; but, let God be true, whatever effect the admission of his veracity may have on human affirmations. The promises of mercy granted in the Gospel were sustained by its early action in Greece, as well as Rome. In Corinth, Divine truth encountered the combined forces of lascivious idolatry, mercenary adventure, and the vanity which attends redundant wealth labouring for admiration by architectural display and affectations of eminence in literature and taste. To the painful defects recorded of the church formed here, Dr. Halley has referred with too much exultation, as if they proved that Christian disciples were incorporated here and everywhere, without any regard to their character. He must not be accused of rejoicing in iniquity, because it seems to favour his views; but he ought to have seen that the victory won by the truth here forms a most striking demonstration of its power. Paul never seems greater than when he stands against, or rather rises above, the mercenary corruptions and suspicions of that people. It ought to be known, that there adultery was worship; avarice, virtue; luxuriance, beauty; and falsehood, discretion. It was infamous at Athens to be called a Corinthian. That men, supposed to be converted, and recognised as believers, should, in passing from such a society, bring with them some of their heathen deformities, is not so much to be wondered at, as that the holy Gospel should have there obtained any converts at all. It must be remembered, too, that their faults came out, by their own confessions, in sending to ask advice of Paul. The vigour of their discipline, under his direction, is proof, too, that there was, in that assembly, an internal life, struggling with corruption as it appeared. But if they were all wrong; if the Corinthian professors were hypocrites to a man; the Epistles written by Paul, and that which followed from Clement of Rome, reveal the law of their incorporation. They were baptized into Christ, incorporated as men who confessed that they were not their own. They were subjected under Christ, as the Jews were under Moses; and they were answerable to Christ for the vigour, kindness, and purity, of their internal discipline. They had a strong testimony of their faith in those spiritual gifts with which that assembly was endowed. Like other Christians, they also were baptized on the hope of a resurrection from the dead. The same principles appear, combined with commendation, in the Epistles sent to Thessalonica and Philippi. And, that these were the true and not the evanescent principles of their fellowship, is proved; since, after one thousand years had elapsed, these border lands of Thrace retained the doctrine, and Theophilact declared its truth, in his commentaries on these very Epistles, while labouring in Bulgaria.

THE TESTIMONY OF THEOPHILACT.

To this author a particular attention should be paid, because he is himself a Greek commentator, and may therefore be supposed to understand the works which were before him in his own language. He also follows, with considerable exactness, the opinion of Chrysostom, who was certainly a master both in eloquence and criticism. Both these authors were powerful teachers of Divine truth, and so situated as to have their whole attention given to the discipline of Christian churches; and their writings contain unquestionable proofs of the doctrine which was taught and prevailed in Greece and in Asia Minor, with little variation, for one thousand years at least. The following examples contain both the text quoted by Theophilact and his explanations;—

" Heb. vi. 2, '*A doctrine of baptisms.*' Paul speaks in the plural number, not as if there were many baptisms, for there is but one, but as if this followed from the conclusion supposed: for if he again taught, and baptized again, and baptized the persons who had failed in their profession, by necessity also there would be again, (as with the Jews,) many baptisms, but this is absurd. It does not behove, therefore, that you should be (anabaptized) baptized again; but it behoves you to continue acting upon the former baptism."

" '*And of a resurrection from the dead.*' For this also took place in the baptism through the figure of the immersion received, and in the confession it becomes confirmed; for we confess, that we believe a resurrection from the dead." " But observe, that the baptism is after the repentance, for since the repentance is not sufficient of itself to show that we are purified, therefore we are baptized, in order that the favour of the Christ may be perfectly enjoyed."

" Coloss. ii. 12, ' *Having been buried with him in baptism.*' That which he (Paul) designated a circumcision before, now he calls a burial—exhibiting to us something greater than the circumcision . . . he, therefore, who has been baptized, has been buried with the Christ."

"'*In whom also ye were raised through the faith of the operation of the God who raised him from the dead.*' The baptism is not a burial only, but a resurrection also; but how? through the faith (we exercise); for believing that God is able to raise up, and having an example of this that he also raised up the Christ from the dead, we are thus raised in two ways; both because we, expecting a resurrection, seem already to possess it, although it may be future; and because spiritually we are delivered from the death which is involved in the works of sin."

"Rom. vi. 3, 4, '*Or are ye ignorant that we, as many as were baptized into Christ, were baptized into his death? Therefore we are buried with him through the baptism into his death, in order that as Christ was raised from the dead by the glory of the Father, so we also might walk in a newness of life.*' He (Paul) is explaining how we die to sin, and saith, that (it is) through the baptism; for we are baptized into the death of the Christ; that is, to this end, that they who are baptized might die as he did. For as the cross and the sepulchre were to the Christ, so also the baptism is to us, even though the cross and sepulchre be not themselves endured. For he, indeed, died to the flesh, and rose again; but we, dying to sin, are raised to virtue, in order that as the Christ rose in flesh from the dead through the glory of the Father—that is, through his proper divinity (for the Son is a glory of the Father), so we also rise by another resurrection, the new course of conduct. For when the fornicator becomes chaste, there is both a death and resurrection—a dying of the evil, and a resurrection and life of the virtue in the man."

"Rom. vi. 5, '*For if we have become plants growing together with him in the likeness of his death, we shall certainly become so also of his resurrection.*' Paul saith not that we have fellowship in the likeness of his death, but that we have become plants growing together; by the noun which describes the planting, he indicates the fruit which results from it. For the body of the Christ, having been buried in the earth, brought forth a fruit of salvation. But since we, indeed, were buried in the water, and he in the earth; and we to sin, but he to the body; he (Paul), therefore, saith not in the death, but in the likeness of his death. And we ourselves, inheriting an everlasting life, shall become partakers of his resurrection, because the resurrection (we have obtained) is exhibited in good works."

"Galatians iii. 25, 26, '*But the faith having come, we are no longer under a schoolmaster. For ye are all sons of God through the faith which is in Christ Jesus.*' The faith having come, he saith, which maketh a perfect man; if so, we who have become perfect thereby, and have passed through our childhood, should be no longer under a schoolmaster. For since we are perfect men through our faith, it is obvious from what cause we are also sons of God by the faith we exercise in Christ, for so is the construction. But universally he who is deemed worthy to become a son of God, is neither imperfect, nor an infant. So that the supposition (against which Paul reasoned) that having become men, they should be placed under the law, which is the schoolmaster, is ridiculous: as also this, that the day having risen, they should not use the light of the sun, but that of a lamp. But observe how, above indeed he showed that the faith made men sons of Abraham, but now he shows that it makes them sons of God."

"Galatians iii. 27, '*For ye, as many as have been baptized into Christ, have put on Christ.*' (Paul is explaining how we are sons of God, and saith, that it is through our baptism. But he doth not say, Ye, as many as have been baptized, have become sons of God, (and as the consequence required); but that which is more solemn, 'Ye have put on Christ.' For, if we have put on Christ, the Son of our God, who have also obtained a likeness with him, we have entered into one relationship and one condition, having become, by grace, that which he is by nature."

Galatians, iii. 28, '*There is not in one man a Jew, and in another a Greek; nor in one a slave, and in another a free man; nor in one a male and in another a female: for, ye are all one in Christ Jesus.*' He (Paul) saith, Every one of those who have been baptized, hath laid aside—put off—the personal peculiarities which belonged to him by nature; but all have assumed one example (τυπον) and one form, not of an angel, but of the Lord himself, exhibiting in themselves the Christ. So that, we are also one in Christ Jesus; that is, as we have one form of the Christ remaining in us; or also, as we are one body, we have one head, the Christ."

"Ephesians i. 13, '*In whom ye also having believed, were sealed with the Holy Spirit of promise.*' He saith, Having believed in the Gospel, or, in the Christ; that is, through the grace of the Christ, ye, having believed, were sealed. So that, it becomes plain that this (the sealed believer) is a portion and an inheritance belonging to God. But the Jews, indeed, were sealed by the circumcision, receiving, as creatures without reason, a fleshly seal; while we, as sons of God, and raised above the flesh, are sealed in the Spirit. But this he calls a spirit of promise, either because it was given by promise, and also because God, through Joel, declared, I will pour out of my Spirit upon all flesh; and the Christ said, Ye shall receive a power when the Holy Spirit hath come upon you, or because the promise of the good things to come is confirmed by the Spirit. For he having been already given to us, establisheth also the things which are future; wherefore, he is also called a seal. For, hear what follows:—

"Ephesians i. 14, '*Who is an earnest of our inheritance,*' God hath negotiated with us our salvation and given to us beforehand, as an earnest, the Spirit; certifying that he will also give the inheritance of the unspeakable blessings. But those who truly become partakers of the Spirit, know from thence already that he is an earnest of the perfect inheritance. Such was Paul. Wherefore, also, he groaned, and sought to obtain the consummation, and to be with

Christ; but we neither have the earnest as we ought, nor do we aim at the consummation as those who have a relish for it."

"Titus iii. 5, 6, '*Through a washing of a new birth, and a renewing of a Holy Spirit, which he poured out upon us richly through Jesus Christ our Saviour.*' Oh, wonderful! that we were so baptized, *immersed* in evil, that we were not able to be purified, but required a new birth, for this is the producing again and the renewing, the second birth, and the new formation. For as a house altogether dilapidated we do not repair, but, pulling it down to the foundations, form it anew; so also God hath not repaired, but rebuilt us. But how? By the Holy Spirit. For in order that thou mightest not question respecting the mode of this operation, the Spirit, he saith, shall put in order the whole. Whence is this perceived? He (Paul) saith, which he hath poured out upon us richly. For he hath not only by that Spirit formed us again; but also largely, abundantly granted him, in order that his former work might be shown by his present gifts. And this is likely, for after that he hath purified, he will also fill us with the Spirit most bountifully. For this is the meaning of 'he poured out.' Because that which is holy entereth not into that which is impure. But these things transpire through Jesus, for he is the Mediator for us, and the agent for effecting all these benefits."

"Titus iii. 7, '*In order that, having been justified by his grace, we might become heirs according to the hope of eternal life.*' Again, observe, the 'by grace,' and not by merit. But this also teacheth humility. For we ourselves have not put in order anything;' and he maketh us inheritors of a good hope concerning things to come: for if, by free favour, he hath saved us when so abandoned, much more will he give his predicted favour to those who are justified; in order that, he saith, they may become inheritors of eternal life, as also we hope; or because we are already inheritors as far as respects the hope."

The brethren will excuse this long series of quotations from an author so deserving of esteem. He may not be always perfectly right; but before he, and such as he, are abused, they ought to be refuted and shown to be wrong. Let the words of Theophilact be taken in their true sense, and his simple testimony is, that sinners become sons of God by faith in Christ Jesus; that, by baptism, they put on Christ; that repentance goes before baptism; and that baptism goes before the full effusion of the Holy Spirit; but that the Spirit so granted to a penitent and baptized believer is an earnest of the promised inheritance of eternal life. Here is neither absurdity nor schism; for it is said that all such persons form one body in Christ. If these doctrines,—taught as well by Chrysostom, in A.D. 398, as by Theophilact, in A.D. 1070; in Antioch and Constantinople, as in Bulgaria upon the Danube,—be not conformable to the meaning of Holy Scripture, they are so clearly stated, and their statements are so connected with the words of Paul, as to admit of easy refutation. Let Dr. Halley follow the expositions of Theophilact, and show, with equal suavity and calmness, where he has missed the meaning of the inspired word: cases of this kind may be found, without doubt; but when a due attention has been paid to all the elements of his reasoning, his errors will be found comparatively few; and from the rich mine of sacred truth which his writings compose, this testimony to believers' baptism will be obtained, which is too clear to be misunderstood, and so conclusive as to admit of no possible refutation.

THE TESTIMONIES FROM ASIA MINOR.

Lesser Asia, extending from the Hellespont to Syria, contained many provinces; and, in most of these, assemblies of disciples had been formed before the Apostle's death. The instructions given to them by Paul are recorded in his epistles—to Titus, who laboured in Crete; to Timothy, in Ephesus; to the Ephesians themselves; to the Colossians, the Galatians, and Philemon. The bare mention of these books will serve to recall those passages in each which bear, as we have shown, on the present inquiry. In these communications Paul affirms that all who had been baptized into Christ had put on Christ, were separated from the world by the washing of their new birth, were buried with Christ in baptism, had risen with him, were sons of God by faith in Christ Jesus; and, against all Judaising and heathen teachers, had only to retain their position in Christ, seeking the things which are above until the Lord come. The directions given to Timothy and Titus, for regulating the assemblies of believers, imply this law of their incorporation, because they can be applied to none other than those who personally profess their faith, willingly embrace the obligation of believers, and cherish the hope of their calling. These communications were all sent before the year A.D. 65 or 66, when Paul suffered martyrdom in Rome.

When Paul, at Miletus, took leave of the Ephesian elders, he predicted the corruption of their fellowship; and most pathetically charged them, on that account, to be the more careful in feeding the flock of God: and, in his letters to Timothy, the same event is foretold; but, in both cases, he indicates that this event would be *against* the law of Christ. In A.D. 96, when John, the last of the Apostles, presided over seven churches in and round Ephesus, this prediction began to be fulfilled. The Zabians, who still adhered to John's baptism, and wished to give him supremacy over Christ, and the Gnostics, who blended the eastern learning with Christian doctrine, injured the churches, destroying the faith of some, and teaching views of the person of our Lord which mar the whole dispensation of mercy. JOHN then produced his Gospel, his Epistles, and the book of his Revelations, in Patmos. In these works, the divine majesty of Christ is shown, his supremacy is witnessed by the very words of John the Baptist, his threefold object of giving light, life, and support to his people, is explained by abstracts of his own discourses; the privilege and hope of his disciples, as sons of God, are beautifully declared; the Lord is said to give that privilege only to those who receive him, to those who believe on his name; and these are required, in his own words, to be born again of water and the Spirit, before their privilege in the kingdom of heaven can be enjoyed. In all these points, John is exhibiting the truth to meet some form of rising error; and in his vision, the Lord himself is seen walking, not in the world, but between the candlesticks, amongst the churches, with eyes of fire and tongue of flame, to give the discrimination of his law a greater force, and to make the brethren feel the weight of their responsibility, and the terrors of his judgment, while the opening seals of prophecy show the extension and conflict of his kingdom till the close of time.

With such declarations of his will, the Lord was pleased to close up his inspired communications with mankind. John the Evangelist died in about A.D. 100, and men were left to use the written word, completed by his writings, as the only infallible guide to salvation in the fellowship of Christ. In the year A.D. 107, or, as some think, 116, Ignatius, the bishop of Antioch in Syria, passed, under a military escort, through Asia Minor, on his way to be martyred in the theatre at Rome. His great age, venerable character, and personal docility, under the blessing of God, secured him a kindly treatment from his guard; and, by their permission, his intercourse with the brethren who formed churches in the cities through which he passed, was considerable. When he came to Smyrna, where Polycarp was, he wrote to the churches in Ephesus, in Magnesia, and in Trallium; he wrote also to the church in Rome; and, removing from Smyrna to Troas on his way, he wrote to the church in Philadelphia, and in Smyrna, and to Polycarp in particular. It is not so much to any one passage in these letters, written in haste, by an aged man, under military guard, and receiving consolatory visits and communications on his way to martyrdom, that we refer; the total character of the whole is proof, that the baptismal incorporation of believers, exhibited in the writings of Paul and of John, as the ordained fellowship in Jesus Christ our Lord, is the very thing which, with all its personal freedom, responsibilities, and hopes, existed in Asia while Ignatius was on his journey. He wrote, spake, acted, hoped, and suffered, as a member and citizen of one vast republic of faith, where every soul was, by his own confession, subject to the law, and under the care of one Almighty Lord. The martyr acts and writes as one who had a right to assume, that those who formed these assemblies were believing men; he prescribed no limit to his own subjection in Christ, and supposed none to theirs; he refers to the baptism of our Lord* in a way which sustains the character already given to that event, and makes an appeal to the baptism† of believers, as one who assumed its intelligent, confiding, and public moral engagement. In fact, these letters, and the references to them in Eusebius, show that they must have been sent to assemblies of men who could have been regarded in no other light than that of baptized believers.

The sphere of Ignatius' labour was beyond the extreme east of Lesser Asia. The church and residence of Polycarp was at the extreme west. He affirmed, in his confession, that he had been a

---

* Ad Smyr., Sect. 1.   † Ad Polycarp, Sect. 6.

servant of Jesus Christ for eighty and six years. He is supposed to have been martyred in A.D. 148, certainly not later than A.D. 168. His letter to the Philippians appears to have been written in the year A.D. 108, very soon after the martyrdom of Ignatius. In this document we have, not only a distinct testimony borne to the labours and writings of the Apostle Paul, who founded the churches in Philippi and Thessalonica, and the epistles which he sent to those churches, but every admonition and advice is given in the spirit, and on that principle of incorporation, which Paul taught, and on which we have already seen that he acted. Polycarp writes as a believer addressing believers. He individualises his instruction, as one concerned to obtain that personal and dignified devotion in the conduct of believers to which they were pledged in their baptismal covenant. His distinction between the initiated and the world, and between true and false brethren, and the merciful fidelity he urges in reference to those who erred from the truth, are proofs of a discriminating fellowship, which defy contradiction; and the account of his martyrdom, which was sent by his bereaved church in Smyrna, to their brethren in Philadelphia, soon after his decease, not only exhibits a rule of devotion in the cause of the Redeemer, which rises to absolute majesty in the storm which then raged, but shows with what propriety and force Trypho, who was ignorant of the grace in which believers stand, could plead that the law of Christ was one which human nature was unable to fulfil.

Thus, from the two extremes and all the intermediate provinces of the Lesser Asia, a testimony is gained which harmonises with that of Greece and Rome, in justifying our interpretation of the sacred oracles; and in proving that the fellowship of believers, discriminated in their baptism, is of God, and not of man. At this period, the fellowship of Jesus had been maintained, with steadfast adherence to Divine precept and example, at least for one hundred years. The province of Asia Minor was so important to the empire, and the active parties of its population were so often at variance, that it became the scene of most rigid legal action whenever the supreme authority called for a persecution of the Christians. Moreover, the artists, the merchants, the landowners, and landholders, were all suffering, with the heathen priesthood, through the neglect of idol worship, by which the market for produce in sacrifices, a popular source of individual wealth and power, was absolutely dying out before their eyes; and that, too, by the means of this uncompromising body of believers baptized into Christ. It was also the practice of Roman Proconsuls, who held their power in the provinces but a year, to make that official tenure as profitable as they could, by serving for bribes the complaining part of the community. Nothing could be more favourable for this than the persecution of Christians in favour of the priesthood and dependants of idolatry. These and other circumstances of like nature made the Lesser Asia a place in which Christian principle became, by necessity, subjected to the most fiery and the most diversified trial. The wonder is that it retained an existence at all. The next one hundred years continued both its trials and its victories. It not only distinguished its possessors from the world, it formed a basis on which they were recognised by each other, and loved each other, even to the death. The heathen rulers seemed not so anxious to destroy the people, as to disgrace the system; for if, when brought to the torture or place of execution, the sufferers failed, their failure dishonoured the faith they had professed, which could not have been, if men, baptized into Christ, had professed no faith at all. The Christians of that time knew their own position; and knew that their position could only be sustained by an obedience unto death. The feebleness and the sinfulness of human nature were, as Paul foretold, exhibited in the failure and even the apostacy of individuals; this is more conceivable than that such a struggle should be undertaken without any profession or regard for faith at all; but the rule of the fellowship, and its required obedience, cannot be better shown than in the action and words of Polycarp, who, when waiting prayerfully in his hiding-place the will of God, turning to those who were with him, said, from the impression on his mind, but with holy calmness, "*It behoveth me to be burnt alive.*"* The words, the action, the spirit of the martyr, and the record of the event, set before us, beyond all dispute, the great practical reality

---

* Martyrdom of Polycarp, Sect. v., p. 17. Ed. Oxf., 1644.

which was then thrilling the heart and changing the constitution of heathen Asia. Under that law of self-devotion, multitudes were advanced to the tribunal, stood under the torturing scourge, until the whole economy of their sinews and arteries became visible to the human eye; and then, basted with melted wax, or roasted in fire, they found repose in death. This was no trifling superficiality. Christian profession was a thing so serious, that none but serious and believing men could sustain it. They could not sustain it except by the constant communication of power from God. It presented phases in its action which confounded the most intelligent observers, who did not know the faith of Jesus, and its conquering power: the conduct of these disciples can be explained only by that which Chrysostom has affirmed—they, when baptized into Christ, were baptized on the hope of a resurrection from the dead. Their faith laid hold on eternity.

TESTIMONIES FROM SYRIA.

The witness of Ignatius connects the evidence from Asia Minor with that of Syria, in which country, his own church, in Antioch, was situated. That assembly was formed in A. D. 42, by brethren, who, being scattered by the persecution, went into Phenice, Cyprus, and Antioch.* They bore their testimony with them; and in Antioch the hand of the Lord was with them, and a great number

---

* Acts xi. 19, 21.

believed and turned to the Lord. These were the first elements of that assembly; and, when the Apostles heard of it, they sent Barnabas to go as far as Antioch, who, when he had seen the grace of God, was glad, and exhorted them all that with purpose of heart they would cleave unto the Lord; for he was a good man, and full of the Holy Ghost, and of faith.* The subsequent history of this church confirms the fact that this believing and turning to the Lord were no superficial results of mere excitement, but operations of Divine power attending the administration of truth. From thence, and from Damascus, the truth extended through Syria, where its early successes became both splendid and permanent. If no other evidence of this fact existed, the old Syriac version of Sacred Scripture, made for the use of Christians in that country, is of itself sufficient. It was made as early as A. D. 150. The multitudes who came from the borders of this country to hear the Redeemer himself, were prepared for the declarations of truth which were made, in his name, by the first teachers who penetrated this region, soon after Pentecost. His deeds of mercy were known in Syria; and the congregation of believers must have been large and numerous to call for such a translation of Scripture for their use. In making that translation, the passages that relate to baptism are so translated, as to prove that, in the view of these churches, the disciples were to be initiated by an immersion in

---

* Acts xi. 22—24.

water, as Baptists now observe it; and, that this initiating immersion was never administered except upon the ground of an accredited faith.

THE TESTIMONIES FROM PALESTINE.

Theophilus, at Antioch, in A.D. 181, states to Autolycus, that the churches of Christ were like islands in the troubled sea of life, to which the lovers of truth might flee for refuge; that believers were as fixed stars; the prophets and apostles, of the first magnitude; eminent uninspired teachers, of the second; and the rest, of all degrees, yet fixed and luminous in the spiritual hemisphere; and that the recipients of truth were the persons born again, and receiving blessing of God in baptism. His great attention to figurative analogies had, no doubt, its object in his time; and requires extreme care in the interpreters, who use his writings now; but the requirement of faith, in the subject of baptism, and the responsible devotion of the baptized, are clearly recognised by him as the law of Christ. His testimony is sustained by that of Eusebius, the historian, who was Bishop of Cæsarea, in about A.D. 315.* From the destruction of Jerusalem, in A.D. 70, to this date, includes a space of about 245 years. About the year A.D. 164—that is, at about half of this whole space of time—Justin Martyr suffered for the truth.† He was then about seventy-four or seventy-six years of age. He was born in Samaria, and presided over the

---

* Lardner, vol. iv., p. 71. † Lardner, vol. ii., p. 126.

church in that city. The time of his conversion is not known; but his learning, and, after his conversion, his devotion to the truth, combine, with his advantage in residence and intercourse with the body of Christ, to give his testimony the greatest importance. Before the fall of Jerusalem, the law of Christ, as holden and taught in Palestine, is explained and proved by inspired writers, and the example of inspired witnesses; about twenty years after that event Justin was born; and about seventy years from the fall of Jerusalem some of his most important writings were produced. His apologies have been already noticed, as written at Rome in behalf of all the Christians who were living in his time. These, with his other writings, show that the whole community of Christians was one, as in the time of Paul, meeting in various countries, and cities, and from house to house; the same responsibilities being recognised, and the same privilege being enjoyed by every accredited believer in each place. Justin and the disciples of his time contended against the heathen, that there was only one God, who, being invisible and eternally perfect, exerted a providential control over all events, and all created things; against the Jews they contended that this God was to be approached only in the one name, and by the merits and mediation of Jesus, the Christ, and their Lord. They contended, that only those who come to God by him could be saved; that those who believed the truth, and felt prepared to live as Christ ordained, were initiated under his rule by an immersion in water, and brought into their assembly with laying on of hands, fasting, and prayers. Justin clearly shows, that in these special exercises of devotion a peculiar and prominent regard was given, both by the candidate and the brethren, to the forgiveness of his sins. When received into the church he was no more regarded as a criminal, unless he committed sin after baptism; he was, by the law and merits of Christ, justified from all past sin, as well as in all the hopes and privileges enjoyed in the fellowship of saints. The initiating immersion, by which a person professing faith was united with the body of believers, is called by Justin a new birth; and the persons so born again were required to be faithful even unto death. He gives a particular description of the Sunday worship of these believers, their breaking of bread together, and their careful regard for brethren in prison, banishment, affliction, and poverty; he proves that this society of believers, in the hand of Christ, was the great central thought of ancient prophecy, and the closing dispensation of mercy to this guilty world. Indeed, the works of Justin are invaluable, as affording the clearest testimony to the sense in which the instructions of our Lord respecting the conduct of his dominion upon earth were taken and acted upon in Palestine and Syria, after the destruction of Jerusalem, and during the period of his active life.

The church in Samaria was formed in A.D. 32;[*]

[*] Acts viii. 1—17.

and that in Cæsarea, at the conversion of Cornelius, in about A.D. 41.* The exceptionable case of Simon, at the former place, shows that no one, whatever his profession, could have any part in this fellowship of Christ in the Spirit, whose heart was not right with God; and the extraordinary descent of the Spirit on Cornelius, to prove the admissibility of his faith, forms a divine testimony to its sincerity. The case of Ananias and Sapphira, who were struck dead for lying against the Holy Ghost, shows the solemn sacredness of the fellowship, which they were the first to defile and to dishonour. The evidence from Justin shows the same discriminating rule of fellowship, by which all were excluded from participation in the supper of our Lord who were not born again in baptism, or who were not living as Christ ordained; and the approval of his works in Eusebius, with passages of his own expressing the same principles, proves that this discipline was received by the churches, as by the law of Christ required, down to the year A.D. 313. For 281 years, therefore, this discriminating church fellowship, with its baptism, was maintained in Samaria, Cæsarea, and in Palestine, which they represent. But the point from which these testimonies derive their greatest importance is, at the present time, the light they throw upon the meaning of the word, "born again," and its derivatives, as used in Holy Scripture. This word, though used

* Acts x. 1—47.

there with some latitude of meaning, expresses, for the most part, the act by which a human being is brought forth to be registered in society, and from which we begin to reckon his age. This is to be born: to be born again, is to pass through another event, from which a new age may be reckoned, and of which a new register may be taken. It is in this sense that baptism is called a new birth, in Justin, and in all the authors to which we have referred. Justin describes the process so exactly, that no doubt can be entertained of its import and nature. By mistaking the sense of the word, and supposing that it refers to the event by which a human being is produced before it is born, the Tractmen have supposed that these Fathers, and the Scripture with them, teach the doctrine of baptismal regeneration; and that faith, or grace leading to its production, is communicated in baptism. Dr. Halley commits the same error, though he denies the conclusion. He should have shown how, on his premises, it can be avoided. This he has not done; most likely, because he could not. He is not singular in this. No other man has done it; and, from the evidence before us, it would appear, that no person ever can. It is a singular, one might almost say, a providential circumstance, that, by the use of this one word alone, in its various connexions, during the first three hundred years of the church, Christians are absolutely bound to admit, either an efficacy in baptism to produce faith, or an obligation resting on the church, to ascertain, as far as possible, the profession and reality of faith, before baptism is administered.

THE TESTIMONY OF JUSTIN MARTYR.

The foregoing statement is strong, and, therefore, notwithstanding the length of this exercise, requires a little further attention to the proof. The passages which follow are, many of them, found in Dr. Halley's work. By considering them in the order in which they are here presented, any individual may judge for himself, what the conclusion is to which they lead.

"If any one have not clean hands, let him wash, and he is clean; but observe, Isaiah did not send you into the bath, that you might there wash away the murder and the other crimes which all the waters in the sea were insufficient to purge away; but, as it was proper, anciently, the saving initiation was this very same, which he declared to those who repented; and who are no longer purified by the blood of goats and sheep, or the ashes of an heifer; . . . but through the faith of the blood of the Christ, and of his death; who died for this end, as Isaiah himself declares."—*Works of Justin Martyr. Paris Ed., p.* 229.

"Therefore, by the laver of repentance and the knowledge of God, which, on account of the sins of the people of God, hath been instituted, as Isaiah proclaims, we believe, and we declare, that this, the very baptism which he names, is the only one able to purify those who repent; this is the water of the life (we seek); but these cisterns, which ye dig out for yourselves, are cracked and useful to you for nothing; for what advantage can result from that baptism which purifieth the body only? Baptise ye the soul from wrath and from avarice, from murder and from hatred, and behold, the body will then be clean."—*Ibid., p.* 231, C.

"We do not receive this, the circumcision of the flesh; but that which is spiritual, which Enoch and those who were like him observed. But we, since we had become sinners, through the mercy which comes from God, receive it by our baptism, and in like manner we are permitted to partake of every ordinance."—*Ibid., p.* 261, D.

"For the Christ, being a first-begotten of every creature, became also again a beginning of another race, of those who were born again through him by water, and faith, and wood, which possesseth the mystery of the cross; and in the same way as Noah, in wood (*the ark,*) was saved, being borne with his family on the waters."—*Ibid., p.* 367, D.

"But he saith through water, and faith, and wood, those who were before prepared, and had repented of their sins, escaped the judgment which is about to come upon us from God."—*Ibid., p.* 368, A.

"But in what manner we, having been made anew through the Christ, devote ourselves to God, I will narrate, in order that I may not, by omitting this, seem to commit an error in the discourse. If such there be, as believe that the things taught and spoken by us are true, obey them, and profess that they are able to live so (as these things require), these persons are instructed, fasting, to pray and beseech from God a pardon of all their former sins; we fasting and praying with them. After that they are led by us to where there is water, and are born again in that kind of new birth by which we ourselves were born again. For upon the name of God the Father and Lord of all, and of Jesus Christ our Saviour, and of the Holy Spirit, the immersion in water is performed; because the Christ hath also said, 'Except a man be born again, he cannot enter into the kingdom of heaven.'"— *Ibid., p.* 93, D.

"But this immersion is called an enlightening, since those who are learning these things are instructed as to the mind; and he who has been enlightened, is immersed by the authority of Jesus Christ, who was crucified by the command of Pontius Pilate, and on the authority of the Holy Spirit, who, through the prophets, proclaimed all the things which relate to Jesus. And, observe, this very same immersion, the demons having heard proclaimed by the prophet, procured that those who were entering their temples should sprinkle themselves, and that those who were about to approach them should perform libations and offerings of incense, but they also procured that departing they should be perfectly washed or immersed before they entered to set down at the sacred rites within."—*Ibid., p.* 94, D.

" And as we have before written, it is stated by Isaiah in what way we who have sinned and repented may escape from sin. But it is stated thus, Wash you, make you clean, put away the evil from your souls ; learn to do well, judge the orphan, do justice to the widow ; and come let us reason together saith the Lord ; and though your sins be as scarlet they shall be white as snow, though they be red like crimson, they shall be as wool ; but if ye be disobedient to me, ye shall die by the sword, for the mouth of the Lord hath spoken it. But from the apostles we have learned a reason for this ; since being altogether ignorant of our first nativity, we were produced and born by a necessity of nature . . . and continued in vain conversation and corrupt habits ; but in order that we might not remain children of this ignorance and corrupt necessity of nature, but by choice and knowledge obtain in the water a forgiveness of the sins we have committed, the name of the Father and Lord of all is pronounced on him who chooses to be born again and has repented of his sin. Those who lead to the laver (place of baptism) the individual to be immersed pronouncing this the name of God only."—*Ibid., p.* 94, A.

" But after having been so immersed (baptized) we lead the person who had been convinced, and who had been made to agree with us, to those who are called brethren, where they, having been collected together, are offering up prayers for themselves and for him who had been enlightened, and with one voice for all other men universally; that, learning the things which are true, we may be counted worthy (of the kingdom), and by our works be found good citizens, and keepers of the commandments imposed upon us, in order that we may be saved with an everlasting salvation. When the prayers are ended we salute each other with the friendly kiss; after that, a loaf of bread, and a cup of water, with a mixture of wine, are brought to him who presides over the brethren; and, taking these, he offereth praise and glory to the Father of all through the name of the Son and of the Holy Spirit; and continued thanksgivings are presented, because we have been deemed worthy of these things which we receive from him. When he has finished the prayers and thanksgivings, all the people present say, Amen . . . but when the presiding brother hath given thanks and all the people present have responded, those whom we call deacons grant to every one of those who are present to partake of the bread, and the wine and water, which have been blessed, and they bear away portions for those who are not present. And this food is that which we call the eucharist, of which it is lawful that no one shall partake, except he believe that the things which are taught by us are true, and hath been washed with the immersion, which (is administered) on account of a forgiveness of sins and for the new birth, and be living as Christ hath commanded."—*Ibid., p.* 97, B.

" And on the day which is called Sunday a gathering together is made, in the same place, of all who dwell in the cities or rural districts, and the narratives of the apostles, with the writings of the prophets, are read as long as the time will permit. Then, the reading having terminated, he who presideth, by a living discourse, maketh an admonition and exhortation of imitating the good things which have been read ; then we all rise up together and offer prayers. And, as I have before stated, when the prayers have terminated, bread with wine and water is brought in, and he who presides offers prayers and thanksgiving as long as he is able, and the people respond, saying, Amen. And the distribution and participation of those elements which have been so blessed are granted to every one, and to those who are not present, portions are sent through the deacons. Those who are prosperous and willing, but every one according to his own choice, give that which they are willing to give ; and that which is collected is confided to the presiding brother, and he relieves the orphans and the widows, and those who, from disease or other causes, are in want, and those who are in bonds, and those who are in banishment, and universally, he is made the protector of all who are in necessity. But on the Sunday we all collect together, since it is the first day, in which God, changing the darkness and material element, formed the world; and Jesus Christ, who is our Saviour, on that same day rose from the dead, for on the day before the Saturday they crucified him, and the day after the Saturday, which is the Sunday, appearing to his apostles and disciples, he taught those things which we have presented to you for your inspection. And if, indeed, it appear to you that these things have reason and truth, honour ye them; but if they appear to you absurd, treat them as things to be despised, and do not, as if dealing with enemies, decree death against those who have done no injustice, for we tell you beforehand, that ye shall not escape the judgment of God ; if ye continue in your unrighteousness, we also will continue to say, the will of our God be done."—*Ibid., p.* 98, D.

By carefully observing these passages, any one may see the terms, " enlightened" and " born again," with others, now made the sport of ridicule and the subjects of censure, used in connexion with Christian baptism and Christian fellowship; but all clearly implying, that repentance and faith had been produced by rational teaching, before the baptism, to which these terms are joined, could be administered. In saying that the first birth resulted from necessity, Justin merely speaks of it with regard to the child that was born, and the results which follow from our universal depravity. His object in leading the thought to that fact is, to show that in the second or the new birth, the person born again has a choice in the event; it is his own act to solicit and receive the baptism so designated. The physical necessity of the first birth, therefore, is contrasted with the moral and voluntary character of the second birth, or the new birth, which leads to fellowship in the body of Christ. What is it, then, that makes the language of this, and of other ancient Christian writers like him, appear so confounding and absurd to our modern polemics? It is answered, a cherished aversion to that believer's baptism on which the whole system of Justin Martyr is based, and a stern adherence to infant baptism, with which his statements cannot be reconciled, must inevitably give an appearance of absurdity to this, and to every other author of his age and school.

THE TESTIMONY FROM EGYPT.

The supposition that faith is produced in baptism, all experience flatly and unanswerably denies. The ordinance has been administered under all possible variations of form and circumstance, without producing the effect affirmed; on the contrary, and on this very account, the doctrine of sacramental efficacy has, in every nation, formed a precursor to infidelity. The moment when faith has been first produced, by the hearing of the truth, can never form the beginning of social action; because it cannot be ascertained by other than the person in whom it has been produced. The existence and the action of faith is first between the man himself and God, who seeth the heart; for, "with the heart man believeth unto righteousness." The existence of faith will justify its possessor in confessing it; but cannot be acted upon by other men until he has confessed it; because, till then, it cannot be known. It was the personal and credible confession of faith, therefore, which formed the basis of action in these early churches. While this remained unimpeached, teachers, and pastors, and people, inspired and uninspired, after its lawful recognition in baptism, continued to regard each confessor as a believer; he bore the obligation of his calling, and the privilege of his justified condition, in all the parts of Christian fellowship, until some cause, approved by the law of Christ, was shown for his expulsion. The social action rested on a basis which lay within the reach of social observation. The fellowship thus became tangible, and had an immense power of testifying to the world how much the truth of God deserved the confidence of all mankind. The incorporated mass of believers formed a body, crying with one unanimous voice, "It is a faithful saying, and worthy of all acceptation, that Jesus Christ came into the world to save sinners." We know it, for we have obtained mercy. That this credible profession of faith and consistent observance of the truth formed the basis of all fellowship in the body of Christ is clear, not only from the writers of Palestine and Syria, but also from those of Egypt in the same age.

Pantænus, in A.D. 180,* presided over the school in Alexandria; this is distinguished from the church, but yet called the school of the faithful. Though this date is only eighty years after the death of John, that school is said to have been long in existence. Pantænus was succeeded in that office by Clement and Origen. It included all persons who were candidates for baptism, until they were sufficiently instructed in Divine truth to justify the acceptance of their profession of faith. Inquirers from the heathen, and children of Christian parents would find, in these schools, the most important personal aid in forming that character which the confession of faith required them to sustain. The scholars in these schools were called catechumens. The best instructors of the age were employed in conducting their studies; the inspired writings were prepared for their use, with extreme care: and the existence of such a school, with its discipline, so near to, if not within the Apostle's time, is demonstration that,

---

* Eusebius, book v., chap. 9.

right or wrong, the Egyptian churches did not baptize without a careful regard to the acquirements, as well as the faith, of their candidates.

Clement of Alexandria appears to have succeeded his master Pantænus about the year A. D. 190.* He was afterwards bishop or pastor of the church in that city. His writings are copious, and very rich in the information they supply relating to those times. The difficulty in reading his works originates in the great difference there is between the manners and tastes of our age and country, when compared with his. This may account for some, but not for all, the blunders which have been made respecting his sentiments and practice in the church. In some cases, it will be seen hereafter, that eloquent reprehensions are poured out upon his head for using words which he had quoted or borrowed from holy Scripture, from the discourses of our Lord and the Epistles of Paul. This has been done when the precise meaning of those words in Scripture formed the very basis of Clement's reasoning. This fact will not prove him right in all he did, or wrote; but it ought to produce caution in forming our estimation of this author and his times.

Alexandria, where he presided, first in the school, and then in the church, was not only important in itself, but more so from its situation and relationships. By the Nile it was connected with Ethiopia in the Upper Egypt, and through it with India, to which it

---

* Lardner, vol. ii., p. 217.

sent Pantænus as a teacher or evangelist; and by the sea, it was united with all the Christian churches on the north coast of Africa; and by these and its own commerce, with the churches of Spain and Gaul. Not only did the school of Alexandria afford many pastors to distant churches, but the transcripts of Scripture obtained from thence were more numerous, in the early times, than those obtained from any other source. The doctrine and practice of this church, then, is a key to those of nearly one-third of the churches which then existed. The writings of Clement are exceedingly adapted, also, to supply the information required. His "Pædagogus" is a work written to explain the relation in which Christians, through the church, are united with Christ, who is thus designated the chief Teacher. He calls Christians, children, youth, babes, sons, and infants; because he finds all these terms used in Scripture, to describe the new people,* or the *renewed* people, the *peculiar* people of the Lord. They are not called so from their childishness, but from their moral sensibility and tenderness of spirit,† and their reliance on God their Father; ‡ they are not only new now, but always renewing with increased knowledge and advances in maturity.§ They were made perfect in baptism, as Jesus was, by being set apart to their proper work in the kingdom of heaven; || when

* Pæd., Lib. I., p. 86, C.   † Pæd., Lib. I., p. 89, C.
‡ Pæd., Lib. I., p. 87, D.   § Pæd., Lib. I., p. 89, C.; p. 91, D.
|| Pæd., Lib. I., p. 92, B.

baptized, they are enlightened; when enlightened, they are made sons; when sons, they are perfect, and, being perfect, death can do them no injury.* Their baptism is variously called an act of Divine grace, an enlightening, a perfection, and a washing. It is a washing, because we therein renounce and put away our sins; it is an act of grace, because those sins are forgiven; it is an enlightening, because therein they penetrate the reality of the Divine mind and will; it is a perfection, because those who are thus received in the truth, shall never come into condemnation. As those who are roused from a dream are prepared to exercise wakeful thought, and receive correct information, and, as the removal of a film leaves the eye exposed to the proper action of light, so we who are baptized, by putting away those sins which, as a cloud, justly obstruct the communications of the Spirit, are enlightened by an attentive and free use of his teaching. Since like is lovely to its like, the holy disposition thus evolved is lovely to the Spirit, which is, in the highest sense, called a light. Thus it is said, Ye were at one time darkness, but now are ye light in the Lord. Whence, Clement adds, "As I conceive, by the ancients, the man was called a light." And further, to leave no room for doubt, he says, "Faith is the perfect result of teaching, as the Lord saith, He who believeth in the Son hath everlasting life." "The elementary instruction leadeth into faith, but, at the same time, faith is evolved, disciplined by

* Pæd., Lib. I., p. 93, A.

a holy spirit in baptism;"* it is thus, as in the case of the Redeemer, made to complete the solemn personal compact of devotion in the kingdom of heaven.

Tertullian is supposed to have been born something earlier than A.D. 150; he flourished in Africa between A.D. 194 and A.D. 216, and is supposed to have died about A.D. 220. His treatises are numerous; and the evidence they supply, in confirmation of our doctrine and practice in Christian baptism, is most clear and unanswerable. Some remarks on the treatment of this author by Dr. Halley must be referred to the next exercise, to which, in fact, they belong. His Tract on Baptism deserves to be translated and brought into wide circulation, as a whole document on our side. It is only possible to add now the following from his Treatise on Repentance. The words are intended to reach that state of mind in which men evade the duty of repentance, because they are not professors of religion. To such he says (in this case), "What can distinguish you from a perfected (baptized) servant of God? Is there one Christ for the immersed (baptized), and another for the hearers? Is there any other hope, other reward, other fear of judgment, any other necessity for repentance? (than is found in him, and which refer to all?) That laver (of baptism) is a seal of faith, which faith is begun and commended by a faith of repentance. We certainly are not baptized (washed) in order that we may desist from sin, but because we have desisted, because we have been washed in heart."† This not

* Pæd., Lib. I., p. 95, C.   † Tertul., p. 144, C.

only affirms the positive doctrine of believer's baptism, but positively and formally repudiates the prospective and indiscriminating baptism now urged by the opponent. This evidence is strengthened by a fact recorded in Eusebius.* " When Gordianus had been Emperor of Rome six years, A.D. 246, Philip, together with his son Philip, succeeded him. Of this man it is reported, that he, being a Christian, and desirous to be a partaker and joined with the multitude in the ecclesiastical prayers upon the last day of Easter Vigils, could not be admitted until he had first rendered an account of his faith, and coupled himself with them who, for their sins, were examined and placed in the room of the penitents; for except he should have done this, he could not be admitted; therefore, because he was faulty in many things, he willingly obeyed, and declared by his works his sincere and religious mind towards God." Here the expression, " being a Christian," includes his previous faith and baptism; while his subjection to the discipline of penitents plainly proves that, by the law of the church in those days, no respect of persons was admitted in its application.

CONCLUSION.

Such, then, is the evidence which these witnesses supply. The appeal is made to them in vain for any case or statement favourable to the doctrine of baptismal efficacy, or the proposed scheme of a prospective and indiscriminating use of that rite. The

* Eccl. Hist., vi. 34.

one point on which the evidence of all these witnesses, inspired and uninspired, unite and harmonise is fatal to infant baptism in any form, or on any ground whatever. Testimonies have been collected in Rome, in Greece, in Asia Minor, in Syria, Palestine, and Africa. These have been selected chiefly by the guidance of those who wish to sustain infant baptism, with its attendant and defensive theories. Where they appeal for means of defence, they find nothing but means of destruction. The character of these churches, often praised and blamed with almost equal rashness, is not the question: whether in practice they were right or wrong, we have to ascertain what these ancient writers deemed the law of Christ. Did their interpretation agree, or not agree, with the one now advocated in believers' baptism? The affirmation here, as far as the discriminating requirement of repentance and faith in each candidate for Christian baptism is concerned, is unqualified; in this they did agree with us; all declare that this was the meaning of their Lord, and the law of his kingdom. Their evidence is also so combined with that of the Apostles, that the inspired and uninspired witnesses speak together as with one voice. In their regard to moral feeling before baptism, and the consistency of action after baptism, these ancient churches have no parallel in modern times; in this respect, the trial of persecution, and the order of their worship in the church, exerted an influence over them greatly to their advantage. If in some practical points, and through some media of information, they appear to disadvantage, this does not affect the reality of their united testimony. It might be pleaded and admitted, that they are not authorities; but this will not destroy their unanimity. If it be said, that these witnesses cannot be heard in favour of baptizing professed believers only; then it must be answered, how can their words be taken, against themselves, to support the theories of infant and promiscuous baptism? If they are not to be heard in what they *do* say, how can their testimony be taken for what they do *not* say? From the confidence with which he writes, and the eloquence of his censures, it is rightly presumed, that if one passage favouring baptismal efficacy, infant, or indiscriminate baptism, could have been found in these ancient authors, Dr. Halley would have produced it. The authorities to which he himself appeals all show a discriminating regard to penitence and faith, both in administering the baptism, and in all the fellowship in which the baptized became united. The circumstances, too, are very remarkable. One law was given by one Lord to twelve inspired men, with many others acting under their instructions. These go forth enriched with gifts of the Holy Spirit, God working with them in signs and wonders. They spread in their labour, and occupy the civilized world; and most of these twelve men die for the truth they taught. Wherever they came, churches rose; each country having its own peculiarity of character, language, and physical and moral associations. By different hands this same law was translated into different languages, diverse in their construction as the nations by whom the languages were used. The truth of the Redeemer, so translated, had to encounter idolatry and treason which, in every form, were incorporated with the interests and sympathies of nearly all mankind. At the beginning, the advocates of this holy law were so few and feeble as to seem beneath contempt; the result was that, in three hundred years, all society was so changed that Constantine secured the empire by favouring its advocates. The great body of mankind had either gone over to its fellowship, or regarded it with respect. In Rome, Greece, Asia, Syria, Palestine, and Africa, churches were formed in the name of Christ, and by his law; but in each and all of these countries, whatever the variation of circumstances and national taste, the churches produced by this law were, in constitution and discipline, the same. It is the more remarkable, that the law was considered and acted upon by individual judgments as well as assemblies. How should this be, that millions give the document the same interpretation, and often under the most powerful motives to change its sense? The only answer that can be given to this inquiry is this,—the law must have had a defined and fixed meaning, and the interpretation so generally and effectively received must have been the right one. It is not only morally certain, it is absolutely and mathematically certain, that any wrong interpretation of the law, could never have been so universally and so unanimously received.

LECTURE VIII.

ON THE GENERAL APOSTASY.

"He that is not with me is against me." These words of our Lord apply, first, to a believer in the world; and, secondly, to an unbeliever in the church. The Redeemer supposes that something in the case has been granted to him and to his kingdom; but that something is still withholden from him; and his affirmation teaches us that the withholding this neutralises all that has been conceded. The believer in the world, if such an anomaly may be supposed, has given the Lord his heart; but, as far as his actions are concerned, lives only to testify against the Lord in whom he trusts; and the unbeliever in the church, whatever the motive or artifice that brought him there, by not being with the Saviour in heart, the profession he makes is turned against the Lord in whose name he makes it. The supposed believer in the world declares, that his Redeemer, how great so ever his person and work, cannot be trusted in everything; while the supposed unbeliever in the church declares, by the state of his mind, that, however useful the external relationship may be for the present, the Saviour is, in reality, to be trusted in nothing. It is easy to see that both cases are, as far as their individual influence is concerned, absolutely against, to the moral and spiritual power of the Redeemer upon earth. The believer in the world withholds the confession of his faith and his testimony to the truth of the Lord, just at the time and in the place where his witness becomes of the greatest importance; while the unbeliever, professing religion, is, in himself, a living, organised, and practical falsehood, obtruding on forbidden ground, stealing the incidental advantages which result from faith in others, and yet, in the midst of believers, and in the presence of a faithful Lord, withholding that very confidence on which the whole relationship and communion in the body of Christ has been based. It is clear from the cases supposed, that this must have been the work of an enemy; for, by either subterfuge, the very law of the kingdom of heaven is, by a malignant dexterity, turned against its founder and Lord.

It has been shown, that the rule of Christian discipline, as exhibited and maintained in the early churches, was removed to an equal distance from each of these unprincipled and God-dishonouring courses of procedure. It required that each individual admitted into or retained in fellowship should be with the Redeemer in heart, and in action, and without reserve. From the ministry of our Lord, and his forerunner, it has been shown, that a society formed on the recognition of this personal devotion to his service, was the very object they laboured to secure; and in securing which, they realised the leading idea of ancient prophesy, the substance of Jewish rites, and the spiritual kingdom of Messiah. At the time when our Lord, having wrought the atonement, and risen from the dead, declared that all power was given to him in heaven and in earth, we have seen that he gave his final instructions to his people in this world, took his seat at the right hand of God, and sent forth his Spirit to be with and dwell in his servants, directing and comforting them to the end of his dispensations. The Apostles went forth with these instructions, and under the guidance of this Spirit, formed assemblies of individuals, who, on a personal, and practical, and open declaration of their obedience to the Redeemer, were recognised in baptism as recipients of his mercy, as instruments of his rule, and as believers on his name. Such were the persons who, in the apostolical churches, were baptized into Christ, baptized into his death, separated from the world, had put on Christ, were children of God by faith in Christ Jesus, heirs according to the promise of eternal life; and, being baptized on the hope of a resurrection of the dead, formed one community, one peculiar people, one new man, an incorporated body of Christ. The testimony which proved that this was the doctrine and practice of the Apostles, and that this was the discipline and law of the churches they formed, was, in the last exercise, collected from witnesses obtained in Rome, in Greece, in Asia Minor, in Syria, in Palestine, and in Africa, whose unanimous voice, in favour of this interpretation of the Saviour's commandment, was borne, without any counteracting evidence whatever, from the age of Paul to that of Eusebius, in A.D. 315.

Dr. Halley points to this period as one in which the church or body of Christ underwent an important change in its constitution. If this be intended to point out the fruits of certain principles which individuals had imbibed and mingled with the holy doctrine, the affirmation may, with some modification, be received as true; but if Dr. Halley means to affirm, that the elements unfriendly to Christian purity were then originated, his affirmation must, without qualification, be denied. Paul, in his address to the elders of Ephesus,* clearly predicts this corruption, and warns them to a faithful resistance of its approach. In writing to Timothy, who remained at Ephesus, Paul again refers to the same event, and points out the wrong use of Divine law, and the genealogical absurdities out of which the corruptions would spring.† In his second epistle he expands the prediction, showing, with other features of its malignity, that one in which all unite, having the *form* of godliness, but denying the *power*.‡ When

---

* Acts xx. 17—38.   † 1 Timothy i. 3, 4.
‡ 2 Timothy iii. 1—9.

writing to the Thessalonians, Paul paints the monster crime, the *man* of sin, whose ripened strength should appear in the assumption of Divine rights, and the reception of Divine honours.* He declares, that the guilty element was already in existence and at work, though at present hindered. The prophetical expectation seems to have filled the minds of the inspired teachers; and, in the last pages added to the sacred canon, the actual existence and working of the evil is not only shown, but the vision of John's revelation unfolds the growing mystery of gospelised crime, until no figure seems too loathsome for its description, and no words sufficiently strong to state its terrible adulteries. The man of sin is thus transformed into a whore, riding on a beast, drunk, stained with the blood of many murders, holding forth the cup of her bewildering abominations until she falls for ever by the hand of God.

It is not true, therefore, that the third century of the church originated the evils under which she fell. These evils were none other than the treasonous rebellion of the world, from which the church was by law separated. The corruption was effected by giving that treason a Christian form, bringing it within the circle of Christian society, and turning that very society itself to its foul and blasphemous service.

* 2 Thessalonians ii. 1, 12.

DR. HALLEY'S MISTAKES.

Where there is any doubt respecting Dr. Halley's meaning, the whole advantage of the doubt should go on his side. This rule, however, will not protect him from just blame in several particulars: and, *first*, in neglecting to supply the names and writings of those authors in whom he thinks that he has traced the corruptions which marked what he calls the transition age. He says, I find this and I find that; but he does not say where. This is wrong. If he had, in many cases, given references instead of rhetoric, his readers would have been more fully instructed in his argument.

Secondly, It was quite a mistake in Dr. Halley to affirm, that the expressions and practice of authors who lived in the second century, and, in some cases, in the first, were characteristic of the third and fourth century, in which he says the transition took place. The nature of this transition should be shown by the writings and acts of those who were engaged in producing it; not by referring to men who had died a hundred years before he supposed it to have begun.

Thirdly, Dr. Halley pleads, and his whole argument implies, that the transition which led to the apostasy commencd with catechetical schools and believers' baptism. But these did not begin in the third and fourth centuries. The catechetical school we have traced, through Pantænus, to within eighty years of the Apostle John—it was then called an ancient school; and believers' baptism has been traced to the Lord himself and John the Baptist. Besides, supposing that these were features of corruption peculiar to these times, in his argument the Doctor should have explained in what way it seemed to him that believers' baptism led to the general apostasy. A few of the words which might have been spared in his volume would have been sufficient to make this point very much more clear than it is at present.

Fourthly, Tertullian is treated as though he were the first authority in favour of baptizing believers only, and for conducting with care the introduction of its members, and their discipline in the church of Christ. Dr. Halley had probably forgotten the authors and evidence adduced in the last lecture; or, perhaps, he could not find them; but he ought to have shown how his personal remarks on the moral character of Tertullian, his extravagance and undue severity, could affect the point of inquiry. Whatever his faults, Tertullian's arguments stand, as far as they conform to Divine truth; and, however amiable in himself, Dr. Halley can maintain his ground in no other way. To this point, therefore, all attention ought to have been confined.

Fifthly, Dr. Halley is very hard on Clement, of Alexandria, and condemns him with much severity and ridicule, because he calls the baptized believers, (*teleioi*) perfect, and (*photizomenoi*) enlightened; the use of these terms is called tumid, and traced to the heathen oracles and mysteries. This is pointed out as one corruption of the time. If Dr. Halley had been more careful, he might have found that these Fathers had quoted these very words, in the very sense, and in reference to the very same subject, from the writings of the Apostle Paul and the Epistle to the Hebrews. Was Paul, then, the author of the apostasy?

Sixthly, Another mistake, equally glaring and improper, relates to the violation of the baptismal compact. Because Tertullian and the ancients treated the crime with great seriousness, Dr. Halley becomes merry at their expense. This is doubly wrong; for, first, no good man ought himself, or on any account induce others, to laugh at sin, whether it be committed before or after baptism; and secondly, a doctor of divinity should have known that, in the sixth of Hebrews, in the very language quoted by the Fathers, this very distinction of sin after baptism has been made the basis of a discriminating severity.

In stating what he supposes to be the objectionable views of Clement, Dr. Halley makes but little use of the author's own works, which are copious and greatly to the point; but infers his sentiments from an abstract of doctrines taught by Valentine and Theodotus, which is printed with Clement's works. Dr. Halley ought to have stated that the former of these teachers was an excommunicated heretic, condemned three times by the church in Rome. It is not improbable that this abstract might have been the statement of facts on which his excommunication was considered and approved at Alexandria. Can anything be more unjust, than to pass by a man's own writings and infer his sentiments from such a document as this? And yet, as if an infatuation had seized our brother, he passes by the numerous errors contained in this document, and rests his principal charge on a passage which proves to be an almost literal quotation from the Gospel of Mark, the words being uttered by the Lord himself just before his ascension.*

* It is believed that the Theodotus here meant lived as early as A.D. 130.* Valentine died about A.D. 160.† In this year Clement is said to have succeeded Pantænus in the school of Alexandria. In this city Valentine had been a resident; and some think it was the place of his nativity. Many individuals were attached to his person, and some were influenced by his doctrine. While conducting the school, to the presidency of which he had been appointed, Clement must have encountered both the tenets and the friends of Valentine. To discharge the duties of such a station rightly, a concise and authentic statement of this doctrine was indispensable. Clement might have obtained it with this view; with this view he might have preserved it, and it might thus have been transcribed first, and afterwards printed with his works. But however it came there, and by whomsoever it was prepared, the document shows that the sentiments of Theodotus and Valentine are not those of the person who writes the abstract, but of the heretics themselves. In ascribing them to Clement, therefore, Dr. Halley has committed an error, for which the best apology that can be afforded rests on the supposition that, through precipitancy, or the pressure of other duties, this imputation on Clement of Alexandria was written without acquiring an exact knowledge, either of his writings, or of his character, or of the abstract from which the slander has been fabricated.

---

* Lardner, viii., p. 577.   † Watkins' Dict. Moschemii De Rebus, &c., p. 371.

THE PRINCIPLES COMBINED IN THE APOSTASY.

These discrepancies show that if Dr. Halley's statements be received, the blame of the general apostasy must fall upon the Lord himself, his Apostles, and the Spirit which inspired them. This, it is certain, whatever his mistakes, our opponent will not ask us to admit. Besides, whether it be considered in the light of New Testament prophesy, or whether it be studied in the fruit which it has yielded for twelve hundred years in Europe and every quarter of the globe, this apostasy, this man of sin, this harlot of the nations, presents something more deeply influential, and more fascinating in its action on fallen nature, than believer's baptism could ever be. They do not move in the same direction, and have nothing in common. One is paying its court to fallen nature and its passions; the other is rebuking and even setting them at defiance. The apostasy has destroyed the discrimination between believer and unbeliever; but the object of believer's baptism is to restore it. The law of baptizing only on a credible profession of faith agrees with the law of Christ, and the practice of the Apostles and of the Fathers who lived before this transition age; but it accords with nothing called Christian that lies between that age and the present time. The question is, How did that intermediate mass of horrible discrepancy that lies between us and the early churches, come into existence? Can it be ascertained where this filthy fungus joins the healthy flesh, and how it came to be generated in the body of Christ?

THE LOVE OF POWER.

Before the disciples were entrusted with his kingdom upon earth, the question, Who should be the greatest therein? became more than once a subject of discussion. They did not appear conscious that the feeling involved any impropriety or, at least, anything directly hostile to the Redeemer; it was for the Lord himself to detect its terrible possibility of wrong, even when combined with feelings the most friendly to his dominion. Out of this corruption has proceeded the war-spirit of all times, making slaughter-fields of empires, and cities desolate: and, He who knoweth all things, must have foreseen that when this disease had assumed a gospelised form, and found a recognised place in his kingdom, its nature would change; and, instead of a uniform obedience to himself, his own church would produce, in his name, the most cruel and blasphemous treason that ever existed upon earth.

THE SACRAMENTAL EFFICACY.

The very fact that this extensive crime was to appear in the body of Christ, and, as God, exalt itself in the house of God, suggests a reason for some of its most repulsive emblems. Its mercenary character must have some lucrative basis on which to rest its operations. The disgusting emblem of a harlot is used to represent a practice of giving to others and receiving in return a personal attention which is due only to the Lord himself. All these painful features are realised in the doctrine of sacramental efficacy, on which the whole antichristian power is based. It raises a man into the place of God, as one on whose official act eternal life depends: it thereby creates an influence over the minds and actions of other men; the power so generated becomes the most absolute that ever existed amongst men, and its illicit barter in the policies of mankind is amongst the most loathsome productions of earth. Dr. Halley himself shows that this is the element of this great religious imposition and wrong, and predicts that if this can be exploded popery and semi-popery will vanish as a mist from the region of theology. Whatever comes of the prophesy, there can be no doubt that the supposition of sacramental efficacy has been an element in those causes which have led to the general apostasy in the body of Christ.

STATE ALLIANCE.

During the early struggle of the believers, in their persecutions and poverty, it was a consolation to them to remember that the kingdom of their Lord was not of this world. This truth being forced on their attention by all events, they were led to fix the eye with more precision on the joy that was before them in the world of spirits. The contemplation of this, aided by the indwelling Spirit, fed that martyr courage by which they lived and died. But, when their victories were multiplied, and worldly flattery was added to the difficulties of their calling; when ministers became tried with their people, and people with their ministers; and when the use of violence from without could be procured by a repayment of moral influence from within; when the earthly ruler saw that the church had something to sell that was useful in his design, his policy was constructed so as to secure, with the least possible offence to religious feeling, the purchase so essential to his advancement and security. This was formally effected in the reign of Constantine, by some called the Great; and from that time, in the body of Christ, might be seen the tolerated and even reverenced love of power, the extending assumption of sacramental efficacy, and the influence of worldly policy in alliance with the state. These united their operations to produce, in the name of Christ, a community, not formed of his disciples, not imbued with his Spirit, not influenced by the principles he inculcated, not subject to his laws, not observant of his ordinances, not careful for his glory; but, regardless of all that he appointed or loved, and reckless of all results, in time or in eternity, feeding and fostering that ambition which he condemned by prostituting the symbols of that mercy for which he died. This is Antichrist. It is a habit of mind, producing a social compact and government amongst men, so utterly opposed to the Christ of God, that it usurps his authority, prostitutes the symbols and rites of his worship, turns the hope of salvation cherished in his name into pernicious moral poison, constructs a blasphemous absurdity out of that very ordinance by which we are reminded of his suffering for sin, and, with a boldness which no other system of iniquity has ever yet exhibited, repels the charge of absurdity by urging the obligation of faith, and appeals to the word of the Redeemer in confirmation of a lie invented to overturn his holy and merciful dominion.

THE BEGINNINGS OF THEIR ACTION.

In the first action of these moral errors, they presented a tenderness and simplicity which concealed their malignant nature and secured for them the approval of good, though mistaken, men. The disciples did not seem much astonished at the desire to be greatest in the kingdom of heaven; and, in multitudes of cases since, it has appeared as the exuberance of Christian zeal, desiring to be first in service and danger. The idea of sacramental efficacy presented itself first as a physiological explanation, designed to diminish the mystery, and give a permanence and vigour to the life of faith. Valentine and Cyprian, who were partners in this work, do not appear to have designed any inroad on personal religion and its culture in the body of Christ. The former would have made the discipline very severe, and the latter was anxious to combine and concentrate the forces of the church, to meet with vigour, if they could not prevent by social influence, the persecution which was dreaded, and even suffered in his time. The principal teachers of their time saw a pernicious error in the theory they advanced; but the authors used so much of Scripture language, and this was in so small a degree modified in its sense, and they retained at the same time so fully the force and sacredness of the baptismal compact, that, even when reprehended or excommunicated, they still made a strong appeal to the sympathies of individuals. The same thing appears in the introduction of state alliance. The spread of divine truth, the multiplication of churches, their differences of opinion, the general want of competent teachers, and the frequent injury to which those who presided in the assemblies were subjected from the want of a more perfect knowledge of the divine will in individual believers, made many desire some regulating and restraining power which all must be compelled to respect. The arbitrations of the pastors, who decided in disputes between believers and believers, had produced the model of a bishop's court, the procedures of which might often seem to need the sanction of some higher power. In fact, the pastors and people, who had passed through the conflict of persecution and adversity with success, had now to pass through the dangers of growing prosperity. The fire of persecution which tested the early professions of faith were extinguished; and, lighted with the smile of an emperor, the church had now to deal in a more extensive degree with unsound, and even mercenary, candidates for its fellowship. Her catechetical schools did much, but could not do all. Individual instruction required to be carried farther, and the perfecting of individual character by effective discipline required the development of other energies than those which sustained the conflict with idolatry and persecution. The church was troubled, and ought to have sought assistance at the feet of her Redeemer, and in the perfection of his laws. Many remembered the promise, "Lo, I am with you;" but the feeling, the position, the power, and the overtures of Constantine, seemed so providential, so like an intervention of the Lord—it seemed so opportune, so useful, it could not be refused. He was a student of Scripture himself; it seemed uncharitable to treat him as an enemy. He submitted to the pastor, and asked for no authority in divine ordinances; he only offered the help of his sword, and the use of his wealth, to remedy one or two defects which no one could conceal. It was an evil hour, and the enemy prevailed. Jesus was dishonoured, as if insufficient to direct and preserve his people in prosperity; while order, protection, and a perfecting of his spiritual favours, were sought at the hands of civil and even military government. The character which was formed, in the embraces of the Saviour, had now to become perfect in the lap of the emperor. It seemed but the union of kindness with discretion; but the consummating of that one act sealed for the empire an irrevocable ruin, and plunged the church into her long defilement.

THE PRINCIPAL CAUSE OF THE APOSTASY.

The love of power seems to be so inherent a feature of our fallen state, that every good man is compelled to watch against its appearance, whenever an opportunity is presented for its gratification. It forms, perhaps, a natural result of voluntary action, and the pleasure which attends it, and cannot be condemned with justice, unless where it breaks in upon the rights of others, or takes a position which belongs to God alone. Whenever the love of power becomes thus defined and obvious, the moral sense of mankind rises so firmly against it, that without physical force, or some means of concealment, it cannot be extended to any great result.

Moreover, the alliance between church and state, though it afforded help to those who were influenced by ambition, yet, it could never have effected the apostasy, without first corrupting the discipline and constituency of the church. If none were admitted to its fellowship but those who made a credible profession of faith, and if every one who professed faith had been held responsible for its consistent fruits, as by the law of Christ ordained, the occasions for correction would have been so numerous, and the difficulty of combining, through successive generations, the actions of the church with that of the state would have been so overwhelming, that the influence thereby obtained in favour of earthly governments would never even seem to repay the labour of acquiring it. If each had acted in his true character, the two parties, so united, would, by mutual consent, have moved for a separation in less than fifty years; nor could the union have continued to produce the terrible results which are now deplored wherever the Gospel was at first made known.

It is clear, therefore, that the love of power in the church, and the love of power out of the church, in worldly governments, must have had some medium by which their operations could be united. Without this the man of sin could not be revealed in his maturity. This, therefore, was supplied in the doctrinal assumption of sacramental efficacy. By its means the church could be extended at pleasure, without waiting for the development of faith. If, by any logic, it could be shown that baptism produced faith, or brought the individuals baptized within the limit and corporation of the body of Christ, then their privilege and obligation might be pleaded and enforced by appeals to Scripture; thus the inhabitants of an empire might, possibly, be reduced so far to uniformity as to bear being treated, through their teachers, as a whole. By this means the numerous and conflicting claims of heathen gods would be laid aside to great advantage; and the baptized multitude might be treated with, and directed through their religious feeling, as occasions might require, and circumstances might admit. Through the same vehiculum, the social influence might be conveyed from generation to generation. If the church consisted only of believers in Jesus, it might so happen, that these would be numerous at one place, but few in another; in one age they might preponderate, in another they might form only a small minority. On this rule, therefore, the earthly policy could never stand; but if sacraments have power to produce faith, or to incorporate without faith, which amounts to the same thing, then children can be incorporated as fast as they are born; the civil and the ecclesiastical powers can unite, they can transfer their influence from the one to the other, and from age to age; the priest can help the monarch with his Bible, and the monarch can help the priest with his sword. Where they cannot persuade, they can enforce. The messenger of mercy can then assume an attitude in which his word must be respected. Protected by civil power, his property may be defined and augmented from age to age; that property may become great, the greatest in the empire, and the disposal of religious offices may comprehend the chief patronage of a government. All this has taken place. The pastor of a believing flock has become the bishop of a people baptized without discrimination, and defined only by their place of residence or place of meeting; the bishop has thus become an archbishop: and he a patriarch, a cardinal, or pope. In fact, the love of power in the church, aided by state alliance, covered with the fraudulent assumption of sacramental efficacy, and strengthened by the prostitution of its influence, has both generated and brought forth the predicted Antichrist. It stands out before the eye of all mankind, realising every hateful feature painted in the ancient and inspired prophesy.

THE ORIGIN OF SACRAMENTAL EFFICACY.

The body of Christ is a social system formed for his service in the present world; and all its rites and ordinances are either Divine appointments, or inventions profanely introduced by men. The doctrines relating to those rites are the same; they are either the declarations of God himself, or inventions profanely obtruded by men. Such is the doctrine of sacramental efficacy. It is either a clear declaration of God, or otherwise a human invention profanely uttered in his name. But we have shown, that, in the Divine law, baptism is exhibited and enforced as the solemnising of a covenant with God in Christ, which did not produce faith, but supposed its existence and personal declaration. If this be the law of Christ, therefore, the doctrine of baptismal efficacy, or of a spiritual gift in baptism, where no faith has existed before, must be an assumption profanely uttered in his name. Is it possible to ascertain, therefore, where and how its existence in the church of Christ began?

In writings which have been already considered, the Apostle Paul refers to systems of error which, in his time, so influenced the opinions of mankind as to endanger the purity of this Christian association. His expressions, "old wives' fables" and "endless genealogies," and "learning so called," are all intended to convey a reprehension of the system they so justly describe. The fables on which they were built related to invisible worlds, by which the present world in which we live was said to be produced and governed. The genealogies were made up of supposed successive generations by which the invisible existences were first produced themselves, and then produced the things that live on earth. This could not be properly called learning, because it formed a vast jungle of unfounded suppositions, and unjustifiable conclusions. It was learning, falsely so called. It seems to have grown out of that sinful curiosity by which men plunge with rebellious determination to know what God has thought proper to conceal. It found an apparent authority in the figurative language of Holy Scripture, and proffered its explanations wherever the Christian student found a difficulty in the word, or works, or ways of God. The theory appears to have been constructed out of fragmentary thoughts, partly collected from nature, and partly from Old Testament revelations, scattered over Persia and its provinces, soon after the age of Daniel and the Jewish captivity. Designed, at first, to explain the mysteries of nature and providence, it so encompassed the mind with wild imaginations, that its professors were induced, by their application, to explain the actions and mysteries of Divine mercy. The person of Christ, the personal character and position of his forerunner, the production of men, and the production of believers—their direction, support, comfort, and final deliverance from all the pollution and conflict of this sinful world—were topics on which, with vast ingenuity, but with the most absurd infatuation, the teachers of these dreams concentrated their energies. Theodotus is supposed, by some, to have conversed with Paul, and to have received from him secret instructions. The first supposition, if true, will show how early the brethren were exposed to this malignant corruption; the existence of the last supposition proves where, and in what cause, the idea of unwritten traditions began in the Christian age. A theory less corrupt than this could never have required a supposition for its support, by which the secret instructions of Paul were placed in positive hostility to his published writings. Valentine, who gave the views of Theodotus a wider diffusion and greater celebrity, taught in Rome about A.D. 144, and was, for his errors, twice deprived of communion with the brethren; and then, on a third impeachment, expelled, as an incurable advocate of error. His native country is supposed to have been Egypt; and, having been much known through his gifts and labours there, his judgment in Rome could not have passed without notice by his friends in Alexandria; and, it is conjectured, that circumstances rendered it advisable, if not necessary to peace, that the abstract of his doctrine, now found in Clement's works, should be prepared. After his condemnation in Rome, he retired to Cyprus, and is supposed to have died there about the year A.D. 160.

THE ANTICHRISTIAN ERROR.

A theory may be very erroneous and pernicious in its operation on the mind, and yet not deserve to be designated the Antichristian error. It is this that we wish to find; and this we do find in the theory proposed by Theodotus and Valentine. The latter did not hide the sources from which his sentiments were derived; and by no means refused to be called a Gnostic, or one adhering to the Asiatic theory. This was constructed to explain by natural causes and generations the creation and conduct of the visible world; and when applied to Christianity, its object was to explain, by the analogy of natural causes and generations, the creation and conduct of

THE ANTICHRISTIAN ERROR. 397

the visible church. As nature, in all her fields, presented facts that excited curiosity; so the church, in all her assemblies, presented facts that excited curiosity; and in each case the facts were explained by supposing that unseen agencies were employed in producing them by natural generations. Through their influence it was attempted to show how children bore the features of their parents both in the body, in the intellect, and in the state of their moral inclination; and the preponderance of either was said to depend on that element which exerted the greatest influence in the parental nature and action. This result was said to be effected through the man, not by him; an unseen agency being employed, to which he became an instrument. The same appeared in Christian ordinances. The spiritual influence, called seed, and fire, and so forth, conveyed to the soul of a believer in baptism, was said to be given to the soul, not to the body; and through the ordinance, not by it. In fact, the hereditary and the ritual claim to the covenant of grace might both be made out, from this author, with more perfection than most of his modern imitators seem to suppose.

In the law of Christ it has been seen that he contemplated and enforced the formation of a society, based on personal character, and incorporated by the mutual recognition of a personal and moral compact. Valentine did not appear to deny this. Indeed, he clearly recognises this fact in the abstract before us. But the moral compact did not seem to him sufficient to meet the import of Scripture passages, to explain the facts before him in the church, or to sustain the character in which a disciple of Christ was committed. The school to which he belonged led him to look for some physical element to which the operations of moral principle might be assigned. The perception and reverence of truth, the fear of its Author, and the hope of his fellowship and favour, did not appear to him sufficient to sustain the operations of faith, and to evolve the results which it presented in the life of man. It might be favoured in the movements of Providence, fostered by the teaching and discipline of the church, and energised by the moral power of the Holy Spirit, but these were not sufficient; he must have some "angelical juice," some heavenly fire, some refined material element which he might call a seed, and by which the operations and facts in the church of Christ might be conformed to his theory of universal existence. It was this which, in his view, gave the power to baptism, and made the devils shudder at the baptized; and it is astonishing with what wonderful exactness the language he uses to introduce his theory, the arguments he employs in its defence, and his method of appealing to Scripture for proof, coincide with what we now find in popular writings issued in the defence of sacramental grace and infant baptism.

THE FIRST IMPRESSION.

Of all the errors taught in the first ages of Christianity, no one has so fully occupied the attention of contemporary Christian authors as this, the doctrine of Valentine and Theodotus. The action of the church in Rome, the writings of Clement, of Tertullian, and even of Cyprian, in Africa; those of Irenæus, in Gaul; and Justin, in Palestine, show how great the danger was which they apprehended, and with what uniformity and unanimity the error was condemned in all the principal churches of Christ. In this, the followers of Jesus did but repeat the judgment, and follow the instructions of Paul and of John, the last apostle. The application of the theory to explain the mysterious person of the Lord, the Christ, the Immanuel, God with us, seems to have produced, by its blasphemous tendency, the first shock; and, when applied to explain the use of sacraments, by ascribing the grace, or supposed material communication therein, to other supposed existences than the Holy Spirit, so clear a violation of Divine law was involved, that the first impression could not be overcome. The poison administered was too strong to be retained until its fatal operations could be effected. It was cast out with loathing; and its advocate was excommunicated as a hopeless man. The monster was presented with too much nakedness, and had to be clothed in a dress that might conceal its deformity and grace it with charms, before it could obtain the embraces of beguiled humanity.

THE SUCCESSFUL MODIFICATION.

Tertullian is an author on this subject deservedly represented as of great importance. In his view, the church of Christ was based on personal and moral compacts, sanctioned by the highest authorities, and leading to the greatest possible results. His condemnation of Valentine, therefore, is not only carried to the whole extent of its principle, but it is sustained by a consistent advocacy of personal religion which strikingly coincides with the requirements of Scripture. In Cyprian, a similar condemnation of Valentine is found; but without the same consistency in submitting to the dictates of inspiration. He has more of the politician, indicates a greater laxity of moral principle, and, in another form, enforces the very physical or material notion he condemned in Valentine. This is obvious in his works on both the ordinances of our Lord. The material of the Eucharist is supposed by him to have undergone so great a change in the benediction, that when received by a girl, after secretly submitting to illicit embraces, it would not remain in her polluted body; but produced effects too painful and too filthy to be translated. The water of baptism appears, from his words, to undergo a change, and to exert a power, and to communicate a substantial and material good to each recipient of that rite. The eighty-eight pastors, who met in what is called their council, argue, that no man who has not the Spirit, can give the Spirit in baptism; and, therefore, persons baptized by

THE SUCCESSFUL MODIFICATION. 401

heretics, not having the grace of that rite, must be baptized again. Their verdicts are given, and recorded one by one; and, from the various forms in which the argument is put, it is quite clear that much allowance must be made for the use of figurative language; but Cyprian unquestionably used the doctrine of sacramental efficacy. The case of the Eucharist already named is indisputable. As a general rule, he advises, like Tertullian, that baptism should not be hastily administered to persons not prepared to comprehend its import, or to sustain the character therein recognised; and this must be yielded in his favour; but his decision on the case of sickly children and penitents in affliction, clearly shows that he taught the doctrine of a spiritual gift in baptism. This was separated from the grosser speculations of Valentine, combined with the ministration of the Holy Spirit, and his words would in some cases seem to imply that the thing conveyed in baptism was the Holy Spirit itself. Hence, his argument, Let them be baptized that they may not perish. The age of the infant is not material; and the incapability of the sick man to be immersed is of no moment; the form and circumstance are but adjuncts. The principal thing is the grace, the Spirit, the actual supposed communication in the rite, without which men cannot be saved. Let them be baptized, therefore, as they can, that they may not perish.

THE RISE OF INFANT BAPTISM.

A drowning man will catch at a straw. The advocates of infant baptism may, therefore, cling to this authority of Cyprian. Whatever aid it can legitimately afford them ought also to be used; but nothing can excuse the way in which so many of these writers have concealed the true nature of the evidence which Cyprian and his works supply. Do the Evangelical Independents baptize sickly children only, and baptize them that they may not perish? Does Dr. Halley baptize them with that view?—then what becomes of his renunciation of baptismal efficacy? Does he confine his baptism to those that are likely to die?—then what becomes of his indiscriminate baptism? Such special pleading seems to imply that readers are too idle, or too ignorant, to examine the authorities so daringly adduced. For what, after all, is the weight of Cyprian's testimony, supposing it were full and direct, when compared with that which has been adduced from earlier authorities, inspired and uninspired? He stands before us as the first clearly-convicted and successful advocate of sacramental efficacy in the Christian community. The thing he condemns on one page, he enforces on another. He begins the dominion of Antichrist. The sacramental efficacy for which he pleads is material, like that of Valentine, whom he himself has cursed; and, from his time, its operation is traced in *the canons relating to baptism*, in the *multiplication of supposed sacraments*, and in the *monopoly of sacramental power*.

THE CANONS ON BAPTISM.

Dr. Halley says, that from the date of Cyprian, downwards, there can be no doubt that infant baptism existed; this is part of the truth, but not all. From the date of Cyprian to the Reformation, the practice of infant baptism became more general; and the canons passed in its favour show that it was invariably admitted, as a new thing, in each case that presented itself, and that it was admitted on the ground of its necessity to salvation. In A.D. 256, as recorded in the words of Cyprian; in A. D. 438, as recorded in the decree of the council then holden at Carthage, and in every other case, the basis of the argument is everywhere found in the supposition that baptism conferred a substance or grace, without which salvation was impossible. This was not only administered to foundlings and orphans, therefore, but also to abortions; and, moreover, the Cæsarean operation was performed on dying mothers that the unborn infant might be baptized and saved. The rising Antichrist pressed this application of sacramental power with such determination, that objectors to the delusion were defamed, persecuted, chased to mountain retreats, and hunted down like deer; the Scriptures to which they appealed for the support of their doctrines were prohibited; and, within the pale of that community which professed to be of Christ, tortures and the most cruel deaths were deliberately inflicted by the highest authorities, on persons who dared to assert, or even to obey, the Redeemer's law: this overt treason was perpetrated until, at last, the open affirmation of the principle obtained its record in the Council of Trent. The decrees there passed in A.D. 1547 are as follow:—

" Whosoever shall affirm that the sacraments of the new law (gospel) are not necessary to salvation—that they do not contain the grace they signify—and that the Church of Rome has not the true doctrine of baptism, let him be accursed."—*Council Trent, Canon on Sacraments*, 4, 5, 6, 7; *on Baptism*, 3.

THE MULTIPLICATION OF SACRAMENTS.

It is easy to see that the operations of a community formed of men who are still imperfect, but yet united by a law of unlimited subjection, must have required not only a rule for recognising its members and edifying them in their faith, but also for treating their offences and trials, and for regulating their conduct in respect to the world. The first two points of practice were provided for by Baptism and the Supper of the Lord; the confession of faults was enjoined on all who committed them; repentance was the term of forgiveness, and forgiveness formed the term of restored fellowship. The laying on of hands was a form by which believers united in imploring especial mercy towards a new convert in his profession, and a minister entering on his office; and the anointing with oil was an act by which they marked an individual, for whose recovery from affliction united prayer was made. In the use of these simplicities the associated believers, in the apostolical age, appealed to him they trusted and served, and signal were the operations of Divine power by which

MULTIPLICATION OF SACRAMENTS. 405

the prayer-hearing God revealed his compassionate attention to his people. Out of these domestic arrangements of the church, the first that became polluted by a supposed sacramental power were Baptism and the Eucharist. By these the constituency of the body of Christ was so prepared, that four others were selected for the same use, and designated, respectively, confirmation, penance, extreme unction, and orders. By a judicious extension of their use, the operations of sacramental power were made to penetrate the whole mass of religious society, with all its relationships. The theory was not yet perfect. Domestic life contained the home feelings and the dearest sympathies of humanity. To subject this, marriage was exalted to the nature of a sacrament, and, when solemnised by a priest, was said to communicate the sanctifying and fruitful grace. Here the Antichrist resolved to stop. At its birth, the infant was presented to the priest in baptism; in confirmation, the youth; in marriage, the man; in orders, the candidate; in penance, the culprit; in extreme unction, the afflicted and dying. The Eucharist, changed into the Mass, exerted its influence over all the living; and, being offered for departed souls, grasped all the sympathy with which the living are accustomed to regard the dead. This seemed to be enough; it was wise to go no further; and at Trent, in A.D. 1547, it was decreed thus, "Whoever shall affirm the sacraments to be any more or less than these seven, let him be accursed."—*Canon on Sacraments*, 1.

THE MONOPOLY OF SACRAMENTAL POWER.

In all the earliest writers who enforce this pernicious doctrine, a power of communicating, through the sacraments, the supposed material element, was claimed in behalf of all ordained ministers. Some churches were more ancient, and had a greater social influence, than others; but the sacramental power was not supposed to depend on any earthly centre of ecclesiastical authority. Jerusalem, in the Apostles' time, was the place to which questions of difficulty were referred; because there the greatest number of inspired authorities could be, with the greatest facility, convened. After the destruction of Jerusalem, and the decease of the Apostles, inspired authority was sought in their writings, wherever they could be found. When the church was brought into alliance with the state, it was desired to combine the different assemblies of believers in one organisation, of which the highest authority should have its place in the new metropolis of Constantinople. The empire then became divided, and the conflict for supremacy between the Bishop of Rome and the Bishop or Patriarch of Constantinople became severe and most disgraceful. The time of keeping the Easter festivals, and the return to image worship, were amongst the questions on which this point of supremacy was tried. The calamities of the Eastern empire brought it down to utter weakness; and the rise of European nations, who, one by one, claimed the right of independent government, reduced the empire of Rome to a mere shadow. While these changes were in progress, the inundations of barbarous hordes first exhausted the military strength, and then occupied the provinces of Rome by rulers who reigned by warlike force alone, and to whom all learning was despicable. The pastors of the churches in those provinces had a moral influence over the people, which each conqueror found it necessary to employ; and the ordinances of worship were changed to suit their barbarous taste. The Eucharist was made a scenic exhibition of the crucifixion; and baptism, the means of producing the beginning of the Christian life. The sacramental power was urged, until the corrupted church conquered the barbarous rulers, as the rulers had used the church to subjugate the people. While these changes were in progress, the falling empire found no means of communication in the provinces so effective as the clergy; and in the use of this, the pastor of the church in Rome acquired increased importance. It was advantageous that all should make him the centre of communication; and when he became a civil and military ruler, his influence with other princes enabled him to claim supremacy. The resistance of this claim was extensive and strenuous even in the council of Trent; and never was as fully conceded as, in spiritual matters, it is at the present time. The whole system has ever presented the character and action of a spiritual treason, shrinking from the light of Scripture, and shuddering at the voice of conscience in the breasts of men. Its aggressive and defensive action, in this warfare with human reason and Divine truth, forms the most skilful, refined, extensive, and determined exertion of a prostituted intellect that history has recorded. The events by which other powers would have been dishonoured and broken became the means of refining this, by deepening its policy, and imparting a greater subtlety to its fraud. As the Gospel it perverted bears the mark of Divine invention and origin; so this perverting of that Gospel is so perfect, so co-ordinate with the corruption of Divine truth in former ages, and so subversive of its whole design, that it seems to require more than the genius of human nature to produce it. This monster of crime bears on its forehead, therefore, the designation "mystery," because it is the symbol of a hidden power. Its agencies have, therefore, acted with a moral daring which implies more than human strength. In this resource of sacramental power, it seemed to have an expedient which laughed at reason, and enabled man to act and speak as if he were God. It thus became a practical exponent of the primæval lie, "Ye shall be as gods." The nations became drunk with the delusion; and, in its confidence of victory and forgetfulness of God, proclaiming its absurdities, and selling with effrontery its indulgencies for all transgression, the great central monopoly of this sacramental wrong, growing grievous in its demands, and bloody in its wrath, provoked the reaction which appeared in the early martyrs, and the more general conflict of the Protestant Reformation.

INTERNAL EFFORT TO REFORM.

It must never be forgotten, that some of the greatest difficulties which the Papacy had to overcome originated with members of its own body. Individual teachers, such as Wickliffe, John Huss, Jerome of Prague, and Father Paul, of Venice, without separating from the so-called Roman Catholic church, raised their voices against its terrible corruptions; and some in flames, but more in tortures and in prisons, sealed their protestations with the sacrifice of their lives. The highest authorities in Rome were compelled to admit the necessity of the reformation thus required; but they pleaded for time; and with all determination contended for the element and use of sacramental power. One after another the monastic fraternities rose into existence, each proposing a remedy for obvious and existing evils, in some new method of using the laws and discipline of the great confederacy. Each was regarded with fear and jealousy at the first; but each was authorised, when its perfect subjection and incorporation with the central monopoly was secured. The authors of these fraternities were often men of great genius; and some, without question, were men of devoted piety. Some were men given to the culture of the intellect, and learning is indebted, even now, to their labours; others relied more on Christian doctrine, and in some of their works the sweetest exposition and use of evangelical truth may be discovered; while others gave such attention to the formation of habits, and the exercise of human policy, that nothing in those departments has yet exceeded their productions. The object of all was, at the first, to procure an internal reformation in the so-called church. By their several laws of exclusive fellowship, each fraternity formed a church within the church; and, in their monastical retreats, the brethren had the advantage of separation from the world. Here, unquestionably, many devout minds were prepared for heaven; and many, endowed with eminent gifts, were trained for positions and times of great importance, but the object of their formation was not gained. The church in which they were contained, and to which they were subjected, turned each one of them into an instrument of its own sacramental corruption. The supposed baptismal regeneration, by which all members became incorporated in the church, was, from necessity, honoured by all the monastic fraternities of the church. They urged the necessity of personal conversion to God, but could not act upon it. The consequence was inevitable. The baptism which professed to regenerate, did not regenerate; the so-called Catholic church was, therefore, composed of unregenerated men. Unregenerated men contended for and gained its places of trust, the command of its patronage, the streams of its wealth, the manifold resources of its power, and turned to their own use the energies of every monastic or regular fraternity. The Catholic body could not be reformed by any element generated within itself; its own law of incorporation involved the evils which all were obliged to confess. If the

Catholic church had become as pure, in his time, as St. Bernard would have had it made, by incorporating, without discrimination, all the children that were born, the church of the next generation would be made to contain all the depravity that existed in the world. This same depravity flowed, by the same means, into the priesthood, the monasteries, the conclave, and the Papal chair. All were, professedly, regenerated in baptism; but that regeneration was fabricated. It was not a truth. No practical result followed. All classes in the church revealed the fruit of an unregenerated nature. The highest and the most sacred were the worst. The history of no dominion upon earth is so abhorrent to humanity, so directly opposed to all things just and true, as that of the Papal chair. The conclave of Cardinals, once the evangelising elders of the baptized brethren in Rome, grew, under this indiscriminating discipline, to be the most corrupt and profligate body of politicians on the globe; and those very monastical orders which sprang from an unhealthy effort to reform, became, through the same indiscriminating discipline, too base to be described. They were not to be endured. They perished through the general abhorrence of their avarice and defilement; and the ruins of their once princely establishments pronounce, to all succeeding ages, the absolute impossibility of preventing, by any human effort, the corruption of a body, so formed in the name of Christ, but in contempt of his holy law.

THE REFORMATION.

Luther was a monk of the Augustine order; and the history of his mind is but the history of many others, to whom the same amount of practical energy and advantageous circumstances was not granted. Indeed, great changes cannot be forced by man before their time. Society must be prepared for them; and then the leaders who become celebrated in their progress assist in giving birth to the reformations which bear their names. It was manifest from the advance of learning, the influence of commerce, the operation of papal policy on national interests, and the obvious corruption of the clergy, that some great change must come. It seemed to be near when Wickliffe rose, but the time was not yet. It seemed still nearer when John Huss, of Bohemia, bore his flaming testimony to the truth; but the nations were not prepared. When Luther was excommunicated, nothing could have prevented a change. He was the noble and happy instrument; but if he had never been born, the change must have transpired. The action of Leo X. gave such ripeness to the criminalities of papal policy, that it must be exposed and judged. It was no longer a question of logical dexterity and proof, but one of pungently sensible practice. The resources of governments and their people were flowing away to Rome for paper indulgences, for permissions to commit crime against God and man with impunity. This was done in the name of Christ, and manufactured out of that power which he was said to give his sacraments. The Redeemer of sinners was thus made the originator and protector of crime. It was just then that letters had revived, and the Redeemer's own words had been brought into more general use. The two things could not then stand together. The light of truth shone on the very point where men were feeling the pressure of this sacramental tyranny. Luther was convinced, and others were convinced with him, that the sacramental power of Rome was not of God, but opposed to God's truth, and, therefore, deserved the reprehension and not the reverence of mankind. It was a happy moment; the interests of nations and those of Divine truth were seen to harmonise. Luther acted on this conviction, the reformers acted with him; the princes joined with them, and the Reformation was effected. The event of the Reformation was then determined; but it was not determined how far this Reformation should proceed. They did not like the sacramental power of Rome; but the church was a powerful aid to princes, and the source of her power, in assisting them, could only be secured by her sacraments. If all the sacraments of Rome could not be retained, some were clearly authorised, and these must not be reduced in value. The people must be secured, and, therefore, they must be baptized in infancy, and regenerated in their baptism. Some penetrating minds found in Scripture, to which all now appealed, another system; they pleaded for it, but they could not be heard. The idea of baptizing believers only, though found in the word of God, accorded with no purpose, and favoured no interest, sought by the political agents of Protestant Reformation. It involved a separation of church and state, by breaking that sacramental power by which the people might be managed through their pastors. This was going too far. Luther rejected this proposal, the reformers rejected it, the princes rejected it. In all the creeds and confessions, with little modification, the doctrine of sacramental efficacy was retained. They broke down the monopoly, and each prince set up for himself. Instead of one great store for vending sacramental grace, each nation now had one of its own; and each reformed church, formed on this basis, has worked out a new experiment by which it is proved that, on a small as well as on the largest scale, this terrible assumption is fatal to all religious interests and principle whatsoever. The churches of England, and of Saxony, were professedly founded on the assumption of sacramental efficacy; and in the results which have followed, each nation exhibits its pernicious tendency. In Germany the spirit of practical religion has given place to intellectual pride, vain conjecture, and the coldest formality; while in England, with all the counteracting influence of religious freedom, this vain assumption has saturated the community, defied the widest circulation of Holy Scripture, appealed for its confirmation to the sacred page, and pioneered the way for a returning popery.

THE PROTESTANT DISSENTERS.

In all these three great practical cases, one particular calls for especial regret. Each hierarchy contained, at its beginning, and in the growth of its power, many good, great, and greatly devoted men. The unprincipled politicians, who acted in those times, could never have effected the results which have ensued without that influence of character which was thus obtained from mistaken individuals, who were better than themselves. It is this which preserves them still. If there were no good men in the hierarchy of England, it would soon fall by the force of its own corruption. The same may be affirmed of that which bears the name of Luther; and Rome owes more to the pious that have remained in her communion than to all her policy and power. The testimony of a few good men gives greater strength to these delusions than legislative enactments and pecuniary advantages. By these they became rooted in public esteem; and, by the same influence, that public esteem is preserved long after it has been justly forfeited. In their position they do infinite harm; and the melancholy fact is, that there they can accomplish no substantial good. No individual effort ever could produce a spiritual reform in the church of Rome. The indiscriminate principle of incorporation, however concealed by the theory of baptismal regeneration, was absolutely fatal to all internal reform. The cases of Rome and the Lutheran church are decisive evidence on this point; and the energetic piety of those who founded the latter, is so near to us in point of time, that while we admire its splendour, we are more perfectly prepared to deplore the entire frustration of its chief design. In England the sacramental error was felt from the beginning of the Reformation, by some who rejected the baptism of infants altogether, and by others who have wished to retain the practice, and yet avoid the general doctrine out of which it sprang. The former went the whole length of scriptural principle at once, and, confining the ordinance of baptism to accredited believers only, embraced the odium of their great cause, and waited, in the social disadvantages assigned to them, the appearance and protection of their mighty Lord. The latter could not advance so far. They wished to avoid the sacramental error, and yet retain the practice which that error had embalmed in the sentimental affections of mankind. Language was subjected to the rack, in order to produce some form of speech so refined and delicate in its meaning, that the advocates of sacramental efficacy on the one side, and those of believers' baptism on the other, might have no cause for complaint, or ground for objection. The position was purely defensive on both sides, and every effort which the genius of those times could make, was put forth to its utmost limit, in the Westminster Assembly, which sat from 1643 to 1652; and, in the Savoy Conference of A.D. 1661.

THE LAST RESOURCE.

To name the various modifications of theory and defensive argument put forth and used by Protestant Dissenters in this case, is by no means necessary to our object; it is enough to say, that on neither side has the defence been made secure.

The practice of infant baptism has been attended with a constantly increasing boldness in the affirmation of the doctrine of sacramental efficacy; and it has been shown, that when the practice is received, the Scriptures must be rejected, or the power of that rite to produce faith must be allowed. On the other hand, the defence of infant baptism, against those who baptize accredited believers only, by every investigation, appears to be increasingly insecure. For many years, the arguments founded on Jewish law and Jewish covenants, and that resting on a supposed hereditary claim to the covenant of grace, assumed in behalf of children born of believing parents, seemed satisfactory, at least, to those who urged the baptism of infants. In the face of all these pleadings, however, the advocates of baptizing accredited believers only, have increased; and this fact becomes explained, when Dr. Halley affirms that none of those arguments for infant baptism will bear investigation. This is true; and it explains the reason why the wider circulation and more general study of Scripture, have invariably led to an increase of the practice these arguments were intended to destroy. The reasonings fail on three grounds: first, they are not founded in truth; secondly, they are implicated in the theory of sacramental grace, which it is intended to avoid; and, thirdly, the substituted hereditary claim to the covenant of grace, is as fatal to the doctrine of justification by faith only, as the theory of sacramental efficacy itself. In practice, they amount to the same thing; for the baptismal regeneration is nothing; and the hereditary claim is nothing; and each of these fictions only serve to conceal the act of incorporating persons in the body of Christ, in whom the existence of faith has never been ascertained. Dr. Halley makes an advance upon both these theories; he proves that the concealing fictions of sacramental efficacy, and the hereditary claim, are untenable; and, therefore, he proposes that the indiscriminate incorporation, by which every church which has admitted it has perished, should now be enforced openly, without any disguise, as a command of the wise and merciful Redeemer.

PROTECTING MODIFICATIONS.

The commission of our Lord, his practice, that of his messenger, and the Jewish baptisms, to which Dr. Halley appeals, have been examined; and, instead of affording a support for the bold proposition he makes, they all unite to enforce that discriminating baptism and fellowship of believers, which he condemns. The practice of the apostles, and of the ancient churches, down to Eusebius, in A.D. 315, elucidates the law of Christian fellowship; and clearly proves that Dr. Halley's indiscriminating theory is absolutely wrong. The passages in the Apostolical Epistles, which Dr. Halley refuses to consider, demonstrate that, on the theory which he proposes, no church can be formed to which the apostolical language and treatment can be applied. Further repetition is needless; but Dr. Halley conciliates his brethren, by professing to retain the exploded appeal to Jewish covenants and hereditary claims whenever they may seem to be serviceable for defence. This is absurd. The hereditary claim is either valid or fictitious; if valid, why has he so justly exposed its fallacy? But if fictitious, why should he, how could he dare to retain its use? The same may be said of arguments drawn from Jewish law and covenants. They are sound or unsound. If sound, he should not have exploded them; if unsound, he should use them no more. It is not the part of a Christian disciple and teacher, to act upon the errors which other men may be disposed to entertain; each witness for Christ is bound to bear his testimony to the truth as far as he has ascertained it. In some parts of his work, also, boldness in affirmation is followed by vacillating hesitancy, as if the subject before him were not fully considered; hence, after calling the rite of baptism both a badge of discipleship and the initiating rite of the Christian church, he nevertheless reasons on the supposition that apostolical churches were assemblies of believers discriminated after baptism, and in some other way, which he has not shown. It is clear that no such subsequent discrimination, as a term of fellowship, can be traced in Holy Scripture; and some expressions of Dr. Halley which imply it, might be attributed to inadvertency; but other expressions, compared with the actual discipline of independent churches, indicate, by the introduction of this test after baptism, for which no authority can be found in Scripture, that the indiscriminate theory, concealed or unconcealed, however proposed and advocated, is one so fraught with pernicious consequences, that though it may be used for defence, yet even its own advocates dare not carry it out to a legitimate and practical result.

To become all things to all men for their good is a Christian duty, when nothing is sacrificed in the act but personal convenience, and that which may be properly called our own. This is not the case when truth and Christian principle are involved. These gracious bestowments are committed to the servants of Christ as stewards who are expected and bound to be faithful in their sacred trust. Before any proposed interpretation of the Saviour's law can be admitted, therefore, something more of consistent evidence must be given to show that it is the one which the Lord intended that we should receive and act upon. Statements produced in mutually-destroying variations cannot be received. Those who urge us to baptize infants, because the Lord has commanded it, are bound to show the ground on which they rest the affirmation " thus saith the Lord." The leading feature of the times renders an attention to this rule the more important. Men are not now beginning the experiment of sacramental efficacy and misappropriation; we are surrounded with its pernicious results; and in every sphere of Christian action, at home and abroad, its agencies and activities are found perverting the right ways of God, and resisting the work by corrupting the doctrine of Divine mercy. It is not enough for the enemy that this sacramental delusion should be revived in almost every form, and used in almost every parish of England; it is sent out into the colonies, presented to the heathen, and joined with the open agencies of Antichrist, resisting, at all times, in every place, and by all means, the great cardinal doctrine of justification by faith alone. At such a time the advocates of Divine truth should bring the whole force of their genius to its diffusion and defence. If the practice of baptizing infants and unbelievers, generated as it was by the sacramental delusion, and moulded into the very form and constitution of Antichrist, still retain a charm for advocates of personal and vital religion, its alliance with the general apostasy ought to be broken, and some statement of Divine authority should be given, in which the adherents to that practice can unite. The attempt of Dr. Halley was well designed, and in making that attempt he has shown considerable ability; but his absolute failure, and the force of his reasoning in breaking down the former defences of infant and indiscriminate baptism, combine with the character of the present times in claiming from the brethren who retain that practice, a serious and radical revision of their whole system.

THE APPEAL TO CHRISTIAN CANDOUR.

That this appeal to the candour of Christian brethren is worthy of their regard, may be proved by the effects which follow from one single line of argument to which they have been driven in their defence of infant baptism. It has long been pleaded, and Dr. Halley has shown, unjustly, that βαπτιζω means to purify; and, like καθαριζω, to purify in many ways. This cannot be sustained. It has already been proved,* that baptize, meaning to immerse, if at any time it be used to signify a purification, the use of that word would prove that the writer meant thereby a purification by immersion. In one of the latest works published in defence of Pædobaptism,† this argument is carried out with a boldness that shows, most fully, the necessity for revising the whole subject. Mr. Godwin makes the interpretation of the word to bear on the subjects of baptism, as well as on the definition of what baptism is. In order to effect his object, he is compelled to explain the passage in which our Lord saith, "He who believeth and is baptized shall be saved," and others, in which the word baptize is joined with other subjects of great solemnity and importance. To make it appear that baptize means to purify, he brings together passages in which the words purify, sanctify, and make perfect, occur in the English version, as though these terms were all designed to translate one word, and to express one idea; whereas they stand for different words, which have different meanings. Καθαριζω is the generic word for purify; άγιαζω means, to consecrate; and τελειοω means, to perfect. Thus Christ was *made*

* Appendix I.

† Godwin on Christian Baptism.

perfect through suffering,[*] for thereby he wrought his atonement; he also *consecrated* himself[†] when he gave himself up for us in his great work of mercy; and the leprous person was *purified.* [‡] The argument which confounds all these actions with each other, can never be deserving of confidence with persons who revere the truth. In what sense can it be said, that Jesus, the Holy One, required to be cleansed or purified? and yet Mr. Godwin, because the Saviour is said to be made perfect through suffering, and he himself said that he had consecrated himself, concludes that he was purified by his sufferings on the cross; and then advances to infer, that when the Lord said,[§] "I have a baptism to be baptized with, and how am I straitened until it be accomplished;" he intends to say, I have a purification to be purified with, and how am I straitened until it be accomplished. Considering that every sin-offering must be spotless, and that Jesus died for us all, the brethren may well be prepared to revise so terrible an inference as that which makes his atonement for us to become a purification of himself. But this is not all. In the next case considered, the Lord said to the sons of Zebedee,[‖] "Are ye able to drink of the cup of which I drink, and be baptized with the baptism with which I am baptized?" &c. They answer in the affirmative, and Jesus replies, "Of the cup of which

---

[*] Hebrews ii. 10.   [†] John xvii. 19.   [‡] Matthew viii. 3.
[§] Luke xii. 50.   [‖] Mark x. 38.

I drink, ye shall drink; and with the baptism with which I am baptized, ye shall be baptized," &c. And after assuming that this refers to the sufferings of our Lord, and that these sufferings were a purification of the Lord himself, Mr. Godwin advances to affirm, that by the cup is intended the intensity, and by the baptism (purification) the design, of those sufferings; and that the Lord affirms to these disciples, that they should partake in that design—that is to say, that these disciples should personally partake in the purification of the Saviour's person and his atonement for sin. Is it too much to ask, that a method of pleading which leads to this result, or rather which is based on such an assumption as this, should be most seriously reconsidered? and that the system which requires such defence might be subjected to a renewed examination? And, further, Mr. Godwin says, that when the Lord said, " He who believeth and is baptized shall be saved,"* " it is unlikely that baptize means *to dip*, and it is likely that it means *to purify*." He, therefore, proposes to translate the words, " He who trusts to it and is purified shall be saved." If this be admitted, then no one has a right to hope for salvation until he is purified—that is to say, until he is in heaven—and yet the Apostle Paul says, " We are saved by hope."† On the words of our Lord, " Go ye forth, make disciples through all the nations, baptizing them into the name of the Father, of the

* Mark xvi. 16. † Romans viii. 24.

Son, and of the Holy Ghost,"* Mr. Godwin says, "We conclude that the words of our Lord mean, 'Purifying them for the Father, and for the Son, and for the Holy Ghost.'" But why must he so conclude? He says, because "purifying for God is a combination of very frequent occurrence; but dipping for God, or immersing into God, or into his holy name, is a combination not found in the Bible." Should such affirmations pass without being revised? Is not the very expression, "Immersing them into the name of the Father, and of the Son, and of the Holy Spirit," before him, in the very passage which he is forcing from sacredness into absurdity? If it be there, how can he say, "It is not in the Bible?" Is not the twenty-eighth chapter of Matthew in the Bible? and are there not other passages like it? Is there no such passage as baptized into, or *immersed into Christ*, in the Bible? Is not the third chapter of Galatians in the Bible? But, to avoid digression, suppose the rendering of Mr. Godwin be admitted, what can be its meaning? and how were the Apostles to perform the act? Can man purify man, in the sense required for fellowship with God? Is not the purification wrought by the Holy Spirit himself? But this author concludes that the minister must, in some way not defined, purify the sinner before the Spirit is received.

On the Sixth of Romans, 1—13, forcing the application of his theory onward, he proposes that the

* Matthew xxviii. 18—20.

words of Paul, " As many as were baptized into Christ, were baptized into his death," should be rendered, " As many of us as were purified for Christ, are purified for his death." The minister of mercy, therefore, must, in some way not defined, purify the sinner for Christ, before the advantage of his death can be enjoyed; and, therefore, the blood of Christ doth not cleanse from all sin, but the sinner must be cleansed from all sin before the blood of Christ can be applied. Who, then, of all the sons of men can hope for eternal life? It is the leading and principal artifice of Satan, now, to make men suppose that good works are an essential qualification to their acceptance of the atonement; and the soul of Popery is found in the assumption, that sacramental observances are the qualification required. To escape the argument for believers' baptism, Mr. Godwin confirms both these terrible conclusions. On 1 Corinthians xv. 29—32, he assumes that Paul is speaking of persons who were "*purified*," and not baptized " because " of the resurrection of persons that were dead; as if the doctrine of the resurrection were the cause of purification, and not the eternal Spirit. Why, then, were not the Pharisees purified? They and the Mahometans believe that doctrine as well as we. Galatians iii. 27, he renders, instead of " As many of you as were baptized into Christ," &c., " Such of you as are purified for Christ have put on Christ," &c.; making the effect which follows from an appropriation of the atonement to become a qualification for its use. Thus again he affirms that, in Colossians ii. 12, Paul says, "We are buried with Christ by *purification* into his death." It is not the object of this exercise to answer Mr. Godwin; these specimens of his reasoning, and their results, are adduced to show that the system which requires such a defence claims a most serious reexamination. If Mr. Godwin's book were *his* only, the appeal might be made to him alone; but the substance of this work has appeared in the "Congregational Magazine," and these dogmas are heard from many pulpits: they are retailed as ingenious expedients for defence; the brethren who use them and reiterate them to satiety are bound to consider that the dark ages have no such perversion of Holy Scripture as that contained in this one section of Mr. Godwin's work, entitled, "The Baptism of the Christian Life." Its quiet sarcasm is unworthy of its author; and its daring assumptions lead to results that are most terrific.

It is obvious that Mr. Godwin is labouring with the difficulty into which the advocates of infant baptism are forced by the Tractmen, through their appeal to these passages in favour of baptismal regeneration. Mr. Godwin is obliged to admit the relation which is here exhibited between the acts of Divine mercy in the kingdom of heaven, the essential character and hope of its subjects, and the baptism here spoken of. Instead of striking the Tractmen alone and directly, he aims to wound them by forcing the weapon through his Baptist brethren. This would be clever, if he could only do it: but displays of dexterity are seldom friendly to the discovery of truth. Such bold experiments betray their authors more frequently than they subdue their adversaries. It is thus in the case before us. Mr. Godwin pleads that the things affirmed in these passages, of baptized persons are such as "dipping" in water could never produce; and, therefore, infers that dipping cannot be intended. He might go further, and say that the affirmations here made of baptized persons are such as no immersion, or sprinkling, or washing, or ceremonial rite whatever, can produce: but, when he has stated his position in the strongest and most respectful terms possible, the Tractmen are not answered. They allow that these affirmations of Paul and of Jesus relate to operations of mercy and their results, which are so sublime in their nature that no human act whatever can produce them; they positively affirm that these operations of mercy can be performed and produced by God only; but they plead, further, that God will produce these results in his own sovereign way. Clay is not a natural unguent for the eyes; but if the Redeemer chose to heal the blind man by that means, who shall forbid him? So baptism is not a natural cause of faith; but, if God hath made it the means by which he will produce it and the elements of spiritual life, who shall dare to dispute his sovereign right and power? The Tractmen, therefore, are not answered by this contrivance of Mr. Godwin, neither are his Baptist brethren. To make it appear that "baptize" in these passages must mean to purify, and not to immerse, he assumes that the putting on of Christ, being buried with Christ, being crucified to the world, becoming dead unto sin, and being sons of God, &c., which are all affirmed of baptized persons, must be secured either by the immersion itself, or by the state of mind to be produced in the persons said to be baptized; and all his argument goes on the supposition that his Baptist brethren ascribe these splendid and vital realities to the immersion alone, which he vulgarly calls "a dipping." This is slander. The Baptist brethren, or rather the Apostle Paul, declares that the persons baptized were sons of God by faith in Christ Jesus. It is to the operation of their faith, therefore, that he ascribes their putting on of Christ, their being buried with Christ, and their privilege in the body of Christ. The question is not whether they were the subjects of faith *or* immersion: the affirmation of the Apostle and of the Baptist brethren is, that they were the subjects of *both;* that is to say, the persons who were baptized into Christ, did put on Christ, and become sons of God by faith in Christ Jesus. They were believers in Christ before they were baptized, and their baptism was an act and a recognition of their faith; or, in other words, the baptism here spoken of is believers' baptism, and nothing else.

If the Independent brethren, therefore, have any regard for their consistency, and would not wish to be met on every side with refutation and the trials which attend it, they must revise their whole system, with its proposed defence. This is seen, as much in the line of official action, as it is in that of argument and criticism. With so many injunctions, on the sacred page, to be observed in Christian fellowship, nothing can be more important than a definite perception of the sphere in which those duties are to be performed. What, then, is the body of Christ, and what are his assemblies? The direct appeal to Scripture gives a plain and satisfactory answer. The body of Christ consists of those whose faith in Christ has been credibly avowed and lawfully recognised. The assemblies of Christ are those recognised believers who meet in different places, to perform, in company with each other, their worship and service to the common Lord. By this rule the path and sphere of Christian duty become plain; but this will not satisfy the advocates of infant baptism. Some must have the children of believers incorporated, and affirm that they were born in the church; others will have all children incorporated and treated as parts of the church; by some the profession of individual faith is examined, and by others it is neglected altogether; the plea for Christian union is urged until promiscuous fellowship has blended the church and the world; Divine ordinances and Christian fellowship are reduced to contemptibility by those who profess to be their advocates; where God saith, " Come out from among them and be ye separate," the cry is, Unite, and compromise the difference; the prevalent opinions of men are to be holden in reverence, while the law of Jehovah is set at nought, by those who bear his name; human speculations are followed with recklessness, and the appeal to Divine truth is regarded with suspicion, with fear, and, at times, with marked aversion: this is wrong, and wherever it exists, calls loudly for revision and amendment.

PRACTICAL INDUCTIONS.

Beloved brethren, in repelling these new attacks made upon the practice and constitution of the Baptist churches, it is found that, not merely in this form, as in every other, investigation shows the stability of our principle; but the more this investigation is extended, the more is this principle of fellowship found to combine with other realities that are spiritual, divine, and everlasting. Dr. Halley, as an opponent, is more gentlemanly than many who have pleaded on his side; and, therein, we have an advantage in the present case; yet, even here, we are justified in asking for amendment. With all his learning and advantage, our brother is, nevertheless, betrayed at times into a use of satirical and unjust appeals to prejudice. This is wrong; and those who do this wrong, ought to remember with what ease, if Christ had not forbidden it, these weapons might have been returned, barbed and made burning, into their own breasts. What, for instance, have the " ragged anchorite," the " solitary Donatist," and the other disreputable characters named by Dr. Halley, and required by him as ancestors, to degrade his Baptist brethren, to do with his argument? If he would trace our fraternity to its origin, he will find it written by St. Luke; and where the author and beginning of our fellowship are named, he might see claims to his reverence, rather than his ridicule. When such efforts are made to desecrate what cannot be destroyed, it seems to be forgotten that a diamond cannot be laughed out of its lustre; or does the pious doctor think that the sweetness of our fellowship has been enjoyed, until we are ashamed to look its Author in the face? External accidents, how degrading soever, can never change a real gem. When buried in earth, or trampled with the shoon of base vulgarity, it retains its value and brightness still, and it is destined to shine on the bosom of loveliness, or to grace the crown of royalty. By this same rule the ancient and divine law of incorporating believers in the body of Christ, remains unchanged by all the slander, vituperation, and ridicule with which at various times it has been assailed. The body, so incorporated, is still dear to him who hath ordained it, who watches over it in deepest degradation, and is already preparing for its final exaltation and purity. Ridiculed and defamed as it may be now, in it shall be realised the great conception of the ancient prophecy; in its production, the labour of our Lord, of his forerunner, and his inspired apostles, all concentrate; in its advancement and protection the holy energising martyr-spirit of antiquity revealed its patient and devoted power; its pure and spiritual victories, and their fruits of love, shall, in the Lord's esteem, repay the anguish of Gethsemane and Golgotha; the perfection, the glory, and fellowship of this body of

Christ, formed the joy that was set before him, when he endured the cross and despised the shame: and, when his purposes therein have been completed, their holiness, wisdom, beauty, and grandeur shall fill the anthems of his praise for ever, adversity and derision notwithstanding.

PRACTICAL DANGERS.

But modesty is natural to the great and the true; and this should always induce a careful attention to practical difficulty and danger. The truth of our principle is not to be doubted. That Jesus designs to have a believing people set apart for himself by baptism, and used on this earth in his service and for his glory is clear from his word, and verified in his providence. The reality is before us. It is not a doctrine, but a fact, effectuated by his power and confirmed by his authority. But those who are thus set apart for himself are yet on earth, and are yet but men; and hence, to maintain the character of their holy calling, they need a constant supply of mercy from the Lord they serve. He who is their head is also their life, and no one can live without him. This dependence on the mediating Lord is not their weakness, but their strength; in Him they shall have life, and have it more abundantly. In the observance of his law, they have nothing to dread; the fear is, lest, by some misapplication of Divine law, new disease should be generated where health was sought. The points on which this danger is most imminent now, are three: *First*, The moral nature of faith has, in some cases, been neglected; if this be allowed, the law is broken which demands a prostration of the heart, and corruption enters the church through its own initiating institution. *Secondly*, The initiated disciples of the first age were much in company with each other, and were trained by careful discipline; the neglect of this has long been felt by Christian brethren, and the perpetuating of this neglect will paralyse the church and cause every member to be unfitted for his calling. *Thirdly*, A gospelized selfishness, resting in the joy of a personal hope, and treating with contempt the destruction of a world, is a direct and habitual violation of divine law. These are the dangers against which the baptized believers should be on their guard, and from which their preservation should be sought with watchfulness, fidelity, and constant prayer.

THE NATURE OF CHRISTIAN FAITH.

Three expressions are used in Scripture, by which the moral feelings which Christian faith includes may be clearly ascertained. To "*believe in*," is to take the word of any one, to receive his statements as true; this may be done from the evidence adduced, without any reference to personal character, as we take the affirmation of a child, whose cry declares its pain, or that the habitation is on fire. The fact is received in that case; but the idea that the child is competent to meet the declared emergency never enters the mind. To "*rely upon*," includes more; it is an act by which one person reposes, what he feels to be important, on the character and competency of another. It implies a sense of personal insufficiency on the part of the believer, and a personal all-sufficiency on the part of him who is entrusted with the matter in hand. The former kind of faith is needful in receiving the doctrine which our Lord declares; the second is required in confiding to him, in his action and office, the great work of salvation with which he is entrusted. To "*believe into,*" means something more even than this; for a person "*in Christ,*" is not only dependent on his aid, but subjected to his authority; and is, actually and willingly, in the power of Christ. The sense of the expression requires the introduction of a verb of motion, as if written, *he believed (entering) into Christ*, when the action is in the present tense; or, *he believed (having entered) into Christ*, when the action is in the past tense; and cases occur in which it might be written, *he believed (to enter) into Christ*, when the person named was in a state of mind, wherein the confidence he had in Christ prepared him to place himself, for time and for eternity, in the hands of the Redeemer, without any reservation. In these three forms of expression, the threefold aspect of a disciple's faith is placed before us. By a subject of this faith, the word of our Lord is admitted as true; the personal character and attributes of our Lord are admitted to be perfect; and the directions of our Lord are received as legitimate and authoritative. These are not three kinds of faith; but three aspects or actions of the same faith—the faith of a Christian disciple. By these features, too, it is distinguished from all merely intellectual states of mind. The most capacious knowledge of Divine truth may exist, where this moral subjection to the Saviour has never been yielded; but, however ignorant or sinful a man may be, if this believing subjection to the Saviour be attained, professed, and accredited, he shall be saved, and ought to be received as a subject of saving faith. It is this which makes him look back on his past life with contrition, to the future with hope, and to show a grateful devotion in present obedience. To the ascertaining of this condition in the heart, therefore, all attention ought to be directed in admitting members to the Christian church. The cant of liberality and the slang of sectarian strictness, may, by the worst of men, be acquired with equal facility; but when used to veil the deformities of an unrenewed heart, they can only lead to increased corruption. It is the heart that must form the place of the Redeemer's throne; and before he takes his dwelling there, the heart must be broken. It is the broken, the contrite, the new heart, with all its delicate moral sensibilities and griefs, which forms the seed-bed of Christian virtue. This childlike disposition in the presence of the Saviour, which receives his doctrine, reposes on his personal perfections, and submits to his authority in all things, known and unknown, for time and for eternity, is the new creation of God; and, of those who are such, he forms his family, his church, his kingdom, that shall remain for ever. Let the builders of Zion find and use these living stones, this gold and silver, these precious stones, and, come what will, the work shall never perish; but if, through impatience or worldly policy, they build into this holy fabric wood, hay, straw, stubble, or icy conglomerates of polemical dogmas frozen to consistency, smeared with the compost of formal profession, and marked with the watch-word of sectarian interest, the work shall not stand, baptized or unbaptized; it is vanity, and the day shall declare it.

MODERN TECHNICALITIES.

Rising as Europe is, or has been, from Popery, as from a quagmire, it is natural to expect, in its present state, some marks of its former position and defilement; and, therefore, every one should be on his guard when entertaining a fellowship with popular prejudices. It is, on the first view of the case, improbable that truth should be very popular in a state of society given, for so many ages and so absolutely, to the domination of error. Besides, many of our modern technicalities have been originated by the enemies of truth, and were at first admitted by the disciples of our Lord only in sufferance. The word *Christian* did not originate with the Redeemer, nor with any of his inspired Apostles; the disciples were called Christians first at Antioch, and most likely by heathens, who conformed therein to the usages of their own schools. It is a fearful fact, that the influence of the general apostasy is seen in nothing more strikingly than in changing the sense of terms found in Scripture, even when their meaning and use have been determined by Divine authority. What, then, may we not expect in technicalities that have not been so defined or authorised? Hence the title Christian is now taken by any party that chooses to assume it; and it is assumed generally with the greatest effrontery, where the most vital truths taught by our Lord and the Apostles are denied, and where the most obvious duties imposed by God in the administration of his mercy are to be trampled under foot. The word "charity," and the phrase "Christian charity," are thus made to conceal habits of compromise which are most unjustifiable. "Christian liberality" is a phrase which often means a contempt of all truth. The word "conscientious" is frequently so used as to show a habit of voluntary and determined self-deception, which, in its rise and operation, clearly indicates the maturity of self-will. Persons are now found ostentatiously appealing to Scripture who have never studied the passages which throw their light on the duty in question, and who, when the meaning of those passages is, by their own confession, stated, will not submit to that authority. The error in all these cases consists, in paying to the sentimental feelings of men a deference which is not paid to the teaching Spirit and his written authority; and in withholding from the Divine will, however expressed, that supreme regard which, as the will of God, it justly claims. In the simple language of inspired writers, the designed application of moral principle is clearly kept in view; and those who suffer themselves to be drawn away by modern technicalities from the sublime and gracious realities conceived in the mind of eternal wisdom, and so revealed in the action of dying and redeeming love, ought to bear in mind, that one of the chief devices used by Satan has ever been to draw by degrees the population of earth into positions which, being taken, the truth of God becomes changed into a lie, and the use which is made of it is rendered ridiculously absurd. The greater the truth which thus becomes perverted, the greater the evil to which that perversion leads. The more endeared, by indirect associations, the term which is thus chosen for debasement may have been, the greater is the calamity which its debasement inflicts. When surrounded by such moral catastrophes, and such triumphs of Satanic fraud, the followers of Jesus should be prepared to go all lengths in dealing with popular delusion, and to make all sacrifices that may be required in order to attain and promulgate the pure and imperishable reality which their Lord has so clearly enjoined. Christians, if they be really what they would have their name to indicate, will, unquestionably, unite in obedience to the laws of him they serve; but it remains for him who makes the affirmation, to prove that any one, knowingly rejecting the law of his Redeemer, can, with propriety, be so named. If the right of private judgment be allowed—as it is due to every individual—yet the obligation of uniform reverence, docility, and submission to Divine law, may be enforced on individuals, and tested in church discipline. This state of heart towards God—which is, at the same time, the greatest and the most merciful production of Divine power—forms, and ought to form, the basis of all fellowship in the body of Christ. The first act of that subdued heart is to embrace the Christ whom God hath given and exalted; and every subsequent action of such a heart is taken in obedience to that Christ. Hence the union is a union in Christ, and the members are one body in Christ; and thus by him, the common centre, they become members one of another. The common subjection to the common Lord is, therefore, the pledge and compact of the whole with all its parts. But subjection to the Lord, is a subjection to his commandments; and his commandments enforce some things that influence individuals principally, as, "Keep thyself pure;" and others, which principally influence these united brethren collectively, as, "Neglect not the assembling of yourselves together." Neither class of duties can be absolutely separated from the other, for the whole body is affected by each of its members, and each member has an interest in its general movements and condition. Being one body, it has one interest, and that one interest is acknowledged by each member on his entrance; and each member devotes himself to that one interest, under that one Lord, by the one Spirit, and in conformity with that one written law, which is granted by inspiration of God. It is in this compact of mutual and combined subjection that the fellowship of men in Christ begins; and the sincerity with which this compact is made, with the faithfulness evinced in fulfilling it, constitute the chief objects of discipline in the body of Christ. Murder, theft, falsehood, fornication, and drunkenness are not, or ought not, to be expected in such a fraternity. If such things do occur, the perpetrators are cast out, until they repent; but to reserve the discipline of churches and their fellowship for such acts only, is to prove that its positive object has been abandoned, that the vital reality of fellowship in Christ exists no more. The more general or the more restricted technicalities of party will be used in vain wherever this vital moral element has been forsaken. The society without this is, call it what men please, no more a church of Christ, than straw, when tied into any shape, and however labelled, can become a man. With all its grotesque formalities, it is straw, and nothing more. Paste it and adorn it as we may, it has no human internal organisation or life. It has no thought, soul, or energy: it is an idol. Such things may be made, and made all alike; and they may be all called by the same name; but they have no life or reality, notwithstanding. Wherever the living principle can be found, its fellowship should be sought and granted as the law of Christ ordains; but, in the present day, and with all our neglect of ulterior discipline, to accept without scrutiny whatever garnished things presume to call themselves Christian, is not only a departure from Divine law, it is perfecting the ridiculous by degrading the sublime.

OF INDIVIDUAL CHURCHES.

The oneness of the whole community in Christ has been shown in all the foregoing discussion. The design of our Lord is to form, conduct, and perfect, one kingdom under his own authority and administration; and through all succeeding ages he is bringing this kingdom to that result in which he shall be glorified in his saints and admired in them that believe. An individual devoted to him in the covenant and hope of Divine mercy is one of that number, who, in all the earth, are given to him on the same principle, by the same law, in the same recognition, and for the same end. The assembly of such individuals meeting in any one place, by meeting together as individuals *in* Christ, are not thereby separated from the body of individuals who are in Christ, for their meeting together is an express command of him whom they all serve. It is clearly written, " Neglect not the assembling of yourselves together, as the manner of some is." This duty is enforced on the believers in Rome, Corinth, Ephesus, and in Judea, if not in the same words, yet with the same intent, by the Apostle Paul, who by no means urged thereby the separation of the believers in each place from the general community of disciples. By perfecting the discipline and union to each other of disciples in Rome, he felt that he was perfecting the union of these same disciples to all other disciples of the Lord in what place soever they were found. The more respect he obtained for the law of Christ in each place, the more he was consolidating the reign of Christ there, and over those who met there in his name and for his service. The Christ is one, his dominion is one, his law is one; his atonement, mediation, and Spirit are the same in Rome, Corinth, Ephesus, and Judea; and the persons who revere him in all these places are, by necessity, one people, live and meet in what city they may: but the neglect of him, and of his laws, ordinances, and gifts, cannot produce or augment the union of persons in Christ. Hence, to meet in any one city, or in any one town, or in any one street or house, for the purpose of conducting his worship, obeying his laws, sustaining his ordinances, bringing sinners to the knowledge of the truth, and training converts for his fellowship and service, is no separation from the general body of disciples; it is only doing what the disciples of Jesus are commanded to do in every place. Neither is the using of a local or distinguishing designation an act of separation from the whole body of believers in Christ; they may meet in London or in Liverpool, as they met in Corinth or in Rome, and yet be believers still. They meet in those places because they are believers, and because, being believers and disciples, they are bound thus to serve the common Lord. Moreover, by strictly adhering to the law and ordinances of their Redeemer, these assemblies of disciples commit no act of separation from the body of Christ; they thus give a social visibility to the rule of their common Lord, and the principle which actuates the body of his people. The more strictly they conform to his will, the more strictly may these assemblies and the persons who compose them be said to be one. It is not obedience, but rebellion, that divides. Disciples are one, because they are learning in the same school, under the same tuition and discipline, and acting under the same authority, for the same end. The more sacredly they reverence this authority, cultivate this discipline, study this lesson of redeeming love, and seek the end of their fellowship in their own assembly, the more will those disciples who compose it become influenced by the principles and governance which unite the whole kingdom of heaven. The discipline of an army includes the discipline of all its troops; and the oneness of that army is produced by each man's filling his place, with orderly obedience to the general command. Neither the existence nor the discipline of particular assemblies, therefore, can with propriety be dishonoured with the charge of schism; the assemblies are called assemblies of God because their existence and actions are authorised of God, and their fellowship is aggrandised with his presence. It is by his mercy and under his authority that each convert is admitted; it is by his ordinance that each confessor is received and recognised; it is subjection to his law that each believer, in fellowship, professes and promises; the assembly is a visible and local development of the union which repenting sinners have in God. Instead of being a departure from, it is a practical exhibition of, the unity obtained in

Christ. The more careful and firmly conscientious in their observance of his law these brethren become, and the more they are united to each other, the more will their development of this unity in Christ be perfected. It is absurd to plead for union in the whole body of disciples, by proposing to relax the bond of union in their particular assemblies; a politician might, with as much propriety, propose to secure the union and prosperity of an empire by urging on every parent the neglect and desertion of his own family.

Every assembly or church, so called, is either a church of God, or it is not. If it be a church of God, it is because the assembly is formed of persons who believe in God, embrace the Saviour he has given, submit to his law, rely on his providence, and are, in his own ordained incorporation, devoted in each other's fellowship to his service. If these affirmations do not apply to it, the assembly or church, though called by the name of Christian, falls not within the present inquiry. If the assembly be composed of believers, incorporated and devoted by his law to the Redeemer, and under him to God, then all the business and aim of the assembly must be to promote the glory of God in the extending of his dominion, and in promoting the edification of his people who are so united. They may have to ask the sympathy of other brethren, and they may hold fellowship with other brethren; but they have also a privilege and an engagement with each other at home. To extend the influence of divine truth in any locality, and to advance the edification of recognised brethren there, are parts of a work in which great exertions must be made, great responsibilities must be incurred,—and by possibility, great resistance may be encountered. But it cannot be said that these responsibilities devolve on one more than another; these undertakings belong to the whole assembly. That which belongs to each disciple, is what he is able to do in the common work, with what he can use of the common privilege; and he enters the assembly of brethren to become a brother and a partaker with them. But the law of their incorporation is the law of God; and the end of their incorporation is the glory of God; while each one is admitted on the authority of God. He comes to the door of the assembly and asks admission on the mercy of Christ and the authority he has given. He thus asks to be recognised as a brother, a partaker in the common privilege, and a sharer in the common service for the Redeemer's glory. On this fraternal compact, formed by Divine authority and protected by Divine law, they proceed to elect their pastor, appoint the deacons, form their schools, send out their evangelists, and incur, perhaps, a large but necessary debt in the erection of the place in which they worship. Indeed, by the command of God, and under the protection of God, they have formed a moral and spiritual partnership. They are not separated from the general body of disciples; but, in that general body of disciples, they have fellowship in a given work. They have all confided in

God; and under him each has trusted the other. In this mutual faith they have undertaken their several works, and cherished their individual and united expectations. It is quite conceivable, that in this partnership of mercy and obligation, some individual may be imprisoned; and that others may be forced to the verge of pecuniary embarrassment or ruin. Here, then, is the question: Is that compact of partnership in privilege and service binding, or is it not? In forming it, the brethren did not withdraw from the general body of disciples; and, in continuing it, they are not cut off from the body of the disciples. The particular church is as a portal to the mighty temple. On these questions there is no doubt. The only point brought under dispute by modern casuists is, whether this compact, formed in obedience to Divine law, may not, when convenience or caprice dictates, be broken with levity, whatever the effect on brethren whose confidence has been solicited, and on the glory of God, by whose authority it was obtained?

If this question occurred in mercantile associations, and came to be the subject of ordinary arbitration, it is perfectly plain to any one what must be the award. No partnership, when legally formed, can be dissolved without a proper notice of the act, a due regard to mutual interests, and a just submission to the forms of law. The person retiring must be justified in the act by the partner he leaves and the government under which both parties reside. This, then, is the case in hand. A penitent sinner is received into the assembly of brethren, that he may there become a brother; if he wish to retire, he must be justified in the act, both by the brethren he leaves, and by their common Father, Redeemer, and Lord. Having become a party in a joint concern, he must act as a party, and regard the interests of all the parties with whom, at his own request, he became united. He entered by the law of his God and Saviour; and before he can retire, he is bound to show, first, that the law of his Saviour justifies the act; and, secondly, that, in taking the action, he fulfils the law of fraternal kindness.

It is strange that while fidelity used to be expected among thieves, apostasy should now be justified among brethren. If anything could make this anomaly more remarkable, it would be the fact that poor mistaken humanity has urged this species of unfaithfulness as a means of promoting more general union in the body of Christ; that is to say, stripping the statement of all its obscurities—by loosening and even dissolving the bond of union between himself, his pastor, and the brethren who received him into fellowship, this beguiled victim of error is urged to promote a closer union with supposed brethren, whom he has neither seen nor known. Where he has received the offices of Christian love and confidence, he is taught to hold himself at liberty to betray the one and refuse the other, that thereby he may be greeted as liberal by all mankind. His brethren, whom he has seen, he may forsake in their difficulties, betray in their confidence, and in their tenderest feelings penetrate with deepest sorrow. And why?—because the man is exceedingly charitable to others, whom he has never seen, and with whom he has entered into no fellowship of service whatsoever. It often occurs that these unseen brethren are known to be the subjects of error; the system of their incorporation is confessed to be unscriptural, and it is known that their character has been subjected to no scrutiny, their commendation being principally found in their wealth or worldly station; and, with the sentimentality thus generated, the known obligations of home are abandoned, and brethren, to whose kindness may be traced the greatest spiritual advantage, are, in the face of a world, covered with the shame of open desertion. If the object were merely to convey an advantage defined and authorised by the law of the Redeemer, and to do this for other real or supposed brethren, without neglecting the engagements of home, there could be no objection. The wider and more bountiful these operations of Christian love are made, the more closely will his disciples conform to the law of their Redeemer. The objection lies not against what these mistaken brethren propose to do; but against what they determine to leave undone. It is not merely other Christians that they are bound to love; they are bound to cherish and exercise the love which is in Christ Jesus towards all mankind. The more guilty and wretched the victim of sin may be, the more powerfully and justly he appeals to the compassion of those who believe in Jesus. The more refined and perfect the piety may be which is discerned in other men, the more are believers in Jesus bound to glorify God in them and on that account. But the love of Christ for saints or sinners never induced him to abrogate, for personal convenience, the known law of God, or to forsake the particular work which God had given him to do. It was by perfecting his own work that he revealed his reverence for the Father, his delight in the saints, and his pity for the world. He thus made all the elements of moral principle in his mind harmonise in one great service, done to God and men. Those who follow him must read his law in the light of his example. By this they are led to express their charity, not by forsaking, but by fulfilling, the engagements of their fellowship in the body of Christ. It is not by doing less than we undertook for him, but by doing more, that the fulness of love and zeal will be manifested. By neglecting the place of prayer, the gathering together of the brethren who have been received by us and whom we have received, by leaving our portion in the work of God at home unfulfilled, by withdrawing our succour from its pastorate, our sympathies from those who are afflicted, our advice from the young, and our energy from the aggressive action on the world, we do not perform a service to other saints, but inflict an injury on those with whom we have been personally united. Whatever we propose to do, these things should never be left undone. The plea founded on the right of private judgment, is of no use, when brought to cover a neglect of duty, which no judgment whatever can justify. If the disciple has a right to do these things against the voice of brethren, whose confidence he has solicited and gained, it is no other than the right he has to commit any flagitious crime and take the consequences. The plea of universal charity, when brought to shelter these home and positive neglects, is both absurd and false; for if the whole body of Christ be loved with all the intensity that is professed, by neglecting and injuring the members with which he has been united, the victim of this error cannot advance the welfare of the body he professes so highly to esteem; the plea is, therefore, absurd; but it is also false, for he who loveth not the brethren whom he hath seen, how can he love the brethren whom he hath not seen? Hence it follows, that from this source proceed not the love and succour which brethren are to expect from brethren in the service of their Father and Lord, but the neglect and the ill-treatment which reason might lead us to expect from arguments so utterly superficial and unsupported. It is only while the gratification and praise of the present moment, or of a particular circle, are to be enjoyed, that this ostentatious and inconsistent appeal to general love is maintained. It becomes modest, as the reality from which it has purloined the name, whenever a real common-sense and self-denying service is to be performed. It is clamorous when praise is to be obtained, but quiet and cowardly when good is to be done, and when self is to be denied. All the true and universal love of the saints is found in those happy and noble spirits who, first in their own assembly, feeling the power of Divine love enrich it with spiritual service and benefits, which, being made to overflow, produce a fountain at which strangers may be refreshed. This is the real course through which our Lord designs the oneness of his people to proceed, and the fruits of that oneness to reveal his glory. This result can never be produced by personal neglect or local infidelity. A man, to be lovely abroad, must first become faithful at home ; and all fictitious catholicity, not having this basis of faithfulness on which to rest, produces no good that can be called substantial, but fills the society of believers with mutual wrongs. It is hence that many seek to overturn the organised assemblies of believers, and to break up the discipline altogether; while many, when individual members of these churches have done wrong, will give them shelter from discipline which the Lord himself ordained. Let it be called charity, or candour, or what men please ; by this means the churches are set against the churches, and division, not union, is the result. Moreover, it is not to love that any such action can be traced, but rather to a respect of persons, which James forbids; or to a love of obtaining gain, which is, by Paul, designated idolatry. It is the hope of a subscription or of praise which ordinarily leads to this exercise of *charity* towards a culprit, and of *cruel unfaithfulness* to brethren who have never been impeached. Let brethren who thus wrong each other, bear in mind, that no misapplication of words can change or conceal the true nature of this vile transaction, by which, through despising each other, they invite the derision of all mankind; and, for Him whom they profess to serve, obtain, not reverence and glory, but the rudest blasphemies.

ON THE DISCIPLINE OF DISCIPLES.

When this work was undertaken, it was intended to give more attention to this particular; but tracing the error we had to expose has left but small space to accomplish the design. The brethren may find a more extended view of this subject in the author's "Hints on the Regulation of Christian Churches," and the outline of Christian virtues contained in his first book of the disciple class. Here now it is possible only to suggest the utter improbability that God should first renew—rather, regenerate—the souls of men by his Spirit and his word, and then cause them to be born again into a new social relationship, separated from the world in which they live, and destined to inherit a place at his right hand, and yet leave them without fellowship, education for the future, or discipline to fit them for present action. The most superficial reader of the New Testament may see that, in ancient times, it was not so; and the clear instructions of our Lord, as well as his example, prove that it ought not to be so. The disciples under his care were not left dependent on those general instructions which were given in promiscuous assemblies. They met together in their newly-recognised character. They met to recognise the grace of God exhibited in each other. In those assemblies, where the baptized believers gathered round the feet of their holy Lord, they were taught to expect the action, the comfort, and glory of a present and eternal Spirit. They were not less energetic than we in labouring to convince the world, by testifying that Jesus was the Christ; but they possessed a high advantage in the worship of the churches, the communion of their members, and the mutual fostering of that martyr-spirit by which so many sealed the truth, and, by their deaths more than their lives, widened and deepened its influence. Without dogmatically affirming any peculiar view of Divine truth, it is plain, that many words and phrases of Holy Scripture have ceased to bear any meaning in many assemblies of baptized believers. The miraculous gifts are gone, and, whether irrecoverably or no, since the evidence of their existence is not shown, the effects of their existence in the early churches can form no rule for our investigation now. But leaving these all out of the question, the almost entire neglect of church meetings for worship, and fellowship in mutual edification, involves a clear departure from the ancient practice which must be pregnant, if it has not been productive, of terrible results. The inaptitude of Christians to improve such opportunities is a clear and positive proof that their discontinuance has been attended with pernicious consequences. To edify one another in love, must have a strange, unmeaning sound on those who never meet at all, who often *would* never meet at all, and who, by pride of station or other motives, are more separated in the church than either party in the church has become separated from the world. To bear each other's burdens, and so fulfil the law of Christ, has almost become confined to acts of pecuniary charity, which seems to have been scarcely comprehended in the ancient meaning of those words. Our churches are remarkable for the clatter of business; the ancient churches, not neglecting the duty of attending to this, were eminent for their deep and elevated devotion. "*It is only a prayer-meeting*"—a phrase which ancient Christians would not have understood, because prayer was the element of their being, its life, and joy—regulates now the conduct of thousands; while the meeting itself, so spiritless and insipid, and absolutely dependent on the pastor, or some one or two individuals, explains the mystery, proving how easily believers themselves may sink below the practical requirements of their high and holy calling. In those three great points, to which this culture was directed—personal peace and joy in God, personal usefulness, and preparation for heaven—the want of more communion and discipline in the churches is made unquestionable. Many Christians would now derive the evidence of their personal religion from their doubts and fears; many have never been useful, and scarcely ever tried to be useful, since they professed to be converted; and more have never conquered their love of ease, or denied themselves one gratification for the cause of the Redeemer or the love of souls; while the high-toned fervour of Paul, "I have a desire to be with Christ, which is far better," his yearning for the unseen world, is now confined to a sphere too limited and secret to be described. The profession of these things is not wanting, and their propriety is not doubted; but they either do not suit our taste, or seem to be impracticable. Many have been so beclouded, that they cannot see the difference, and think themselves as good as the Apostles; while others, lamenting the languor of our fellowship, seek for its revival by unlawful means. Men, with the Bible in their hands, are continually startled by the fact that our experience does not realise the blessings that it promises to believers upon earth. What is the remedy for this evil? Brethren, you will find it in a perfect conformity to the law of the Redeemer; and a practical, constant, and social communion with his Holy Spirit in the churches.

THE CHRISTIAN ENTERPRISE.

All the foregoing observations show, that the body of Christ was formed for some great moral purpose; such an association of men, so organised and preserved as this is, for nothing, would be little other than an infinite absurdity. The commission of our Lord proves that this elected body, this association of consecrated persons, was entrusted with a great work. The believers, so recognised and united, are the heralds of his mercy, and witnesses to the truth of God, who declares its richness, granting and fulfilling its covenants and promises. The corrosive and agitating question, whether the action of believers on the world should be performed in the way of direct invitation, or by a positive and formal testimony to the value of those mercies which are granted in Christ, will not affect the matter in hand. Whether we testify or invite, or combine in our labour the influence of both, the commission has been given, and believers are responsible to Him they trust for every instance of its neglect. With the affirmations, or rather the injunctions, before us, Go into all the world, proclaim the glad tidings to every creature; carry the proclamation into all the nations; make disciples, baptizing them into the name of the Father, and of the Son, and of the Holy Ghost: he that believeth and is baptized shall be saved; ye are my witnesses; and lo, I am with you alway, even to the end of the world. With all these injunctions and affirmations before us, whatever scruple we may have respecting the form of the action, to neglect its performance in the way we think it should be done, must involve us in the guiltiness of disobeying the Lord we serve. Whether we appropriate the designations significant of liberality or strictness; whether our creed allow of promises, or testimony, or of both; whether our view of the atonement be general or particular; to look coldly on, where sinners perish in ignorance of the great salvation, and the Author of that salvation, in which we hope, is dishonoured every day, can never be a matter of indifference to the Searcher of hearts. If the event which sinks so many souls in perdition, and produceth so much blasphemy upon earth, be in itself inevitable, a cold-hearted contemplation of the event can, in the followers of Jesus, never be justified. The Lord himself knew, more perfectly than we can know, the vastness, grandeur, justness, wisdom, purity, and benevolence of his ulterior design; yet, when he knew that Jerusalem must perish, he wept over the city and said, "Oh, that thou hadst known, even thou." If his servants be now and hereafter called to occupy a similar position, and look on similar objects of wrath, with all we may see to admire in his righteous judgment, he does not forbid a participation in his deep and pure compassion. Nor can we justly assume the power of seeing beforehand where and when the door of mercy shall be closed against the guilty. It is not our business to know this: the Sovereign Author of mercy alone knows where and when the operation of mercy shall terminate to nations or individuals. Our own age has set before our eyes wonders of grace and victories of truth, exceeding the most sanguine expectations of mankind; as if, with exuberance of love and power, he determined to chastise the insufficiency of our utmost zeal. While men are crying, There is no hope! he streaks the dark horizon with the tinge of morning, and perfects their reprehension with the light of day. All these things declare that the limitation of his purpose can never be the rule for human action. Men who are under orders must act upon the word they have received; and whether this mean, invite or testify, or both, it saith, " Go into all the earth, proclaim to every creature." It is strange that any difference of opinion should exist amongst believers respecting the import of words so solemn and so plain; but if there be a difference of opinion, and that difference of opinion be conscientiously held on either side, this does not prevent the preparation of each party to perform, as he understands it, the command of his Redeemer. The neglect of this is what we have at present to deplore. There be some who plead for gospel invitation, who never invite sinners to repent; and others, rejecting the invitations, plead for a gospel testimony, but yet never testify for God. On his own showing, each of these is wrong; and God is making each party a rebuke and an admonition to the other. The humble and devoted, though more general labourer, is crowned with success before his particular opponent; and the humble, devoted, particular labourer is seen, blessed with usefulness in the face of his general reprover. Each is honoured by the common Lord, as if to show, that those who are his indeed, shall, when devoted and sincere, be blessed of him, the differences permitted to exist among his people notwithstanding. All the subjects of Divine grace are his workmanship, created anew in Christ Jesus; and he who made each one, made it for his own use, for the good work to which he hath called us; and, with all its defects, it is used by him to effectuate his purpose and reveal his glory. Each instrument, therefore, should be ready, in its place, and filled with the temper adapted to its use. In the work of God, however he may view it, each Christian is bound to be as true as steel. The church and its fellowship has this for one main object of its institution. By mingling with and acting on each other, Christians are prepared to act upon the world. Whether they invite, or testify, or do both, it is in the church, and in communion with the Spirit, that each should be prepared, in what he does, to become, in the hand of God, an effective instrument. To rest in our own hope, take the joy of our own salvation, and, as if therewith satisfied, to shun the conflict, and let things take their course, whatever view we hold, is utter infidelity. Every member in the body of Christ is called to perform its function, and the discipline and fellowship of the church ought to be so conducted as to secure the functional efficiency of every member. The world is our battle-field, and every church is bound to fill its place, bring up its resources, and maintain its order, as though the victory of redeeming love must be lost or won by the failure or perfection of its own service.

THE VICARIOUS SERVICE.

Nothing can be more clear than the Divine authority, by which the officers and delegated servants of the churches are sustained. The pastor, the deacon, and the evangelist are not only given; but directions are given for their guidance, and for the guidance of churches in their appointment. The messengers of the churches might, with perfect propriety, be made to meet every requirement of circumstances in any age. The definiteness and flexibility of the order plainly show that our Lord intended the fellowship of his people to be carried through all time, and to act upon all generations. If so, its essential character must be evolved in all generations. This, then, being based on personal religion, must consist in personal responsibilities. The church may have pastors, and deacons, evangelists, messengers, and missionaries for foreign lands; and each of these may have a peculiar responsibility; but the existence and responsibility of any or all these officers can never release from their obligations the individual members of the churches. If this could be assumed, it were easy to show, that the cause of the Redeemer would gain advantage by an utter extinction of every office which the Lord appointed when ascending up on high. It cannot be assumed. The words of our Lord have nothing, and the churches planted and approved by the apostles have, in their constitution and practice, nothing to approve or justify the assumption. Official appointments were designed to guide and to render more effectual, not to supersede, the exertion of individuals. Each member in the body has not the same, but each member in the body has its own function; and Paul affirms, that even the least is essential. So each member of a church has his place and duty; and in his place, that duty must be performed. Our departure from original practice may be seen more obviously in nothing than in this. Multitudes seem to demand praise, when, by a poor subscription of some pounds a-year, they have purchased a substitute to fill their places, and presented a vicarious service to the Lord. This is absolutely wrong. The Lord we trust, redeemed us with his own blood, and suffered for us in his own person; his personal service for us is, even now, continued at the right hand of God; and on this our personal salvation depends. What, then, can return this mercy without our personal love and labour? For us he gave himself, that we to him might give ourselves. It is not our money, but our hearts, that he demands. Not our substitutes, but the service of our own hands. Rightly considered, the supposition of vicarious service has no place in the body of Christ. Each Christian is the Lord's, with all that he possesses; he, therefore, has nothing to sell or to transfer to his brother's account. Whatever he can do in the service, he owes in the service; every brother, like himself, owes whatever he is able to perform. Besides, the moral benefits which attend devotedness can only be received by each in his own person. The trial of faith and patience, the increase of fortitude, the perfecting of love, the joys of victory, and all the balmy blessings which attend our labour in bringing sinners to God, or gathering in his elect, can only be received and enjoyed by the labourer himself. It cannot be purchased and sold. This fruit is gathered out of every man's own field. The interest of each believer, therefore, declares this supposed exemption from the work of mercy to be an injustice. Such an exemption would be banishment. Besides, if only pastors and evangelists act upon the world, the testimony of the church would, by the supineness of its members, tend to frustrate all their labour. The silence of twenty, who ought to speak, would neutralise and almost falsify the word of one who bears his testimony alone. Out of this fountain streams of evil flow into the churches. These streams of evil flow out of the churches into the world. Members lean on members, shifting the burden of service on each other; deacons become encumbered and lean upon the pastor. Some pastors, in their trouble, flee for refuge to the state; others lean on operations conducted by unscriptural associations. The country leans on town, and town upon the country; the error has pervaded our missionary churches so far, that where the disciples are numbered by thousands, a pastor is not found amongst them all. The evil is unlimited; and the pernicious consequences are mourned by thousands. Against these results, which provoke both grief and shame, the evil can present no shadow of Divine authority, or one particle of good. The inaction of individuals can be of use to none but those, who, hiding ambition with professed zeal, labour to be great at the expense of others. Such would take money for service, to a limited extent; but, even they must have service at the last. It is not only wrong, therefore, but absurd. The hired agency may be good; but the personal agency is indispensable. A living body must have life in every limb. Whether it be considered in respect to home or foreign labour, the evil resulting from the habit of personal neglect is indescribable; and the hope which invites its correction, is filled with the highest felicity that can be here enjoyed.

THE LABOUR AND PROSPECT OF HOME.

The present condition of our English churches is solemn, but yet encouraging. They have an amount of moral energy, not yet appreciated, which waits to be called into effective action; and no age has ever presented greater incentives to awaken and employ every resource. The freedom of the press, the cheapening of literature, the wide distribution of Bibles, the multiplication of tracts, the organisation of schools, especially of those taught on the Lord's-day, of town and country missions, and other societies for the diffusion of Divine truth, give to the time and country in which we live features that will render it illustrious to all future generations. The churches of our order and constitution have never been so numerous and powerful since the Reformation began. Our forefathers thought themselves happy when able to escape from prison-houses and shameful deaths; and, in our own time, the denominational odium has been felt in every circle of society to which we have gained access, and followed us in every labour of our hands. Under every trial the Lord hath been our refuge and strength, and, by his blessing, the churches have increased, their operations have extended, blessings have descended on their labour, and God hath bestowed on his people greater privilege, and on his ordinances a more general esteem, than have been known in England for many centuries. A moral and social status has been granted, as if to prepare for future results. During the comparative increase of our churches, an advance has been made in their character and discipline; and clearer light has been poured on the sacred page. These and other features of our case are full of encouragement and hope. But one fact is full of instruction. In most of the churches, as in the denomination at large, the work has been done by a comparatively small part of our whole strength. A few men do the labour, while others are looking on. If the comparatively few have, by the blessing of God, effected what is done, what might we not expect if from eighty to one hundred thousand of our members, each in his place, would rise up, in the strength of God, and act with equal decision, prudence, and zeal? There are no miraculous gifts now; and, therefore, other things being the same, what is done by one man may be effected by another—in nature, if not in degree. It is granted that each cannot perform the same work; but it is pleaded, that each may be doing some work for God, and testify in some way to the word of his grace. The bees are not all queens; but, in their hive, they protect no *drones*. It is this individual and practical efficiency that ought to be sought in all the churches. Each baptized believer ought either to be a man in Christ Jesus; or, if not, aim to become one. The knowledge of a Christian should be combined with his feeling, these followed by the action, and in every sphere the action should be rendered habitual and easy. Such men, straining their whole resource, and laying hold on God, might move the world with their moral energy, and make the advocates of error and of sin afraid. Let the English baptized churches set their hearts on this; take the advantage of their organisation; meet as in the presence of the Comforter, the Holy Ghost; use the intimations of his Word, and its application by the Spirit; and they, with all the imperfections they confess, shall yet renew the ancient victories. Effective official agencies, however important in their places, cannot perform the task; the members must be roused, individuals must be trained, the churches must awake. It must be seen in their fellowship, activity, peace, and joy, that in the constitution they receive from God, these churches have received from him more than a form, a creed, a ceremony; that they have received a life, a spirit, an indwelling soul. In a word, let the churches rise to the dignity of their privilege; then shall the body of Christ they form, become, in the eyes of all observers, "fair as the moon, clear as the sun, and terrible as an army with banners."

Brethren and fathers, what is the spectacle before us in our native land? I speak not of antiquity, but of to-day; nor yet of Palestine, or India, but of home. Here, where our fathers lived, and our mothers nursed our infancy, what do we see, in our own time? Compared with the Apostles' time, the change is wonderful. At first it would seem that heathenism and Judaism had passed, or almost passed away, from all our hemisphere. It is no such thing. The heathenish idolatry has not passed away: it has been incorporated. It was first overturned, and then embraced by the victor. Piece by piece, both the error of the heathen and that of the Jews have been appropriated by the followers of Jesus. The Popery, the semi-Popery, and the various fractional mixtures of that poison, have brought into our society all that was base amongst Gentiles and Jews. These elements of religious corruption, assuming the name of Jesus, have been hardened into confederacies, and strengthened by denominational interests, properties, refined polemics, and national alliances. Policies have followed policies in churches and in governments, goading the multitudes to all but madness. The maladies of heathen Rome, with more than all her crimes, have now returned in Christian countries, and in the name of Christ. What the future may unfold, no prophet comes, at present, to describe; but now we see a people distressed and impoverished, loaded by the incubus of a vast establishment, which rose in darkness, rules by force, and retails her poison in every family. What should we do in such a case? We are here, living in the pestilence, and, by sovereign grace, separated from its fellowship: what shall we do, while generations rise and fall into perdition at our doors? The least that can be asked of us is, the perfection of our own fellowship. This is, at first, but caring for ourselves;

yet this will be a service done to others too. These churches, once made perfect, shall become a bulwark to our peace in time of national calamity; and every member, when trained to usefulness, will become an evangelist to the darker places of our country, and a foe to its manifold corruptions.

THE MISSIONARY FIELD.

Of all the peculiarities which mark our time, no one is more interesting than the wide extension of our colonies, and the planting of Christian churches among the heathen. The former fact has already given a moral power to the English language never before granted to any spoken by mankind. The Greek and Latin tongues exerted, at particular periods, a power that was felt by many nations, and both of these were used as instruments for extending the knowledge of Divine mercy; but neither extended its influence over so wide a space, and through the population of so many, so large, and such diverse nations, as the English. By making this the vehicle of Divine communication, the Lord has shown the universality of his merciful design. He has also facilitated the execution of his purpose; for whatever is printed in the English tongue, will exert an influence through all the regions affected by the government, the commerce, and the colonial descendants of our country. Already may be seen, in the case of North America, the fruits which follow from this national procreation and alliance. British influence is, even now, felt in every zone, and in both hemispheres; it hath literally encompassed the globe. This fact imperatively claims of British Christians the utmost care in rendering the versions of Scripture they use as perfect and as permanent as human power can make them; and in giving to their works on divinity, and the constitution and fellowship of their churches, the utmost possible exactness of conformity to scriptural instructions and examples. What is, in this way, done for England, is, in fact, done for the world. Besides, the planting of our churches hath already commenced in almost every land, and, through them, the gospel is already seen exerting its influence on every kind of heathen population. The English settlers, the Boors, the Hottentots, the Caffres, the Negro race, and mountain tribes of Africa, are now seen sitting at the feet of Jesus to hear his words. The Mussulman, the Brahmin, and wretched devotees of Hindostan, are turning from their Koran and Shasters to the sacred page. The regal princes of Burmah, and the millions of China, are already feeling the light and influence of English learning and our holy gospel. New Zealand, and the islands of the Southern Seas, have felt the vitalising and transforming power of Divine truth. American aborigines have owned the Saviour, and, in the Caribbean Archipelago, the love of Jesus and his ruling power have overturned an English slavery. Through all these regions infant churches, formed of emigrated Englishmen, or converted heathen, are rising to existence or maturity in the light of heaven. By this feature of our times, we realise the most distinctive features of apostolical times. It hath come upon us suddenly; for from the death of the Apostle John (A.D. 100), to the close of our last century, the Gospel almost ceased to spread, and all its energies became engrossed on the territory that it occupied. Now it spreads again; and this feature of the Apostles' time recalls to our observance the apostolical examples. Nor is this all. The bitter reign of Antichrist, by whom the labour of apostles, and of martyrs, and of the Lord himself, with all the credit of their names, have been turned to base and pernicious purposes—hath been shaken through the whole of Christendom. Its fraud hath been exposed, its adulteries have been condemned, the national participants in the abomination have been brought to extremity; and whatever comes in future, Christians may now see the beginning and results of those corruptions by which our holy religion was first brought into alliance with worldly corruption, and then reduced to imbecility and disgrace. In our foreign labour, every new church that is planted presents an opportunity of using, to the greatest advantage, whatever the experience of eighteen hundred years gone by have given to elucidate the nature, application, and working of our principles. The Bible, with all the advantage we possess for its explanation, forms a written law; and the Spirit, the Comforter, is a Divine and living agent in the living church. A thoughtful observance of the past shows all fanciful experiments wrought out to perfect failure, and then rejected with Divine disapprobation; it also shows a steadfast adherence to Divine law, living through all adversity, receiving the Divine approval amidst all reproach, conquering every obstruction, and, in the strength of Him we serve, rising from the ashes of martyrdom to bless the nations. Such incentives should make us fix our own, and also the attention of every missionary convert, first, on the written word, then on the living Spirit, which dwelleth in the churches. If these two authorities can be followed from the first, as Christ ordains, no present imperfection or resistance can prevent the advancing improvement of our churches, and the wider extension of their holy victories.

THE CONFLICT.

One test of principle exists in the present day, which was not known in the time of the Apostles. They had dangers from the heathen, and from the Jews, and from false brethren, who crept in unawares; they were not let in knowingly, but crept in unawares, and thus they became a source of trial; but the apostles had no national or papal hierarchies, bearing the Christian name, and teaching pernicious errors in the name of Jesus, to oppose their work, standing between them and the people. The only thing approaching to this feature of our case was the position and conduct of the Jews, with respect to their ancient Scriptures. Here the example of our Lord is full of admonition and instruction. In his treatment may be seen the true spirit of mankind, when roused by the opposition of religious prejudice and interests, formed and protected by corruptions of Divine law. His case unfolds the trial, and his conduct the duty of brethren who, in their sphere of labour, meet and encounter the agents of ecclesiastical corruption. Covered and concealed, as it may be, by present policy, this is the point at which the death-struggle of the Antichrist will be maintained. All experience proves that he will die hard, and present events show, with all possible distinctness, that the struggle will be felt wherever Christianity is known or taught. Side by side with every missionary of the truth, you have, or soon will have, the missionary and agent for its perversion. As the Jews of their time followed and resisted the apostles in every land, so now the papist, the semi-papist, and every partaker of its delusion, will follow and resist your missionary labour throughout the world. In principle, they have nothing to lose, and, therefore, they combine with the heathen on any terms, and desecrate the name of Jesus, in the name of God. It is not the heathen so much, as these corruptions of our holy doctrine and solemnities, that we have to oppose. These stand between us and the object of our compassion. The habits and interests of these men prepare them to treat the revelation and ordinances of our Lord as heathen never would. How, then, shall such adversaries be overcome? We have no fire, or sword, or civil penalties with which to overcome their manifold resistance. We can do nothing but by conviction, and act on nothing but on faith. How, then, can we prevail? It is answered, Let our conformity to the written law be unimpeachable, and let our maintenance of that conformity commend us to the living Spirit. Then shall the feeble be as David, and the house of David shall be as God.

THE INDIVIDUAL REQUIREMENT.

Let for one moment Tahiti speak. This much and justly-admired scene of missionary labour shows both the spirit of Antichristian resistance to the truth, and the one indispensable requirement for its defence and promulgation. It was not by argument only, or principally, that the advocate of Popery sought to effectuate his pernicious aim on that island. He landed there in a pacific spirit, pleaded his claim to apostolical descent, inverted the overtures of mercy, declaring that individual salvation depended on rites which the Redeemer never ordained. This was evil; and the resistance of that evil demanded the vigour of a well discriminated and disciplined church. If the brethren had simply appealed to the word and spirit of their Lord, the conflict might have been severe and long; yet victory would certainly have crowned the purposes of mercy: but when they appealed to human law, expelled the enemy by force, and guarded a promiscuous assembly by a royal mandate, the brethren revealed their own weakness, and the adversary unclothed his true character. Against force he appealed to force, kindled the flame of war, and, as in former times, in the name of Jesus the meek and lowly Mediator, summoned the military governments to mortal combat. Such is the fruitfulness of religious wrong, and this example is but a symptom of what we may expect. The agencies of Popery, which are spreading everywhere, form an organisation which waits for nothing but the opportunity, to muster and embroil, in one universal conflict, all the nations upon earth. Prophecies and facts indicate alike this terrible event. Against this combination in behalf of error and religious policies, the followers of Jesus cannot repel force with force. They can be discriminated by their faith, they can be recognised in their baptism, they can be disciplined in the fellowship of their churches, they can be armed with the holy word, and they can appeal to the living Spirit; in this attitude they can plead with God and men, but they can do no more. The great thing is, therefore, that they should do this perfectly—that they should all do it; and that each should do it with stability and success. The battle is, or will be, all along the line; and every soldier of the cross ought to be prepared, in discipline and armour, in skill, courage, and devotedness, to maintain his post. If the necessities of the time, and the law of the Redeemer, require a discriminated and organised people, let us never forget, that this organised people must be perfected in discipline and attainment. Let this be done, and the missionary churches will produce their own pastors, and occupy advanced posts; they will stand also in the evil day, proving the faithfulness of him they serve; and every new position which is taken, will prove an advance to the ultimate design. Besides, the action of the enemy may be concentrated on a single believer; and great work is often to be performed by one man; each, therefore, ought to be prepared in such emergencies, to labour or to fight alone. Moreover, it is to each believing disciple that the Redeemer addresses his inspiring word, " Be thou faithful unto death, and I will give unto thee a crown of life."

Brethren and fathers, we labour and contend, in this enterprise of mercy, under the observance of the Lord himself, and in actual communion with the Holy Spirit. He who redeemed us is pleased or offended by every action we perform and every word we speak. The Spirit, the Comforter, is grieved when we are negligent and supine; he is honoured and delighted with our wisdom and devotedness. By infinite mercy, we have been raised to be fellow-workers with God; and Deity sympathises in all our movements, conflicts, and cares. Exalted to such a fellowship in action, we should add to our faith, virtue; and to virtue, knowledge; and to knowledge, temperance; and to temperance, patience; and to patience, godliness; and to godliness, brotherly kindness; and to brotherly kindness, charity: for, if these things be in us and abound, they will make us that we shall neither be barren nor unfruitful in the knowledge of our Lord Jesus Christ. These things should be and abound, not in one, but in all: the minister should be filled with them; the deacon should abound in them; the Christian parent and relative should bring their full force into the domestic circle; tradesmen should carry their Saviour into business, and the pleasures of friendship should be sanctified by this means; the visitor, the Sunday-school teacher, the missionary, and the evangelist, at home and abroad,—all should be furnished with the full advantage of Christian virtue and Christian habits. We need the inspiring zeal which may animate each individual in his place, give him a healthful vigour in its action, and make the service of each day a preparation for future advance. No one can predict what service the Redeemer may demand of him by to-morrow's dawn. Every soul, therefore, should be preparing to yield the utmost possible devotion. The condition of mankind never presented such promise of success; and yet, with all the hope which shines upon the future, we are admonished to work while it is day, for the night cometh, in which no man can work.

Awake! awake! put on thy strength, O Zion! Shake thyself from the dust, loose thee from the bands of thy neck, and put on thy beautiful garments, O Jerusalem, the holy city! Hear thou the call of thy Redeemer, and be not afraid. If it be inquired, Where shall the work begin? let him that asketh begin with his own heart, with his own defects, and his own duties. A threefold light shines upon the path, to lead and comfort the sincere. *First*, the intimation of conscience, let it not be resisted; *secondly*, the written word, let no one turn from its healthful teaching; and, *thirdly*, the living Spirit in the living church. If the way to perfection in the fellowship of our churches be at the present never so obscure, with these three sources of instruction no one need, or ought to be, discouraged. The cause is not ours, but God's; and can anything be too hard for the Lord? He bringeth the blind by a way that they know not, and leadeth them in paths that they have not known. Behold, he is gone up before us, and his glory is already flaming in the rear; the tokens of his presence and the working of his power, have become to us visible on every hand. The docile regard due to conscience, with its holy sensibilities, the solemn reverence of his written Oracles, and the subjugation of our souls to his teaching Spirit, are but parts of his just demand. Yield him the whole, brethren, individually and collectively, then shall the light spring forth from darkness, and judgment as the noon-day; then the crooked shall be made straight, and the rough places plain, and the glory of the Lord shall appear, and all flesh shall see it together, for the mouth of the Lord hath spoken it.

A MOTIVE TO FIDELITY.

During this discussion, the thought has been guided particularly to the past. There we have seen all evil resulting from violations of the Saviour's law, which seemed at first to be but trivialities. Such features always mark Divine arrangements. In the organisations which are extended through all nature, the same perfection is found in what God hath ordained; and similar ruin follows from every human interference. While he in mercy prolongs the hope and postpones the final judgment of mankind, the widest observation clearly proves that no evil, introduced by sin, can be remedied without a penitent return to the Divine commandment. Hence the direct and indirect importance of that discipline which first realises to the obedient themselves the social benefit which their Lord designed, and then becomes an indirect means of softening the darkness and misery of others. Imperfect as they are, it is yet difficult to say how bereft of personal religion this world would be if once without the witness and activity of baptized believers. But, besides the past, without the aid of a prophetic spirit, the future will supply an argument for faithfulness and constancy. The final corruption of the body of Christ is destined to terminate the Divine forbearance; and all the judgment which shall then fall upon the hopeless victims of that transgression, should urge believers to avoid a participation in that crime. On the other hand, as long as the final judgment is postponed, a pure church, conforming to the law and living to the praise of the Redeemer, is assured of his presence and care, and cheered by his promise with the hope of victory.

Therefore, beloved brethren, be ye steadfast, immovable, always abounding in the work of the Lord, forasmuch as ye know that your labour is not in vain in the Lord.

APPENDIX.

I.—ON THE ACT OF CHRISTIAN BAPTISM.

THE question, Who are the persons that ought to be baptized? is considered in the body of the lectures; that subject, involving the constitution of Christian churches and their discipline, being deemed of sufficient importance to claim so much attention. The question, What constitutes that baptism itself? is sufficiently proved by Dr. Carson's work, entitled "Baptism, in its Mode and Subjects." The only object of this note is to place before the reader one or two facts, by observing which, an English student of Holy Scripture may determine for himself the nature of that act which Christ the Lord hath enjoined, under this name, on all who build their hopes of salvation upon his merciful mediation and governance.

In this case it is most important to consider, that the discussion has no reference to the honesty or dishonesty of different parties engaged in the dispute. The opponent may be very conscientious, and yet be perfectly wrong in his conclusion; the whole inquiry, therefore, relates to the import of the Saviour's law. The thing that He commands his people to perform, it is their duty to do, and not some other thing, which men may think will do as well, in its place. It is the duty of subjects, acting under Divine authority, not to legislate, but to obey; and in order that they may be obedient, the utmost care should be taken to learn the meaning of the Saviour's words.

Words that belong to a language which has for ages ceased to be used in ordinary intercourse, have a fixed meaning, their import being determined by the sense in which they were used when the language formed a medium of ordinary intercourse. This is an advantage, as it prevents the change of meaning to which words are liable through the changes which are taking place in active life; but it imposes a tax on patient study, because it is difficult to place one's-self in precisely the position of those who used the language spoken by our Lord and his Apostles, or that in which the books of Scripture have been preserved. On this account the student of Scripture should be always prepared for fresh discoveries: delicate modifications of speech will often present themselves in new aspects, and with new evidence of their import; and when this is really the case, when the evidence collected is conclusive, the discovered meaning is the law.

This argument for modesty of judgment and diligent docility in study, derives a still greater force from the fact, that, in these times, the churches of Christ have risen from a state of darkness and corruption, the duration and perfection of which justify a reconsideration of Divine law on every point of practice. The most vital and the most circumstantial parts of Christian duty have all been baptized in pollution and error; and, in rising from this filthy submersion, it requires an equal care, not to retain an adhesive wrong, and not to reject a Divine right through the undue influence of general and popular intervening customs. If it were possible, advantage would be derived from absolutely forgetting all that has intervened, and realising the actual presence, communion, and converse of the Lord himself; not, as if in the present time and the country in which we live, but, as at the time when and in the country where, the beloved Redeemer conversed with and instructed mankind.

The sacredness and merciful importance of the object ought to prevent discouragement arising from difficulty. No pains can be too great, when taken to ascertain a Redeemer's will, and to promote his glory in the midst of sinners whom he died to save. Still less should apparent difficulty induce the conclusion, that he who spake as never man spake has chosen a word to express his meaning which could·not with ease be understood by those who heard him. If this were true, in every case of disobedience the Legislator himself would be to blame. Had Jesus expressed his will in words, the meaning of which the men of his time could not comprehend, faith in his word now would be perfect madness. The very object of his coming was to call men away from obscurity, falsehood, and all the elements that induce distrust; and to utter in their ears a word, of which none could mistake the meaning, and the stability of which should be greater in experience than that which is found in the ordinances of nature. "Heaven and earth shall pass away, but not one jot or tittle of his word shall fail." If there appear to us, in laws designed for general observance, an obscurity of meaning, that fact itself is proof that we are wrong, rather than that He, the wise and merciful, has chosen words of doubtful import.

Were this the only inquiry that suffered obscuration in the dark ages, some of the rhetoric, employed in setting forth the supposed unintelligible character of the Saviour's words, might have admitted an apology; but nothing could justify it. If the supposition were true, the premises would call for universal mourning, not for exultation. If, in ordaining this initiatory rite, to be observed by all his followers, the Lord had used words that mean anything or nothing, he might have done the same in his promises, in the declaration of his atonement, in describing his mediation, and in predicting its results. If his words were ill-chosen in one case, they might have been so in another. Indeed, the same supposed obscurity has been alleged in almost every case, at different times, and on different occasions; and, by some with exultation, not unlike that which now provokes rebuke in writings on the nature of baptism. In the Council of Trent it was as hard to see the meaning of those words in which the Lord has covenanted salvation to each believer, as Dr. Halley now makes it out to be to comprehend what was intended by commanding every believer to be baptized. Those ages of corruption spread their gloom, not only over the page of revelation, but it was made to cover all existence. The clearest facts of nature were denied in the very face of absolute demonstration. The operations of earth had none to understand or admire them, and heaven expanded her deep blue bosom to mankind in vain: the glory was still a secret, because the observer was blind.

By thus glancing at the evil we may learn its cure. The mind, though not altogether free, has, notwithstanding, in some departments, been considerably emancipated; and the rule by which its liberty has been so far gained for natural investigations, must work out its freedom in divinity. Where man has laid aside the use of plausible conjectures, and confined his attention to facts, by becoming a servant and interpreter of nature and nothing more, knowledge has extended; it has become more definite and clear, and every human resource in action has been augmented beyond the utmost boundary of ancient thought. Let the same rule be applied to revelation, and every desirable result will be obtained. When preconceived notions have been laid aside, and the facts of revelation have been carefully collected and arranged, instead of exulting over its obscurity, reason will be found for using the words of David: "The entrance of thy word giveth light, it maketh wise the simple."

An English reader should also bear in mind the fact, that the version of Holy Scripture now in general use, was made under the instructions of King James, as guided by his Pædobaptistical clergy. In other points, as well as this, that version has been modified to meet sectarian prejudice. James said, "No bishop, no king!" and, therefore, his version was made to favour episcopacy. He relied on a state religion; and, therefore, the version was made to favour the union of church and state. The state religion required the baptism of infants, and sprinkling was more in favour than immersion; and, therefore, the version was made to shelter both these departures from the law of Christ. The spirit of freedom, as well as reverence for the Divine law, should urge the followers of Jesus, in England, to demand of their teachers an uniform and literal translation of Holy Scripture, wherever the words of God bear on points of so great practical importance.

When persons divert attention from the true point of inquiry, and occupy it with ingenious remarks on denominational consistency, the folly should be reproved, and the combatant left to exhibit his talent and waste his time, alone. Why should Dr. Halley, or any other man, be so filled with concern to make out the fallibility or infallibility of his Baptist brethren? The question is, not what they are, but what they *ought to be?* His Baptist brethren may be shown to be wrong; but this will not prove that Dr. Halley is right. Two forgeries will not make a covenant. The true question is, What are the terms on which the Lord hath made his covenant with men? and what is this rite which he enjoins on those who are his covenanted people? What is the import of the Divine law? Let this be determined, and then it may fairly be considered whether Baptists or Independents are right.

Besides this strict adherence to the point of inquiry, it is most important to bear in mind, that these documents, in which this word baptize is found, all relate to one great business, that of saving sinful men from treason and death; and, further, all are the expressions of one mind, the Holy Spirit who inspired the writers: the writings, therefore, have an unity of design and of authorship, and ought to be treated as a whole. The neglect of this has led to almost infinite absurdities, if to nothing worse. Dr. Halley and Mr. Godwin, the two latest combatants in the field, have erred flagitiously in this particular. They appeal to Scripture, take the passages in detail, speculate on the import of each separately, and make out some plausible meaning for every one, but they do not bring these constructions together. The total character and object of each book is not considered, the state and object of each writer is totally disregarded, and the harmonising object of the Holy Spirit, who inspired them all, is never brought to test the truth of these modern and astounding interpretations. Such matters, so essential to their object, being studiously avoided, it is not wonderful if their reasonings appear perplexing to others, and obscure to themselves. These circumstances will fully account for, but never justify, the sentiments expressed by Dr. Halley in the following words:—

"If I am wrong in all the philological reasoning of this lecture, not in a few instances of the detail, but in the principle and meaning of the word $\beta\alpha\pi\tau\iota\zeta\omega$, I surrender it with no great reluctance, but with a valedictory remark, that the only argument by which it can be shown that immersion is obligatory upon any man, being founded on the meaning and use of a Greek verb, is altogether unintelligible to those who do not understand a dead language; and to those who do, it is the source of endless controversy," &c. —*Dr. Halley's Lectures, &c.*, pp. 436—7.

The facility with which the learned Doctor professes to resign the fruit of his vast researches, will probably be ascribed to his accuracy of judgment in appreciating its worth (for that which is of little value may be resigned with no great reluctance); but to what cause the spirit of his "*valedictory remark*" may be ascribed, is altogether problematical. Why he, who has taken such pains to explain a word, should now rejoice over its obscurity, remains for himself to unfold. There is only one authorised case in which men " love darkness rather than light ;" but this would lead us to suppose, that his studies had convinced him that any further information would show that he was wrong. The laboured sarcasm of the passage, especially of the part not quoted, is beneath contempt. Levity in the peroration of a study in Divine law, is out of keeping, and in bad taste. It is only the object of this sentence, therefore, which calls for comment here. Dr. Halley seems delighted at the thought, that the argument for immersion is thus made " *altogether unintelligible to those who do not understand a dead language.*" The effect of this is, that private judgment must, in this case, be resigned by the common people, and their conduct, in serving the Lord who redeemed them, must be left to the guidance of others, to whom the subject is " *the source of endless controversy.*" Therefore he says, " If I am wrong . . . . in the principle and the meaning of the word, I resign it with no great reluctance." He seems to see the people already subjected to their disputing priesthoods, as though a plain English reader had no way of ascertaining the truth for himself.

Not to quote the following confirmation of this view would be unjust to Dr. Halley :—" If any one can believe that a religious obligation rests upon so faint and fading a letter" [the word baptize,] " as multitudes of honest and intelligent readers cannot see, in the midst of a revelation whose bright and glorious characters he that runneth may read, and the wayfaring man cannot mistake; I cannot but regard him as troubled with a superstition not unlike that of the Jew, who, with religious awe, binds across his brow the frontlet of his ancestors' text, after its sacred words, with the exception of some faint jot or tittle, are obliterated by time. To counterbalance the satisfaction which he feels in the hard lessons of his lexicography, which God has not given me learning or penetration enough to understand, I find consolation in the assurance that the commandments of the Lord are plain to them that fear him; or that, if in these things they are not plain to me, then upon me they are not obligatory."—*Dr. Halley*, p. 437.

If the Doctor has formed a right estimate of his own " *learning and penetration,*" which it were unmannerly to deny, their defect will serve to mollify the censure he passes on the " *superstition*" of his Baptist brethren, who *do*, as he is fully aware, "*believe that a religious obligation rests upon so faint and fading a letter,*" *as this word baptize*. But it is very difficult to perceive how, with this confessed impenetrable obscurity upon his mind, he can say, "*I find consolation in the assurance that the commandments of the Lord are plain to them that fear him.*" He knows that the Lord did command his disciples to baptize; this, therefore, is a commandment of the Lord; and, "*the commandments of the Lord are plain to them that fear him.*" But the Doctor says, that this commandment of the Lord is not plain to *him*; it would follow, therefore, that *he* did *not* fear the Lord, and that the *want* of this fear had already obscured to him the Lord's commandment. This may be true; but how can it be consoling? It is submitted, that if his attempts at wit have in them any truth at all, that truth should lead to penitential self-examination, rather than to self-complacency. Moreover, this Greek word $\beta\alpha\pi\tau\iota\zeta\omega$, now called a "*faint and fading letter*," is found "*in the midst of a revelation whose bright and glorious characters he that runneth may read, and the wayfaring man cannot mistake.*" But to what revelation can this refer, unless it be the New Testament, which is altogether composed of Greek words? If this one Greek word be so obscure, "*so faint and fading,*" may not other words in that revelation be faint and fading likewise? Who is to distinguish between the "*bright and glorious characters,*" and these "*faint and fading letters?*" If a Greek word be so contemptible, as a means of communication in one case, how shall a Greek word become respected in another? or rather, how can we respect the Spirit who hath chosen to express his Divine command by a word which even those who understand the Greek language cannot explain? This plea of obscurity in the words of God is the ground on which the Papal church has ever based her claim to official interpretation; it is not confined to this one word, $\beta\alpha\pi\tau\iota\zeta\omega$, but extended to others, as occasion may serve. The fallacy of the assumption consists in its falsehood; but it strikes, with what force it has, the very foundation of our faith; and it implicates the character of the Lord himself, by supposing that he taught our duty in words which none of his servants could understand.

It is hoped that Dr. Halley is right in saying, "If I cannot understand this word, it is not my fault." Other persons might have stated it with more humility and self-distrust; but this is not the matter in hand. Since Dr. Halley and the learned cannot in

Greek find out the meaning of the word baptize, it remains to be considered, whether there be not within the reach of English readers, even in our sectarian version, evidence by which a plain man may ascertain the meaning for himself? Is there a short and easy method with the word baptize?

All the books requisite in this study, are an English New Testament and the Englishman's Greek Concordance; which any one may use by simply learning the Greek alphabet. Cruden's Concordance might do; but the reason for preferring the former is, that it gives the passages arranged under the Greek words; so that the reader has before him all the passages in which the same Greek word occurs, with the various translations given to it in our version; but Cruden's Concordance gives the passages under the English words; and consequently, it often happens, that many passages, in which the word under consideration occurs, are lost sight of in the study. Thus many passages, in which the word $\beta \alpha \pi \tau \iota \zeta \omega$ occurs, cannot be found in Cruden under the word *baptize*, because, having been so translated, they are arranged with other passages under the words *wash*, and *dip;* the same remark applies to the word *baptism*, which is derived from the verb *to baptize.* It is sometimes borrowed, and sometimes translated; and, therefore, all the places in which it occurs cannot well be found without the Englishman's Greek Concordance.

The *first* material point the English reader will learn by this means is, that the divers *washings*, so called in Heb. ix. 10, are divers *baptisms;* and that while there were, in the Jewish temple, these divers baptisms, in the Christian society or church there was but *one:* for in Eph. iv. 5, it is expressly said, that it had " one Lord, one faith, and *one baptism.*" If sprinkling were a baptism, and pouring a baptism, and washing a baptism, and dipping a baptism, then there would be many baptisms in the Christian church; but Paul says there is but *one.* The question, therefore, relates to one thing : What is its nature? And hence, it is clear that those who begin by inquiring whether baptism should be administered by sprinkling, by pouring, or by dipping, &c., are wrong at the outset. Those who state the question in this way never mean to *immerse* by pouring or by sprinkling: they intend to enforce a pouring or sprinkling instead of an immersion. Moreover, it is impossible to dip by pouring, or to pour by sprinkling; and, since there is but one baptism, it must be *one* or *other* of these acts, it cannot be *either* or *all.*

The *second* question is, What constitutes the real subject of the action? *what* is to be baptized? The answer is, *Persons*. The required character of those persons is discussed in the lectures; all we have to consider here, is that the apostles were commanded to baptize *persons*. They do not baptize *water*, but *persons*. Water, blood, and so forth, are said to be sprinkled and poured; but persons entering the church, are said to be *baptized*. Men are not poured or sprinkled, as water is poured or sprinkled; before any such expression can be used, the subject of the action must be changed. John did not baptize *water* into the Jordan; but, going down into the Jordan, he baptized *men* and *women in the water.* Matt. iii. 16, 17; Acts viii. 38; Mark i. 9—11.

Thirdly, Where is baptism to be administered? The commission of our Lord gives no instructions on this particular; and this leaves his servants to perform it wherever a decent and orderly accommodation can be obtained. But if we change the question, and ask, Where did his servants baptize persons in the early age? several passages answer to the inquiry:—

1. John baptized in the Jordan, Matt. iii. 6.
2.   in the river Jordan, Mark i. 5.
3.   in the wilderness, or uninclosed pasture grounds, where accommodation could be obtained, Mark i. 4.
4.   in the Jordan, or (going down) into the Jordan, Mark i. 9.
5.   in Bethabara (the ford) beyond Jordan, John i. 28.
6.   in Ænon, near to Salim, because many waters were there; the many waters affording an accommodation for the rite, John iii. 23.
7. Philip baptized on the way as you go down to Gaza. They found water on the road. There are pools in the waddy, or mountain torrent bed, through which the road runs; "and they went down into the water, both Philip and the eunuch, and Philip baptized him," Acts viii. 25, 38.

From these passages it is clear, even to an English reader, that any place, in which the suitable accommodation could be obtained, was used for administering this rite. The descriptions are more or less particular. If baptism was administered in the wilderness, or in the city, in the prison-house at Philippi, or on the way to Gaza, there must have been conveniences there for that purpose. Moreover, John went down *into* the Jordan, the river Jordan, and Philip and the eunuch went down (εις) *into* the water. It was after he went down (εις) *into* the water, and before he came up (εκ) *out of* the water, that the minister baptized; and, it was after he went down (εις) *into* the water, and before he came up (εκ) *out of* the water, that the candidate *was* baptized. Philip went down (εις) *into* the water to baptize the person, and the person went down with Philip (εις) *into* the water to be baptized. While they were in that place, the *person*, not the *water*, was baptized.

Particular attention should be paid to the expression, "went *down into*;" the same word is used in Mark i. 10, 11, to describe the descent of the Holy Spirit when the Lord was baptized. It is said that the Holy Spirit (literally) "came down upon" him. Both these expressions are used in reference to water. When Philip baptized the eunuch, both he and Philip went down (*eis*) *into* the water; but when Jesus saved his disciples from the storm, he came to them " walking (*epi*) *upon*"* the water or sea, which is a gathering together of waters. To go, or walk (*epi*) *upon* the water, therefore, is a different act, from that expressed by, To " go down (*eis*) *into* " the water; for Peter, having gone down from the ship to go to Jesus, walking (*epi*) *upon* the water, perceiving the strength of the wind, was terrified, and beginning to sink, he cried, " Lord, save me."† When he was beginning to sink he went (*eis*) *into* the water; before he began to sink he walked (*epi*) *upon* the water. The difference of the two facts, or actions, is often felt in winter, when persons *upon* the water, the ice breaking, go *into* the water. If any one, the subject of such an accident, should rudely contend that there is no difference,—that his going *into* the water was no more than walking *upon* the water, or going *to* the water, he may be left in his catastrophe until his clothing and the elements have chastised his stupidity. Only keep his head safe, that he be not drowned, and he will soon confess that, compared with walking *upon* the water, his going *into* the water has a marked peculiarity. It is strange, that even in the heat of controversy the difference should not be perceived. When reasoning and illustration fail to convince in such a case, the only other resource that remains is that of actual

---

* John vi. 19. † Matt. xiv. 29, 30.

experiment. Let the advocates of sprinkling, &c., who say that going down *into* the water is no more than going to the water, choose their own men, and their own witnesses, and their own river or sea; they shall take Dr. Halley himself, if they please, and let him, with all his discernment, go down as far as he conceives is going to the water; and when he has confessed that he has gone *to* the water, his Baptist brethren shall be ready to lead him *into* the water; and, with the approval of all observers, he shall be led further and further into the water, until he confess, in plain English, without the "faint and fading letter" of a Greek word, but in bold and substantial Saxon speech, that going down into the water is a different thing from walking upon, or going to, the water. When this is done, with all the eloquence and emphasis that a cold and biting air can give to his confession, he may be dismissed for the present; and while the Doctor is drying his boots, it being confessed by him that going down into the water has a peculiarity in the action, we shall conclude, from the case of Philip and the eunuch, that the baptism, which the one administered and the other received, was something which required that peculiar action in its performance, for they *went down into the water*, both Philip and the eunuch, and then Philip baptized him.

Fourthly, The element in which the person was baptized is clearly stated by John: " I, indeed, have baptized you (εν) *in* water, but he (who cometh after me) shall baptize you *in* a Holy Spirit."* The words are addressed to the disciples he had baptized, and these were to be baptized again ;† they *had been* baptized *in* water, and were *to be* baptized *in a Holy Spirit*. The whole question relates to this first baptism in water; for, if the English reader can ascertain what a baptism in water is, this will enable him to learn what a baptism in the Spirit is. The people of Jerusalem were baptized by John, in water, in the river Jordan; and Jesus (going down) into the (river) Jordan, was baptized by John, in water; and Philip went down *into* the water with the eunuch, and baptized him *in* water. The going down *into* the water is an act preparatory to being baptized *in* water. It is not to be concluded yet what this baptizing *in* water is ; and a mere English reader may be well reconciled to the exercise of patience, since, to those who understand Greek, it is a subject of endless controversy; and Dr. Halley

* Mark i. 8. † Acts i. 5.

says, that God hath not given even him "learning and penetration" to understand the mystery. Yet, from this evidence, it is clear that the action enjoined by this word, baptize, is neither to sprinkle nor to pour; for, to say that they went down *into* the river Jordan, and *poured him* in water—they went down *into* the water, both Philip and the eunuch, and he *sprinkled him* in water, would be most outrageous. To go down into the water, to sprinkle water *upon* him, would be strange and useless; but, to go (down) into the water, and sprinkle or pour the *person in* water, is a form of expression which one who *understands Greek* may, without any dishonour, confess himself unable to comprehend.

. *Fifthly*, The action immediately succeeding baptism increases the evidence: "And going down (εις) *into* the Jordan, Jesus was baptized by John* (εν) *in* water; and immediately coming up from the water,† he saw the heavens opened, and the Spirit, like a dove, coming down (επι) upon him; and a voice came out from the heavens, saying, This is my beloved Son, in whom I am well pleased."‡ The action which followed the baptism is the *coming up* (εκ) *out of*, which answers to the preceding act, *the going down* (εις) *into* the water. The fact stands thus, therefore: Going down into the river Jordan, he was baptized in water; and having been baptized in water, in the river, he came up (απο) *from* the water. In the case of Philip, it is said, "And when they (both) came up (εκ) *out of* the water, a Spirit of the Lord caught up Philip, and the eunuch saw him no more."§ They, therefore, went down *into* the water; Philip baptized him *in* the water, and then they came up *out of* the water. The act of *baptizing in the water* is distinct from the acts of going down into it, coming up out of it, and coming away from it. Moreover, the two first actions explain each other; for, he who had gone down into the water would, when the action designed was performed, naturally have to come up out of the water; and he who came up out of the water must first have gone down into it.

In Mark i. 9, the received text has (απο) from, which has been made a great argument in this controversy; but the MSS. B. D. L. b. 13, 35, 69, 124, have (εκ) *out of*, and this reading would seem to be confirmed by the sense. But Matthew iii. 16, whose words Mark is supposed to be abstracting, has (απο) *from* the

---

* Mark i. 9. † Mark i. 10. ‡ Mark i. 11. § Acts viii. 39.

water, and also adds, The voice came (εκ) *out of* the heavens. By observing the difference of these events, we may see the relative force of these two particles. (Απο) *from,* answering to the words, "went down *to,*" describes the point from which the action began to leave the edge or surface of the water; but (εκ) *out of,* answering to the expression, went down *into,* describes the point from which a body, subjected to the influence of the water, begins to rise above it. The απο implies the εκ, for a body cannot leave the edge or surface without first coming out of the element. The procession of the voice began at the throne, in the heavens, from whence it was uttered; and, since it was heard on earth, it must have passed through the whole intervening space, and is, therefore, said to come out of the heavens; but it reached the hearers while Jesus was coming up the bank from the water, that is, after he had come up out of the water.

Sixthly, In Mark i. 4, our translators give us " John did baptize *in* the wilderness;" at verse 5, it is said, " The inhabitants of Jerusalem were baptized *in* the river Jordan." But at verse the 8th it is written, " I, indeed, have baptized you *with* water, but he, who cometh after me, shall baptize you *with* the Holy Ghost." Here the question should be put to any Greek scholar, Is the word rendered *with,* in one place, the same, yea or no, with that rendered *in,* in the other? We must not ask the Grecian to explain its meaning, but only to testify the fact whether in these four places the word used in the Greek be, or be not, the same? Any one that can read the Greek *letters* will see that in all the four cases the word *is the same.* It is εν, *in,* and, by turning to the concordance before referred to, we find that this word εν, which is rendered *in* in the two first examples contained in this passage, has been, in almost every case in which water is named as the element in which the person is to be baptized, rendered *with,* so that the expression, " baptized *with* water," is given to the English reader for the phrase, " baptized *in* water." It is impossible to censure this too severely, because, by thus altering the word of God, the translators have produced the difficulties which attend this whole inquiry. For baptize means nothing in English; it is not an English, but a Greek word; and, when this Greek is borrowed and joined with a wrong preposition, a difficulty is created, which no English reader is prepared to expect, and which it is unjust to require him to overcome, especially in the face of ridicule heaped upon his effort by a Doctor of Divinity. Indeed, whether the evils of this expedient were perceived or not, it is so great that the action in the verb is transferred from the *person* baptized to the *element* of baptism. The expression, " I baptized you *in* water," implies that John moved the persons when he baptized them; but the expression, " I baptized you *with* water," as plainly implies that in the act of baptism *the water was moved*. This subterfuge bears upon its face the mark of a controversial expedient, for thereby the way is prepared for affirming that we may baptize *with* water, by sprinkling. To affirm that he went down *into* the water, and sprinkled him *in* water, or baptized him *in* water by sprinkling, is a jungle of mere words, which, when carefully examined, can mean nothing.

Seventhly, It is quite clear, therefore, that the argument founded on the meaning of the word baptize is not the only argument for immersion. From every other word with which the word baptize may be grammatically joined, a separate argument may be derived. Instead of inserting the untranslated Greek word, write the sentence thus : I going down with you into the Jordan, ——— you *in* the water ; and having ——— you *in* the water, we came up out of the water, &c.; and let any one judge what word should be supplied in the blank space.

Eighthly, Where the meaning of a Greek word is so disputed that diplomatic scholars find consolation in the thought that an obscurity in Divine law has already delivered them from the obligation of obedience,* an English reader has a right to say, Give me, then, an uniform translation of the passages in which the disputed word occurs, and let me determine the meaning for myself ; or, at least, clear my conscience by making the attempt. On this principle, therefore, let the translation of Mark be written uniformly in both ways.

First, with *in* for εν.	Secondly, taking *with* for εν.
" John was baptizing *in* the wilderness, and all the inhabitants of Jerusalem went out and were baptized by him *in* the river Jordan, confessing their sins ; and (he said), I, indeed, have baptized you *in* water, but	" John was baptizing *with* the wilderness, and all the inhabitants of Jerusalem went out and were baptized by him *with* the river Jordan, confessing their sins ; and (he said), I, indeed, have baptized you *with* water, but

* Dr. Halley, p. 437.

he (who cometh after me) shall baptize you *in* the Holy Spirit."—Mark i. 4—8.

he (who cometh after me) shall baptize you *with* the Holy Spirit."—Mark i. 4—8.

From this comparison of the two translations, it is clear that the first alone can be received; for, in the second, the borrowed word baptize, when joined to *with,* in the first two cases, is reduced to absurdity; and there has been no translation proposed in this controversy which will not suffer the same condemnation; on the other hand, the first case retains an uniform translation of *in* with the borrowed word; and it admits the same uniform translation, when the borrowed word is translated *to immerse.* John was baptizing or immersing *in* the wilderness, *in* the river, and *in* the water; but if, contrary to the record, it be said, John was baptizing *with* water, how shall it be said that he was baptizing with the river Jordan, or baptizing *with* the wilderness?

Ninthly, Let the English reader apply the same rule to all those passages in which the expression "baptize in water" occurs in the New Testament; and it will be found that *with* being taken for *in,* to accommodate the controversialist on the word baptize, alters the sense, and destroys the uniformity of the translation; while *in* retains the uniformity, and therewith compels the rendering of baptize by immerse. Where the particle occurs in other connexions, evidence may be obtained; but, then, it must be received *with caution*, because, in relation to other objects, and under other circumstances, the word may have a different modification in its meaning. But when it is used by the same author, in the same sentence, in reference to the same action, and without any change in form or circumstance, it is scarcely possible to conceive that it was not used in the same sense. To baptize *in*, must mean the same thing, whether the word *in* be followed by water, the Jordan, the river Jordan, the wilderness, or a gaol. It being known that the person was baptized *in* water, to say he was baptized *in* the river, only implies that the water was *in* the river; to say that the person was baptized *in* the wilderness, implies that the water was *in* the wilderness, and the person was baptized in the water there. So, also, in every case. The examples, which are not very numerous, are here :—

Matthew iii. 6, (the people) were baptized of him (John) *in* Jordan.

   11, I (John), indeed, baptize you with (*in*) water.

   ,, he shall baptize you with (*in*) the Holy Ghost.

Here, to change the meaning of the word baptize, it is written *with* water, and then it must be added, *with* the Holy Ghost. But the plausibility is removed when the word is translated. Who could bear, sprinkled with the Holy Ghost, sprinkled with the wilderness, they were poured with water, they were poured with the Holy Spirit, or, they were poured with the wilderness? What Englishman can help seeing the difference between these expressions and the following:—and the people were immersed by John *in* the Jordan, *in* the water, and the Messiah shall immerse them *in* the Holy Ghost?—
Luke iii. 16, I, indeed, baptize you *with* (*in* understood) water.
    ,, but he shall baptize you *with* (*in* expressed) a Holy Spirit and fire.
Acts i. 5, For John, indeed, baptized you *with* (*in* understood) water.
    ,, but ye shall be baptized with (*in* expressed) a Holy Spirit.*

In this form of the expression, which is used by Luke three times, the εν, *in*, is understood in the first clause, and expressed in the second. If it be said, "I, indeed, baptize you *with* water," the water is put in motion in the act; and in the other cases the Spirit and the fire are set in motion by the act, while the person is at rest. By this assumption Luke is opposed to Matthew, and the statement of Luke inverts the order of Divine treatment in the dispensations of mercy. For the person is brought under the Saviour's teaching *first;* he is led by the Saviour into the knowledge and faith of God and his atonement; he is then led down into the water and baptized in it; he is brought up out of the water into his new life, in this new life he is subjected to the Spirit in his ministrations, he advances under them till he is immersed in the Spirit; led by the Spirit he advances into tribulation, the fiery trial which shall try his faith. The whole process is one of personal advance; and if this controversial expedient be admitted, of taking *with* for *in,* this personal advance under the Saviour's conduct, is changed into mere passivity.

John i. 26, I baptize with (*in*) water.
    28, John was baptizing *in* Bethabara beyond Jordan.
    31, on this account I come baptizing with (*in*) water.
    33, he who sent me to baptize with (*in*) water.
    ,, he it is who baptizeth with (*in*) the Spirit.
  iii. 23, But John also was baptizing *in* Ænon near to Salim.

These cases all coincide with those of Matthew and Mark. The persons are baptized by John *in* various places, but *in* one element,

---

* Again in Acts xi. 16.

in *water*. The water is *in* the places, and the persons are baptized *in* the water. It is not said that the water was baptized *in* the persons, or *upon* the persons. The act, therefore, is not sprinkling or pouring, for in these acts the motion takes place *in* the element, and the motion of the element ceases when it comes *upon* the man; but the motion takes place in the man, and ceases when the man is baptized *in* the water. The uniform translation of the particle (εν) *in*, enables the English reader to judge what must be the meaning of the word baptize. The uniform translation of the particle *with* is absurd; *with* water and *with* the Spirit, may be borne, while baptized is left untranslated; but who could bear to read, he shall *wash* you *with the Spirit*, or sprinkle you *with* the Spirit? and what Grecian could extract a rational meaning from the expression, John was washing, or sprinkling, or pouring *with* Ænon near to Salim, or with Bethabara? But let the word baptize be translated *immerse*, and *in* be substituted for *with* in every case; then we have, " *I immerse in* water; " " On this account I come *immersing in* water; " "He who sent me to *immerse in* water, &c.; " " he it is who *immerseth in* the Spirit; " " John was *immersing* (*in* water) *in* Bethabara, and *in* Ænon, near to Salim, because there were many waters there," fitted for his purpose. The total character of this uniform rendering is a proof of its accuracy, and the effect of any other is a demonstration that it is wrong.

Tenthly, By turning to the concordance again, it will be found that the word under examination appears in two forms—βαπτω, *bapto*, and βαπτιζω, *baptizo*; the latter being the same word, with *iz* before the final *o*, which gives the word a causal force: if the first mean to immerse, therefore, the second will mean to cause to immerse. Hence we have—

Luke xvi. 24, that he *may dip* the tip of his finger *in* water;
John xiii. 26, to whom I shall give the sop when I have *dipped* it;
Rev. xix. 13, the woman was clothed with a vesture *dipped* in blood.

It is easy to see, that in each of these cases the sense of the simple form is retained by the Spirit; for Lazarus was not to cause his finger to *be* dipped, it was asked that he should *dip* it himself; the Saviour also did not cause the sop to *be* dipped, he himself *dipped* it—this was an especial compliment from the head of the table; and, lastly, it is the very gist of the description, that the woman's garment had been *dipped* in blood by her own murderous havoc of God's people. Moreover, the baptizing of John always implied the act of another, the believing subject, as well as his own, and might have been performed entirely by other hands under John's direction.

Lastly, by uniformly translating the original verb, *to dip*, in the cases last mentioned, the translators have given their judgment of its simple meaning. These are facts, which thus come before the English reader. Here is the word, in its first and primary form, translated *to dip*, in every case; and in this sense it retains the motion of the subject, the same element is named, and the same preposition, εν, *in*, pointing out the element in which the action is performed, just as they are found in cases where baptize is used. Lazarus was to *dip his finger in* water; and John said, I baptize you in water. The direct conclusion to which these facts lead us is, that the sense of the original must be retained in the causal form of this verb; and if it be right to say, Let Lazarus dip his finger in water, it cannot be wrong to say, John caused the people to dip, or to be dipped, in water. The causal verb must retain the sense of the simple and original verb, otherwise it could never convey the additional idea of causation.

The facts of the case form the best defence against polemical obscurities; for it must not be forgotten, that the passages containing the two forms of this one word are found in the same author, and in the same work, the Gospel of Luke; and the two parts of that book relate to the same history of Divine love. Luke iii. 16, and Luke xiv. 24, are not to be treated, therefore, as if one belonged to classical Greek, and the other to Hebraistic Greek. It is the same author who, at the same time, writes, "Let him dip the tip of his finger in water," in one passage; and "I baptize you in water," in the other: and he uses two forms of the same word in two passages. If we follow the plain dictate of common sense, and translate the word immerse in both cases, the whole matter is plain, for Lazarus must immerse the tip of his finger in water, in order to do what was requested of him; and John did cause the people to be immersed in water, both when the action was performed by his own hands, and when it was done under his authority. If the learned, who talk about Greek, are not satisfied with this, the English reader should require some other translation, which will, in the prescribed forms, produce an equally natural meaning in both the cases. Let wash, sprinkle, purify, or pour, be used for the sake of experiment. How would it appear if written, Let Lazarus wash his finger in water, and come and cool my tongue;" and "he to whom I shall give the sop when I have *washed* it ;" or, "a vesture washed in blood"? What sense could be obtained from the cases, by, in the same way, using sprinkle or pour? How could an English reader understand, "Let him purify his finger in water, and come and cool my tongue;" "he to whom I shall give the sop when I have purified it;" or, "her garment being purified in blood," when that blood was shed in the murder of God's people? For John to have said, I caused you to purify in water, would have been strange, when the blood of Christ alone cleanseth from all sin. To say, I caused you to sprinkle or pour (yourselves) *in* water, is absolutely wonderful; but to say, I caused you to wash in water, when baptism does not profit to removing the filth of the flesh, and Christ hath washed us from his sins in his own blood, is confounding. It produces not the *obscurity* in which Dr. Halley professes to find consolation (p. 437); it produces an obvious contradiction of the truth. It places Scripture against Scripture in grotesque hostility; and, without producing that blissful release from responsibility in which our opponent rejoices, it rebukes and puts to shame all reverence whatever for the Sacred Writings.

In Acts xxii. 16, we find the expression, "Arise, and be *baptized*, and *wash* away thy sins;" and in Mark vii. 4, "Except they *wash*, they eat not." In the first passage, the word baptize is borrowed, and the word *wash* stands for $\alpha\pi o\lambda o\upsilon\omega$; by turning to that word in the Concordance, we shall find that it occurs in one other place, 1 Cor. vi., "But ye are washed, but ye are sanctified, but ye are justified, in the name of the Lord Jesus, and in the Spirit of our God." The three expressions stand thus:—

Acts xxii. 16, Arise, and be baptized, and *wash* away thy sins.

Mark vii. 4, Except they *wash*, they eat not.

1 Cor. vi. 11, Ye are *washed*, ye are sanctified, &c.

This looks as though *wash* in Mark vii. 4, were the same word, or had at least the same meaning, with wash in the other passages. But the words in Mark are, "Except *they baptize*, they eat not." Corresponding with this rendering, we have other passages in which wash is put for baptize, and washings for baptisms. Thus, in Luke xi. 38, Jesus had not washed (baptized) before dinner; in Mark vii. 4, 8, we have the washings (or baptisms) of pots and cups; in Heb. vi. 2, the doctrine of baptisms; and in Heb. ix. 10, we have different *washings*, for different baptisms. Here the English reader has just ground for complaint. If the meaning of the word be so difficult, that it forms the subject of endless controversy to those who understand Greek, why was it translated at all? If rightly translated *dip* in its primitive form, why should it be translated *wash* in its causative form? Lastly, if it were rightly translated wash, a rendering for which Pædobaptists plead, why was not the word so translated in all the cases which relate to the rite of initiation? They would then have had, " Arise, and be *washed*, and *wash* away thy sins," with other absurdities, which have been already pointed out.

The injustice involved in this process, may be seen by turning to the word *wash*, in Cruden's Concordance; there we find, " *Washed* their robes, and made them white in the blood of the Lamb;"* Greek word, *pluno*. " Who *washed* us from our sins in His own blood;"† Greek word, *louo*. " If she have *washed* the saints' feet;‡" Greek word, *nipto*. " She hath *washed* my feet with her tears;"§ Greek word, *brecho*. If any one should turn to these passages to ascertain in what sense the word *wash* was used by the sacred writers, he would thereby be utterly deceived, and led away from the import of the word baptize. Indeed, it is to this neglect in the translators, of that precision which is observed in the original, that most of the great practical errors which prevail in the church in modern times, must be ascribed. In ancient churches, error grew up from the want of Scripture; but Christians are now showing how the same errors may be fostered and perfected by its perversion. If the New Testament were in the hands of Englishmen perfectly translated, before the judgment of its godly readers, and the Spirit that is in them, imaginations which now command reverence, would fall like monsters frightened into apoplexy.

Another illustration of this injustice to the English reader is found in the proposal which is made, to render baptize by purify. It was not intended to translate it at all; but the borrowing of this Greek word has excited curiosity, and, to meet the inquiries thus provoked, it is proposed to translate it *purify*.‖ Turn, therefore, to the Testament itself, and there we find, " Many went up into Jerusalem to purify themselves;"¶ Greek word, *agnizo*. This same

---

* Rev. vii. 14.   † Rev. i. 5.   ‡ 1 Tim. v. 10.   § Luke vii. 44.
‖ Mr. Godwin, on Christian Baptism.   ¶ John xi. 55.

word is found in six other places; we have, " The ashes of an heifer sprinkling the unclean sanctifieth to the purifying of the flesh;"* Greek word, *katharotes*. And just after, "nearly all things are by the law purified with blood;"† Greek word, *katharizo*; which word occurs thirty times in the New Testament; and has there, at least, three different translations: to *cleanse*, to *purge*, to *purify;* and of these, some uses are of the most serious nature, as, " The blood of Jesus Christ cleanseth us from all sin."‡ Thus, difficulty rises behind difficulty; and the English reader is confounded. But this is not all: to those who understand Greek, as Dr. Halley affirms, the meaning of this word " baptize," becomes a " source of endless controversy." By thus obscuring it to the English reader, therefore, they have obscured it to themselves; and those who have so used their own countrymen, and the word of God, have justly deserved the terrific task of making their expedient plausible to others.

The principal forms in which baptize is found in Scripture, are these:—

SCHEDULE A.

Matt. iii. 11.	I indeed	*baptize you*.....	*in* water.
Mark i. 8.	I indeed	*did baptize you*	*in* water.
	He	*shall baptize you*	*in* the Spirit.
Matt. xxviii. 19.	Make disciples, &c.	*baptizing them*..	*into* the name of the Father, &c.
1 Cor. i. 15.	{ Lest any should } { say that ...... }	*I had baptized*..	*into* my own name.
John iii. 23.	John	*was baptizing*..	*in* Ænon near to Salim.
John i. 25.	Why	*baptizest thou*..	then?
Acts xix. 4.	John indeed	*baptized*	a baptism of repentance.
John iv. 1.	Jesus	*baptized*	more disciples than John.
2.	{ Though Jesus } { himself ...... }	*did not baptize*..	but his disciples.
Mark vii. 4.	Except the Pharisees	*baptize*	they eat not.
Luke xi. 38.	Jesus	*had not baptized*	before dinner.
Matt. xx. 22.	Are ye able	*to be baptized*	according to the baptism.
23.	With which	*I am being baptized*	?
Mark xvi. 16.	He that believeth and	*is baptized*	shall be saved.
Luke iii. 7.	The people came out	*to be baptized*	by him, &c.
Matt. iii. 6.	The people	*were baptized*	in the Jordan.
Luke vii. 29.	................., ...	*having been baptized*	with the baptism of John.
30.	Not	*having been baptized*	by him.
xii. 50.	I have a baptism (with which)......	*to be baptized*......	and how am I straitened.
Acts ii. 41.	As many as received the word	*were baptized*.	
viii. 16.	Only they	*were baptized*......	*into* the name of Jesus.
1 Cor. x. 2.	The Jews *in* the cloud and *in* the sea	*were baptized*......	(entering) into Moses.
Acts xix. 3.	Into what then	*were ye baptized?*	
viii. 13.	When he	*was baptized*	he continued with, &c.
1 Cor. i. 13.	....	*were ye baptized*....	*into* the name of Paul ?
Acts xix. 5.	Hearing this.....................	*they were baptized*..	*into* the name of Jesus.
Rom. vi. 3.	As many of us as	*have been baptized*..	*into* Christ.
	Were...........................	*baptized*	*into* his death.
Gal. iii. 27.	As many of you, have put on Christ, as	*were baptized*......	*into* Christ.
1 Cor. xv. 29.	Else what shall they do who	*are baptized*	for the dead.

* Heb. ix. 13. † Heb. ix. 22. ‡ 1 John i. 9.

In glancing over this schedule it is perceived that *with* is retained in two places only: Luke vii. 29, and Matthew xx. 22, 24. The reason for this is, that in these two cases neither εν, *in*, nor εις, *into*, is used, but the word *baptisma*, *without* a preposition. The Saviour is not speaking of the element in which he was being baptized, but the doctrine or rule of the baptism through which he was passing, and through which his people must pass with him into the kingdom of heaven,—the rule of unreserved self-consecration. In the same manner, those who were not baptized with the baptism of John are not supposed *not* to have been baptized at all: the Pharisees always baptized before dinner; but it is affirmed that they were not baptized in conformity with the rule of John's baptism, that is to say, on a credible profession of their faith and repentance. The nature of those cases, and the necessity for using *with* or *according to*, that their meaning may become obvious, shows how wrong it is to confound these forms of speech with others in which the idea is essentially different, and the word (εις) *into* or (εν) *in* is used. The preposition *with*, in these passages, stands for *para* or *kata*, which is, in the Greek, understood.

The cases in which (εν) *in* is found plainly relate to the element or the place in which the person was baptized, and answers respectively to the interrogatories, Where, or in what, were you baptized? The words, "with the wilderness," or "with water," do not answer to the words, "where," or "*in* what;" and when brought into comparison with the expression "with," or "in conformity with the baptism of John," these expressions confound the element with the law or doctrine of baptism, which cannot fail to produce obscurity. The fact is, the people were immersed *in* water, *according to* the law of immersion observed by John; and, refusing obedience to this, the Pharisees rejected the council of God against themselves.

The cases in which (εις) *into* occur, have all, in the New Testament, a reference to the action performed by the person baptized. Thus the Jews were immersed *in* the cloud and sea while they were entering *into* Moses. Before their passage through the Red Sea, they might have returned into Egypt if they chose, though not without a sinful rejection of Divine mercy; but, after the passage, they had entered *into* Moses, and, under God, were in his power; they were not then permitted to return, they must go forward or perish. They thus became examples to us, and the Apostle uses their chastisement as an admonition to baptized believers in his day, implying that they had been baptized into Christ with a no less solemn intention than the Jews had been baptized into Moses.*

The personal and prospective nature of the act performed by disciples in their baptism is explained by two other forms of speech constantly recurring in the New Testament. *First*, They are said to be persons *in Christ*, they are, therefore, "*new creatures*," and "*to them there is no condemnation.*"† Seeing, therefore, that they are in Christ, and that being in Christ they are new creatures, there must have been a time when they were newly created and personally entered into Christ Jesus. This coming out from the world and entering into Christ, is the act of conversion; when this has taken place, they are persons in Christ; and when this has been recognised, they are recognised as persons in Christ. The facts of the case, therefore, explain the meaning of the words. It is not intimated, that as many as were baptized *into* Christ had not been baptized in water, but that they were baptized *in water* when they *entered* into Christ. The act of entering into Christ was so declared on their part, and recognised on the part of the brethren to whom they thus became united. They were immersed (entering) into Christ, and such persons must have entered "into his death," for this was the ground of all their hope; and they must have "put on Christ," for his example and authority thus became the law which ruled them and formed their character.

But, *Secondly*, When the Apostles were brought before the tribunal for having healed the lame man, the priests said, "In what power, or *in what name*, have ye done this?" Peter replied, "*In* the name of Jesus Christ of Nazareth, whom ye crucified."‡ This explains the principle of all their action. Acting in the name, they acted by the authority, of Jesus; and where *their* action was dictated by *his* authority, there *his* action was revealed for their support. The authority to which they thus became obedient is variously called, the authority of God (the Father), of Jesus the Son, or that of the Holy Spirit. In attempting to go into Bithynia, the Spirit forbade them, and they submitted; while the intimation of the Spirit within him must have led Peter to say, "In the name of Jesus Christ of Nazareth, rise up and walk;" and, in his subsequent defence, Peter said, "It is our duty to obey God rather than

---

* 1 Corinthians x. 1—14. † Romans viii. 1. ‡ Acts iv. 7—10.

man."* In receiving and obeying the Saviour, they had reference to the authority of God the Father, who sent him: "This is his commandment, that ye should believe on his Son Jesus Christ."† In negotiating with men, the disciples acted in the name or by the authority of Christ: "We beseech you, in Christ's stead, be ye reconciled to God;"‡ and, in obeying the instructions of Christ, they were subject to the Spirit whom Jesus sent, and spake as that Spirit gave them utterance.§ Here, therefore, is a threefold, but harmonising exercise of Divine authority, under which the operations of the church were conducted. By this subjection to God the Father, God the Son, and God the Holy Spirit, the church was distinguished from the world; and there must have been a time when each believer retired from the world, and thus became willingly subjected to Divine authority. In this particular, that was the time of his conversion. It is conversion itself, viewed in respect to Divine authority. When this action transpired in his own mind, the person entered into the name, the authority, of the Father, of the Son, and of the Holy Ghost; he then became a person acting in the name, or under the authority, of the Father, the Son, and the Holy Ghost; but, when this subjection to Divine authority became avowed and accredited, he was *recognised* as a person acting under the authority of the Father, the Son, and the Holy Ghost. Thence followed the sacredness of the Christian community: "Know ye not that ye are the temple of the Holy Ghost, which is in you, which ye have of God, a habitation of God through the Spirit." It is to this point that the expression refers in Acts xix. 5, "Hearing this, they were baptized *into* the name of Jesus," &c. It is not intended to say that they were not baptized *in water*, but that they were baptized in water (entering) into the name, or authority, of Jesus; and then they were "sealed with that holy spirit of promise," &c., Eph. i. 13. To the same point must be referred the *into*, in our Lord's commission, Matt. xxviii. 19. The words do not imply that the persons should be baptized *in the name* of the Father, &c., instead of *in water;* nor are the words, *into the name*, &c., intended to form the disciples' authority for baptizing the converts, for this is expressed in the imperative verb, *go;* but it is intended to describe those persons who are to be baptized. The whole meaning is expressed thus: *Go*, make disciples, baptizing in

---

* Acts v. 29.   † 1 John iii. 23.   ‡ 2 Cor. v. 20.   § 1 Cor. xii.—xiv.

water those who enter *into* the name, or resign themselves to the authority, of the Father, the Son, and the Holy Spirit, &c. "*Enter into the name,*" is even stronger than the expression, "*resign themselves to the authority;*" it expresses an action, which, being performed, leaves the person no more his own property, but absolutely the property of another, in whose name every action is to be performed, every inheritance is to be possessed, every privilege is to be enjoyed, and every hope is to be cherished, through time and through eternity.

There is, therefore, a distinct difference in the meaning of the three words, in, with, and into, which our translators have concealed by changing the one for the other, in order to make the English version fit the borrowed word baptize. If for that borrowed word any other that has yet been proposed to express its meaning, be placed in its stead, before the reader has passed down half the cases in the schedule, he will find difficulties which are insuperable. The literal translation of εν, *in*, and εις, *into*, and the using of *with* for κατα, understood, guards the meaning against any wrong word that can be proposed. If an English reader could bear to read "I purify you in water," and "purifying men into the name of the Father, the Son, and the Holy Ghost;" "why *purifiest* thou then?" would imply that no one *purified* but the Messiah, while the expression "Jesus *purified not*, but his disciples," would be absolutely *false*. If the word *wash* be substituted for baptize in the schedule, who could understand or bear the combinations which would be thus produced? It might be said, "I *wash* you in water;" but what could be intended by "He shall *wash* you in the Spirit," and yet "Jesus *washed* not, but his disciples"? *Washed* into the name of Jesus, washed into Christ, washed into his death, are all expressions which either have no meaning at all, or a meaning quite opposed to that of the Holy Spirit. If these difficulties intimidate, and recourse be had to the other words by which the Greek word purify has been rendered in the English version, the case becomes worse. What should we do with "I purged you in water," or "he was cleansing in Ænon"? To go through the trial of these words is dreadful. With the schedule of literal renderings, the English reader may test any of the Greek, semi-Greek, or anti-Greek coinages that have yet been forced on public attention. If they pass in one clause, they will not pass in the other. Like counterfeit coins, they are detected either by their bulk or weight, and generally by both. It is not to be borne, that such things should pass current through boastful declarations, that the learned cannot settle the question; it is, therefore, the more important, that common sense should be placed in requisition before public confidence is gone for ever. While the one word *immerse* passes through the schedule of literal translations, according with each passage, and requiring change in nothing, its claim to adoption as a current coin of the Saviour's kingdom is indubitable. With this word, but with none besides, all the forms of speech can be harmonised with the known arrangements of our Lord. Other words change the subject of the action, for the element in which the action is performed, and produce untruths in the supposed words of the Spirit. In isolated cases, plausibilities may acquire respect through ingenuity and precipitate generalisation; but where so many examples are at hand to act as witnesses, an appeal to general use can scarcely be deceptive.

It is scarcely right to conclude this note without presenting to the eye a schedule of literal renderings, with the word baptize translated *immerse*.

SCHEDULE B.

Reference			
Matt. iii. 11.	I indeed	*immerse you*	*in* water.
Mark i. 8.	I indeed	*did immerse*	you *in* water.
	He	*shall immerse*	you *in* the spirit.
Mat. xxviii. 19.	Make disciples, &c.	*immersing*	them *into* the name of the Father, &c.
1 Cor. i. 15.	Lest any should say that	*I had immersed*	*into* my own name.
John iii. 23,	John	*was immersing*	*in* Ænon, near to Salim.
John i. 25.	Why	*immersest thou*	then?
Acts xix. 4.	John indeed	*immersed*	(administered) an immersion of repentance.
John iv. 1.	Jesus	*immersed*	more disciples than John.
2.	Though Jesus himself	*did not immerse*	but his disciples.
Mark. vii. 4.	Except the pharisees	*immerse*	they eat not.
Luke xi. 38.	Jesus	*had not immersed* ..	before dinner.
Matt. xx. 22.	Are ye able	*to be immersed*	with (in conformity with) the *immersion*
23.	With which	*I am being immersed* ?	
Mark xvi. 16.	He who believeth and	*is immersed*	shall be saved.
Luke iii. 7.	The people come out	*to be immersed*	by him.
Matt. iii. 6.	The people	*were immersed*	by him in the Jordan.
Luke vii. 29.	....	*having been immersed*	with the immersion, &c.
30.	Not ....,	*having been immersed*	by him.
Luke xii. 50.	I have an *immersion* (with which)	*to be immersed*	and how, &c.
Acts ii. 41.	As many as received the word	*were immersed*	
viii. 16.	Only they	*were immersed*	*into* the name of Jesus.
1 Cor. x. 2.	The Jews *in* the cloud and *in* the sea....	*were immersed*	(entering) *into* Moses.
Acts xix. 3.	Into what then	*were ye immersed*....	?
viii. 13.	When he	*had been immersed* ..	he continued with, &c.
1 Cor. i. 13.	....	*were ye immersed*.....	*into* the name of Paul?
Acts xix. 5.	Hearing this	*they were immersed* ..	*into* the name of Jesus.
Rom. vi. 3.	As many of us as	*have been immersed* ..	*into* Christ,
		were immersed	*into* his death.
Gal. iii. 27.	As many of you have put on Christ, as....	*were immersed*	*into* Christ.
1 Cor. xv.	Else what shall they do who	*are immersed*	*for** the dead.

* ὑπερ, not εις.

The schedule A is designed to place, in one view, the literally translated connexions, with the word baptize untranslated; the schedule B brings these same literal renderings of the connexions, at one view, into union with the word immerse, proposed as the translation of baptize. When the advocate of sprinkling, &c., brings his plea of obscurity, and pleads that the words of our Lord cannot be understood, let him be put into schedule B, and there pressed to say where the obscurity is to be found? to what it must be ascribed, in any one, or in all these cases? Is there not a definite meaning in the word, the words with which it is combined, and in the sentences which they form? and does not the sense in which these are used in one place, allow is to be transferred to all the rest, without violating the truth of history or the harmony of Christian doctrine? If it be pleaded, in Dr. Halley's words, that we have an account to settle first with the classical writers respecting the sense in which they used the word baptize, which he says is the occasion for endless controversies, the English reader may safely reply, Before you confuse me with that evidence, you who know Greek, or think that you know it, ought to decide among yourselves what is its nature and value. I cannot hear your testimony until you are yourselves satisfied as to its import. The English Christian may well say, I am not studying heathen songs and plays, but the law of my Redeemer; and from these passages, I find one meaning in which the word may be used, which you confess to be a right one, and this renders the communications of my Lord intelligible, and consistent with all that I know of his intentions and ordinances. Perhaps, if other Greek writings were subjected to a similar process, and the passages fairly arranged in literal translations, the sense of the word would appear, to plain English people, as obvious as it does in this schedule of Scripture passages; and, from these, the sense of immersion is so clear, that I am bound to observe it, until something more than evidence, which is the subject of "endless controversies," has been brought for its refutation. If the learned doctor still urge, that because he understands Greek, he ought to be, and must be heard, let him be brought into schedule A. There are the borrowed word and its connexions literally translated; and let him be required to find some other term which may be substituted in all the places, giving as distinct a meaning as this word immerse gives, and uniting, with equal facility, with all the other parts of speech in the schedule, and harmonising as perfectly with Christian doctrines and ordinances, which are admitted by all. To this requirement he should be holden with a firm hand. He must not be allowed to take the passages in detail, without securing, at the same time, their perfect harmony; for truth is ever consistent with itself. Appeals to charity are worth nothing; for those who claim to be heard because of their learning, are bound, at least, to support their own affirmations. Each proposed translation, therefore, must pass the trial of common sense in this schedule A; and whenever it fails, in conformity to the rule, it ought and must be rejected. If it fail to make sense in any one passage, it cannot be received in preference to a word which makes an evangelical sense in each and all. If the proposed word, like sprinkle or pour, require a change in the order of nature, by putting the subject of an action where the element is named, this will be fatal to its adoption. Immerse requires no such change, and no such change ought to be allowed. The Lord never could say, Sprinkle a man in water, if he intended that water should be sprinkled on a man. In fact, this use of the schedules is nothing more than an application of the law of induction to scripture studies. The power of this law in emancipating the mind has been observed and praised, in every department of human learning; but its benefits and victories are yet to be augmented, if not aggrandised, on the sacred page. Here, where the greatest blessings have been turned into malignant evils, the greatest emancipation will be effected, and the greatest reparation will be made. The value of having a fixed and written law will be again perceived, when once the principle of induction has drawn forth its true and certain import. Only let this be used with care, and with prayerful reliance on the Holy Spirit, and the time is not far distant when the obscurities, in which our opponent now exults, will be no more. It will then, as it may now, be seen that, after all the controversy maintained in its resistance, *one* argument by which it is shown that immersion is obligatory, is founded on the meaning and use of a Greek verb, which, when its connexions are literally translated, conveys its import with such precision and obviousness that a mere English reader can scarcely misunderstand it.

II.—ENGLISH RENDERINGS OF ΜΥΣΤΗΡΙΟΝ.

From "Bagster's Hexapla."

		Wickliff.	Tindall.	Cranmer.	Geneva.	Rheims.	Authorised.
Matt. xiii. 11.	τα μυστηρια	the privities	the secrets	the secrets	the secrets	the mysteries	the mysteries
Mark iv. 11.	το μυστηριον	the privity	the mistery	the mystery	the mystery	the mystery	the mystery
Luke viii. 10.	τα μυστηρια	the privity	the secrets	the secrets	the secrets	the mysteries	the mysteries
Rom. xi. 25.	το μυστηριον	this mystery	this secret	this secret	this secret	this mystery	this mystery
Rom. xvi. 25.	μυστηριου	of mystery	of the mistery	of the mystery	of the mystery	of the mystery	of the mystery
1 Cor. ii. 7.	εν μυστηριω	in mystery	in secret	in secret	in a mystery	in a mystery	in a mystery
1 Cor. iv. 1.	οικονομους μυστηριων	dispensers of the mysteries.	disposers of the secrets	stewards of the secrets	disposers of the secrets	dispensers of the mysteries	stewards of the mysteries.
1 Cor. xv. 51.	ιδου μυστηριον	a privity	a mystery	a mystery	a secret thing	a mystery	a mystery
Rev. i. 20.	το μυστηριον	the sacrament	the mystery	the mistery	the mystery	the sacrament	the mystery
Rev. x. 7.	το μυστηριον	the mystery	mistery	mistery	mystery	mystery	the mystery
Rev. xvii. 5.	μυστηριον	mystery	a mistery	a mystery	a mystery	*Mystery*	Mystery
Rev. xvii. 7.	το μυστηριον	the sacrament	the mistery	the mystery	the mystery	the mystery	the mystery

By observing these renderings it will be seen, that in these six versions, the English translators have all rendered the word *musterion*, so as to prove that in their view it signifies a symbol of truth, to be used in the church of Christ; and the word sacrament is so employed to translate it as to prove that it was used in the same sense.

III.—ON THE ELLIPSIS IN THE COMMISSION.

From the considerations advanced in the text of Lecture VI., it is clear that the words, "Go forth, disciple all the nations, baptizing them," &c., must contain an ellipsis, since the discipling of a nation is not a work consistent with the facts of sacred history, the intentions of Divine love, or the powers with which the Apostles were entrusted. Moreover, "*them*," in the sentence, cannot agree with "all the nations," because the former is masculine, and the latter is in the neuter gender; and yet the verbs, disciple, baptize, and teach, all relate to the same persons.

In Acts xiv. 21—23, almost all the expressions employed in this commission are used in reference to the same work, but without the disputed phrase "*all the nations*." The whole passage describes the operation of the apostolical ministry in a more limited sphere. Paul had just been stoned at Lystra, and was left by his persecutors for dead; but the disciples standing round him, he rose up and entered the city; on the morrow he departed, with Barnabas, into Derbe. Here the event transpired to which reference is made for illustration of the Saviour's words. Luke says, "Having evangelized that city, and having discipled a great number, they returned into Lystra, Iconium, and Antioch, confirming the souls of the disciples, exhorting them to continue in the faith, and (urging) that, through many tribulations, we must enter into the kingdom of God." Here, the kingdom of God is the same that Jesus preached, declaring that it was at hand; entering into that kingdom is the great solicitude of individuals; the persons supposed to be entering into that kingdom of God, are the apostles and the disciples, and these disciples are urged to continue in the faith, notwithstanding their trial, in order that they might enter into the kingdom of God. But if they were to *continue* in the faith, it must have been supposed that they were in the faith, or that they were believers.

Moreover, the disciples in Lystra, &c., could not have become disciples otherwise than as those which were made at Derbe; and, further, these were made by evangelizing the city, for it is said, "Having evangelized that city, and discipled a great number, they departed."

This was doing, in the city of Derbe, what the Lord commands his disciples to do throughout all the world; and Clement of Rome states the same thing in the following words, "The Apostles having preached *through* regions and cities, being directed by the Spirit, ordained the first-fruits of their ministry to be bishops and deacons of those who might hereafter believe," p. 325. The words of Clement and the words of Luke have this difference, that in the one there is an ellipsis which is supplied by the other. Luke says, The Apostles evangelized, or joyfully proclaimed, *the city*, making many disciples. Clement says, "The Apostles joyfully proclaimed that the kingdom of God was at hand, and preached *through regions and cities.*" In each author the word city is in the accusative case. In each case also, though the word city comes after the word evangelize or proclaim, it does not mean the subject of the proclamation. Paul did not proclaim *the city*, but he proclaimed in or through the city, that the reign of God was at hand, and that believers must enter it through much tribulation. Hence Clement supplies the ellipsis, by adding to the word proclaim, the subject of the proclamation; and by prefixing to the words region and city, the word κατα, *in*, or *through*, which governs them, in the accusative case, and makes them describe the sphere of the action. To say, that Paul evangelized the city, therefore, is the same as saying, that Paul proclaimed the joyful tidings in that city; and the result was that he discipled a great many: not a great many cities, but a great many persons, who thus became believers, because they were afterwards exhorted to continue in the faith.

Paul did two things in Derbe: first, he proclaimed the kingdom of God; and, secondly, he made many disciples there; the latter action being consequent upon the former. The first was the means, the second was the end.

The words of our Lord, taken together, and the ellipsis being supplied, stand thus: "As the Father hath sent me, so send I you," John xx. 21; "Going into all the world, proclaim ye the joyful tidings to every creature," Mark xvi. 15; " Because so it hath been written, and so it behoved that the Christ should suffer, and be raised from the dead on the third day, and that on his authority a proclamation of repentance and a forgiveness of sins should be made, beginning from Jerusalem (and proceeding) into all the nations," Luke xxiv. 46, 47; "All authority is given to me in heaven and upon earth. Going forth, therefore, disciple ye, (individuals) (through or in) all the nations, baptizing them into the name of the Father, of the Son, and of the Holy Spirit, teaching them to observe all things whatsoever I have commanded you (to observe); and lo, I am with you at all times, even to the end of the world," Matthew xxviii. 18, 20.

Mark is supposed to have written his Gospel with that of Matthew before him, and his account of this commission supplies the means to be used in making disciples of individuals. Taken together, and avoiding repetition, the words would read, "Going forth into all the world, proclaim ye the joyful tidings to every creature; (in or through) all the nations, disciple (individuals), baptizing them into the name of the Father, and of the Son, and of the Holy Spirit." The words of Mark, thus read, show how persons were to be convinced and made disciples; the words of Matthew show how these disciples were to be incorporated: the action enjoined is just what Paul did in Derbe; and the extending of this work through all nations, and into all the world, prepares us for the result seen by John in the Apocalyptic vision: "After this I beheld, and lo, a great multitude whom no man could number, out of all nations, and kindreds, and people, and tongues, stood before the throne, and before the Lamb, clothed with white robes, and palms in their hands; and cried with a loud voice, saying, Salvation to our God which sitteth upon the throne, and unto the Lamb," Rev. vii. 9, 10. The apostles and their successors proclaimed the gospel, and discipled individuals in all the nations; and, therefore, the redeemed are brought out of all the nations.

The statement of our Lord in Luke, that the proclamation was to begin from Jerusalem, and proceed into all the nations, naturally combines with the command recorded by Matthew, "Going forth, disciple ye (through) all the nations;" for by making the proclamation of repentance and forgiveness of sins in all the nations, they would, if successful, convince persons of sin, lead them to repentance, and thus make disciples in all nations; just as Paul and Barnabas proclaimed the joyful tidings, and thus discipled individuals in the city of Derbe: but the proclamation of forgiveness was never made to any national corporation whatever, and could, by no means, begin at Jerusalem; for the corporate body seated there was formally and absolutely rejected. The mercy was proclaimed to individuals; it required individual repentance; it proposed individual forgiveness: and by separating individuals, and setting them apart for God, the corporations were to be, and were ultimately, dissolved.

The ellipsis supplied by Clement, before the accusative case, is by no means an unusual way of describing the sphere of an action. Hesychius says, that κατα is used for εν, which means in, and we find it expressed or understood in that sense three times in one sentence of Pindar, I. Pyth. 25, Heyne's Edition, where it expresses "through earth, and sea, and Tartarus;" and since the nations cannot be discipled as incorporated communities, the disciples must have been made κατα, *in* or *through* the nations; for the phrase "all the nations" being in the accusative case, and not governed by the verb, it must be governed in that case by κατα, which is understood.

That this use of κατα, *in* or *through*, employed by Clement in describing the action enjoined by our Lord in his commission, is not altogether at variance with the usage of the Greek language, may also be seen from several cases in the Septuagint or Greek version of Scripture, which was used by our Lord and his Apostles. In Numbers viii. 2, the lamps are said to throw their light κατα, *through*, the space before the lamp-stand; in Exodus xxvi. 9, it is ordered, that the sixth covering should be folded κατα, *in*, the front of the tabernacle; in Genesis i. 20, the waters are said to have produced the fowls that fly κατα, *through*, the firmament of heaven; in Esther ii. 11, Mordecai is said to have walked κατα, *through*, the court of the women, to see what would become of Esther; and in 1 Chron. v. 10, it is affirmed, that the people who dwelt κατα, *through* or *in*, the parts east of Gilead fell into the hands of Saul and his soldiers. In each case, κατα, with an accusative, describes the sphere of the action; for if it be asked where the people dwelt who fell into the hands of Saul? the history answers, In the parts east of Gilead. Where did Mordecai walk? In the court of the women. Where did the lamps cast their light? In the space before the lamp-stand. Where do the birds fly? In the firmament of heaven. And where, then, were disciples to be made? Certainly, in all the nations.

Joshua i. 10, 11 presents a singular resemblance to the injunction of our Lord, now under consideration, both in the act to be performed, and in the words used to describe it: "And Joshua commanded the scribes of the people, saying, Go ye, κατα, *through* the midst of the camp, and command the people, saying, Prepare ye substance, because in three days ye shall pass over this Jordan," &c. Here the scribes, like the apostles, were to convey a message; their communication had to produce a practical result on the people; this also had an ulterior aim, and the sphere of action is in each case described: the scribes were to communicate their message and secure its effect "*through* the midst of the camp;" in which clause κατα is expressed; and the apostles were to execute their task "*through* all the nations;" in which clause κατα is understood.

The form of speech under consideration, is used in the New Testament to describe the sphere of various agencies, when in action. Their poverty is said to extend κατὰ βάθους, "into the depths."* The apostle and his companions went into a ship of Adramyttium, being about to navigate the places κατὰ τὴν 'Ασίαν, "*in* Asia."† Having passed κατὰ Μυσίαν, "*through* Mysia," they attempted to go κατὰ τὴν Βιθυνίαν, "*through* Bithynia," when the Spirit forbade their progress.‡ Jesus himself went κατὰ πόλιν καὶ κώμην, "*through* city and village," proclaiming and declaring the kingdom of God.§ This is the very thing he commanded the apostles to do, and the meaning of his words is shown by the healed dæmoniac; who departed, proclaiming, καθ' ὅλην τὴν πόλιν, "*through* all the city, what things Jesus had done for him."∥ The disciples, on receiving their charge, went *through* the towns, κατὰ τὰς κώμας, proclaiming the glad tidings, and healing everywhere.¶ Paul taught the Ephesians in the public assembly, and κατ' οἴκους, "*in* their families."** He had also imprisoned and bound those who believed, κατα τας συναγωγας, "*through* the synagogues."†† The people brought out on beds the afflicted *along* the streets, κατὰ τὰς πλατείας, "that the shadow of Peter might fall upon them."‡‡ With a genitive, as well as with an accusative, κατὰ is used to show that the action was extended "*through* the whole of Judæa."§§ The churches existing "*through* the whole of Judæa and Galilee,"

---

* 2 Cor. viii. 2.   † Acts xxvii. 2.   ‡ Acts xvi. 7.   § Luke viii. 1.
∥ Luke viii. 39.   ¶ Luke ix. 6.   ** Acts xx. 20.   †† Acts xxii. 19.
‡‡ Acts v. 15.   §§ Luke xxiii. 5.

is a designation formed in the same way, to express those which had peace when Saul, the great persecutor, had been converted and removed.* Intimations are said to be given, κατ' ὄναρ, "*in* a dream."† Pestilences and earthquakes are foretold κατὰ τόπους, "*in* places."‡ The Saviour went into the mountain to pray, κατ' ἰδίαν χώραν, "*in* a retired place." In the parable of the Prodigal Son, a grievous famine was said to prevail "*through* that region," κατὰ τὴν χώραν ἐκείνην.§ With these cases before us, it is hard to think that Jesus would have violated the genius of the language by saying, "Going out, make disciples," (κατὰ) πάντα τὰ ἔθνη, "*in* or *through* all the nations;"‖ or that Clement was wrong in using that form of speech to describe the action which our Lord enjoined.

In two cases relating to the Apostle Paul, in which we may suppose that his own expressions are recorded, the foregoing evidence is strengthened. It was reported of him in Jerusalem, that he taught an apostasy from Moses.¶ If we ask, In what this apostasy consisted? the history tells us, in teaching the Jews not to circumcise their children. He does not seem to have been suspected of proposing their baptism instead, or this would have been named; but he is said to have taught, that they should not circumcise them, nor conform to the customs. But whom did he teach this? It is answered, "All the Jews," κατὰ τὰ ἔθνη, (scattered) "*through* the nations." And further, of himself he said,** he knew not the things that might befall him, in going into Jerusalem; he only knew that the Holy Spirit testified to him, that bonds and afflictions abided him; but where was this testimony of the Spirit given to him? He says, κατὰ πόλιν, "*in* every city." It mattered little to him, therefore, which way he turned; the same trial, and the same hope, were before him on every side.

Dr. Halley seems to have been misled by the use of τὰ ἔθνη, in Acts xv. 7. Let this case, therefore, be considered in connexion with the facts to which it refers. The disciples were then convened in Jerusalem to consider and decide upon the case of those who had been gathered into the church from heathen nations. It was pleaded by some, that these ought to be circumcised like the Jews. To this, Peter objects; and he supports his objection by the case of Cornelius, and those who with him heard the Gospel

---

* Acts ix. 31. † Matt. xxvii. 19. ‡ Matt. xxiv. 7. § Luke xv. 14.
‖ Matt. xxviii. 19. ¶ Acts xxi. 21. ** Acts xx. 23.

and believed at Cæsarea. These persons were men belonging to the heathen nations. The question is, Why should Peter call them " *the nations,*" or " *the heathen,*" when they formed but a small part of *the heathen nations?* The answer is, by their treatment in sending to them the Gospel, and by giving a divine and miraculous acceptance of their faith, God decided the case of all the heathen nations, as far as their admissibility to salvation, through faith in Christ Jesus, was concerned. It is, therefore, said that in them "God chose that, by the mouth of Peter, *the heathen* should hear the word of the Gospel and believe; "* while, in the same chapter, the believers of that class are addressed as brethren κατὰ τὴν, &c., through the Antiochean, Cilician, and Syrian (districts), ἐξ ἐθνων, from the nations.† Peter himself also, declaring his feeling in reference to Cornelius, and those who heard and believed with him, says, "In truth I perceive that God is no respecter of persons; but ἐν παντὶ ἔθνει, *in every nation*, he who feareth him, and performeth a term of justification (believeth in Christ), is acceptable with him: for all the prophets testify to this, that every one who believeth in him shall receive a forgiveness of sins. ‡

Peter concluded his speech in the assembly with these words, "Now, therefore, why tempt ye God to place a yoke upon the neck of the disciples," (from the nations) "which neither our fathers nor we were able to bear? but we ourselves believe that we may be saved through the grace of our Lord Jesus Christ," καθ' ὃν τρόπον, "*in* the same manner as they."§ "Then all the multitude became silent, and heard Paul and Barnabas narrate what wonders and signs God had performed through them," ἐν τοῖς ἔθνεσι, "in the nations." When these had concluded, James continued the discussion, saying, "Men, brethren, hear me; Simeon (Peter) hath narrated how God first looked to take *from the nations,*" ἐξ ἐθνων, "a people (to call) upon his name." This people was composed of those persons whom Peter pronounced acceptable to God, for the gathering of whom the gospel was proclaimed through all the nations. They were the persons who believed the glad tidings proclaimed, and confided in Jesus who sent them. These were the disciples made in every nation upon earth. To support this view, James refers to Amos ix. 12. God there promises his people,

---

* Acts xv. 7.   † Acts xv. 23.   ‡ Acts x. 34, 43.   § Acts xv. 10, 11.

first, a purification of their own assembly; *secondly*, a restoration of the tabernacle of David; and adds, *thirdly*, "They shall inherit the residue of Edom, and all the nations, or assemblies of men, that are called by my name." This, he says, is just what the prophet foretold; and this is just what Paul means by "the gathering of Israel with the fulness of the Gentiles." If God's word be true, the last days shall see believing Israel purified and exalted in the midst of multitudes from every nation, who are, by repentance and faith, united to "Jesus the Lord of all."* The Son of David shall thus accede to David's throne. It was the beginning of this great work in which the disciples were then engaged: they were going out and proclaiming the gospel in all nations; disciples were being made *in* or *through* all the nations; churches of those disciples were formed, or forming, in all the nations; the kingdom was come, and extending in heathen lands. This work had only to take its natural course, and then the question before them was decided; for, believing Gentiles had no need to become Jews, the house and Son of David would possess them by their faith, and thus the prediction of Amos would be fulfilled.

The reasoning of James is clearly founded on the sense of the Hebrew; and to that the events of the history recorded by Luke conform. In addressing the multitude of believers, James quotes the prophecy from the Alexandrine MS. of the Septuagint version, which is identified by the readings, and which it may, on that account, be concluded was in most common use with the people. To make this agree with the Hebrew is very difficult. The word *Edom* is mistaken for *Adam*, and hence they write, "The remainder of men," instead of "The remnant of *Edom*." *Secondly*, instead of the prediction, "My people shall possess the remnant of Edom," they write "The remainder of men shall seek the Lord." It is not impossible that this expression was intended as a paraphrase or explanation of the words, "My people shall possess;" for, the house of David will, through the Son of David, the Christ, possess those who seek the Lord. If this be the case, the words, "My people shall possess," would be understood in the last clause, and the whole would read, "After these things I will return, and rebuild the tabernacle of David, which hath fallen down; and I will restore its ruins, and set it in order, in order that the remainder of men may seek the Lord

---

* Acts x. 34.

(therein), and (through) all the nations (my people shall possess) those upon whom my name hath been called." This will realise the sense of the Hebrew text, the spirit of the whole prophecy, and its fulfilment in the commission and victories of the Redeemer. On the other hand, if πάντα τὰ ἔθνη be taken for all the heathen, it makes three classes of men,—" my people," " the rest of mankind," and " all the heathen," which is absurd; as if we should say that this world contains men, and women, and Chinese. And, moreover, if these words be so transferred to the Lord's commission, its meaning would be, Going forth, make all the heathen disciples, baptizing them, &c. ; in which sense the Jews would have been virtually excepted, and the work could not, in that case, have begun in Jerusalem. Indeed, it is clear that, until the conversion of Cornelius, the idea of admitting the heathen as disciples never entered the minds of the Apostles at all.

The work enjoined on the disciples, by our Lord, being so extensive and relating to all future time until the last judgment of earth, it is obvious that its performance would involve a succession of advances towards completeness; and the record of its progress would require a description of the action to be performed in the whole world, as the apostles performed it in different places. This, then, is the case, as we find it in the sacred histories. The proclamation of Divine truth was made in families, in villages, in cities, in regions; and these are only parts of the nations. Each of these progressions made in the performance of that one work is described with κατα, and the accusative case; the preposition being sometimes expressed, and sometimes understood. Jesus went, κατα, *through* cities and villages, proclaiming the kingdom of God. Paul taught at Ephesus, κατ' οἴκους, from house to house; he proclaimed the joyful tidings κατα, through the city of Derbe ; he went, κατα, *through* Mysia, performing the same work ; he is sometimes said to have done it through one city or region, and at other times through more than one. And Peter, when the full scope of the commission was opened to him, said: " I perceive that God is no respecter of persons; but in every nation, he who feareth him, and performeth a term of justification" [believeth in Jesus], " is accepted of him." The work, therefore, which he and his brethren were performing in each part, had to be performed in the whole; and, by going from house to house, from village to village, from city to city, from region to region, and, by going through them all, they had to go *through* all the nations, penetrating every organised community with the truth, and everywhere performing the work of love.

That κατα before εϑνη is no exception to the rule may be seen from the following passage in Demosthenes (*Oratores Attici*, vol. v., p. 209):—

" Olynthus, indeed, mark ye, and Methone, and Apollonia, and two-and-thirty cities of Thracia, I pass over, all which he (Philip) so cruelly spoiled, that it would not be easy for any one approaching them to say whether they had ever been inhabited; and, though so great, I will not speak of the extirpated nation of the Phocians: but how is it with Thessalia? Hath he not taken away their administrations and their cities, and appointed tetrarchs with them in order that not only κατα, *through* the cities, but also κατ' ἔϑνη, *through the nations*, they might be enslaved?"

Here, as in the words of our Lord, the pronouns *them* and *their*, which are forms of the same word in the Greek, are plural and masculine; and are preceded by Thessalia, which is singular and feminine. To what, then, do *them* and *their* refer? It is answered, To the people of Thessalia; for the nations of Thessalia were composed of the people of Thessalia, as the nation of the Phocians was composed of the people of Phocis. Who, then, did Philip wish to be enslaved in Thessalia? Plainly, the people who inhabited Thessalia. But how were they to be enslaved? Philip took away from them their civic administrations; and, dividing the country into four εϑνη, *nations*, he appointed a tetrarch over each. What were these tetrarchs to do? Demosthenes says, to enslave the people; but where were the people to be enslaved? Demosthenes adds, not only *in* or *through* the cities, but also κατα, *in* or *through*, the nations of Thessalia; just as the Lord sent his Apostles forth to disciple individuals, not only κατ' οἴκους, *in* families, from house to house, κατὰ κώμαι, through villages, κατὰ πόλιν, through cities, and κατὰ χώρας, through regions, but, also, κατὰ πάντα τὰ ἔθνη, *through* all the nations, not of Thessalia, but of the world.

It has been stated already, that both Peter and James, when arguing the case of the Gentile converts, urged the purpose of God to take for himself a people *out of* the nations. In conformity with this statement, the letter from Jerusalem was sent to the brethren *from* the nations; and Clement of Rome calls the community of believers in Christ, *a nation* taken *out of* all other nations; while

John describes the church in her final glory as a great multitude taken *out of* every nation, kindred, and tribe, &c. ; and, as if to prepare for this, the Lord sent his proclamation of repentance and forgiveness *into* all the nations ; and the event predicted could scarcely be secured unless disciples were made *through* all the nations. It then follows, of course, that the glorified church would be an assembly gathered *out of* all the nations ; and the harmony of the statements so explained, is proof that the construction proposed, by supplying the ellipsis with κατα, is at least admissible, if it be not the only way in which the meaning of the Spirit can be harmonised with the grammar of the language he has used in recording the Divine commandment.

Should time and the advance of biblical criticism, supply other elucidation of these words than that which the cases presented in this note afford, all parties will be bound to examine it with care, and receive it with candour. Meanwhile, however, as the reasoning in the text shows, the authorising of a separated fellowship among believers, and the appointment of his immersion in water as the means by which the repentance and faith of each convert should be professed by himself, and recognised by the brethren in Christ, have, by the other instructions of our Lord, been placed, if not beyond all resistance, yet certainly beyond all plausible dispute.

LIST OF SUBSCRIBERS.

ENGLAND.

LONDON.

Name	No. of Copies
Peto, S. M., Esq.	6
Fletcher, Joseph, Esq.	6
Soule, Rev. I. M.	6
Bowser, W., Esq.	7
Bowser, Mr. W.	1
Tritton, Joseph, Esq.	2
Kelley, Mr., and friends	9
Hoby, Rev. Dr.	2
Carey, Rev. E.	1
Morris, Mr.	1
White, Mr. R. J.	1
Baker, Mr. J.	1
Le Maire, Rev. R.	2
Fennings, James, Esq.	3
Bowser, Mr. A. T.	1
Mulley, Mr.	1
Stanger, Mr. S.	1
Wallis, Mrs.	1
Steane, Dr.	1
Gurney, W. B., Esq.	1
Orchard, Mr.	1
Pegg, Rev. G. W.	1
Poole, Mr. John	1
Frances, Mr.	1
Godwin, Mr.	1
Pettit, Mr.	1
Stevenson, Rev. J.	2
Aphed, Mr. J. H.	1
Hawson, Rev. G., Staines	1
Skerrett, Mr. James	1
Read, Mr. C.	1
Gustarson, Mr. G.	1
Ware, Mr. R.	2
Strong, Mr. G. W.	1
Lowe, G., Esq.	3
Jones, Rev. J. A.	1
Randall, Mr. F. S.	1
Saffery, Rev. P. J.	1
Kent, Mr. J. K., F.S.A.	1
Bargerbur, Mrs.	1
Keighley, Mr. J.	1
Freeman, Mr. G. S.	1
Blake, Rev. W. A.	1
Overbury, Mr. B.	1
Gordelier, Mr. W. J.	1
Curtis, Rev. S.	1
Miller, Mr. R. V.	1
Allingham, Mr.	1
Barrett, Mr.	1
Williams, Mr. W.	1
Vickess, Mr. J.	1
Dixon, Mr. R.	1
Daniell, T. P., Esq.	2
Kemp, Mr. G. T.	1
Bale, Mr. H. A.	1
Deane, G., Esq.	2
Payne, Mr. E.	1
Marlborough, Mr. E.	1
Phillips, Mr. W. H.	1
Murch, Rev. W. H., D.D.	1
Banister, Mr. J.	1
Heriot, Mr.	2
Dawson, Mr.	1
Ashton, Mr. J.	1
Chesterman, Mr.	1
Revel, Mrs.	2
Creswell, Mr. H.	1
Webb, Mr. John	1
Webb, Mr. W.	1
Hatchard, Mr.	1
Cartwright, Mr.	1
Olney, Mr. T.	1
Gale, Mr. S.	1

LIST OF SUBSCRIBERS.

Name	No. of Copies
Burgess, Mr. John	1
Owen, Mr. B.	1
Smith, Rev. James	2
Whitehorne, James, Esq.	1
Cheetham, Mr.	1
Pike, Rev. G. S.	1
Walton, Mr. H.	1
Aldis, Rev. J.	1
Burles, C., Esq.	1
Pontifex, Mr. R.	1
Crisp, Mr. John	1
Furguson, Mr.	1
Dickerson, Rev. P.	3
Moore, Mr.	1
Williams, Mr.	1
Hinkley, Mr.	2
Brace, Mr. E.	1
Cressweller, Mr. H.	1
Woolley, Mr.	1
Spurden, Mr. C.	1
Warmington, J., Esq.	4
Warton, Mr. R.	1
Wright, Mr. James	1
Wadman, Mr.	1
Palmer, Mr. T.	1
Russell, Mr. A.	2
Bentley, Mr. J.	2
Ransom, Mrs.	1
Watson, W. H., Esq.	1
Gifford, Rev. J.	1
Blakeborough, Mr.	1
Cowell, B. B., Esq.	3
London, Mr. E.	2
Kitson, G., Esq.	2
Kelson, Mr.	1
Benson, Mr. S.	1
Carto, Mr. B.	1
Callard, Mr. T. K.	1
Starkey, Mr. J.	1
Lush, Mr. R.	1
Jones, Mr. C., sen.	1
Bligh, Mr. Samuel	1
Kitson, Wills, Esq.	1
Weston, Mr. W.	1
Hill, Mr. John	2
Hughes, Mr. T.	1
Elliott, Rev. R.	1
Clarke, Mr.	1
Stanger, Mr. W. W.	1
Salmon, Mr.	1
Howard, Mr. S.	1
Brooks, Mrs.	1
Sangster, Mr. J.	1
Eyre, Mr. Erasmus	1
Whorlow, Mr. G. G.	1
Moore, Mr. G.	1
Murphy, Mr. M.	1
Harris, Mr. R., Maze Pond	2
Gregory, Mrs.	1
Burt, Miss	14
Stark, Mr. R.	1
Redington, Mr. T.	1
Brown, Rev. J. J.	1
Pulsford, Rev. E.	1
Mannell, W., Esq.	2
Rogers, Mr.	1
Henderson, Mr.	1
Branch, Mr.	1
Read, Mr. John	1
Middlemore, James, Esq.	5
Herriot, Mr.	2
Eives, Mr. John	1
Hammond, Rev. E. R.	2
Merthens, Mrs.	1
Nash, W. W., Esq.	1
Meggs, Mr. James	1
Shelton, Mr. Thomas	1
Attersley, Mr. R.	1
Newling, Mr. W.	1
Dunch, Miss E.	1
Matthews, Mr. R. G.	3
White, Mr. W.	1
Beddome, W., Esq.	2
Bishop, Mr. James	1
Haddon, John, Esq.	1
Hawkins, T., Esq.	3
Nicholson, Mr.	1
Adcock, Mr. J. C.	1
Powell, Mr. T.	1
Dovey, Mr. G.	2
Swinstead, Mr. Charles	1
Swallow, Mr. B.	1
Watts, Mr. John	1
Doulter, Mr. Henry	1
Doulter, Mr. Frederick	1
Meredith, Mr.	1
Edger, John, Esq.	1
Cameron, Mr.	1
Trestrail, Rev. F.	1
Cook, Mr. T. T.	1
Watkins, Mr. R.	1
Martin, Mr. H.	1
Hearne, T., Esq.	2
Harris, Mr.	1
Smith, Mrs.	2
Elliot, Mr.	2
Davis, Rev. S. J.	2
Davis, Mr. John	1
Bligh, J. S., Esq.	1
Orchard, Rev. G. F.	1
Norton, Rev. W.	2
Angus, Rev. J., M.A.	2
Peacock, Rev. J.	1
Daft, Mr.	1
Bennett, Thomas, Esq.	1
Russell, Rev. J.	2
M'Laren, David, Esq.	1
Price, Rev. Dr.	1

LIST OF SUBSCRIBERS. 521

	No. of copies.
Lehmann, Rev. G. W.	2
Allen, J. H., Esq.	1
Woollacott, Rev. C.	3
Danford, Warren, Esq.	2
Chandler, Mr. John	1
Hawkes, Mr. John	1
Ridsdale, Miss	1
Chew, Mr.	1
Swinstead, Mr., sen.	2
Williams, Mr.	1
Skean, Mr.	1
Archer, W. E.	1
Higham, Mr. D.	1
Parker, Mr. Samuel	1
Trickett, Mr. John	1
Goodman, Rev. W.	1
Jackson, Rev. Mr.	1
Dunning, Mr. R.	1
Vines, Joseph, Esq.	1
Smart, Mr. J.	4
Burn, Mr. Thomas	1
Edmonds, Mr. James	1
Cole, Miss	1
Bugby, Mr. F.	1
Pugh, Mr. S. S.	1
Turner, Mr. James	1
Keane, Mrs.	1
Cook, Mr.	2
Wiggins, Mrs.	2
Davis, Rev. S.	2
Dunch, Thomas, Esq.	2
Clarke, Rev. Owen	1
Rothery, Rev. J.	1
Bugby, Mr. Wm.	1
Standring, James, Esq.	2
Millar, Mr. W. H.	1
Knight, Mrs.	1
Oliver, Mr.	4
Moore, Rev. T.	1
Cartwright, Mr.	2
Woodrow, Rev. G.	2
Danford, John, Esq.	2
Feler, Mr. John	1
Toswill, C. S., Esq.	1
Swinstead, W., Esq., Oxford-st.	2
Fraser, Mr., Gloucester-terrace	2
Wiggins, Job, Esq., Bow-road.	1
Benham, Mr., Welbeck-street	2
Davis, Rev. Dr. B., Stepney	1
Watkins, Mr. R., Islington	1
Kempton, Mr. F., Burton-crescent	1
Ware, Rev. R., Potter's-bar	2
Young, Mr. T., Fore-street	1
Oram, Mr. B., Kennington	1
Lowe, Mr. J., Leadenhall	1
Gladding, Mr., Mile-end	10
Saunders, Mr. R.	1
Smith, W. L., Esq.	3

	No. of copies.
Kemp, Mr. T.	1
Hall, Mr. Enoch	1
Worley, Rev. V. C., Addleston	1
Vickery, Mr., London	1
Pewtress, T., Esq.	3
Cox, Rev. F. A., D.D., LL.D.	3
Freeman, J., Esq.	1
Salisbury, Mr.	1

BEDFORDSHIRE.

Kent, Rev. Mr., Biggleswade	1
Foster, J., Esq., ditto	1
Foster, B., Esq., ditto	1
Gutteridge, J., Esq., Dunstable	1
Rogers, Mr. C., Oustly Mills	1
Owen, Rev. T., Cranfield	1
Collier, Mr. T., Sharnbrook	2
Daniel, Mr., Luton	1
Williams, Mr. J., Sharnbrook	2

BUCKS AND BERKS.

Marten, Rev. R. H., Abingdon	1
Tomkins, T., Esq., ditto	1
Collier, Mr. J., ditto	1
Leader, Mrs., ditto	1
Carryer, Rev. W. H., Buckingham	1
Payne, Rev. W., Chesham	1
Bartlett, Rev. B., Chenies	1
Simmons, Rev. J., Olney	1
Birt, Rev. C., Wantage	1
Drew, Mr. J.	1
Granger, Rev. Mr., Waddesdon	1
Buckland, Rev. W. T., Wraysbury	1
Lillycrop, Rev. S., Windsor	1
Hooper, H., Esq., ditto	1
Tyler, Rev. P., Haddenham	1

CAMBRIDGESHIRE.

Foster, R., Esq., Cambridge	2
Foster, E., Esq. ditto	2
Brimly, A. G., Esq. ditto	1
Adams, Mr. W. ditto	1
Tupling, Mr. ditto	1
Burditt, Rev. T. ditto	1
Barham, Mr. W. P. ditto	1
Roffe, Rev. R. ditto	1
Flood, Rev. J., Melbourne	1
Halford, Mr. C., March	2
Roberts, Rev. J., Chesterton	1
Booth, Mr. E., Marsh	1
Cantlow, Rev. W. W., Shelford	1

CHESHIRE.

Gill, Mr. J., Tarporley	1
Harling, Mr. W., Chester	1
Hattersley, Mr. W., Woodhead	1

LIST OF SUBSCRIBERS.

CORNWALL.

	No. of Copies.
Osborne, Rev. J. H., St. Austell	1
Stocker, Mr. E., ditto	1
Sexcombe, Mr. J., ditto	1
Samble, Mr. P., Truro	1
Allport, Mr. W., Padstow	1
Pallin, Mr. S. R., Launceston	2

DERBYSHIRE.

Pegg, Mr. R., Derby	1
Stevenson, Mr. G., ditto	1
Tagg, James, Esq., Riddings	1
Tomlinson, Mrs., ditto	1
Hardy, Mr. T., ditto	1
Goulder, Mr. W., ditto	1
Goulder, Mr. John, ditto	1
Knight, John, Esq., ditto	1
Davis, Rev. I., Swanwick	1
Gee, Mr. John, ditto	1
Johnson, Mr. B., Pentrich	1
Ward, Mr. T., Ripley	1
Argyle, Mr. R., ditto	1
Argyle, Mr. G., ditto	1
Burrows, Rev. J., Alfreton	1
Bowen, Mr. D.	1
Ward, Mr. R.	1
Parsons, Mr. T.	1

DEVONSHIRE.

Horton, Rev. T., Devonport	3
Radford, Mr., ditto	1
Trend, Mr. S., ditto	1
Radford, Mr. I. C., ditto	1
Anstie, Rev. P., Brixham	1
Bagshot, Mrs., Great Torrington	1
Dyer, Mr. J., Bideford	1
Vessey, Mr. C., Torrington	2
Randall, T., Esq., Kingsbridge	1
Wills, Miss A., ditto	2

DORSETSHIRE.

Froud, Mr. J., Dorchester	1
Sincox, Mr. S., ditto	1
Pitt, Mr. J., Wareham	1
Greenway, Mr., Netherton	1
Trafford, Rev. J., Weymouth	1

DURHAM, &c.

Moffatt, Mr., South Shields	1
Carrick, Rev. J. D., ditto	1
Sneath, Rev. J., ditto	4
Imeary, Mr. R., ditto	1
Marshall, Mr. T., Shotley Field	1
Wilkinson, Mr. H. A., Newcastle	1
Wilkinson, Rev. T., ditto	1
Angus, Rev. H., ditto	1
Adam, Mr. D., ditto	1
Angus, H., Esq., ditto	1
Bell, Mr. J. W., Newcastle	1
Fenwick, Mr. J., ditto	1
Hatherley, Mr. R., Morpeth	1
Bone, Mr. W., Whitehaven	1
Wilkinson, Mr. J., ditto	1
Paxton, Mr. John, Berwick	3
Anderson, Mr. Hugh, Maryport	1
Hamilton, Mr. S., Workington	1

ESSEX.

Tubbs, Mr. R., Ashton	1
Hodgkins, Rev. B., Bishop Stortford	1
Garrington, Rev. J., Burnham	1
Langford, Rev. R., Colchester	1
Harvey, Mr. J. B., ditto	1
Souls, Mr. S. H., Langford	1
Gould, G., Esq., Loughton	1
Brawn, Rev. S., ditto	1
Pilkington, Rev. J., Rayleigh	1
Wadman, Mr. J. D., West Ham	1
Bentall, Mr., Halstead	1

GLOUCESTERSHIRE.

Sherring, R. B., Esq., Bristol	8
Probyn, Mrs. R., ditto	3
Leonard, R., Esq., ditto	3
Cuzner, J. H., Esq., ditto	1
Probert, Rev. E., ditto	1
Gotch, Rev. F. W., ditto	1
Harris, Mr. E., ditto	1
Winter, Rev. T., ditto	1
Jones, Mr. R., ditto	1
Cummings, Mr. J., ditto	1
Baptist College, ditto	1
Crisp, Rev. T. S., ditto	1
Bompas, Dr., ditto	3
Fox, Joseph, Esq., ditto	2
Darkin, Rev. C., Cirencester	1
Cubit, Rev. J., Bourton	1
Battew, Mr. T., Coleford	1
Trotter, Mr. T., ditto	1
Herbert, Mr. Jas., ditto	1
Nicholson, Mr. W., ditto	1
Penney, Rev. J., ditto	1
Berge, Rev. John, Tewkesbury	1
Knight, Mr. W., ditto	1
Lewis, Rev. T., Wollaston	1
Rose, Rev. W., Stembridge	1
White, Mr. R., Hellsby	1
Breeze, Mr. R., Leeklode	1
Underhill, E. B., Esq., Nailsworth	1
Holloway, Mrs., Yate	1
How, Rev. T., Sodbury	1
Wood, Mr. Isaac, Nolgrove	1
Tyndale, Mr. R., Littledean	1
Ely, Mr. S., Wotton-under-Edge	1
Nicholson, Mr. T., Lydney	3

LIST OF SUBSCRIBERS. 523

	NO. OF COPIES.
Soloman, Leo., A.M., Woodchester	1
Newman, Rev., Nailsworth	1

HERTFORDSHIRE.

Knighton, Mr., Stoney Stratford	1
Forster, Rev. E. L. ditto	1
Pratten, Rev. B. P., Boxmoor	1
Chater, Mr. J., Watford	1
Wycherley, Rev. T. E., Tring	2
Clayton, Mr. G. R. W., ditto	1
Broad, Rev. J., Hitchin	1
Jervis, Wm., Esq., ditto	1

HUNTINGDONSHIRE.

Simmons, Mr. I. E., Colne	1
Crofts, Rev. W. H., Ramsey	1
Palmer, Mr. I., ditto	1
Peck, Mr. John, Kimbolton	1
Foster, Mr. M., Huntingdon	1
Pulsford, Rev. T., Ubique	1
Stapleton, Mr. T., Old Weston	1

HAMPSHIRE.

Millard, Rev. J., Lymington	1
Mursell, Mr. W., ditto	1
Blake, Mr. R., ditto	1
Furnell, Mr. I., ditto	1
Toone, John, Esq., Salisbury	2
New, Rev. I., ditto	1
Rhodes, Mr. W., Damerham	1
Wavell, Mr. R. M., Newport, Isle of Wight	1
Vernon, Rev. C. W., ditto	2
Cakebread, Mr., Portsea	1
Robinson, Mr., ditto	1
Baker, Mr. J., Andover	1
Heretage, Mr., Winchester	1
Morris, Rev. T., Southampton	1
Mayos, Mr. A. F., ditto	1
White, Mr., sen., Hartley-row	1
Young, M. S., Ryde	1
Scorey, Mr. G., Whitchurch	1
Burt, Mr. J. B., Beaulieu	1

KENT.

Clark, Rev. T., Ashford	1
Scott, Rev. T., ditto	1
Lepine, Miss, ditto	1
Linsom, Mr., ditto	1
Heyward, Mr. H., ditto	1
Heyward, Mr. G.	1
Flint, Mr. A., Canterbury	1
Flint, Mr. B. F., ditto	1
Flint, Miss, ditto	1
Flint, Mr. F. L., ditto	1
Davis, Rev. W.	1

	NO. OF COPIES.
Kingsford, Mr. A., Dover	2
Clark, Mr. John, Folkestone	1
Parkins, Mr. D., ditto	1
Jenkins, Mr. F., Maidstone	1
Dobney, Rev. H. H., ditto	2
Gamble, Rev. H. F., Margate	3
Flint, Mr. T., ditto	1
Pope, Mr. W., Meopham	1
Daniell, Rev. M., Ramsgate	1
Spencer, Miss, ditto	2
Gould, Miss, ditto	1
Davis, Mr. E., ditto	1
Kewell, Mr. H., Tunbridge Wells	1
Farmer, Rev. J., Romsey	1

LANCASHIRE.

Bowker, Mr., Accrington	1
Bury, William, Esq., ditto	2
Griffith, Rev. William, ditto	2
Bury, Mr. T., ditto	1
Ellison, Mr. J., ditto	1
Kenyon, Mr. O., ditto	1
Entwistle, Mr., ditto	1
Haworth, Mr., ditto	1
Baptist School, ditto	1
Walmsey, Mr. T., Ashton	1
Leen, Edward, Esq., ditto	2
Jackson, Mr. W. E., Haslingden	3
Chatterall, Mr., Westham	1
Henry, Mr. G., Bolton	1
Brooks, Mr. A., Stalybridge	1
Potter, Mr. J., ditto	1
Brooks, Mr. J., ditto	2
Nichols, Rev. A., Goodshaw	1
Chapel Library	1
Butterell, Mr., Colnfield	1
Taurberton, Mr., ditto	1
Casson, Mr. E., Heywood	1
Caycock, Mr. B., Sabden	1
Foster, Mr. G., ditto	1
Griffiths, Mr. S. P., ditto	1
Foster, Mr. W., ditto	1
Burry, Mr. J., Pendleton	2
Evans, Edward, Esq., Charlton	2
Lindsay, Mr., Manchester	4
Bannerman, Mr., ditto	1
Hull, Mr. J., ditto	1
Garside, Rev. J., Ogden	1
Howarth, Mr. S., Bacup	1
Howarth, Mr. Thomas, ditto	1
Ashworth, Mr. R., ditto	1
Lord, John, Esq.	1
Haythornwait, Mr., Fleetwood	1
Burnett, Mr. T., Lytham	1
Banks, Mr. J., Coaker Marston	1
Lewes, Mr. T. H., Preston	2
Catterall, Mr. C., Preston	1

LIST OF SUBSCRIBERS.

	NO. OF COPIES.
Dewhurst, Mr. T., ditto	1
Powell, Mr. T., ditto	1
Lamb, Mr., ditto	1
Jolly, Mr. T., ditto	1
Hamilton, Mr. J., ditto	1
Robinson, Mr. T., Rochdale	1
Burchell, Rev. W. F. E., ditto	1
Kelsall, Henry, Esq., ditto	1
Ormerod, Miss, ditto	2
Palethorp, Mr. A., Liverpool	1
Roberts, Mr. J., ditto	1
Johnson, Mr. Robert, ditto	2
Johnson, Mr. Richard, ditto	1
Coward, John, Esq., ditto	1
Francom, Mr. Joseph, ditto	1
Park, Mr. W., Wigan	1
Birrell, Rev. C. M., Liverpool	1
Davies, Rev. J. J., Bootle	1
Medley, Mr. W., Liverpool	1
Medley, Mr. Guy, Liverpool	1
Jones, Mr. Josiah, ditto	1
Jones, Mr. Robert, ditto	1
Lyon, Mr. John, ditto	1

LEICESTERSHIRE.

Mursell, Rev. J. P., Leicester	1
Beales, Mr. John, ditto	2
Robinson, C. B., Esq., ditto	1
Brooks, Mr., ditto	1
Carryer, Mr. J., ditto	1
Baines, Mr. C., ditto	1
Bowser, Mr. Henry, ditto	1
Baines, W., Esq., ditto	1
Davis, Rev. Joseph, Arnsby	1
Bassett, Mr., Countesthorpe	1
Bassett, Mr. W., ditto	1
Bassett, Mr. R., Cosby	1
Coleman, Mr. Joseph, Leicester	1
Jarrom, Mr., Leicester	1
Soar, Mr., Castle Donnington	1
Staddon, Rev. James, Quorndon	1
Preston, Mr. I., ditto	1

LINCOLNSHIRE.

Hills, Miss M. A., Lincoln	1
Craps, Rev. J., ditto	3
Philips, Mr. J., Boston	1
Baptist Library, Fleet	1

NORTHAMPTONSHIRE.

Abbott, Mr. W., Cranford	1
Gough, Mr. T. T., Clipstone	1
Collier, Mr. H., Thrapstone	1
Stapleton, Mr. T., ditto	1
Randall, Mr. W., ditto	1
Phillips, Rev. T., Northampton	2
Cave, Mr. G., Piddington	1
Williams, John, Esq., Ringstead	1

	NO. OF COPIES.
Knighton, J., Esq., Wollaston	1
Baker, Mr. R., Spratton	1

NOTTINGHAMSHIRE.

Edwards, Rev. T., Nottingham	1
Robinson, Mr. T., New Basford	1
Edge, Mr. J., Sutton-on-Trent	1
Wallis, James, Esq., Nottingham	1
Vickers, W., Esq., ditto	2
Heard, John, Esq., ditto	1
Felkin, W., Esq.	1

NORFOLK.

White, Mr. W., Hellasden	1
Lewes, Mr. J. P., Diss	1
Mines, Mrs., ditto	1
Fyson, Mr. J., Fakenham	1
Gooch, Mr. S. B., ditto	1
Thompson, D., Esq., ditto	1
Lord, Rev. J., Norwich	1
Brock, Rev. W., ditto	1
Griffith, Rev. E., Neeton	1
Symonds, Mr. T., ditto	1
Bunn, Miss M., ditto	1
French, Mr. R., Norwich	1
Claydon, Mr. C. F., ditto	1
Scott, Mr. T., ditto	1
Wegner, Rev. J. T., Lynn	3
Graves, Mr., Brouden	1
Hobson, Rev. J., Boston Mills	1
White, Mrs. E., Diss	1
Cates, Mr. R., Fakenham	1

OXFORDSHIRE.

Smith, Mr. J., Bicester	1
Merrick, Mr. D., Banbury	1
Payne, Mr., Banbury	1
Blakeman, Rev. J., Hook Norton	1

RUTLAND.

Whitelock, Rev. H., Uppingham	1

SUSSEX.

Davis, Rev. E., Lewes	3
Hammond, Mr. N., ditto	1
Edger, Mr. J., Forest Row	1

SALOP.

Onslow, Mr. R., Wem	1
Hares, S., Esq., Prees	3
Wittingham, Mr. T., Whitchurch	1
Roderick, Mr. E. O., Pontisbury	2
Lee, Mr. Thomas, Wem	2

LIST OF SUBSCRIBERS. 525

SUFFOLK.

	No. of Copies
Burton, Mr., Ipswich	1
Webb, Rev. J., ditto	2
Hitchcock, Mr., ditto	1
Neve, Mr. J., ditto	1
Harvey, Mr. J., ditto	1
Skeet, Mr. R., ditto	1
Lacy, Mr., ditto	1
Everett, Mr., ditto	1
Gooding, Mr. J., ditto	1
Cowell, Mr. S. H., ditto	2
Pollard, Mr., ditto	1
Mathews, Mr., Aldboro'	1
Cooper, Rev. J., Wattisham	1
Elven, Rev. C., Bury	1
Mathew, S., Esq., Lindsey	1

SOMERSETSHIRE.

Middleditch, Rev. C. J., Frome	1
Allen, Mrs., ditto	1
Rawlings, Mrs. S., ditto	1
Coombs, Mr., ditto	1
Porter, Miss, ditto	1
Badcox-lane School, ditto	1
Shepherd, John, Esq., ditto	1
Jones, Rev. W., ditto	1
Thompson, W., Esq., ditto	1
Houston, Mr., ditto	1
Edwards, Mr., ditto	1
Payne, Mr., ditto	1
Bunn, Mrs., ditto	1
Edwards, Mr. E., Chard	1
Bridgeman, Rev. D., Horsington	1
Winter, Mr. W., Wincanton	1
Day, Rev. G., ditto	1
Hannam, Mr., ditto	1
James, Mr. J., ditto	1
Hoopell, Rev. R., Winscombe	1
Horsey, Mr. D., Wellington	1
Price, Mr. H., Wells	1
Fyte, Mr. C., ditto	1
Mason, Mr. John, ditto	1
Burnett, Mr. G., Stogumber	1
Jackson, James, Esq., Bath	3
James, Rev. R., Yeovil	1
Reeves, Mr. S., Clevedon	1

STAFFORDSHIRE.

Evans, Mr. D., Burton-on-Trent	1
Port, Mr. Alonzo, ditto	1
Morris, Rev. D., ditto	1
Kyte, Mr. W., Rugeley	1
Sing, Mr. J., Bridgenorth	1
Roberts, Rev. E., Mould	1
Greenway, Rev. G., Netherton	1
Greenway, Mr. W., Netherton	1
Thomas, Rev. T., and Friends, ditto	6
Abington, Mr. L. J., Hanley	1
Carryer, Mr., Burslem	1
Barber, Mr. Gerard, Bilston	1
Sing, Mr. W., Swancote	1

YORKSHIRE.

Dowson, Rev. H., Bradford	1
Pottinger, Rev. T., ditto	2
Cole, Mr. J., ditto	1
Stead, Mr. William, ditto	1
Murgatroyd, Mr., ditto	1
Illingworth, Mr. D., ditto	1
Saunders, Rev. M., Haworth	1
Ash, Rev. J., Golcar	2
Atty, Mr. J. W., Bedale	2
Hepper, —, Esq., Shipley	2
Smith, Mr. E., Sheffield	1
Smith, Mr. H., ditto	1
Chapman, Mr. S., ditto	1
Hill, Mr. J. H., Hull	1
Palmer, Mr. D., ditto	1
Aked, Mr. F., Shipley Grange	1
Everson, Mr. James, Beverley	1
Voller, Mr. J., ditto	1
Patterson, Mr. G., Driffield	1
Normanton, Mr. J., ditto	1
Town, Mr. John, Keighley	3
Illingworth, Mr. M., Harrowgate	1
Johnson, Rev. R., Beverley	1
Crook, Mr. J., Halifax	1
Byles, Mr. H. B., Bradford	2
Russell, Mr. A., Scarborough	1
Purnell, Mr. G., ditto	1
Evans, Rev. B., ditto	1
Barry, John, Esq., ditto	2
Andrews, John, Esq., ditto	2
Wheldon, Mr. J., ditto	1
Garbutt, Mr. C., ditto	1
Morgan, Mr. Thomas, Leeds	1
Wylde, Mr. J., ditto	1
Town, Mr. J., ditto	1
Richardson, James, Esq., ditto	2
Fox, Mr. William, ditto	1
Waddington, Mr. J., Leeds	1
Goodman, Mr. B., ditto	1
Fennie, Mr. J., ditto	1
Heaton, Mr. W., ditto	1
Greesham, Mr. H., ditto	1
Fletcher, Mr. W., ditto	6
Stocks, Mr. J., ditto	1
Billrough, Mr. B., ditto	1
Wilkinson, Mr. J., Whitehaven	1
Bailey, Rev. R. S., Sheffield	1

LIST OF SUBSCRIBERS.

WARWICKSHIRE.

	No. of Copies
Edmonds, G., Esq., Birmingham	2
Roe, Rev. C. H., ditto	1
Hopkins, T. H., Esq., ditto	1
Tipping, Mr. T., ditto	1
Lardner, Mr. C., ditto	1
Edger, Rev. S., ditto	1
Morgan, W., Esq., ditto	1
Makepeace, Mr. C. D.	1
Middlemore, W., Esq., ditto	1
Barnett, Mr., ditto	1
M'Evoy, Mr. H., ditto	1
Davis, Mr., ditto	1
Mills, Rev. J., Kidderminster	1
Nutter, Mr. J., Leamington	1
White, Mr. J., ditto	2
Kitts, Mr. J., Thurlaston	1
Scroxton, Mr., Bromsgrove	1
Scroxton, Mr. T. H., ditto	1
Bale, Mr. H., Kidderminster	1
Harrison, Mr. W., Birmingham	1
Bury, Mr. John, Kidderminster	1
Nickson, Mr. James, ditto	1
Nicholls, Mr. John, ditto	1
Watts, Rev. J., Coventry	1
Booth, Mr., ditto	1
Newsome, Mr. Henry, ditto	1
Franklin, Mr. W., ditto	1
Dine, Mr. G., ditto	1

WORCESTERSHIRE.

	No. of Copies
Smith, Rev. James, Astwood	1
Crumpton, Mr. D., Atch Linch	1
Crowe, Rev. W., Worcester	1
Reynolds, Mrs., Paxford	1
Tring, Mr. J., Stourbridge	2
Newman, Mr. S., ditto	1
Wright, Mr. Joseph, ditto	1
Andrews, Mr. E., Pershore	1
Fletcher, Mr., ditto	1
Overbury, R. F., ditto	1

WILTSHIRE.

Wassell, Rev. Mr., Bath	1
Ricketts, Mr., ditto	1
Sims, Mr. J., ditto	1
Spackman, Mr., Corsham	1
Sillefant, Mr., ditto	1
Stubbings, Rev. S., Great Sherston	1
Lonsdale, Mr., Westbury	1
Wilkins, Mr., ditto	1
Evans, Rev. S., ditto	1
Starling, Mr. J. P., Warminster	1
Phillips, J. J., Esq., Melksham	1
King, Rev. T., Semley	1
Barnes, Rev. W., Trowbridge	1
Page, Mrs., ditto	1
Salter, S., Esq., ditto	1
Gouldsmith, J., Esq., ditto	1
Back-street School, ditto	1

WALES.

Bardsly, E., Esq., Builth	1	Thomas, Mr. J., Merthyr	2
Hopkins, Mr. T., Cardiff	1	Evans, Mr. B., ditto	1
Owen, Mr. J., ditto	1	Richards, Mr. J., Newbridge	1
Jones, Mr. J. J., Cardigan	1	Reynolds, Mr. W., Solva	1
Roberts, Mr. J. N., Darkgate	1	Rees, Mr. William, ditto	1
Spencer, Rev. J., Llanelly	3	Jones, Mr. D., ditto	1
Jones, Rev. R., Llanllyfni	1	Jones, Rev. J. G., Haverfordwest	1
Pritchard, Mr. W., Llandudno	1	Phillips, Mr. M., Pembroke	1
Thomas, Rev. T., Newcastle Emlyn	1	Jones, Mr. E. S., Llangollen	2
Cawker, Mr. T., Swansea	1	Ellis, Mr. R., ditto	1
Davis, Rev. D., ditto	3	Pritchard, Rev. J., ditto	1
Pughe, Rev. D. L., ditto	1	Coward, Mr. W., ditto	1
Walters, Mr. J., ditto	1	Evans, Rev. E., Cefn Mawr	1
Thomas, Mr. D., Pyle	1	Kelley, Mr. John, Bont Newydd	1
Jones, Mr. J., ditto	1	Williams, Mr. J., ditto	1
William, Rev. E., Merthyr	1	Jones, Mr. J., ditto	1
Protheroe, Mr. H., ditto	1	Jones, Mr. Joseph, ditto	1
Davis, Mr. Rees, ditto	1	Hughes, Mr. John, Llanrwst	1
Lewis, Rev. D., ditto	1	Noulkes, Mr. R., Denbigh	1
Williams, Rev. B., ditto	1	Owen, Rev. G. J., Ruthen	1
Jones, Rev. J., ditto	1		

LIST OF SUBSCRIBERS. 527

HEREFORDSHIRE.

Name	No. of Copies
Smith, James, Esq., Ross	1
Child, Mr. E., Hereford	1
Thomas, Mr. T., ditto	1
Jennings, R., Esq., ditto	1
Conway, J. W., Esq., Abergavenny	1
Williams, Rev. D. R., ditto	1
Thomas, Rev. M., ditto	1
Conway, Mrs., ditto	1
Edwards, Mr. J., ditto	1
James, Mr. B., ditto	1
Havard, Mr. W., Abergavenny	1
Jenkins, Mr. W., Pontheer	1
Phillips, W. W., Esq., Pontypool	1
Thomas, Rev. T., D.D. ditto	1
Evans, Rev. D., St. Mellows	2
Turner, Mr. C., Ironbridge	1
Price, Rev. S., Abersychan	1
Rowe, Rev. J., Risca	1
Conway, C., Esq., Pontnewydd	3
Thomas, Mr. G., Pontypool	1
Morris, Rev. T., Newport	1
Penney, Mr. W., ditto	1

SCOTLAND.

Name	No. of Copies
Macallen, Mr. D., Aberdeen	1
Taylor, Rev. James, Airdrie	1
Macleod, Mr. Alexander, Glasgow	1
Stobie, Mr., St. Andrew's	1
Downs, Mr., Ayr	1
O'Neil, Mr., Lochgilphead	1
Winzor, Mr., Combmartin	1
Robertson, Mr. R., Dunfermline	1
Dickie, H. D., Esq., Edinburgh	1
Evans, Mr. R., ditto	1
Innes, Mr., ditto	5
Craig, Mr. R., ditto	2
Clark, Mr. J., Edinburgh	1
Clark, Mr. A. M., ditto	1
Tennant, Mr. A., Paisley	3
Coats, Mr. W., ditto	1
M'Naughton, Mr. A., Islay	1
Pullar, John, Esq., Perth	1
Thompson, Rev. R., ditto	1
Goudy, Mr. A., Serwick	1
M'Dougald, Rev. Mr., Tyne	1
M'Donald, Mr. D., ditto	1
Macdonald, Mr. P., Elgin	1
Thomson, Mr. S., Spiggie	2
Armstrong, Mr. A., Stirling	1

IRELAND.

Name	No. of Copies
Berry, Mr. T., Abbeyliex	1
Eccles, Rev. W. S., Coleraine	1
Bates, Rev. J., Dungannon	1
Thomas, Rev. W., Limerick	1
Burr, Mrs. W., Nenagh	1
Burr, Mrs. R., Nenagh	1
Hardcastle, Rev. C., Waterford	1
Scroder, Mr. C., ditto	1
Bowman, Mr. E., ditto	1
Elliott, W., Esq., Letterkenny	1

GUERNSEY.

Name	No. of Copies
Nant, Mr. T., Mount Carmel	1
Burroughs, Mr. J., St. Peter	1
Torode, Mr. D. J., Bourgs	1

A Biographical Sketch of Charles Stovel (1799-1883)

by
John Franklin Jones

A BIOGRAPHICAL SKETCH OF CHARLES STOVEL (1799-1883)

Charles Stovel—"strict communionist Baptist minister, leader, and writer"—was born in Southwark, London in 1799. Initially apprenticed to a baker, Stovel was baptized by Joseph Dawson of Staines, Middlesex, ca. 1891 (*DEB*).

He was educated at Stepney (now Regent's Park) College (1823-1826) and served with William Fletcher as copastor at Swanwick, Derbyshire (1826-32). He also served as pastor at Prescott Street, London (1832-83). The Prescott Street church removed to Commercial Street, Whitechapel in 1865 (*DEB*).

A founding member of the Society for Diffusing the Gospel Through the Continent of Europe (May, 1831), Stovel was an active antislavery advocate with William Knibb. He served the Baptist Missionary Society. He also served the Baptist Building Fund, serving as secretary with Thomas Thomas, and he was the chairman of the Baptist Union (1862 and 1874) (*DEB*).

He authored *Hints on the Regulation of Christian Churches* (1835); *Pastoral Appeals on Conversion* (1837); *Lectures on Baptism Regeneration* (1843); *Lectures On Christian Discipleship and Baptism* (1846); *Lectures on Popery in England, Nineteenth Century* (1847); and *Lectures on Baptismal Reconciliation* (1848). He edited *John Canne's Necessity of Separation* (1849) (*DEB*).

JOHN FRANKLIN JONES

Stovel died at Stepney, London 22 October 1883 (*DEB*).

BIBLIOGRAPHY

Lewis, Donald M. *Dictionary of Evangelical Biography 1780-1860*, 2 vols. S.v. "Stovel, Charles," by Geoffrey Ralph Breed.

Stovel, Charles. *Christian Discipleship and Baptism*. London: Houlston & Stoneman, 1846.

BY JOHN FRANKLIN JONES
CORDOVA, TENNESSEE
JULY 2006

THE BAPTIST STANDARD BEARER, INC.

a non-profit, tax-exempt corporation
committed to the Publication & Preservation
of the Baptist Heritage.

CURRENT TITLES AVAILABLE IN
THE BAPTIST *DISTINCTIVES* SERIES

KIFFIN, WILLIAM   A Sober Discourse of Right to Church-Communion. Wherein is proved by Scripture, the Example of the Primitive Times, and the Practice of All that have Professed the Christian Religion: That no Unbaptized person may be Regularly admitted to the Lord's Supper. (London: George Larkin, 1681).

KINGHORN, JOSEPH   Baptism, A Term of Communion. (Norwich: Bacon, Kinnebrook, and Co., 1816)

KINGHORN, JOSEPH   A Defense of "Baptism, A Term of Communion". In Answer To Robert Hall's Reply. (Norwich: Wilkin and Youngman, 1820).

GILL, JOHN   Gospel Baptism. A Collection of Sermons, Tracts, etc., on Scriptural Authority, the Nature of the New Testament Church and the Ordinance of Baptism by John Gill. (Paris, AR: The Baptist Standard Bearer, Inc., 2006).

CARSON, ALEXANDER	Ecclesiastical Polity of the New Testament. (Dublin: William Carson, 1856).
BOOTH, ABRAHAM	A Defense of the Baptists. A Declaration and Vindication of Three Historically Distinctive Baptist Principles. Compiled and Set Forth in the Republication of Three Books. Revised edition. (Paris, AR: The Baptist Standard Bearer, Inc., 2006).
BOOTH, ABRAHAM	Paedobaptism Examined on the Principles, Concessions, and Reasonings of the Most Learned Paedobaptists. With Replies to the Arguments and Objections of Dr. Williams and Mr. Peter Edwards. 3 volumes. (London: Ebenezer Palmer, 1829).
CARROLL, B. H.	*Ecclesia* - The Church. With an Appendix. (Louisville: Baptist Book Concern, 1903).
CHRISTIAN, JOHN T.	Immersion, The Act of Christian Baptism. (Louisville: Baptist Book Concern, 1891).
FROST, J. M.	Pedobaptism: Is It From Heaven Or Of Men? (Philadelphia: American Baptist Publication Society, 1875).
FULLER, RICHARD	Baptism, and the Terms of Communion; An Argument. (Charleston, SC: Southern Baptist Publication Society, 1854).
GRAVES, J. R.	Tri-Lemma: or, Death By Three Horns. The Presbyterian General Assembly Not Able To Decide This Question: "Is Baptism In The Romish Church Valid?" 1st Edition.

	(Nashville: Southwestern Publishing House, 1861).
MELL, P.H.	Baptism In Its Mode and Subjects. (Charleston, SC: Southern Baptist Publications Society, 1853).
JETER, JEREMIAH B.	Baptist Principles Reset. Consisting of Articles on Distinctive Baptist Principles by Various Authors. With an Appendix. (Richmond: The Religious Herald Co., 1902).
PENDLETON, J.M.	Distinctive Principles of Baptists. (Philadelphia: American Baptist Publication Society, 1882).
THOMAS, JESSE B.	The Church and the Kingdom. A New Testament Study. (Louisville: Baptist Book Concern, 1914).
WALLER, JOHN L.	Open Communion Shown to be Unscriptural & Deleterious. With an introductory essay by Dr. D. R. Campbell and an Appendix. (Louisville: Baptist Book Concern, 1859).

For a complete list of current authors/titles, visit our internet site at:
www.standardbearer.org
or write us at:

he Baptist Standard Bearer, Inc.

NUMBER ONE IRON OAKS DRIVE • PARIS, ARKANSAS 72855
TEL # 479-963-3831   FAX # 479-963-8083
EMAIL: Baptist@centurytel.net   http://www.standardbearer.org

Thou hast given a standard to them that fear thee; that it may be displayed because of the truth. — Psalm 60:4

www.ingramcontent.com/pod-product-compliance
Lightning Source LLC
Chambersburg PA
CBHW021349290426
44108CB00010B/162